GLENN AUSTIN, M.D., is a pediatrician
in private practice in Los Altos,
California, with years of experience both
teaching and practicing medicine for
children.

THE PARENTS' GUIDE
TO CHILD RAISING

GLENN AUSTIN

with

Julia Stone Oliver and John C. Richards

A SPECTRUM BOOK

PRENTICE-HALL, INC., Englewood Cliffs, New Jersey 07632

Library of Congress Cataloging in Publication Data
Main entry under title:

The Parents' guide to child raising.

(A Spectrum Book)
Includes bibliographical references and index.
1. Children—Management.   I. Austin, Glenn.
II. Oliver, Julia Stone.   III. Richards, John C.
HQ769.P273   649′.1   77-28168
ISBN 0-13-650028-5
ISBN 0-13-650010-2 pbk.

A Spectrum Book

10   9   8   7   6   5   4   3   2   1

Printed in the United States of America

PRENTICE-HALL INTERNATIONAL, INC., *London*
PRENTICE-HALL of AUSTRALIA PTY. LIMITED, *Sydney*
PRENTICE-HALL of CANADA, LTD., *Toronto*
PRENTICE-HALL of INDIA PRIVATE Limited, *New Delhi*
PRENTICE-HALL of JAPAN, INC., *Tokyo*
PRENTICE-HALL of SOUTHEAST ASIA PTE. Ltd., *Singapore*
WHITEHALL BOOKS LIMITED, *Wellington, New Zealand*

CONTENTS

8

SCHOOL AND LEARNING PROBLEMS

9

SEPARATION: DIVORCE AND DEATH

BOOKS FOR PARENTS

INDEX

FOREWORD

This book, a unique composite of viewpoints and approaches to child-rearing, is intended to emphasize the concept that parents are capable of developing their own decision-making skills concerning the health and welfare of their children. Indeed, our goal is to strengthen and reinforce these parental decision-making skills in caring for their off-spring. The responsibilities that parents have as educators and as models for their children merit this commitment. In fostering this capacity, the intention is also to insure a sense of confidence and comfort within the parents regarding their roles. These assets are a key to a successful and enriched family life.

In essence, *The Parents' Guide to Child Raising* is dedicted to the growth and development of parents and simultaneously to that of their children—the parents of tomorrow.

SPRAGUE W. HAZARD, M.D., F.A.A.P.
Director, University of Health Services
Brandeis University

PREFACE

How do I and my associate editors thank the over 500 people who have helped form this book and its companion volume, *The Parents' Medical Manual?* They are all sincerely appreciated. You will also appreciate that the person who was the greatest help, who stuck in there with encouragement in good times and bad times, whose inspiration and faith truly made this book possible, is my wife. I dedicate these books to her—with love.

My associate editors are wonderful people who wrote, challenged, argued, and continually worked to improve these books. Julie Oliver did this between being a full-time mother, a part-time piano teacher, a writer, and a compassionate human being who never forgets her family and is always ready to help other people. Her background as a mother, tied to her writing ability, her penetrating intellect, and her unflagging determination to stand up for women and mothers, has flavored the book. My partner in practice, Dr. John Richards, was as demanding of the book as he is of himself. He burned the midnight oil, usually after a long day in the office, writing, thinking, and editing. His intense dedication to parents and children came through time after time and helped us to make these two volumes what they are.

A special thanks goes to a remarkable practicing pediatrician and author, Robert F. L. Polley of Seattle, Washington, whose unique book *Call The Doctor* inspired *The Parents' Guide to Child Raising* and *The Parents' Medical Manual.* Dr. Polley's book is a one-man book. He describes it as a delicatessen representing his special views on some important facets of child raising and medical care. He likens our two books with their hundred contributors to supermarkets. And he cheerfully contributed articles and suggestions. Extra thanks are also due to Dr. Merritt Low, from the quiet little town of Greenfield, Massachusetts. During the writing of these books, he rose in pediatric leadership to become the President of the American Academy of Pediatrics. Yet despite his firm hand in guiding the Academy, he took time to write, and, more importantly, to offer invaluable philosophical and practical pediatric advice. He did this because he is dedicated to the welfare of children and because he wanted these books to be the best books they can be. His wisdom had a major effect upon the character of our two volumes.

Putting this book together has not been easy. At times it looked like a scattered jigsaw puzzle. We are thankful that we had the services and talent of Richard Osborne to help in organizing the books, and the decisiveness of Michael Hunter and Shirley Covington, who changed the manuscripts to books. As the books took shape, building through six successive manuscripts, we had to correlate the writings of all of the contributors from coast to coast and as far away as South Australia and Saskatchewan, Canada. There was, of course, much duplication and variation in styles. Because of the overlap that naturally occurred, and because of the necessity to smooth the books into a more consistent and easily readable style, we had to take a good number of editorial liberties with the material contributed. We strove faithfully to retain the meaning of each article and the character and identity of each author. Because I am not certain that we always succeeded, I will have to take the responsibility and accept the blame if we have inadvertently misrepresented anyone. If we did, it was because it is more important that the reader be given a logical and easily readable exposure to the many divergent views we tried to present than to present the complete position of any single contributor.

One of the great things I got out of these two books was the pleasure of working with a really fine group of understanding, sensitive, and intelligent doctors, psychologists, nurses, mothers, and youths. I humbly admit that much of the good advice in *The Parents' Guide to Child Raising* came from parents in my practice, and from other effective parents like Alicia Herman and Bill Oliver, who worked hard for the book, and from parents in the practice of many of our contributors. I would like to pay tribute to my own parents, grandparents, and teachers of an era now past, whose efforts for me and confidence in me helped shape my life—just as I am certain that most of you would, in retrospect, like to thank your own parents and families and pay homage to your own roots. I thank you all for your companionship and for your contributions to *The Parents' Guide to Child Raising* and *The Parents' Medical Manual*. In the Foreword, Dr. Sprague Hazard makes a slightly less personal and more formal dedication that represents the spirit of our two books—a dedication that really comes from *all* of us—to you, the reader.

GLENN AUSTIN, M.D., F.A.A.P.
Editor

CONTRIBUTING AUTHORS

GLENN AUSTIN, M.D., F.A.A.P., Consultant American Academy of Pediatrics; Pediatrician, Private Practice, Los Altos, California.

"TOMMIE" AUSTIN, mother, Los Altos, California.

DIANA BAUMRIND, Ph.D., Institute of Human Development, University of California, Berkeley, California.

LEO BELL, M.D., F.A.A.P., Pediatrician, Private Practice; Past President National Federation of Pediatrics Societies, San Mateo, California.

ROBERT L. BLACK, M.D., F.A.A.P., Pediatrician, Private Practice, Monterey, California.

HENRY BRUYN, M.D., F.A.A.P., Past Director Student Health Service, University of California, Berkeley; Author, *Handbook of Pediatrics*, San Francisco, California.

ROBERT BURNETT, M.D., F.A.A.P., Private Practice; Chairman, Manpower Committee, American Academy of Pediatrics, Sunnyvale, California.

JAN CANBY, Elementary school teacher; Mother, Rancho Cordova, California.

THOMAS COCK, M.D., F.A.A.P., Bellevue, Washington.

THOMAS CONWAY, M.D., F.A.A.P., Pediatrician, Private Practice, Terre Haute, Indiana.

NANCY COOKSON, reviewing mother, Los Altos, California.

BETTY ANN COUNTRYMAN, R.N., M.N., Professional Liason, La Leche League; Assistant Professor of Maternal and Child Health, Indiana University, Indianapolis, Indiana.

WILLIAM CROOK, M.D., F.A.A.P, Pediatric allergist; President Child Health Centers of America; Author of several books for parents, Jackson, Tennessee.

MARGARET DEANESLY, M.D., Internist, Student Health Service, Stanford University, California.

JAMES DENNIS, M.D., F.A.A.P., Vice President for Health Sciences, University of Arkansas, Little Rock, Arkansas.

JAMES DOBSON, Ph.D., Associate Clinical Professor of Pediatrics, University of Southern California School of Medicine, Los Angeles, California; Author, *Dare to Discipline, Hide or Seek*, and *What Wives Wish Their Husbands Knew About Women.*

MURRAY ELKINS, M.D., Family Practice; Past Chairman Queens County Medical Society, New York, New York.

ANN ENGLISH, Mother, Los Altos, California.

SHIRLEY FELDMAN, Ph.D., Assistant Professor of Psychology, Stanford University, Stanford, California.

WILLIAM FOSTER, M.D., F.A.A.P., Pediatrician, Private Practice, Los Altos, California.

DAVID FRIEDMAN, M.D., F.A.A.P., Professor of Pediatrics, University of Southern California School of Medicine; Chairman, Section on Child Development, American Academy of Pediatrics, Los Angeles, California.

J. W. GERRARD, D.M., F.R.C.P., Professor of Pediatrics, University of Saskatchewan; Author, *Understanding Allergies*, Saskatchewan, Canada.

KAY GRANIERI, mother, Los Altos, California.

DON KERR GRANT, M.B. (Adelaide), F.R.A.C.P., Pediatrician, Children's Rehabilitation Center, Buffalo, New York.

GLEN C. GRIFFIN, M.D., F.A.A.P., Private Practice, Pediatrician: Author, *You Were Smaller Than a Dot*, Bountiful, Utah.

A. S. HASHIM, M.D. (Baghdad), F.A.A,P., Pediatrician, Private Practice, Bethesda, Maryland.

SPRAGUE HAZARD, MD., F.A.A.P., Pediatrician; Director, University Health Services, Brandeis University; Executive Board, American Academy of Pediatrics, Waltham, Massachusetts.

ROBERT HEAVENRICH, M.D., F.A.A.P., Pediatrician, Private Practice; Past President, American Academy of Pediatrics, Saginaw, Michigan

ARVIN HENDERSON, M.D., F.A.A.P., Pediatrician, Private Practice, Palo Alto, California.

NEIL HENDERSON, M.D., Pediatrician, Private Practice; Author, *How to Understand and Treat Your Child's Symptoms*, Boca Raton, Florida.

ALICIA HERMAN, mother, Parent Effectivness Training Instructor, Los Gatos, California.

ROBERT HERMAN, M.D., F.A.A.P., Pediatrician-Psychiatrist, Private Practice, Kaiser Hospital, Santa Clara, California.

CHARLES HOFFMAN, M.D., F.A.A.P., Pediatrician, Private Practice, Flushing, New York.

ALVAN JACOBS, M.D., F.A.A.P., Professor of Dermatology, Stanford University, Stanford, California.

BLACKBURN JOSLIN, M.D., F.A.A.P., Pediatrician, Private Practice; Chairman, American Academy of Pediatrics Chapter; Socio-economic expert, Bellevue, Washington.

RAYMOND KAHN, M.D., F.A.A.P., Family Practice, Dayton, Ohio.

NORMAN KENDALL, M.D., F.A.A.P., Professor of Neonatology, Temple University, Philadelphia, Pennsylvania.

MERRITT LOW, M.D., F.A.A.P., Pediatrician, Private Practice; President, American Academy of Pediatrics, Greenfield, Massachusetts.

MARVIN MCCLELLAN, M.D., F.A.A.P., Pediatrician, Private Practice; expert on sports medicine; Past President, National Federation Pediatric Societies; Consultant, American Academy of Pediatrics, Cincinnati, Ohio.

WILLIAM MISBACH, M.D., F.A.A.P., Pediatrician, Private Practice; Chapter Chairman, American Academy of Pediatrics, Encino, California.

DONALD NAFTULIN, M.D., Associate Professor of Psychiatry, University of Southern California School of Medicine, Los Angeles, California.

Nursing Mothers Counsel, Inc., Volunteer organization of nursing mothers, Palo Alto, California.

BYRON OBERST, M.D., F.A.A.P., Pediatrician, Private Practice, Omaha, Nebraska.

LEON OTTINGER, M.D., F.A.A.P., Pediatrician, Private Practice; Researcher in in learning disabilities; Clinical Professor of Pediatrics, University of California of Los Angeles Medical School, San Marino, California.

JULIA STONE OLIVER, Associate Editor; Mother, Los Altos, California.

IRVING PHILLIPS, M.D., Professor of Psychiatry, Langley Porter Clinic, San Francisco, California.

RUTH POARCH, reviewing mother, Woodland, California.

ROBERT F. L. POLLEY, M.D., F.A.A.P., Pediatrician, Private Practice; Author, *Call The Doctor*; Columnist, Seattle, Washington.

SANDRA PRICE, Certified Pediatric Assistant and mother, Greenfield, Massachusetts.

ISAAC M. REID, M.D., F.A.A.P., Kaiser Health Center, Cleveland, Ohio.

HENRY RICHANBACH, M.D., F.A.A.P., Pediatrician, Private Practice; School Consultant, Burlingame, California.

JOHN C. RICHARDS, M.D., F.A.A.P., Associate Editor; Pediatrician, Private Practice, Los Altos, California.

SID ROSIN, M.D., F.A.A.P., Pediatrician, Private Practice, Beverly Hills, California.

GEORGE RUSSELL, M.D., F.A.A.P., Medical Director Moton (ghetto) Health Center, Tulsa, Oklahoma.

BAMBI SCOFIELD, mother, Los Altos, California.

MAXINE SEHRING, M.D., F.A.A.P., School Consultant, Health and Sex Education, Walnut Creek, California.

EDWARD SHAW, M.D., F.A.A.P., Professor of Pediatrics and Chairman (retired), University of California Medical School, San Francisco, California.

ERIC SIMS, M.D., F.R.A.C.P., Senior Consulting Pediatrician, Adelaide Childrens Hospital, South Australia.

LENDON SMITH, M.D., F.A.A.P., Pediatrician, Private Practice; Author, *The Encyclopedia of Baby and Child Care*; Television Program, Portland, Oregon.

MARTIN SMITH, M.D., F.A.A.P., Pediatrician, Private Practice; Chairman, Council of Pediatric Practice, American Academy of Pediatrics, Gainsville, Georgia.

DAVED SPARLING, M.D., F.A.A.P., Pediatrician, Private Practice; Chairman, American Academy of Pediatrics Chapter, Tacoma, Washington.

BENJAMIN SPOCK, M.D., F.A.A.P., Pediatrician; Author, *Baby and Child Care*, New York, New York.

LOUISE TAICHERT, M.D., Consultant, Child Study Unit, University of California School of Medicine; Private Practice—learning behavior disorders, San Francisco, California.

BRUCE VALENTINE, M.D., F.A.A.F.P., Family Practice, Abbington, Connecticut.

HOBART WALLACE, M.D., F.A.A.P., Chapter Chairman, American Academy of Pediatrics; Pediatrician, Private Practice, Lincoln, Nebraska.

BURTON WHITE, Ph.D., Senior Research Associate, Harvard Graduate School of Education, Harvard University, Cambridge, Massachusetts.

CREDITS FOR ILLUSTRATIONS

PHOTOGRAPHS: Pat Gough
LINE DRAWINGS FROM *Call the Doctor:* Stuart Moldren
CARTOONS: Medical and Graphic Illustrations of Stanford University School of Medicine

Key to Degrees and Honors

D.M.	Doctor of Medicine
F.A.A.F.P.	Fellow, American Academy of Family Physicians
F.A.A.P	Fellow, American Academy of Pediatrics
F.R.A.C.P.	Fellow of the Royal Australian College of Physicians
F.R.C.P.	Fellow of the Royal College of Physicians
M.B.	Bachelor of Medicine
M.D.	Doctor of Medicine
M.N.	Masters in Nursing
Ph.D.	Doctor of Philosophy
R.N.	Registered Nurse

INTRODUCTION

As a new parent or a parent to be, you'll want to be sure you have access to as much sound information on child raising as possible. *The Parents' Guide to Child Raising* brings together this information. It covers everything from transmitting values to the pros and cons of prepared baby foods, and from how to nurse a baby to the dilemma of the child who won't learn—all in a single, useful volume.

The information in this book draws from the opinions and suggestions of a representative cross-section of pediatricians and other experts who were asked to elaborate on those child care issues which cause parents the most concern. Their contributions were then circulated among parents, psychologists, researchers, and pediatricians who responded with additions, criticisms, and further thoughts of their own. The result is a book shaped by over five hundred people whose daily lives are, in one way or another, immediately involved with children and/or parents

If you want to gain ideas on how to improve your parenting skills and your understanding of your children, you will find this book invaluable. But if you are looking for a source to tell you how to raise your children and how to be a parent, you will be disappointed. We, the editors, do not believe that experts, including ourselves, are omnipotent and always right. Experts in child raising and family life differ from generation to generation and from individual to individual. The primary goal of this book has been to present the many divergent views of child care and parenting as objectively as possible so that you, the reader, can

1

decide which philosophy or specific advice best suits your children, your needs, and your own personality. After all, in the final analysis, it is you, the parent, who must make the decisions and take the responsibility in raising your child

Because of the inclusion of many differing ideas in *The Parents' Guide to Child Raising,* you should be prepared for opinions that differ from your own and you should also be equally prepared for your strong emotional reaction against them. We, the editors, found ourselves quite upset over some of the viewpoints contributed on such emotionally charged subjects as discipline, alternatives to the two-parent family, and ways of transmitting values to children. And, furthermore, we often disagreed with one another over these issues.

The often conflicting advice that is presented in this book may tend to confuse you at first. However, advice, even in the form of personal consultations with a professional, only rarely should be allowed to get in the way of your own judgment and perceptions of your child. Your pediatrician may have a vastly greater understanding of your child's physical makeup and of the average parent's emotions and the usual child's response; and your child's teacher may be more aware of specific learning problems. But expecting these professionals to know *everything* about your child can only lead to your ultimate dissatisfaction. *You* are the expert when it comes to your children. You are the captain of the health, growth, and development team. Professionals are the coaches who help you as guides. And as a responsible parent, you should listen to them. However, they do not make the final decisions. That is your job. If you wish second or third opinions, you have every right (and a responsibility) to call in new advisors.

Be careful of advice offered in books, even this one, as well as what you read in magazine articles. Authors write for wide audiences, and they inevitably fall into generalizations about the "average," the "normal," and the "in most cases" child. Words like "usually," "often," and "generally" can lull readers into accepting whatever opinion is offered and often into a wholesale application of the theory to a child. Always look at your own child, his particular needs, and your own situation when evaluating general advice. Your child, and for that matter *every* child, is only rarely "average."

Remember that advice, no matter where it comes from, is useful only as you are able to integrate it with other factors that influence your parenting behavior; how you yourself were raised; the kind of person you are; your resources and needs; the circumstances of your present life; and, of course, the unique personality and needs of your child.

As you read this book, you will see advice that "just fits" your child and yourself. Try it. If it works, fine. If not, then try another approach.

We hope that *The Parents' Guide to Child Raising* presents to you a wide enough range of ideas, advice, and concrete facts that you will at least gain confidence in your own parenting instincts and abilities by realizing that there is no one "right" way to raise your children.

1

YOU—THE PARENT

When we think of parenting, most of us think of families. The family is an old institution with many new challenges. The traditional view, expressed by Rousseau in 1762, is that "the most ancient of societies, and the only one that is natural, is the family. . . ." A modern woman sociologist, on the other hand, wrote me privately that, "I do not believe that traditional family relationships are good for women, nor even for men—although they are relatively comfortable for men." Yet both ancient and modern philosophies recognize that a major purpose of families is to serve as a structure for parents and as a base for raising our children. Somehow, in the face of basic philosophical and practical conflicts, each of us still has to be the best parent we can for our children. Even if you are relatively content in a traditional family, as most parents still are, neither you nor society can escape the influence of the challenges and troubles that face many families, parents, and children today. As parents, we must recognize the abundance of problems and we must also look at an overabundance of talked-about solutions. Most of us feel the same way Mark Twain did about the weather. Everyone talks about it, but nobody does anything about it. It seems likely that if someone *does* do something about it, that that someone will be *you*. We will have to solve our problems person by person and family by family. Although we may not deal with abstract figures about the rising divorce rate, the increase in crime, or the loss of respect of authority, we can learn to deal with ourselves, and each of us can improve the parenting our own children receive.

The first question most parents ask is: "Am I a good parent?" Based on my experience with thousands of parents and children, I can assure you that most people are. New parents are surprised at the growth of their capabilities to love and care for a child. However, like starting any new job, your skill at being a parent develops with time, thought, practice, and study. Australian pediatrician Eric Sims says: "Love alone is not enough. All parents should face the challenge of parenthood as a specialty in its own right, worthy of intelligent study, because the understanding and management of children do not automatically happen in us just because we have given birth to them."

Parents are individual people and individuals are different. For some, parenting comes relatively easily and comfortably. For others, it seems difficult and aggravating. Often this depends upon the circumstances as well as upon the personalities of the parents and children involved. But no matter how well or how poorly the job of parenting is done, it must be done. It is probably the most important factor in your own child's life. So, whether it comes easily or hard, it deserves study.

Of course, study alone is also not enough. You need faith in yourself as a parent as well as love for your children. These will give you confidence in your native ability, and, ultimately, the strength to use what you've learned. In the process, you will more than likely experience growing pains, for there are many dilemmas along with the joys of parenting.

THE DILEMMA OF MODERN PARENTING

I believe that one of the most common problems for a new parent who is trying to do his or her best is deciding just what *is* "best" for the child. In the past, every institution in society—the church, the school, the courts, and a respected body of tradition—supported the dominant father, the domestic and submissive mother, and the seen-but-not-heard children. A parent could simply follow the tradition and have full support from society. Problems such as a child not eating or "talking back" were readily solved by the switch or by forcing the child to stand in the corner.

But this is not so today. Now, the parent seeking outside support or advice in child rearing is as likely to be met with confusion as with help. For every authority in family life and child care (pediatricians, teachers, psychologist, writers, and sociologists) advocating one way to raise children, there is another expert arguing the opposite point of view. One says that children need and even want to be curbed, while another contends that children should be allowed to develop according to their own inner dictates. Still other experts claim that the parent-child relationship is based on authority, and that pretending it isn't only ignores the practical facts of family life. A different but equally vocal group of experts see children as a persecuted minority, much like blacks and women, and is working to accord them greater legal rights in the courts, the schools, and the home.

The fact is that the traditional two-parent family, with mother at home and father at work, while still basic to our culture, no longer exerts the undisputed influence it once did—either by its prevalence, or, some people now claim, by any intrinsic virtues of its own. Many marriages end in divorce, leaving a lot of mothers (and more and more fathers) with the task of running one-parent families. Over twelve million mothers work outside the home, either through necessity or choice. Some parents in the traditional mother-at-home, father-at-work family have begun to question the values upon which their style of life is based. As recently as ten years ago, the woman who opted for a career rather than a family had to "justify" her choice. Today, it is the woman who elects to stay at home and raise her children who often seems on the defensive.

A few parents have completely reversed roles: Mother works and father, the "house husband," stays home with the children. There are parents experimenting with communal arrangements in which responsibility for the children is shared among a group of adults. There is not just one "right" way to live or to raise your children. In America, we have the freedom to shape our lives as people and as parents according to our own ethics, needs and desires, without feeling guilty, unnatural, or out of step. But, along with this freedom comes a massive personal responsibility.

Your Responsibility

Responsibility always comes with personal decisions, and many parental decisions are exquisitely personal. Frequently, they are made in isolation, but are subject to implied criticism by distant experts and to judgment by the people around you. Often there is more judgment and criticism than help. But whether you get too little help or too much help, the decisions are still yours.

How do you make the decisions required in parenting and why do you react as you do to advice? More often than not, it springs from your deep rooted inner drives and feelings. Because of this, it is especially important for each of us to know ourselves and to learn to recognize those drives and feelings which influence our behavior as parents.

YOUR PARENTING LEGACY

By far the most important influence on your behavior as a parent is the way you yourself were raised. Our own childhood is as close to a formal education in how to be parents as most of us will ever receive. Your parents not only gave you the genes and instincts which determine many of the characteristics you possess, but they also passed on to you a complex bundle of traditions, drives, and habits. Consciously or unconsciously, this is a legacy that influences your life as a parent as well as an individual. It is a legacy that has its roots in previous generations and that will continue into future generations. For an example of this legacy, let's say that your grandfather died when your father was a young boy. Then, when it came time for your father to father you, he may have felt ineffective and uncomfortable since he didn't have a model to follow in how to act as a father. As a result, you might have experienced your father as distant and uncommunicative. Now, as a father yourself, the legacy you draw on will include your grandfather's early death, your father's childhood, and your own relationship with your father. You may follow in your father's footsteps, parenting your child as you were parented; or you may bend over backward to give your child the kind of relationship you never had, precisely because you so sorely missed it yourself. Either way, you have been influenced by your parenting legacy and have, in turn, shaped a new legacy to pass on to your children.

The influence of our pasts is subtle and complex. Much of what we think of as natural and instinctive parental behavior is, in fact, the outgrowth of attitudes and reactions which we absorbed more or less unconsciously during our growing-up years. Even our "rational" selves are usually influenced. For instance, an enthusiastic "intellectual" endorsement of a certain child-rearing approach can be more of an emotional reaction to childhood experiences than an exercise in reason. Still, we need not remain the captives of our past, either by following it blindly or by trying to reject it out of hand.

As adults, we have the ability to become aware of our parenting legacy, to look at the way we were raised, and alter those parts that stand in the way of how we want to parent our children now. This doesn't mean we must psychoanalyze ourselves; it does mean we should learn to identify the sources of our feelings and behavior and learn to evaluate, control, and use them rationally. In the long run, we can combine the best of the past and the present into a rewarding relationship between us and our children.

Instincts and Faith

In the process of identifying the source and value of your feelings and of improving your parenting, don't lose faith in your parenting instincts. It doesn't matter whether they are from hormones or from inherited personality traits. Most of mankind has been raised on the basis of parenting instincts which serve as the foundation on which each of our own parenting traditions and values has grown. Usually your instinctive actions, especially those based upon love, will work. If they don't, as measured by the results on your children, then don't hesitate to question and control them. But retain your faith in yourself during the process. Knowing that you are doing the right things or at least *trying* to do the right things for your child is a great asset. A confident parent gives children a feeling of security. A confident parent is happier than an anxious parent, and thus gives children a happier atmosphere in which to grow. Be assured that a lot of experts in child-rearing believe that most parents have the natural ability and commitment to raise their children well. Unfortunately, in the process of reading all the advice the experts offer, you may become confused—even angry enough to "burn all their books."

Burn Those Books?
I will never forget the rainy, winter day when I was so frustrated, aggravated, irritated, and nauseated with four small children that it was wild. Nothing I read in the books on child raising fit or helped. I got so angry at the books that I threw them all in the fire. I thought: "I have read so much that I have lost contact with my natural instinct, and what if I couldn't read?" Then I did what I wanted to do and things settled down.—*Kay Granieri*

The best way to measure your parenting effectiveness, whether it is based on instinct or education, is by looking at the results of your methods upon your children. If the results are good, your feelings were probably correct all along. Whether the results are or are not good, our efforts and effectiveness usually increase. As we mature and clarify our understanding of our feelings, we are able, logically, to improve our behavior. Some behavior may turn out to be based on faulty information which we can replace, or on confused instincts that can be straightened out. Some feelings may be the result of misinterpreting information we already possess. We may be able to re-interpret this information into a more satisfying and useful approach to parenting. Learn to judge for yourself what is good in you and how to express it in parenting. By doing this, you will increase your faith in yourself, and this will be reflected in your increased parenting abilities. In this self-appraisal, we examine our own parenting legacies, our own pasts.

Learning to Parent

Your legacy and personality may be such that parenting comes naturally and instinctively, like fitting into the right size glove. On the other hand, you may not feel especially confident in your ability to raise children: Some parents may even try to reject their parenting legacy. But the best and the worst parents share a common urge to improve their parenting. Probably the most common method of such self-improvement is to learn, consciously or subconsciously, by watching other people we admire as they parent.

There are few courses on parenting offered anywhere. And if such a course is offered, who teaches it, and what are the sources of his knowledge? Is his way of parenting best for *your* children? Personal experience, cultural and religious tradition, and science are the usual sources of the art of parenthood. Personal experience may be helpful, but people and their children are often so individual that what works for one usually doesn't work for all.

HELP FROM SCIENCE

Instinct and tradition as the basis for rearing children is being challenged. Psychologist Rose Zeligs writes: "Today, in the nuclear family, young parents do not have or want the guidance of their elders in child-rearing. They look to professionals for advice in every detail of child care." [1] However under the name of science or the professions, just as under the name of religion, you can get remarkably differing information. Science is a search for truth—it is not necessarily truth. A large portion of scientific and professional literature, however meticulously researched, eventually turns out to be wrong. Most experts in child rearing have been trained in some scientific disciplines: pediatrics, psychology, or sociology. They can be of considerable help to parents. Some experts make it appear that they *do* know just how to raise children "properly." Most of us, however, are a bit more humble. In fact, leading psychologists have become skeptical about many of the pronouncements in their fields. For example, psychologist Diana Baumrind of the University of California at Berkeley is an authority on authoritative versus permissive parenting. Yet she says that, although her interpretations of research findings are probably true for the particular group she worked with, they cannot be used to predict the actions or outcome for an individual family.

There is not such a thing as a *best* way to raise children. Each individual family's total life situation is unique. A generalization which makes sense on a probability basis must be tailored to fit an individual family's situation, if indeed it fits at all. It is each parent's responsibility to become an expert on his own children, using information in books or parent effectiveness encounter groups, or, best of all, by careful observation and intimate communication with the child. [2]

Donald Campbell, President of the American Psychological Association, cautioned against accepting psychological theories or the results of relatively short term scientific investigations. He noted that there is disagreement as to how people should rear their children and how to live their lives. We are unable to experiment or to test even well-developed theories rigorously. Campbell believes that "psychology and psychiatry cannot yet claim to be truly scientific, and thus have special reasons for modesty and caution in undermining traditional belief systems." [3] He argued that traditional "recipes for living" which have been evolved, tested, and winnowed through hundreds of generations have thus been scientifically better tested than the psychologist's or psychiatrist's speculations about how people should live. Dr. Campbell's assessment seems to back up that of Harvard psychologist Burton White, who believes that parents have received little help from the psychological literature in raising their children:

> The entire contents of our experimental psychological journals of the last thirty years have brought us very modest amounts of information to deal with problems of compensatory education, effective child-rearing practices, infant education, or the mental health of children.[4]

What this adds up to is, for some people, the unsettling realization that you, as the parent, have to make your own decisions.

DECIDING THE ROLES

The questions of who "minds" the child, who disciplines, who stays home, and who earns the money are major issues for society and for many parents today. Rapid social change makes it difficult to come up with answers to such questions or with definitions of mothering and fathering which are not sexist and restrictive on the one hand, or totally oblivious to our cultural traditions and to the good of our children on the other. Every man and woman in varying degrees, has an inborn drive to nurture, or parent, which exposure to a child can bring out and develop. Some experts claim that the strength of this drive and the direction it takes are influenced by hormones which create "maternal" behavior. Dr. Merritt Low and Sandra Price, without discounting the possibility of some hormonal influence, believe that most of the differences between mothering and fathering behaviors are learned rather than inborn.

A father has the right and obligation to care, take interest, work, and spend time with his children—to enjoy love and its fruits. If he does not participate fully, he will not receive the share of rewards and time

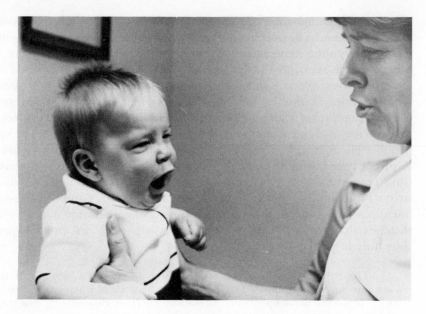

Figure 1   *Whoever "minds" the baby is lucky!*

of parenting which should be his. He is no longer viewed as a germy, clumsy, third-wheel goon. This family role has been kept from father for too long, for he has the right to branch into family life just as mother needs and has the right to branch out. This should be a learning experience which supplements so-called instincts, or supplants lack of them. Father's participation, from the beginning, is now unlimited; he can be more than a disciplinarian and breadwinner. His new horizons give him freedom to love openly and to enjoy love in return, with social and cultural support.

Certainly, the trends of family life in the last decade support the notion that our traditional definitions of mothering and fathering are susceptible to change. This has led some psychologists to believe that the only thing a mother can give a child which a father cannot is the experience of a close and loving relationship with a woman, from which a baby learns the nature of femininity. Obviously, fathers give the same gift to their children—except, of course, that their gift is one of masculinity. Still, tradition is strong, and for many mothers and fathers this minimum definition does not even begin to express their own experiences and feelings.

Many have concluded that, beyond the biologically defined functions of siring, bearing, and breast feeding, the various duties in raising a child are up for grabs by either parent. Regardless, the most important thing is that the child's needs are met, whether they are for clean diapers, a roof over his head, or a loving hug. Of course, in working out whether the mother or the father performs a specific job, a couple will learn the necessity for compromise.

TEAMWORK AND COMPROMISE

In defining your role as a parent in terms of the needs of your child, the needs of your spouse, and your own personal expectations and goals, obviously there are bound to be areas in which everyone must give and take in his personal expectations. If a couple share the same basic values, they are likely to easily reason out a teamwork approach to their mutual philosophy of child raising. However, parents often find that they have differing philosophies or feelings about raising their children. These differences may not be apparent during courtship and marriage. Philosophies just don't seem too important to young lovers. You may not be able to agree on everything, but at least decide what you *can* agree on and build on that. It isn't always a matter of who is right or wrong; it is a matter of trying not to raise a child in conflicting ways. I would almost rather have parents do the "wrong thing" as a team than to do "right things" separately. The reason is that children are opportunists who quite often try to assert their will. If they can play the parents against each other to get their way, they will. This creates problems, including that of one parent and the child taking sides against the other parent. It can hinder the emotional growth of the child, and it can also add to the difficulties in a marriage.

Not all experts agree with the teamwork principle. Psychologist Thomas Gordon, the author of *Parent Effectiveness Training*, says, "Parents don't have to put up a united front." [5] Gordon sees it as an unfair ganging up on the child. Part of his belief springs from his rejection of parental authority in discipline and we will discuss more about this in Chapter 7.

It is worthwhile noting that, as mothers and fathers solve their differences about parenting, they experience significant emotional growth. They learn to know each other better, and in trying to make things work as parents they generally make their marriage better. A marriage requires constant work anyway in order to remain viable. The act of facing up to differences logically and with a positive attitude is a sign of maturity. The diplomacy that one develops in handling interfamily problems is a skill that grows with use and can be applied equally well outside the family. By controlling aggravation and using emotions effectively, a family can become far more harmonious and enjoyable.

Most compromises in how family members deal with each other

work very well. In some families, however, compromises are difficult to arrive at and maintain. This is one cause of the rising divorce rate in our country. Of course, all compromises are not healthy and some families may have problems which are hidden. Some of the people involved may be consciously unaware of their own roles in causing or contributing to such problems.

POSSIBLE HIDDEN FAMILY PROBLEMS

Dr. Donald Naftulin, a psychiatrist in Southern California, has studied and identified some of the common bothersome patterns of family interactions. Any of us may fall into one of these somewhat unhealthy methods of dealing with other people, and it can cause considerable distress within the family. By becoming aware of these self-defeating styles of behavior, we may be able to improve our own behavior and smooth out family functions. Keep in mind that there are hundreds of other stylized behavior patterns and thousands of variations of family behavior patterns.

The Villain and Victims

Sometimes two members of a family blame each other for all the problems. If, say, a child is able to convince the rest of the family that he is the victim of a villainous father, then this relationship can make him the center of attention for all of the family. This behavior can cause a lot of harm to the rest of the family, and it may cause other family members to misbehave in reaction to the donnybrook.

The "All's Well" Family

Many families don't recognize that they have serious problems and yet may actually be very angry with each other. They assume that everything is fine and rarely show their emotions to each other. This sort of emotional divorce is made possible by focusing all their attention on superficial problems such as money, an illness, or whether to put grandpa into a rest home. A few of these families are sick, with schizophrenic or neurotic members. But a lot of ordinary families hide their frustrations and anger behind conformity. They are really isolated from each other and don't understand or appreciate each other's feelings. They never fight, but put on a show of togetherness and sweep their crises under the rug.

The Stylized Family

In this family, each member reacts in a set, stylized pattern to the other members, whatever the problem. They fail to recognize each other's needs and feelings, changes in personality, or future expectations. If they were really able to understand each other, they would be able to relate in richer and more helpful and enjoyable ways.

The Secret
Sometimes family members are very careful with each other, almost afraid, as if there is a family secret which might be disturbed if feelings were discussed openly. Sometimes there may be a "skeleton in the family closet"; but other times there is just a suspicion of fear that there is a secret which might cause trouble if it came out. Usually there is no secret, just unfounded suspicions. But the emotions such worry creates interferes with free and close communication between family members.

The Alliance
In some families, two of the family members form a close alliance at the expense of others. Often the allied members are not consciously aware of their alliance or that they back each other in running down another member of the family. An example is when a husband and daughter team up and support each other in criticizing and deprecating the mother. Such alliances can occur between family members of the same sex, between brothers and sisters, or even between a family member and a pet.

The Double Message
People can say one thing and mean another. This is called a double message. It is accomplished by saying words that mean one thing while giving a different message by using contradictory voice tone, facial expression, or gestures. Thus a mother may say to a child, "Don't do that!" while her tone and facial expression tells the child, "Do that!" Usually all of us, children and adults, respond more to the tone and expressions than to the words.[6]

Dealing with Family Problems

Most family problems are not hidden and are not serious. If you believe there is a serious problem in your family then seek outside professional help. However, most family problems are the result of not meeting each other's needs. Sometimes we have to learn to reduce our own needs and recognize that we cannot always meet all the needs of our spouse or children. So we compromise. Compromise isn't a second best answer —something we have to do because we aren't doing so well. It is a necessary condition of living, even of living with ourselves. It is a solution and a skill that improves the more we learn about it and the more we practice it. Compromise allows us to make the best of a situation. The art of compromise is a form of parental growth and development that can go a long way toward building a happy family.

FATHERING

Parenting is generally fun, whether you are a father or a mother. In the past, mothers traditionally have borne the larger share of daily responsibilities, so it is not surprising that the trend has begun towards equal sharing between mothers and fathers and moving Dad closer to center stage in the parent-child drama. Traditionally, Dad has been the breadwinner, the disciplinarian, the football tosser. Today, however, fathers are being asked to participate more fully in all aspects of parenting, including the pre-natal and delivery stages.

Figure 2

This is a role for which many of today's American males feel unprepared. Their legacy and personal experience as a child may not have exposed them to much active fathering. Other fathers who, deep down, would like to assume a more active parenting role nonetheless fear that doing so somehow will threaten their masculinity. This fear stems in part from our culture's designation of many aspects of nurturing children as feminine and in part from a reluctance to "submit" to the demands of the women's movement.

Sex Roles

The best argument for more active fathering, as Stanford University psychologist Shirley Feldman points out, has less to do with sociopolitical considerations than with the needs of children themselves.

Fathering is more important and produces far more effects than many have realized. A boy develops his male self-concept by identifying with his father; this development takes place most smoothly if the boy perceives his father as warm, powerful, competent, and loved by other people. When father-son relationships are inadequate or missing, especially during the preschool years, this development may be more difficult, requiring the boy to seek male behavior models from among playmates, brothers, male relatives and teachers, and from characters in books, films, and television.

By the same token, girls need fathers in order to try out their feminine social skills, which they will later transfer to boys. Some studies indicate that teenage girls in families where the father was absent showed inappropriate patterns of getting along with boys and men: They became either too anxious and shy, or reacted the other way and became promiscuous or over-assertive. However, some authorities question the validity of such studies. Certainly it doesn't always turn out this way!

Mental and Intellectual Adjustment

Research indicates that warm and involved fathers who spend time with their children, who listen to them and who know how they think and feel, have children who perform well at school, who wish to achieve, and who are analytical and flexible in their thinking. Critical, restrictive, and punitive fathers tend to inhibit the development of scholastic aptitude, especially in their daughters. Interestingly, well-educated, noncontrolling fathers who trust their children tend to have highly creative daughters but not necessarily highly creative sons.

Moral Development

Warm, involved, and affectionate fathers tend to have children who are generous and altruistic, who care for others, and who are able to make moral judgments according to internal standards rather than to external expectations. Conversely, strict and punitive fathers tend to have children who show little concern or consideration for others, and who are more susceptible to external temptations.

Time for Fathering

For a father to learn how to be an *active* father, he needs to spend time with his offspring, and the sooner the better. Fathers who play, cuddle, and help care for their infants from the very beginning are more likely to form a strong, longer lasting, and more intimate commitment to their children than those who assume that the early phases of child care are women's work. The attractiveness of infants can serve as a powerful antidote to the traditional "hands off baby" attitude many men have adopted (although at first Mother may have to go out of her way to make these initial encounters pleasant and nonthreatening for her husband). The baby, too, needs early contact with his father in order to form an attachment to him. Although we have no evidence that a close relationship cannot form later in life, a combination of intellectual and social factors suggests that the second half of the first year of life is the time when such attachment is most successfully formed; some research findings indicate that attachments are best formed right after birth.

Finding the Time

One of the biggest problems facing many fathers is finding enough time to spend with their children. Although it is never too late to start, the later a father starts, the more valuable time is lost. This is time in which children learn about father—his values and expectations, his role. They learn to depend on father, and then, using him as a model, develop beyond this toward self-sufficient men and women. When this time is not given to children, problems can occur. So, if you didn't start fathering at the time of your child's birth, which might have been ideal, then at least start now. Pediatric psychiatrist Robert Herman is especially firm about the need of school age children for *active* fathering:

> If you are a father, you should set aside some time, weekly or bi-weekly, to spend alone with your child, especially after he or she turns seven. By so doing, you begin little by little and without effort to establish a trusting and caring relationship with each child on a one-to-one basis.
>
> Spending time with all the children together is helpful, but during much of that time the children compete for their share of attention. Generally, one or two manage by their tactics to get far *more* than their share, without your being aware of what is happening. The loss may be devastating to the less demanding ones.
>
> What you do on your one-at-a-time visit need not be special, not every time at least. A trip to the store, or even running errands, can be a very special time. Taking a child out for breakfast, a hot dog, or a coke can set the climate for some revealing, interesting conversations that will help you and your child know each other better. Start this when the child is young so that by the time the troubled adolescent years begin you have already established a forum.

My experience with fathers who have not fathered early on is that they are still able to develop a close and significant relationship with their children whenever they start. Some fathers who have seemed unable to relate to infants or small children later relate easily to adolescents. The beauty of all this is that it is never too late to start. The sadness of it for those fathers who start late is that the fathers themselves have lost so much valuable and enjoyable time with their children.

WHAT IS MOTHERING?

Mothering and fathering have never been more important, according to Julie Stone Oliver:

Our homes are not a haven from life, but the primary place where life is actually lived. Our job, as mothers (all of us who care for children), needs no pretty phrases to make it seem important. We have many questions about whether to become mothers, about how to mother, and about how to balance our mothering and our personal needs, but one question we need never ask, and that is whether our mothering role matters. We know that our job is vitally important and worthy of all the maturity, commitment, and effort we can muster.

Like everything else, mothering has its share of problems. We put ourselves down: "Oh, I don't do anything. I'm just a housewife." The experts tell us to mother more; the experts tell us to mother less. We feel guilty if we do stay home to housewife and mother. We feel guilty if we don't stay home to housewife and mother. We're torn between the encouragement of the women's movement to do our "own thing" and the traditional demand of society to do "our duty." Lots of the experts seem to know exactly what we should do and be. Most of us only wish we could be that certain. We're busy finding our own answers, and it is a difficult and complicated job.

For a long while, many of us have mothered "by the book." Perhaps it is time for us to rediscover that we, ourselves, are experts on mothering. Most people give lip service to the glories of motherhood, but at the same time devalue it in reality. Demanding greater respect from society for our role as mothers won't change the downgrading of our importance. We need to convince ourselves first. Ask any one hundred mothers what a mother is and you will receive one hundred different answers as well as one hundred answers that are remarkably the same. We are different things to different people. Our role is living and loving. Our role is to do what is needed in whatever way we can. Our role is giving and receiving. We handle the impossible and the improbable. We have virtues and defects, ups and downs, successes and frustrations. We are not grouped in tidy categories of saints or sinners. We are people, we are women. We are mothers.

MOTHERING

Despite efforts to increase Father's part in raising children, Mother is still what researchers call the "primary parent"—the one who spends the most time with the child; the one who performs the minute-to-minute, day-to-day parenting functions; the one who, as the hub of the family circle, is responsible for the complicated logistics of feeding, care, home maintenance, and family traffic control. It is a challenging occupation, a multi-faceted job requiring many different talents, remarkable energy, and a lot of stamina. Not surprisingly, one of the most frequent causes of family problems is mother's fatigue. Burton White, Harvard child-care authority, points out how rough a mother's life can be: "We allow the quality of everyday life for many of our young families to be far more stressful and far less rewarding than it could be. A great number of our very best put-together 25-year-old women have a miserable average day with two young children. Very few people realize this, and the last ones to know are their husbands." [7] And husbands had better know about the stresses of motherhood.

For some strange reason, writes Dr. James Dobson in his book, *What Wives Wish Their Husbands Knew About Women,* human beings (and particularly women), tolerate stresses and pressures much more easily if at least one other person knows they are enduring it. He files this principle under the category of human understanding and notes:

> It is highly relevant to housewives. The frustration of raising small children and handling domestic duties would be much more manageable if their husbands acted like they comprehended it all. Even if a man does nothing to change the situation, simply his awareness that his wife did an admirable job today will make it easier for her to repeat the assignment tomorrow. Instead, the opposite usually occurs. At least eight million husbands will stumble into the same unforgiveable question tonight: "What did you do all day, dear?" The very nature of the question implies that the little woman has been sitting on her rear-end watching television and drinking coffee since arising at noon! The little woman could kill him for saying it.
>
> *Everyone* needs to know that he is respected for the way he meets his responsibilities. Husbands get this emotional nurture through job promotions, raises in pay, annual evaluations, and incidental praise during the work day. Women at home get it from their husbands—if they get it at all. The most unhappy wives and mothers are often those who handle their fatigue and time pressure in solitude, and their men are never very sure why they always act so tired. [8]

Dobson urges that mother get out of the house completely for one day a week—"Doing something for sheer enjoyment." He counsels that most American families can afford a sitter if they are willing to slow down spending for fancy new furniture or for a new power saw for dad. But his major point is that mothers have a continuing need to have appreciation shown by their husbands.

Fatigued and Bored Mothers

Some mothers don't get out enough, or for other reasons may become fatigued and bored. In fact, some may build up enough pressure and resentment that they "blow up" or break down. If you are a mother (or for that matter, a father), and feel yourself getting too tense, you should get some relief before it really becomes an emergency.

Emergency Relief

When the pressures start to accumulate and to be too much to bear, one of the first things you should do is to seek some time to be by yourself and away from responsibilities. Start by doing the possible. Leave the kids with a relative, friend, or neighbor while you at least go to the store. Get a part-time job and put the children in a day care center or hire a good sitter. Go back to school. Go camping with your husband. If you can afford it, get away for a vacation. But go. If you don't like vacations, do community work or visit friends. (A mother should not be around the children *all* the time.)

Get away and refresh yourself and you may be able to change your emotional attitude toward the children, if not toward housework or your spouse. Don't expect perfect behavior from yourself or from them; but do insist that they stay under control just as *you* must stay under control. That control isn't always easy; one reason is that underneath it all you may feel very guilty about your need to get away and your feelings of rejection. And guilt, especially, tends to make us angry and makes control that much more difficult.

If you are too guilt-stricken or if you are so angry that you always fight with your children rather than discipline them, you may need help. See if your doctor can help you or if he can refer you to someone who can. Don't feel bad about asking. You probably will find that your problems aren't all that awful or unusual and that you can build a satisfying life and function well as a mother. Keep that mother badge!

Some blame housewife-mother's fatigue on the boredom of repetitive daily duties in the home. However, Dr. Estelle Ramey of Georgetown University's School of Medicine found out, in her study of boredom, that:

> Large numbers of stereotypic housewives are *not* bored by the PTA or their daily routines. They enjoy them. There is, in fact, far more potential

flexibility and variety in running a home than in being a file clerk, a bank teller, a sentry at a missile base, or an assistant editor at *Penthouse*. . . . It is not the job itself, but . . . the sense of control, power, and status it engenders that determines whether you'll suffer the pain of boredom.[9]

Of course, there are a lot of women who are not in the mother's role who are unhappy, too.

The Dissatisfied Mother

Dr. Ramey's study makes it very clear that throwing down one's apron and rushing to the nearest employment bureau is by no means a sure cure for boredom. The end result could well be being bored with two jobs instead of with one. To an extent, we can all learn to control and alleviate some of the boredom we feel with our jobs, without throwing them over completely. The first step for housewives is to admit, without guilt, that they are—or are not—bored with homemaking. With today's pressures on women to be something more than "just" a housewife, some will find it hard to admit that they find the job fulfilling, in and of itself. If you do feel unfulfilled as a person, the place to begin to be more fulfilled is with yourself.

Some of the following suggestions from Julie Stone Oliver may be of help to you if you feel you need your batteries recharged:

- Live your own life; don't try to live it through your child.
- Don't make your child responsible for your fulfillment, happiness or welfare.
- Forget working for a martyrdom medal. Get away when you need to, develop outside interests, value your adult relationships, work on your own growth and development.
- Schedule some time every day for yourself.
- Try self-determination instead of self-pity. Concentrate on what you can do about your problems instead of just crying over them.
- Enhance your self-image. Improve your mind, your body, your marriage. Develop a new friendship or rejuvenate an old one. Take on a personal project you feel you can do well.
- Develop a special talent instead of nagging your children to do so. Maybe you're the one who'd really enjoy piano lessons!
- Don't try to "play a role." Be yourself. Develop your own style of parenting; you don't have to mother the same way your mother did. You don't have to *not* mother the way she did, either.
- Learn to say "no" when family and friends seem to be pulling you in all directions at once.

What this all adds up to is that, regardless of division of labors between spouses, and regardless of attitudes or new styles of "families," in our society today children depend overwhelmingly on women, and specifically on mothers. Most mothers enjoy the challenge and rewards of

Figure 3

mothering, even if for many there is little support from husbands, family, or society. Of the reasons for dissatisfaction with the mothering role, probably one of the most serious, is isolation, either within the nuclear family or with no family at all. No mother should be isolated in a home or an apartment away from the rest of the world, for she must interact with and contribute to life outside the home in order to grow as a parent. Isolation, even with the most enjoyable of children, can cease to be healthy. Parents, both mothers and fathers, must keep in touch with the community by living in it if they are to prepare their children adequately for the world. But, on the other hand, the full-time working mother may have too much of the outside world and not enough time to parent as she would like.

The Working Mother

Over twelve million mothers work outside the home. Of these women, more than four million have no choice: They work to support,

Figure 4

or help support, their families. Fifty-five percent of all working mothers choose to do so, in order to find the stimulation and fulfillment they do not get at home. No matter their motivation, however, very few working mothers can completely escape a nagging sense of guilt over leaving their children. Although guilt seems built in to the parenting process, the guilt of working mothers can be particularly acute. If, as a mother, you have the freedom to choose whether or not to work outside the home, be prepared to experience some additional guilt. Justified or not, it can more than offset any gains, financial or emotional, that you had hoped to achieve by taking a job.

How Soon Can a Mother Work Outside the Home?

For mothers who must work or who want to work, the most emotionally charged question is how soon can you take a job outside the home and leave the baby or child. Factually, I have seen many mothers return to their careers or jobs as early as six weeks after a delivery. Mostly this is where a member of the family, usually grandmother, can take care of the baby. I don't approve, because many mothers aren't really physically up to working outside the home all day and then at home half the night that soon after giving birth. It can age them before their time. Most experts counsel against a mother working until at least three months after the baby is born. Early return to "work" can actually be an escape from the greater amount of work at home, but it means that a mother can't continue to breastfeed her child. Even more, mothers miss a lot by not being around, especially after the first three months, when the baby's personality begins to develop. And later, when the toddler begins to explore and learn, is another critical and enjoyable time. It is something like the song from *Camelot*, "If ever I would leave you, how could it be in spring time . . . summer, winter, or fall— No, never could I leave you—at all." [10]

Unfortunately, for too many parents, there is no choice. If you *do* have a choice (and this is dictated by a combination of economic necessity, personal values, and your own feelings and needs as well as your child's), you may wish to heed the advice of Australian pediatrician Eric Sims, who writes: "No one will deny the importance of active mothering, particularly in the preschool years. It is certainly better if a mother's gainful work outside the home can be deferred until a child is at least five years old; but, when that is not financially possible, then a mother can usually still arrange her commitments so that she can be with her infant at critical times."

Psychologist Burton White pinpoints the first three years as critical: "A child needs to get through the first three years with a healthy attachment to his mother. The social patterns he develops with his mother will serve as the basis for his social interaction with other adults and children." This is not to say that a child must spend *all* his time with his mother until the age of three; in any event, for many mothers, this is a luxury they cannot afford—and it is not proof of love to spend every minute of the day with your child. Research has shown conclusively that infants can spend a large portion of their day in the care of warm, nurturing adults in infant day care centers and not show adverse effects. There is even some evidence for positive gains in the infants studied.

Working mothers can also take comfort in this summation of a study of working mothers by Dr. Mary C. Howell, reported in the journal, *Pediatrics*:

- When wives are employed by choice, there are fewer marital tensions.
- If both husband and wife want the wife to work, they are happier about the employment.
- There is a risk that a woman who devotes her entire existence to being a wife and mother will become over-dependent on or over-demanding of, her children.
- Almost no constant, scientifically measurable differences can be found between the children of employed and non-employed mothers.

The summary also highlighted other findings that mothers who don't need to work should consider:

- Marked changes in caretaking procedures when the infant is six to nine months of age may be stressful to him. However, substitute care is not harmful if it is loving and attentive, and given by a person who can enjoy the child and has the time and energy to respond to the infant's moment-to-moment needs.
- If parents feel guilty about sending their children to day care centers or baby-sitters, there is likely to be dissatisfaction with the arrangements for such care. If, however, they feel that good caretakers can be of benefit to their children, then their own parenting may improve.
- When wives are employed through necessity rather than preference, there is more marital tension. This also holds true for wives who are not employed but wish they were.[11]

Everyone's case is different, and generalizations are rarely helpful. I have seen problems occur with children that I believe might have been prevented had mother been home. Mothering—parenting—is really a full-time occupation until the preschooler gets into nursery school, and then it is hardly less than full-time. On the other hand, I am continually amazed at how well so many full-time working women also function as parents. I not infrequently advise some mothers to take outside jobs rather than feel so isolated from the world and so bored at home that they become tense and ineffective parents. Even then, my preference (not necessarily theirs) is that they work outside the home part-time, so that they actually have the time required to be a parent. Such problems or advice may be hard to understand for a mother who fully enjoys her children and her home and doesn't have to work. Such mothers, and you are the majority, should continue your full-time career as mother, house-wife, and community resource person. You are among the most productive citizens in our society even if you don't receive a pay check or have a "glamorous" outside career. But you should still actively do something aside from parenting and housekeeping. Most parents need the stimulation of adult company and other challenges beside children.

If leaving your children makes you feel guilty, don't look on time away from them as self-indulgence; think of it as part of your parenting duties, keeping in touch with the world outside the home which you are preparing your children to face. Such advice is hardly necessary for working mothers. Their needs usually are for a forty-hour-week substitute parent. But working or not, all parents need to get away from time to time. When you do work or get away, a lot of your effectiveness as a parent depends upon your attitude and self-discipline.

Holding Two Jobs Successfully:
Parenting and Outside Employment

Although full time work for mother and day care for the children is not always ideal, I see many well-raised happy children in such families. Part of the secret of success is a parental attitude which accepts the reality of the situation and doesn't waste time on guilt or unhappiness because things are not ideal. This allows parents to enjoy their children and spend what time they have with them effectively. What the whole issue seems to boil down to is this: If you must work, for whatever reasons, do so. Make every effort to see that your child is well cared for in your absence; then, rest assured that your child will be happier than if you stayed at home and were miserable, either financially or emotionally. If you are thinking about working, recognize that some of your ambivalence may stem from feelings of guilt. If you do feel guilty, perhaps it will help to set realistic goals for yourself. You cannot be a perfect parent, so don't be disappointed with yourself when you don't always live up to your goals. Where you do goof, look at your mistake only long enough to teach yourself how to avoid it in the future, then go on with life and forget the error. Learn to expect some guilt and be prepared to live with it and not take it out on the child you feel guilty about. Your child doesn't really want you to feel guilty, and probably accepts better than you do whatever it is you have or haven't done. Don't set impossibly high motherhood standards for yourself, standards which you might like now to revise.

" Tonight for our family hour we want you to turn the set off and introduce yourselves to each other. "

Figure 4a

Making the best use of your time is another key. Successful parents don't waste time escaping via television or moping around; they actively play with, talk with, teach, and discipline their children when they are with them. They share their lives. This can be more than some non-working mothers accomplish. The third key for working mothers is that, since the parents are not able to be with their child at every critical time, they must take steps to assure themselves that whoever is there has similar ideas about child-rearing and will act in ways that are acceptable to the parent and responsive to the child. They must also attempt to insure continuity of care so that the child is not subject to upsetting changes and so that he can develop a meaningful one-to-one relationship with the substitute parent. However, for some there may be options that will make it possible to work and yet still spend enough time with your child. One option is the at-home career.

Earning Money at Home

Julie Oliver, who works at home as a free-lance writer and editor, offers her thoughts on at-home careers:

> The obvious place to begin is with any special talent or training you already have. If you are considering new training, first check out the potential job market in that field. Some jobs can be performed completely at home; others require a minimum amount of time in an office or other place away from home. Many businesses, futhermore, are more receptive to changing the structure of their jobs than they once were. If you have the nerve, you might be able to convince them to try new arrangements—splitting a job between home and office or between two people, for example; or arranging for work which could just as easily be done in the home in the evening as in an office in the daytime.
>
> If you want to start your own business, don't hesitate simply because no one else is doing what you want to do; you may have discovered a real need to be filled. Talk to others who are doing what you want to do, conduct extensive research, do everything possible to ensure your success. Don't give up just because you're very unsure of yourself, or it sounds difficult, or the idea is new. Wanting and needing a thing very badly, combined with a willingness to commit yourself, are tremendous assets for any job. The most important thing of all is to learn to value your own abilities. The fact that you don't have a formal education, training, or a degree does not mean that you have no marketable assets. Many women who do have a college education may feel they are in the same boat you are.

Some of the More Obvious Jobs
That Lend Themselves to At-Home Work

Art instruction
Advertising layout
Architecture, design, drafting
Bookkeeping, accounting, income tax service
Catering: arranging parties or weddings

Child care for other working mothers, including baby sitting agency, nursery
   school
Counseling
Crafts instruction
Dancing, yoga, gymnastics
Dressmaking
Free lance computer programming
Handmade items for sale: art, all manner of crafts, clothing
Illustration
Insurance services
Interior decorating
Laundry
Mending and repairing
Needlework instruction
Phone work (research, sales, answering service)
Private music instruction
Publishing: free-lance copy-editing, writing, research
Remedial or specialized tutoring
Secretarial services
Sewing instruction
Speech therapy

The Option of Half-Time Work

There are many advantages to mother from half-time work. She can
earn money, take an active part in the world outside of the home, and
thus be better able to prepare the children for that world. She can
broaden and use her talents as well as increase her circle of friends. She
might even make a more attractive wife. There can be advantages for
the child. If mother is more content working outside the home part-
time, she will probably be a better parent. And a part-time job allows
her to be with the child most of the day so that the child actually has a
chance to benefit from mother's more effective parenting. The four or
five hours a day the child spends away from the parent are usually a
worthwhile learning experience in how to deal with other adults and
children.

Of course, there is not much point in advising mothers to get half-
time jobs when there aren't many available, and when the amount of
money offered makes the job hardly worth taking. So I am going to di-
gress here and point out the benefits to employers and society of hiring
part-time workers. I urge you to help educate employers, unions, and
government to change their policies and make part-time employment for
mothers both practical and available.

There are many advantages to the employer of a team of two
women on one job, each working four or five hours a day. They are generally fresher and work harder. If one becomes ill or has to leave because
of an emergency at home, the other can usually fill in for her. There is

also better coverage during vacations. If rush work is required, one or the other mother can work overtime better than a single employee. Two workers on the same job can learn from each other and increase each other's efficiency. If continuity is required, each can work four and one-half or five hours with both being on the job at noon without much inconvenience. Then there is less likelihood of quitting because of guilt feelings and worry about the children at home.

However, there can be problems. First, the amount of money earned may not be adequate. Second, employers and unions usually have rigid rules. Third, there are governmental and union contract demands for fringe benefits and paper work that reduce the funds to pay working mothers adequately and that make it difficult for employers to be flexible enough to try new methods of using workers. These problems, however, can be corrected.

Specific changes in government and union regulations can help free enough money to increase the take-home pay of a part-time working mother. For example, employers should not be required to purchase health insurance for a working woman whose husband is covered on his job. This money should be given to the woman as increased pay. Part-time working mothers whose husbands work have less reason to require unemployment compensation, and employers should use such funds to increase pay. Income tax laws could be modified to encourage half-time employment for working mothers and to make it more economically worthwhile for mothers at home to establish their own small home care centers to take care of other children four or five hours a day. American society is flexible, and we have the enterprise and energy to do what must be done without being hung up by outmoded fashions, such as an eight-hour day for working mothers. Here is an area in which American business and government can demonstrate pragmatic compassion and leadership for the good of mothers and children in the longterm interest of our nation. For mothers of children from preschool through junior high school, half-time work or out-of-house activity is an ideal family situation. Our society can ill afford to lose the talents and remarkable industry of the 40 million American women who are mothers. More important, neither our children nor our society can afford to lose the vital mothering time and mothering commitment of love and energy for the children of working mothers.

THE SINGLE PARENT

There are seven million single mothers raising children in this country, and a smaller but growing number of single fathers with the same responsibility. It is no bed of roses: Loneliness, overwork, uncertainty, guilt, and a frequent feeling of being ostracized are common complaints of the single mother or father. The logistics of single parenthood can be tremendously taxing; yet more and more single parents, once they can shed the notion that they have "deprived" their children of a necessary ingredient of growing up, find a great deal of satisfaction in the single-parent experience. And, perhaps surprisingly, so do children in single-parent families, especially if they have felt the tensions of an unhappy marriage prior to divorce. Some children of divorce will "act up" during the divorce itself, but will eventually calm down and will often be much happier than they were before—*if* they are assured of their parents' continuing love, and if they realize that the divorce was not their fault (See Chapter 9 on Separation: Death and Divorce).

If you are a single parent, you may find that the following guidelines will alleviate some of your immediate problems and set the stage for a fulfilling future:

- Don't assume that one-parent families are intrinsically "bad" for children. It's the underlying nature of the parent-child relationship, and not the external trappings, that matters most.
- Don't try to be Superparent; the result could make you a tense, anxious mother or father who snaps at the kids. Share family responsibilities with them as much as possible; take them with you when you can on errands or visits.
- If you are divorced, don't try to compensate for having "harmed" your children.
- Find a way to share your insights and answers with others. By reaching out to help someone else, you will lessen your own isolation as well as theirs.
- Don't get hung up on mother and father "roles." Don't hold back on parenting because of someone else's strict role definition. Fathers can curl little girls' hair and mothers can play catch. But don't do it because you feel you have to be mother *and* father; do it because it needs doing and you want to care for your child. In any case, children can survive nicely without curls or catch.
- You are not alone. Others are in the same boat, and you can help each other with babysitting, shopping, problem-solving. Join one of the many single-parents groups such as Momma, Parents Without Partners, Solo, or Spares. Check with the YWCA, YMCA, churches, temples, college campuses, and community centers for educational, counseling, and social programs. The magazine *Momma*, for single mothers, offers help; it's available from *Momma*, P.O. Box 567, Venice, California 90291. The Journal of Parents Without Partners, Inc., *The Single Parent* is available at 7910 Woodmont Avenue, Washington, D.C. 20014.

If there is no single-parent group in your community, start your own. Single parents need the support and information that other single parents can best provide. Furthermore, it gives the children a chance to get together with other children from single-parent families. Again, churches, Y organizations, and community centers, or even the personal section of the newspaper want ads, are places to let other single parents know of your group.

STEPPARENTS

Like single parents, being a stepparent (or foster parent) may involve special situations and difficulties. Being a successful stepparent calls for the same talents as being a successful blood-parent—and more. Whether from death or divorce, one-parent children can make the life of a new stepparent miserable at first—even if he or she is experienced and understanding. The stepparent role requires real maturity and a willingness to let the children set the pace of the new relationship. Remember, stepparents are additions and not replacements. A stepparent with the patience to be loving and available without appearing to rush in and take over can eventually be rewarded with the love, respect, and affection of his or her new family.

Even so, there can be many problems. Especially with older children or teenagers, there are traps. Girls may be jealous of new mothers; adolescent boys may get a crush. The best thing a new parent can do under these circumstances is to keep a moderate distance and treat the child or children like the adults they are in the process of becoming.

If there was a divorce (or if the parent abandoned the children), spouses and children may carry over their emotional reactions from the natural parent to the stepparent. The children may be emotionally deprived, hungry for love, and yet afraid to demand or accept it. Problems of discipline become common as they test the stepparent to the limit, sometimes exhibiting behavior that courts physical punishment. There is a lot of jealousy to deal with. A child who has, in effect, replaced the absent parent may resent losing that role to the new stepparent. Others, accustomed to spending a lot of time with their remaining parent, may feel abandoned or deserted when the stepparent comes along and requires time with his or her new spouse. On the other hand, if the prior parent died, there sometimes is a mutual attraction between the children (who may be desperately looking for parenting) and the new parent.

Patience may be the most necessary virtue to the stepparent. Other ways to ease the transition and assume a satisfying stepparenting role include the following:

- Be open and honest with all family members' feelings.
- Prepare the child well in advance of taking a new husband or wife. Let the child express all of his or her feelings on the subject.
- Let the child decide how to address the new parent.
- Discuss rules and regulations openly with all members of the family. Make sure that both parents are in basic agreement on how discipline, love, care, and time with the children are to be handled.
- Avoid using the children as go-betweens in parental conflicts between the new set of parents and between former spouses.
- Avoid looking on the child as a living reminder of the past marriage.
- Don't expect that your new family will be the same as your old family.

- All parents need some time for themselves. This is even more important when two families are combined.
- Remember that the new stepparent may want to do some things differently from the natural parent. In the new family, all members have rights which should be respected; frequently family councils may help to resolve sticky questions.
- Don't think single. Stepparenting requires agreement between the new set of parents. The longer either partner has been single, the more difficult it is to remember to discuss problems and consult with the new husband/wife. There is a tendency for remarried parents to continue to "think single." Children will sense this division. Counseling (family counseling, not just individual counseling) should be sought out before problems escalate.

WHEN THE PARENT ISN'T THERE

All parents need to get away from time to time. When they do, they must turn to others to care for their children—the occasional babysitter, grandparents or other relatives, or the more formal child care centers, if a really good one is available. The need to get away exists by the time a baby is one or two months old. By then, most parents are in the market for a babysitter. And, according to Harvard child care authority Burton White, if they're not, they should be:

> Babysitting is essential for the psychological relief of the parent.
> I am not talking about day care, but about a few hours a week when
> a mother can leave her child, without guilt, and just get away. Can
> men envision being in the position of having total responsibility of a
> one-year-old and a three-year-old twenty-four hours a day, seven
> days a week? It is hard to appreciate what that means until you have
> been put in that spot. One of the underlying frustrations of young
> mothers is that they cannot explain the experience very well to their
> husbands.

Baby Sitters

It is too bad that we are saddled with the words "baby sitter" for someone to care for our children when we have to get away. I don't want anyone just sitting when they take care of children. Certainly any mother knows that good child care involves a lot of work and effort, and that there is relatively little time to sit. However, few baby sitters function as substitute parents—as differentiated from the more formal nursery school or day care facilities where many parenting functions must be assured. So, in fact, most baby sitters for young children are neighborhood teenagers. It might be better, on occasion, either to pay a little more and let a neighborhood mother care for your children in her home, or to trade with her and take care of her children when she goes out. But, regardless, both you and the neighborhood mother should get away on a routine basis.

How to Pick a Sitter

There should be some guidelines for picking a sitter. There are some basics for you to consider in making your choice:

- *Age.* The sitter should be old enough to exhibit maturity in action and judgment. If your baby is under a year old, the sitter should be thoroughly experienced and mature, preferably an adult who knows about babies. Grammar school children are too young to sit for more than an hour or so during the day. Junior high school students may or may not be mature enough. High school children should be, but aren't necessarily. Older women are frequently the best.
- *Experience.* It helps if a sitter is from a stable family and has had experience caring for younger brothers and sisters.
- *Recommendations.* The sitter should be able to provide some. Check with her parents; remember that they are frequently back-up supporters for their babysitting children. You might also want to check with a sitter's teachers, scout leaders, and other adults who know him or her.
- *Interview.* Meet the sitter prior to the day you actually need babysitting services. See how the sitter and your children get along together.
- *Personality.* A babysitter should be level-headed, self-assured, friendly, and able to communicate with children, yet firm enough to exert effective control.
- *Training.* Has the sitter had any training for babysitting, first aid, emergency care? If not, you might want to start him or her out on short assignments.
- *Health.* It should be good.

However, at times there doesn't seem to be too much of a choice available. Of course, as parents, we aren't perfect—so don't expect sitters to be perfect, or to take on all parental responsibilities in your absence. If you can think of them as valuable, occasional helpers, you will be less likely to be disappointed. It's a good idea to establish working relationships with more than one sitter. A ready pool of several familiar faces will ease your scheduling problems, and will also reduce your children's need to have to adjust constantly to new people. Your local church might be a good resource center for sitters; often they will be older women who need work and who want responsibility and companionship. If, as is generally the case, your sitters are high school students, you might want to refer to some babysitting training manuals. Three good volumes are *The Cadette Girl Scout Handbook;* "A Manual for Babysitters," by Marion Lowndes; and "GEMS, Good Emergency Mother Substitutes" (Available through the Women's Auxiliary of your county Medical Society).

Another excellent publication is a brief safety guide for teenage baby sitters that parents and sitters should read—*Sitting Safety,* from the

Metropolitan Life Insurance Company. More detailed information can be found in *The Parents' Medical Manual*.

When you do leave your children with sitters there should be careful verbal instruction for the sitter. Make certain that she understands. It is also helpful to post some written rules. Dr. David Sparling offers a brief check list and a list of rules for baby sitting.

For The Sitter
1. No bathing of the children.
2. No food except that provided.
3. No visitors of any sex.
4. No telephoning except about the sitting task.
5. Keep parental rules established for the children.
   a. How much television.
   b. What privileges.
   c. Bedtime.
   d. What discipline the sitter may use.

For The Parent
1. Post an easily visible written list near the telephone of:
   a. The location and phone number where you can be reached.
   b. The number of a trusted neighbor or friend who will be at home in case help is needed and you are not near the phone.
   c. The phone numbers of:
      —the child's doctor.
      —the police and fire departments.
2. Show the sitter your list of rules for sitters.
3. Show the sitter the locations of food, clothing, first aid supplies, and fire extinguishers.
4. Leave appropriate toys and books available, and perhaps something new which will please your child.
5. Explain about the child's bedtime, snacks, clothing, activities, and discipline.
6. Indicate when you will return.
7. A point-by-point debriefing when you return will help you evaluate the sitter and help her to be more skillful the next time.

If you are fortunate, you will have a neighboring parent who can take care of your children while you are gone, or you may have a few reliable teenage girls available. But if there are none, should you use a boy to babysit?

Should Boys Babysit?

Should you employ a teenage boy to babysit? This question may seem to many people to be an affront to that really nice boy next door. And usually it is an affront, for most boys do very creditable jobs as sitters. However, one pediatrician said,

A boy in his early teens should not be given babysitting jobs outside his home regardless of his apparent reliability and past experience with younger brothers and sisters. In early adolescence, every boy is curious, impulsive, rebellious to some degree, and influenced strongly by newly developed sexual drives which he neither understands nor can completely control. It is not rare for a boy, while babysitting, to initiate sexual play with a small child he believes is too young to "tell." Although most boys are reliable most of the time, it is unfair and unwise to expose an immature adolescent to temptations which he may not be able to resist.

I queried forty practicing pediatricians and family practitioners on this point. Half of them knew of instances of boy babysitters engaging in sex with their charges (and a small percentage of girl sitters who engaged in sex play with visiting boyfriends). Overall, however, the number of such instances was low, and most of those queried thought that boys made reliable babysitters. Some thought the subject should not be broached, and felt that it is potentially damaging to some boys who sit. The majority of physicians queried, however, thought that parents should be warned of the possibilities. As a parent, your careful approach to teenagers will allow you to avoid damaging questions and accusations. Each individual is innocent until proven guilty, and should be judged by a history of valuable service, not by suspicions. If you do have a boy sitter, some pediatricians suggest that the sitting situation should be short—maybe just two hours or so—and not involve bathing or changing into night clothes. An occasional phone call might serve to strengthen faltering self control.

Grandparents Can Help

In today's world, the presence of parents or in-laws nearby and available for babysitting is an enviable luxury to young parents, many of whom live in different cities from their parents. In the best of all possible worlds, grandparents are wonderful creatures. To a child, a grandparent is a friend who has time to lend a sympathetic ear, a soft touch who seldom says no, a protector to hide behind when Mom or Dad are angry. Parents can turn to their own parents for guidance, and for freely given babysitting. Many grandparents, in turn, often have the time to spend with their grandchildren, and more than enough love to offer; they welcome the experience of participating in the development of a child without having the primary responsibility. Theirs is the "fun" part of parenting.

Although grandparents usually come close to this ideal, not all do, and none are ideal all of the time. Frequently there are unspoken feelings which can cloud the relationship among generations. What mother has not felt resentment when her mother or mother-in-law took the child's side in an argument, or criticized her methods of child raising? What father has never felt anger and frustration when his child turned to Grandpa for protection from paternal ire? What grandparents have never felt taken advantage of—satisfactory as babysitters, yes, but ignored as sources of advice and wisdom?

As with all human relations, the main ingredients of a successful child-parent-grandparent relationship are cooperation, love, and understanding. Grandparents must understand that their advice, although often valuable, is most appreciated when it is asked for; since they are not primarily responsible for their grandchild's upbringing, they do not have the privilege of calling all the shots. By the same token, parents should understand that their child can easily learn to adjust to different standards of behavior: that, for example, Grandma can indulge her grandchild if she wants to without confusing him unduly or leading him astray. Finally, parents (and grandparents) should realize that grandparents have personal needs apart from their children, and for this reason may have less time available for babysitting than some parents would like. Grandparents should be free to turn down babysitting requests without feeling heartless and uncaring.

Discipline When the Parent Is Gone

Whether your child will be watched by a baby sitter or parented by grandparents or a "substitute" parent in a day care center, discipline is still necessary. Julie Oliver suggests the following:

> Ask for and use all the reinforcement you can get in backing up your behavior rules. Anyone who cares for your child for any period of time should know, understand, and back up the rules you have established. If your babysitter or relative allows everything you forbid, you many have a very confused child and a full deck of discipline problems. Your child's discipline is *your* responsibility, whether you are present or not. You're the boss. Make it very clear to others who care for your child what forms of punishment you will allow for what types of misbehavior. When others care for your child, make it clear that you back up their authority, and that those caring for them must receive the same respect and obedience as a parent. You cannot expect your child to be controlled or even kept safe without delegating this authority and making it clear to your child.

NURSERY SCHOOLS

The difference between some day care centers and a traditional nursery school may be only one of semantics. Even mothers who do not work, however, often wonder if they should send their child to a nursery school. The answer varies with each child. Dr. Neil C. Henderson approaches the question from a practical point of view:

> Nursery schools are not necessary, but they can be to a child's benefit, particularly if he or she lacks playmates in the neighborhood, and if the school has sufficient equipment, space, and trained teachers to provide an interesting and safe environment. Three is a good age to start, although some children at this age are especially susceptible to infections, and so should probably be kept home for health reasons. Unless a child is extremely outgoing, it's probably best for the parent to introduce him to nursery school gradually, staying with him for increasingly shorter periods of time each day until he adjusts. Generally the teacher will be able to judge how the child is adapting. If the child has a temper tantrum when he is left at school, in spite of the adjustment being a gradual one, the solution may be to have the other parent take him to school. Many children get overtired during the first weeks of school; if they attend school at first on alternate days, they may in time become less anxious and not as fatigued. Many children simply may not be ready for nursery school; if the parent has a choice, it's best not to insist in these cases.

DAY CARE: SUBSTITUTE PARENTING

When both parents, or a single parent, must work, then someone must provide substitute parenting during the day. This is a far cry from babysitting, where parents can be relatively relaxed about temporary care. Picking a parent to substitute for you during a significant amount of time is a quantum leap—financially, emotionally, and practically. Financially, we know that money alone cannot buy a good substitute parent. Still, adequate payment may make it possible for a good substitute parent to take on the task. And part of their reward is the reward of parents, the children's affection. Another part of their reward should be your open respect—and very likely you can learn a good deal about parenting from talking with them. It is vital that day care isn't just a holding and feeding operation until the parents take the child home. Some types of day care are, and the head of the California State Health Department, Dr. Jerome Lackner, is against day care for young children. He has been quoted in the news as calling day care centers "nursing homes for little people." He believes children belong at home with their mothers raising them.[12] But for many mothers, that is impossible. The best most working mothers can do isn't too bad. If you work forty hours a week, that means you can be home about 120 hours a week with your children—over fifty active hours plus sleep. But for those forty hours you are gone, you may have to put your child into a day care center. And that could be an advantage to your child.

Advantages of Day Care

Although many day care centers are simply holding operations, good day care centers can be beneficial for many children. Dr. David Friedman of the University of Southern California has outlined many of the advantages of day care:

- A means for children to enrich their experience away from their parents, and for parents to develop their own potential.
- An opportunity for children to learn and explore in a safe environment, and for parents to understand the developmental needs of their children.
- Social and, when necessary, emotional support for the family with special needs (as in the case of single-parent families, and children with special problems).

Responsibilities of Good Day Care Centers

The advantages for children placed in a day care center occur when the center meets its responsibilities. Dr. Friedman's summary, which follows, of how a day care center can meet the needs of children at various ages can help guide parents as well as center personnel.

The Infant (Birth to One Year)

Children at this age are physically helpless and need a lot of feeding, fondling, and physical care. Child care services at this stage can help take the pressure off parents and frequently can help educate parents in how to parent properly. Parents often need relief from the stress of coping with their infant's needs, especially if those needs appear insatiable. They may also benefit from being exposed to good parenting models that day care personnel, in the best circumstances, can provide. Also, some parents may find they can get along better with their infant if they attend to their own needs by working or by some other activity outside the home. In these situations good child care services, which supplement parental care, can provide the infant with stimulation, necessary human relationships, and an opportunity to develop trust in his or her environment.

The Toddler (One to Two Years)

Parents may need help with, and relief from, coping with their child as he or she goes through the "terrible two's." The toddler may find it easier to accomplish his basic developmental tasks (growing independence, tolerating separations from mother, and handling social situations) away from parental influences and with other toddlers and caring adults.

The Preschooler (Two to Five Years)

Children at this age are learning to separate from their parents. Child care centers or nursery schools can help this process along; and they can also help the continuation of the tasks of coordinating motor patterns, developing conceptual understanding, learning how to get along with others, exploring, making choices, and expressing feelings.

The School-Age Child (Six to Twelve Years)

Children at this stage need day care in the hours after (and sometimes before) school. Child care services in these critical hours may spell the difference between success and failure in school and in handling developmental tasks, of acquiring intellectual skills, developing physical prowess, establishing an identity, and building a sense of industry and accomplishment. Organized groups of youngsters of the same age may enhance each other's physical and emotional development and help the child to master interpersonal skills. Even if a child is not exposed to day care services, this is the age when he or she can benefit from such organizations as Boy Scouts, Girl Scouts, Indian Guides, and Camp Fire Girls.

The Teenager (Thirteen to Nineteen Years)

Teenagers and their parents need support as much as or more than any age group. Although some parents will want their teenagers to receive day care in the hours before and after school, the greater emphasis for children of this age is on organizations and groups of their peers. Teenagers are in the process of becoming independent, developing their own ideas, and establishing relations with others their own age.

Disadvantages in Day Care

Day care centers are not good for all children nor are all day care centers good. Not all children of working mothers are happy, nor are all of the families. Some of this is a reflection of negative attitudes by the parents who are really unhappy when their children are in day care—or more specifically, when they are away from the parents. Another disadvantage is the cost of good day care—it can use up almost all the money mother makes. This latter point should also be considered when the government decides to pay for day care. It may be economically unsound in the long run. There are other disadvantages, even though good day care services can help both parents and children. Dr. Friedman points out some problems inherent in day care and some day care situations which should be avoided:

- Day care centers will not accept children with minor ailments, so if her child has a cold, Mother will either have to stay home or make other child care arrangements.

- Few day care centers will accept children under the age of three, nor does it seem in the best interest of the child to be in a large group at such an early age.
- Just putting a child in a room and letting him stay there until his mother picks him up is very harmful. Children do not develop normally, either physically or emotionally, if they are neglected. Women who care for children in their homes need not have professional training, but they should like children, and have the experience and interest to help them develop mentally and socially.
- Equally detrimental is an overemphasis on teaching "facts" before a child is emotionally ready. Many day care centers have become learning mills, to the disservice of their charges. Having children learn at their own pace is one thing; trying to teach them to read before they have mastered certain emotional and social tasks is another.
- Good day care should support, not compete with, the family. The child care worker who operates on the assumption that he or she can do better with a child than the parents can harm both the child and the parent—especially the mother who feels guilty because she has left her child in the care of others. Ideally, parents and day care personnel should make a real effort to brief each other on the daily progress of the child every time he is delivered or picked up. This kind of exchange can help parents see day care facilities as extensions of their home and family, not as rivals.

Types of Day Care

Day care can occur in a neighbor's home or a large governmentally funded center, with many variations in between. The physical facilities and number of personnel per child must be taken into consideration. The American Academy of Pediatrics has established basic standards for day care centers, including the number of personnel needed, space required, facilities to isolate sick children, and sanitary requirements.[13] Even in a neighbor's house, if yours is the only child, you should check on whether or not the house has been poison and accident proofed and on whether or not they have syrup of ipecac on hand in case of possible preschooler poison ingestion (see Chapter 1 in *The Parent's Medical Manual*). Arrangements should be made to have someone take your child to his doctor if needed; and emergency care authorizations should be signed in the doctor's office and the day care center. But physical facilities are not as important as the attitude, values, and philosophy of the people who will take care of your child.

What to Look for in a Day Care Center

Each center has its own personality and flavor. Some encourage independent and small group play whereas others offer firmer direction and organized activities designed to strengthen understanding and character. It is important that your child and the school are compatible, and that each child is treated as an individual. Aside from these important characteristics, pediatrician David Sparling suggests several things to check.

> A day care center for small children must not be overcrowded.
> It must have enough staff to give individual attention, and there should
> be little staff turnover. There should be a place to care for a child
> who has had a sudden illness. Transportation should be available
> to take the child to the doctor if necessary. Children should not be
> insulated from the problems of the kitchen, house cleaning, yard care,
> and even the occasional nonfunctioning plumbing or other household
> crises. Often, children learn to solve problems by seeing adults solve
> them. Most children have ample opportunity to observe women; it is
> particularly fortunate when they have the chance in day care centers to
> come in contact with men, teenagers, and other children.

What to Look for in Your Child

Whether with a sitter or a grandparent, in someone's home, a nursery school, or a day care center, you should check your child to see if it is good for him. Does he look happy when you pick him up and does he go to the center or the sitter reasonably eagerly? Listen to him. Find out how he feels about the personnel, about other children, and about himself. Get him used to telling you all about his day. Ask the sitter or "day-care-mother" or "day-care-father" how things went and what you can do to help. Tell them how you feel, and share your concerns and goals for your child and yourself. Parenting requires team work, and the team includes all who care for your child. The proof of the pudding is the effect on your child. So, each day, take a good look at him and try to follow through to make necessary changes.

NEIGHBORHOOD CHILD CARE COOPERATIVES

If, for financial or practical reasons, you cannot find an acceptable day care facility, why not start your own? If you are responsible, like children and their parents, have the right temperament, are willing to study things like the basic requirements, books on child rearing and care, and can be enthusiastic and innovative, it might allow you to work at home and be paid for it rather than go outside for a job. Possibly you can get a community organization to sponsor you. Keep it in the neighborhood if you can. Enlist neighborhood parents, but don't stop with them. Many retired men and women have the time and would like to help out. Teenagers, too, generally need jobs and can help by cleaning, entertaining, and teaching. Perhaps local schools can be called upon to use your co-op as a place to teach child care to their students, and, in these days of declining school enrollment, to offer the use of a schoolroom or two. Big budgets and large buildings aren't necessary; a home with a yard will do. Keep the business arrangements sound. Some parents can contribute their time and expertise; working parents will be willing to pay if they know their children are being well cared for. It can, of course, create many problems, but if kept reasonably small it may be a real service to the community. Be sure to check with your county family or social service agencies and welfare department for their licensing requirements. Invite social service workers to help you plan, and to make suggestions about how you can do the best possible job.

HOME CARE FOR CHILDREN

You may also want to take just a few children into your own home, rather than start a neighborhood co-op. Here, too, it is a good idea to check with your county social service workers for suggestions and requirements. If you limit the number of children so that you can care for them adequately, you may find this a very satisfactory occupation—offering financial remuneration and long term friendships. More than that, taking care of children helps you grow as a parent.

YOUR GROWTH AS A PARENT

Whether you run a day care center, teach, or take care of a neighbor's child, you function as a parent. And the name of the parenting game is maturation. Maturation is as natural for parent substitutes as it is for parents and children. Of course, parents with their own children have even greater tasks. According to David Friedman, University of Southern California pediatrician and child care expert, parents go through stages just as children do. There are at least seven such stages. In each, he emphasizes not only the changing parental tasks but also the evolving nature of the parent–child relationship as both child *and* parent prepare themselves for greater independence.

Stage 1: Learning the Cues
During the earliest months of their babies' lives, the parents' most bewildering problem is to find out what their youngsters are trying to tell them. Infants are completely dependent on them for all their needs—food, fondling, physical care. They are, in Dr. Benjamin Spock's words, "physically helpless and emotionally agreeable." Throughout this phase—this period of building trust—babies need to establish

confidence in their parents and in their environment. This trust will provide the foundation for further development.

Some babies are difficult to understand. Some parents have difficulty interpreting the individual cues by which their infants express need. Do babies cry because of hunger, fatigue, wet diapers, or are they just plain spoiled? An inability to interpret needs may occur because of parental inexperience, a temperament unsuited for (or initially uncomfortable in) the parenting role, or because of some more deepseated parental problem which interferes with the parent-child relationship.

Stage 2: Learning to Accept Growth and Development

The parents of toddlers can no longer exert total control over their offspring. Although toddlers continue to need love and attention from important adults, they are now fairly mobile and can begin to assert their independence. Spock speaks of a toddler's "sense of his own individuality and will power," and his "vacillation between dependence and independence." Erikson called this the period of "autonomy," since it represents the earliest development of self-reliance and self-control.[14] Many parents who "just love babies" find it difficult or impossible to tolerate toddlers who climb into closets and book shelves, tear up magazines, and break the family china.

This behavior challenges the parents of toddlers to enter a new phase of maturity—learning to accept the growth of their child while still maintaining sensible and necessary limits. Failure to accept growth may result in acute parental discomfort; failure to set necessary limits may jeopardize the safety and well-being of the child, both physically and emotionally.

Stage 3: Learning to Separate

We are accustomed to speak of the separation anxiety of two-year old children as they approach the outside world. Preschool children are increasingly mobile, have an active fantasy life, show an interest in proving their mastery of functional tasks—and develop the positive feelings towards their parents and parent-substitutes which leads them into what Spock calls "imitation through admiration." Erikson refers to this process as developing "initiative." Mothers and fathers are told they must allow their children to assert themselves, but at the same time they are told they must set limits. Understandably, the parent asks, "How do I encourage initiative in my children? Must I let them wreck my home? If not, then what do you mean by 'sensible' limits?"

A two-year-old's difficulty in separating from his parents can be reinforced if his parents are having difficulty separating from him. His tantrums and clinging behavior will diminish when the parents themselves learn to separate. Their task during this stage is to learn to accept and encourage this new direction of their child's development and to be content to model necessary standards—while continuing to involve the child in family activities, communication, and decision-making.

Stage 4: Learning to Accept Rejection Without Deserting

As they enter the middle years of parenthood, mothers and fathers must learn to accept what may seem at times to be total rejection by their offspring. "Middle-aged" children are in school, developing social lives, fitting into groups of their peers, channeling their aggressive and sexual drives into socially acceptable behavior, and developing strict consciences. At this stage, children learn to win recognition by performing and producing results; and the audience they seek to please exceeds their own family to include teachers, friends, and others outside the family circle.

If parents do not understand that this declaration of independence is normal for children at this stage, they may feel hurt, disappointed, or angry—even to the point of appearing to "desert" their children. However, despite bursts of self-assertion, children still need plenty of parental support. It is the parents' duty at this stage to give this support unobtrusively, without heckling, and with assurances of respect for their children's feelings and pride.

Stage 5: Learning to Build a New Life

Having been thoroughly discredited by their teenager, parents need to set about building a life of their own apart from their children and their roles as parents. The behavior of teenagers as they struggle to develop a sense of who they are may seem irrational to adults. Their experimentation and wild behavioral swings as they try to "find themselves" can be very hard on parents. During this stage, parents should confine any necessary conflict to specific and major issues at hand, and should avoid the constant criticism which undermines morale and strains family relationships. Nevertheless, no matter how hard they push, teenagers respect parents who stick to their guns, even though they may not show it.

The ideal parent of a teenager (which, of course, no one can ever be) provides a self-reliant yet communicative model for teenagers to tilt with—and a well-structured, yet somewhat flexible environment for teens to struggle within as they work out their acceptance of themselves, their social skills, and their identity. Parents can best help by rebuilding their lives more or less independently of their children. By themselves adjusting to changing family roles and relationships, parents provide a good example to teenagers. In this process, how parents feel about themselves is probably the most important determinant of their child's maturation and development.

Stage 6: Learning to Appreciate Your Adult Child

Parents don't stop being parents when their last grown child leaves home. Grown children may not need their parents in the way they once did; but this does not mean the end of parenting altogether. The end of active parenthood is also the beginning of a new relationship based on freedom and acceptance of each other's individual and possibly very different styles of life. Parenthood at this stage becomes more of a special friendship between independent adults who enjoy special bonds of love and understanding. Parents and adult children have a lot to offer each other as they travel their separate paths to self-fulfillment. Parents who can establish the psychological distance necessary to appreciate their grown-up children as separate people will be rewarded by returns of love and understanding that they may have despaired of ever receiving when their offspring were teenagers.

With today's trend towards an extended adolescence, many parents would like nothing better than to establish some physical distance from their children as well. They grow up, go to college, "rebel," and then come home again—having found that, in spite of real effort, they cannot find a place in a world that does not seem to be ready for them. When this happens, parental ulcers and youthful frustrations will diminish if there is a clearcut understanding of each other's rights and responsibilities, with financial arrangements and house rules based, as much as possible, on the "child's" ability to function as an adult.

Stage 7: Learning to Be a Grandparent

Grandparents are grandchildren's ties with a past which is as much a part of them as their present and future. By the same token, grandchildren serve as a grandparent's link with the future. Grandparents may be invaluable resources of information on child raising, and can help fill the many needs of their grandchildren in a direct and practical way. By "extending" the two-parent family, grandparents can relieve many parental pressures and add richness to the lives of their children and grandchildren. However, their function extends beyond the merely practical. As Margaret Mead writes in *Blackberry Winter*, "A society that cuts off older people from meaningful contact with children, a society that segregates any group of men and women in such a way they are prevented from having or caring for children, is greatly endangered." [15]

Grandparents function most successfully when they do not attempt to work out their own problems through their children and grandchildren. Increased maturity can make people "better" grandparents than they were parents, but grandparents should not use their grandchildren to make up for failures with their own offspring. Grandparents share the major responsibility of all the previous stages of parenthood dealing with themselves and others as they are *now*.

THE SPECIAL JOY

Putting it together, parents continue to mature as adults. Some parents who had problems with their children may find that, lo and behold, the clouds go away and a friendly and satisfying relationship may develop between them and their children when the children become adults. Difficult children may become marvelous people. But difficult or not, no other relationship has the same special love and gives the same special joy as the relationship between parent and child.

2

THE INFANT

This chapter covers information from pregnancy to diapers to colic—feeding, dressing, sleeping, what you do when baby cries, and other helps. As in the rest of the book, we often offer conflicting opinions on child care. These opinions come from experienced mothers, nurses, pediatricians—all experts in the ways of babies. However, there is no one "right" way, so learn to use your own judgment as to what is the wisest course for you and your baby.

If you haven't yet had a baby, it may be of help to get some idea of what it is like to have a baby at home. This is the province of mothers, so we asked an experienced mother, Alicia Herman, to "tell it like it is" as she saw it.

Infants up to five to six months exist on a survival level. In the womb, every need was met and controlled automatically and the body securely encased. From the moment of birth, when infants are thrust into "life," needs are no longer automatically met. Infants must now depend on themselves and on mother for breath, food, and comfort. Yet, babies have no real self-control. They exist on a reflex, instinctive level of survival. Newborns are "selfish"—recognizing and responding to no needs outside of their own. They are totally dependent. To get their needs met they use the only means possible: crying. Hopefully, someone is there to "provide."

It is normal for the newborn to cry when wet, hungry, uncomfortable, or uneasy. Some—with patience and tolerance—cry only when really in need; others—with more "delicate" systems—cry even at the unexpected movements of their own body parts. The newborn's

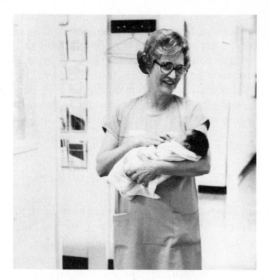

Figure 5   *Ready for mother.*

sucking reflex and the response to touch are strong. Most of the time,
the "normal" newborn sleeps. New mothers will sigh, "All he does
is sleep or cry." There is no give and take with a newborn—just take.
The body needs are urgent; there is a low threshold of patience. If
their needs are met adequately, they begin to make a relationship and
develop a trust in mother.

For the mother, "normal" means getting to know her newborn by
holding (no amount is "too" much), rocking, talking, and singing
to him.

She learns to read the cues in order to help meet the needs "on
time." She provides food and care—more according to the infant's
time schedule in these first few months than to her own. She develops a
good sense of trust in the baby; the baby will survive, will take that
next breath, and will respond to mother and father. She has a tolerance
for baby's needs—eating, crying, and sleeping.

As the infant matures he begins to remain awake some of the
time; and, while awake, he cries less. Slowly he becomes aware of
his environment: room, home, and people. At first, he is aware of "other
people "important" to his life, and then he becomes aware of "other
people." From six months on he becomes more used to the new (out
of the womb) setting and begins to adjust demands, and to develop
self-control and patience. He has better control of his motor reflexes,
and of other body systems and he becomes more aware of and
responsive to his environment. You might say he "looks outside of
himself" for the first time. He begins to develop memory and he looks
forward to things, mimics, and plays a bit.

Now mother too develops more self-confidence: She trusts her mothering abilities more. As she becomes more relaxed, she begins to encourage weaning. She derives great joy and satisfaction from serving her baby, from responding appropriately to baby's signs of distress and expression of needs. She begins to recognize the particular personality emerging. She is patient with him when he is frustrated, and she encourages him when he tries something new. She frequently lets him know of her delight in him—holding him, talking and playing with him, comforting and rocking him. She accepts him and all his peculiarities.

THE COSTS FOR A NEW BABY

It costs a lot—in money, time, and energy—to have and to raise children. Although these costs are relatively little in comparison to the tremendous joys and satisfactions of raising children, they can become a burden, especially if they are unexpected and unprepared for. The monetary costs can add up quickly: prenatal medical checkups and care, delivery and hospital fees, and the newborn's diapers, food, and pediatric bills. If both parents work, the loss of income that will result from mother being home, *at the least* for the first few months, must be taken into account. Of course, some of these costs may be covered by insurance. You will need more funds during the expensive first two to five years when children grow and change rapidly and have relatively little immunity to infection.

Check the costs of delivery and hospital and see what is covered under your own or your spouse's insurance policy. In working out an insurance plan keep in mind that some allow you freedom of choice of physicians while most complete prepaid plans strictly limit your choice. Some plans which look like a bargain may turn out to be unsatisfactory because they cut costs so much that there is little time for personal care. Be sure to go over any clauses that you don't understand with your insurance agent, or, if it is a company policy, with your supervisor or personnel director. Check on your employer's regulations regarding pregnancy. Some companies are very generous about bonuses and leaves of absence, others are not.

You should not feel that you must have all the frills for your child. Many young parents get along very well without a separate room for the baby. Secondhand cribs, strollers, and baby clothing can very readily be picked up for quite a savings from friends, "turn-about" shops, and even garage sales. Just be sure they are clean and in good condition.

Time and energy are the other big requirements. The areas they will influence the most are your personal freedoms and your relationship with your husband or wife. A baby needs full-time parenting and this is best done by you. It is especially critical during the first year not to just give mechanical care, feeding and changing, but to hold, talk to, and play with the baby. However, time away from the baby is just as important as time with the baby—parents should be able, occasionally, to get a break from the twenty-four hour day every day of the year job that's dedicated to the baby. Everyone, even the baby, needs a change and a chance to relate to other people. Arrange for babysitters (p. 34) and find something to do on your own—a part-time job, a hobby, tennis or bowling, or just a plain afternoon out every week.

TEAMWORK FOR PARENTS

What will having a child do to a marriage? It won't save a rocky marriage; in fact, the stress of bringing a third person home to share your lives with you can create a lot of problems. The whole idea of having children should be thoroughly talked out between the couple beforehand. Even so, you may find you didn't anticipate all of the problems that can occur. But then you probably haven't anticipated all the satisfaction it can bring, either. On occasions, new parents, mother or father, will find to their chagrin and amazement that they can be jealous of their own baby. This isn't so surprising when you recognize that none of us ever really outgrow the need to be babied occasionally. In fact, that is one part of marriage. So, if you do have mixed feelings toward your baby, don't be surprised. And don't hesitate to ask for a little babying yourself—and remember to love and baby your spouse as well as your baby. Such feelings can make it a little hard for a teamwork approach between mother and father. But if the feelings can be dealt with openly, you will find it easier.

I see a good number of parents confused about their roles in caring for the baby. Each couple has to work this out for themselves, but there are some facts to be kept in mind. First, Mother should stay home several months at the least, for her own health if for nothing else. Taking care of a baby is a full-time job, and holding down another job is asking too much. If you breastfeed, you will have to have the baby with you anyway. So usually, Mother stays home and works a twenty-four hour day and Dad works an eight hour day outside of the home. To balance things, Dad should help with the housework and the baby. At the same time, regardless of the team approach, someone has to call the shots and make the decisions—to direct the care of the baby. The natural one for this role is Mother—if for no other reasons than that she is there and that she does most of the work. But she needs a lot of practical help, as well as emotional support, from Dad—especially during those hectic first few months.

What if you are not certain that you really want a baby? A lot of mothers and fathers find themselves uncomfortable with the idea of becoming a parent. Some even reject the baby at birth. There is nothing too unusual about this. Even later, when your child is a preschooler or a teenager, most parents ask themselves on occasions why they had children. Luckily, these occasions are overshadowed by the solid satisfactions, comfort, and joy parents receive from raising children. If you do feel negative, disappointed, angry or guilty about your baby it will be wise to discuss these feelings with your doctor. It helps to give and receive love from your husband or wife. Above all, don't lose your sense of humor. After all, it's only a lifetime job you are entering!

BEFORE YOU GET PREGNANT

The best way to assure your baby's health is to make certain of your own good health (and your spouse's) before you get pregnant and to maintain your health while you are pregnant. Most of the points listed below are just plain common sense, whether you're planning a baby or not.

1. Mothers should get a complete physical and gynecological examination by their physician. A cervical culture for gonorrhea may be advisable, as this disease can smolder for years without symptoms. An examination for genital Herpes II virus infection might also be in order since, like gonorrhea, it can be present without symptoms and can both infect the infant and harm the mother. Be sure to tell your obstetrician if you have had genital "cold sores" (and especially if you get them during pregnancy). Overall, gynecological examinations during pregnancy will help you to avoid having a baby that is damaged by an abnormal uterus, too small a pelvis, toxemia, infection, or hypertension in the mother.
2. Get onto a well-balanced diet with adequate vitamins. Get into and stay in good physical health by regular exercise.
3. Stop taking unnecessary drugs and advise your doctor of any drugs that you are taking. Stop smoking: Infants of smoking mothers are smaller at birth than those of nonsmoking mothers. Stop drinking: Recent study indicates that a pregnant mother who averages only two drinks a day may deliver an infant who is abnormally small and jittery. The greater the amount of alcohol consumed, the higher the incidence of mental retardation in the baby.
4. Have your blood tested for syphilis, immunity to rubella, anemia, Rh type, and, if indicated, for the sickle cell trait or Tay-Sachs disease, and, possibly for toxoplasmosis. Active toxoplasmosis infection in the mother during pregnancy can infect the fetus, causing miscarriage or delayed retardation, blindness, or epilepsy. Toxoplasmosis is a parasite carried by cats, dogs, swine, sheep, chickens, and pigeons. Up to 25 percent of raw pork and 10 percent of raw beef and mutton may be infected with toxoplasmosis cysts. Cat feces may contain infective cysts if the cats have eaten raw meat. Especially during pregnancy, avoid possible infection by following these suggestions:
   a. Wash your hands after handling cats.

b. Have someone else empty the cat litter box or clean up any cat feces.

c. Do not feed indoor cats raw meat or let them eat mice. Keep outdoor cats outdoors.

d. Cook all meat thoroughly.

5. Check your family histories for possible significant inheritable or congenital diseases. Information about the odds of passing the disease to your offspring can be obtained from your doctor or from a genetic counseling center. Your doctor can advise you about what diseases to look for in your family history.

WHILE YOU'RE PREGNANT

Having a baby involves many exciting, new, and wonderful experiences. The adjustment from being pregnant to caring for your new baby can usually be eased by learning some simple mechanics about being parents before the big day actually comes. Many courses in how to handle, change, feed, and care for a new baby are offered by the Red Cross, your community center, adult education programs, hospitals, and parent's clubs. (Your doctor can help you find a suitable program.) Most often, the classes are conducted by nurses, and pediatricians are usually invited as guest speakers. But don't stop with classes. If you haven't been around babies, get to know a few. Offer to baby-sit for neighbors or relatives. Ask if you can watch them bathe and feed their babies. Attend demonstration baths in the hospital's maternity ward.

During your pregnancy, you'll also probably want to begin getting together the things—such as clothes, crib, diapers, and bottles—that the baby will need right away. However, don't go overboard. Often, new parents buy or are given more baby things than they can use. Before making a lot of purchases, check with your friends and neighbors and see what you can turn up that could be used. Rarely do baby clothes and furniture wear out after only one baby's use. Then, when shopping, be conservative, for you can easily get whatever you need after the baby has arrived. You will, however, need clothes and blankets to take the baby home in, as well as an infant car seat (see Chapter 1 of *The Parents' Medical Manual*). The following is a list of items needed for the newborn:

Infant car seat.
Blankets
Sheets
Pillow
Bassinet or crib with bumpers
Cradle or rocking chair
Diapers (Pins for cloth diapers or tape for some disposables)
Diaper bag, diaper pail, and diaper soaking solution for cloth diapers

Plastic pants to cover diapers during social events or when you carry the baby
Consider your climate and the season of your baby's birth, when purchasing
  undershirts, socks, booties, hat, nightgown, bib.
Supplemental formula
Bottles and equipment
Breast shield (check with your obstetrician)
Nursing brassieres and pads
Goose neck lamp or high intensity reading lamp to soothe sore nipples
Simple soap (unscented and without additives)
An adequate sink or bathing tub
Cotton balls or pads for cleansing
Rubbing alcohol
Cotton tipped applicators (use for cleaning umbilical cord *only*)
Talcum powder if you insist (use sparingly)
Body lotion to use if needed
Vaseline for coating circumcision area if it is a boy
Ointment Vitamin A and D for initial treatment of diaper rash *if* it occurs
Pacifier (maybe)
Mobiles for baby to watch
Rattles—later

Don't get:
Charming antique cribs or other baby furniture of highly questionable safety
  of design
Clothing in size 0–6 months that your baby may well outgrow before birth
Fancy books to record such things as the baby's headsize and physical examinations
Fancy clothing that will rarely if ever be worn
Other baby books
Rings, necklaces, bracelets, earrings
Shoes
Stuffed animals and expensive toys

ADOPTING A BABY

If you cannot (or if you decide you will not) become pregnant, you
may want to adopt a baby. A considerable part of the total process of
preparing for a baby described above will be the same regardless of
whether you deliver one or adopt one. I have found that, in general,
parents who have adopted a baby enjoy their adopted child and are
contented with their decision. My main concern for couples who adopt
a child is that they sometimes will try too hard to be perfect parents.
This can lead to frustration and resentment for both the parents and
child.

There are a few specific reasons not to adopt a baby or child. As
with a natural child, don't adopt to save a shaky marriage; in such a
case, the marriage often fails anyway. Don't adopt for companionship or
loneliness; adopt because you want to raise a child and set free an adult.
Don't adopt if you or your spouse are really unfit for parenthood and

haven't a "parenting bone" in your bodies. Don't adopt to carry on an esteemed family name or tradition. However, in spite of these warnings, I have seen many couples adopt children for precisely these reasons and be wonderful parents with delightful children. It only goes to show that the academically correct and incorrect ways of being a parent don't always hold true in real life.

Once you get an adopted baby or child it is easy to learn to love him or her. It is also fun—even if it is work. But most important, as pediatrician Thomas Conway says:

> The baby's well-being—now and later—is of greatest concern. He deserves that kind of home known to be best for child-rearing, with warmth and affection from healthy parents. He must be loved for himself and must be allowed to unfold his own personality, however foreign it might seem to his family's traditions. Provide such a home, invest time, love, and energy—and things will work out.

Probably the greatest problem with adopted babies is getting one to adopt. If babies of your own race are very hard to obtain, should you adopt a baby of another race? If your motive is the welfare of the child, then you should consider this. But examine your motives carefully. Be sure you are not just being "liberal" or doing something to strengthen your own ego. You should be able to provide your adopted child with affection, security, and understanding. Talk to a local pediatrician or write to the American Academy of Pediatrics for more information on this and other aspects of adoption.

The Truth About Adoption

Adoption of a child is just as wonderful as it ever was. The "natural mother" has been the giver of the greatest gift she can ever give, and you (the adopting parent) are the God-chosen receiver. This rosy picture has, today, one major qualifier, that is, there are very few newborn babies placed for adoption.

The advent of liberal abortion laws has made carrying an unwanted pregnancy to term unnecessary to all except those with religious or moral commitments against abortion. As a result, if you are dreaming of a cuddly, "picture perfect," healthy baby being placed in your family, think instead of a more special child. Children available for adoption today are older, or of mixed race, or with siblings, or with physical handicaps. But they are children: children in need of parents; children in need of love. There is no greater need—no greater gift. This is the truth about adoption.—*Dr. Margaret Deanesly*

There are other options. Dr. Neil Henderson reminds prospective parents:

Often it is most gratifying to adopt a toddler or older child. They need homes with tender loving care, too. Adopting parents will grow to love the older child just as much as if they cared for him when he was in diapers. The toddler will also grow to love and accept his new parents as his very own. Adopt a baby through a recognized adoption agency. The adoption agency will try to match the ethnic background of the baby with that of the prospective parents and will also try to give prospective parents a choice as to the sex of the child. The baby will have been screened carefully for illness or abnormal development. Usually, only normal babies will be placed for adoption. The adopting parents will receive continuing help from the adoption agency in any problems that may arise.

Most important, says Dr. Henderson, is how can we, as adopting parents, best ensure that we'll be "good" parents.

Before adopting a child, I believe the prospective parents should discuss their feelings with a clinical psychologist or psychiatrist, because either one or both may have certain feelings of inadequacy regarding their own masculinity or femininity if they were unable to conceive together. These feelings must be completely understood if the adopted child is to be raised in a healthy atmosphere.

Many couples have a baby of their own after adopting a child. This occurs so frequently that physicians have drawn the conclusion that anxiety plays an important part in parents' inability to conceive.

The prospective parents should also discuss the reasons why they want to adopt a child. It is amazing how often the conscious reasons we most readily state to our friends or neighbors are really controlled by the unconscious mind, which has entirely different reasons. If parents will take the time and effort to discover these unconscious reasons, how much happier their lives and the life of their adopted child will be. If you already have children, be sure to have a joint discussion about adoption with them. Their feelings should be discussed openly to avoid future problems.

THE DELIVERY

Your obstetrician will thoroughly discuss with you the details of the actual birth of your child. While ninety percent of all deliveries can occur without medical help and probably without complications, expert obstetrical care can make the whole experience a lot easier on both mother and baby. Preparation with courses in natural child-birth is worthwhile, and, for many mothers, natural unassisted birth is ideal. If you aim for a natural birth, don't feel bad if you decide at the last minute to ask for help. The help can vary from a local anesthetic injection into the uterus through the vagina, a caudal anesthetic administered through a small tube low in the spine, or a spinal injection slightly higher up than the caudal. All of these have the advantage that they do not depress the baby. Injections of sedatives or pain relievers into a vein or muscle, or inhalations of gases, may depress the baby if they are in the body very long. Babies born with sedatives or analgesics in them are sometimes a little slow to take a breath. Your obstetrician and anesthesiologist may, however, use these agents under some circumstances without harming the baby. They will explain the details and monitor the effects carefully.

Some new methods emphasize delivery into a quiet and almost dark delivery room, or immersion of the infant in warm water. Others now advocate "natural" home delivery. I find it difficult to believe that it will make much difference to the infant to have a light shine on him after the trauma of many hours of labor and being squeezed out of the uterus. I suspect that anything is welcome after a hard labor. And you do need good light to check the baby's color. The more important things are that the baby's color is good, that the mouth and throat are clear of mucus, and that the baby remains warm.

Should You Deliver at Home?

Although many deliveries can be accomplished at home without major problems, major problems can occur in a significant percentage of deliveries. Some of these problems can be predicted in advance, but many of them cannot. Often there is no warning until a hemorrhage occurs from separation of the placenta, thus cutting off the infant's oxygen supply. Sometimes there is a gush of blood through the vagina. Sometimes problems with the placenta are apparent only if the baby is being monitored closely by the obstetrician either by listening or by a wire attached to the baby's scalp leading to an electronic monitor. In either case, it often becomes essential to do an immediate caesarean section, and mother may require blood tranfusions. At home, such events (and others) are catastrophies for the baby or for the mother. In the hospital, with skilled care, there are excellent chances of averting disasters and of reducing the damage to both mother and child.

Should Father Be in the Delivery Room?

Usually it is worthwhile for father to be in the delivery room, and for him to share the experience of the labor and delivery. If nothing else, it increases the respect a man has for the mother of his child. Perhaps more important is that it allows the father to hold and handle and love the infant early. This seems to reduce the incompetent feeling of many men when they are around a small baby. In any case, mother will want to hold the infant and may even want to offer him the breast—assuming the baby happens to be interested in eating.

Hold Your Baby and Your Spouse After Delivery

Recent research confirms that, when mother and baby have nude contact directly after birth, marked benefits result. In tribal cultures in the past, such contact was a natural routine, and probably strengthened the mother-infant bond. Scientists note that both infants and mothers are particularly alert and responsive right after birth, and that the baby is equipped with a dazzling array of abilities and charms to attract its mother and win her affections, care, and nourishment. Mother is also keyed up, and is acutely sensitive and receptive right after birth—if she isn't "doped up." Further, infants with early close contact with mother tend to breastfeed twice as long and to have fewer skin, intestinal, and respiratory infections than those who were taken away from the mother at birth. Some researchers suggest that, in privacy, mother and baby, both undressed, stay together about forty-five minutes under a heat panel immediately after leaving the delivery room—and father should be included. Such physical closeness seems to greatly strengthen the parent-child bond, thus making parenthood, childhood—and probably marriage —far more enjoyable. It doesn't matter if the bond is fixed, as suspected, because of a hormonal surge and mental inprinting. If the baby is kept warm, no harm can result; and if the research is correct, remarkable benefits occur. Small infants, especially newborns, lose heat very easily, and unless they are kept warm, they can chill quickly. So while you handle, hold, feel, and look at your baby, keep him warm.

Caesarean Section

Caesarean section is as old as ancient Rome. It involves delivery by operation through the abdominal wall of the mother. This now routine procedure is safe for both mother and infant and has made possible the survival of hundreds of thousands who would otherwise have probably died. The disadvantage of this delivery method to C-section infants is that they do not have the fluid squeezed out of their lungs from the uterine contractions that stimulate a vaginally delivered baby. As a result, C-section babies have slightly more lung problems than others. Most hospitals put C-section babies in a special incubator so that their breathing can be easily watched for the first day. However, from the baby's standpoint, the mild increase in respiratory problems is more than offset by escaping the squeezing of the brain and face of those who come through the birth canal.

The Baby's Doctor

Once the baby has been delivered, a pediatrician or family practitioner will be his main source of medical care. It is a good idea to meet your future child's doctor-to-be before the delivery. This gives you all a chance to become acquainted and to size each other up; and offers an opportunity to ask questions and express worries, to check attitudes and compare philosophies. You should trust the doctor you choose—or, if you don't, you should find another one.

THE PREMATURE BABY

Norman Kendall, M.D., Professor of Neonatology, has this to say about the premature baby:

> If your baby is born before the due date and is smaller than average, you are not alone. In the United States, one of every twelve babies weighs less than five and a half pounds at birth. Those born two to three weeks early and weighing over five pounds can be treated

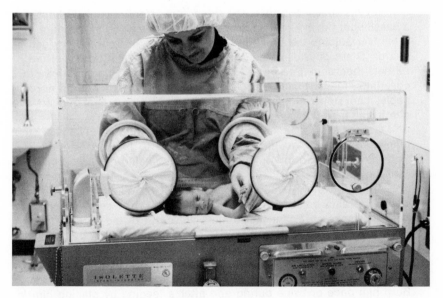

Figure 6 *Mother fondling her premature baby in an incubator.*

as normal babies. Those born weighing less than five pounds usually require special care, an important part of which comes from the parents. No matter how small, if the baby is not seriously ill, you may be able to visit, touch and fondle, and possibly diaper or feed the baby. Why should the nurse have all the fun? This opportunity to become acquainted with the infant helps by stimulating him and by making you realize that you really do have a baby. Such early contacts are definitely beneficial to both parents and infant.

The premature infant usually loses considerable weight during the first week of life; and he may not regain the birth weight until he is ten to twenty days of age: The infant should then gain six to eight ounces a week. Most babies can leave the hospital when they weigh around five pounds. Recently, physicians have been permitting infants to go home at lesser weights, providing (1) no complicating medical condition exists, (2) the parents have become acquainted with their baby while in the nursery, and (3) the parents have received instructions and practice in the care and feedng of their baby.

A "premie" may require some special care, but he should not be so overprotected that the entire family life style revolves around the new arrival.

Frequently, a premature infant is the first child born to a family, which increases apprehension. With such a tiny baby, it is important to realize that his body is complete and will not be easily damaged. He needs to be handled gently, but he needs to be handled just as often as a full-term baby. He should also be stimulated by gentle handling in his crib, by being spoken to, and by placing a mobile over his crib.

For the first few weeks, the premature infant should be kept in a bassinet at the mother's bedside at night. He may be in a separate room if it adjoins the parents' bedroom—so that his weak cry can be heard. [Other physicians believe a premie should not be out of the parents' bedroom. See page 132.] He must be kept warm with extra coverings, for he cannot regulate his temperature as well as normal babies can. However, excessive blankets or bed coverings may make him irritable and raise his body temperature too high.

Visitors should be kept to a minimum: Friends and relatives, other than grandparents, should not be permitted to handle the baby. Persons with respiratory infections or colds should not be permitted near the infant.

An underweight infant has a weak sucking reflex. Plenty of time should be allowed for his feedings. Hold him in a semi-upright position; make sure that the formula flows out of the nipples freely while the infant sucks. If the flow is excessive, control it by changing the position of the bottle from a vertical to a more horizontal position (to a 30 or 45 degree angle). In order to prevent the baby from swallowing air, be sure that the nipple is always filled with formula. Burp him once or twice during and after a feeding by placing him in the sitting position or by holding him upright on your shoulder and patting him gently on the back. If he sucks vigorously enough, breast feeding may be attempted.

One of the most common questions asked by parents is: "Will my premature baby develop normally?" Of course the premature infant's growth and development will lag behind that of the full-term infant. The smaller the infant and the earlier the birth, the longer it will take him to catch up. Every infant is expected to gain a minimum of fourteen pounds during the first year of life. The infant weighing two pounds at birth may not catch up in physical development to his full term playmate till four or five years of age, whereas the one weighing four or five pounds at birth may reach the average at two years of age. When assessing the development of a prematurely born infant, take into consideration the degree of prematurity. A normal full-term infant can sit by himself by the age of five or seven months of age. An infant born two months early will probably not be able to do this until he is seven or nine months of age.

Because of their rapid growth, prematurely born infants require extra vitamin D to prevent rickets, and additional iron to prevent anemia.

Mental and physical handicaps occur more frequently in premies than in full-term infants. The smaller the infant, the more likely it is that a handicap may result. Many of these handicaps are of a minor nature—such as nearsightedness or small stature during childhood—but serious handicaps—such as a low I.Q. or mental retardation—may occur in those weighing less than two and one-half pounds at birth.

The prematurely born infant has a number of handicaps at birth and requires special hospital care in order to prepare him for life. Upon arrival home, he should be treated as a normal infant with a few extra precautions. Relax and enjoy your baby; the few mistakes you may make will do no harm; and the chances are that your score of doing it "just right" will be higher if you relax!

APPEARANCE AND BEHAVIOR OF THE NEWBORN BABY [1]

There is probably no single event in the experience of new parents that is more dramatic and memorable than their first look at the child they have conceived. For most, there is an exhilarating feeling of love, delight, relief, and awe. For many, there are vague feelings of disappointment and alarm when viewing, for the first time, an infant who appears quite unlike the preconceived image they have had of their baby-to-be.

What is the usual appearance and behavior of the baby immediately after birth? There are many normal variations in the infant, as well as changes in appearance and behavior which occur during the first few days after birth.

General Appearance

Immediately after birth, most babies are somewhat blue in color, becoming pink after three or four vigorous breaths. Persisting bluish-red hands and feet with a slight tinge of blue around the mouth for several hours is not uncommon and should cause no concern. Your doctor and nurses will watch this to make certain that the baby receives adequate oxygen, which is vital for the brain.

Before the first bath, there will be some blood from the placenta over the body. Many infants are covered with a film of cheesy white material called "vernix," which is a natural protective substance for the infant's tender skin. It does not have to be washed off.

Some babies, particularly if overdue more than ten or twelve days, have skin which is wrinkled and cracked, resembling a peeling sunburn.

The Head and Face

The head of a newborn is quite large in relation to the body size. The bones of the head are not fused together, and a diamond-shaped soft spot called the fontanelle can be felt at the top of the head. The fontanelle may vary in size from one-half inch to two inches in diameter.

During the process of labor and delivery the baby's head usually leads the way. Consequently, the shape of the head must mold to the shape of the birth canal. Frequently there are some swollen spots on the scalp where a little bruising and bleeding occurred when the head went through the birth canal. These are of no importance and will gradually vanish. One of the things which may cause concern in the mind of a new parent is that the baby's face and head seem terribly misshapen. Often the nose is flattened or pushed to one side. There may be little or no rounding of the forehead. Instead, the line of the nose extends straight back to the top of the head, which is pointed in the back instead of rounded. Occasionally, an infant will be born in a breech position, with the buttocks or feet coming first. In this event, the buttocks and genitalia may be bruised and swollen, the legs will be folded up on the abdomen, and the head will be more rounded or flattened in the back. In spite of all of this, the head and face will be perfectly normal within a few weeks.

The ears of the newborn are soft and pliable, and are often folded forward temporarily. It is not uncommon for the ears to show considerable differences in size and shape. The baby's hearing ability usually can be tested by observing that the eyes blink when a sudden sharp sound is made.

The Skin

A newborn's skin usually has various markings. The most common is a red flush from dilated small blood vessels over the bridge of the nose, the upper eyelid, or the back of the neck. These birthmarks fade out gradually. Some babies have a dark greyish mark low on the back, or on the upper buttocks. Occasional infants have scattered "coffee-with-cream" colored spots on the skin. Hemangiomas, bright red or blue growths of blood vessels, may be present at birth or appear in the first few months. At first they are flat, then they gradually raise and expand. Left alone, they peak in size anywhere from six months to a year and then gradually subside, leaving no scar or mark.

Shortly after birth, many infants develop small hive-like spots that are similar to flea bites. These vanish. Many babies have numerous "white heads" or pores filled with a white oil, especially on the face; occasionally these will bulge, making little bumps smaller than a pinhead. Similar white spots may occur on the gums or the roof of the mouth. These all disappear by themselves. As the baby's face rubs against blankets, against saliva and milk, against his mother's face, hair and breasts, it will frequently become reddened and may develop pimples from the irritated sweat and oil glands. An acne-like rash with raised white heads usually occurs, increasing for a period of six weeks and then subsiding. These rashes often respond to washing the face (and don't forget the soft spot) with soap and water and a wash cloth.

Fingernails and toenails may scratch the face and should be trimmed. Simply hold the finger firmly and carefully cut or clip off the nail with small scissors. It might be easier to do this while baby sleeps. Occasionally, babies are born with peculiar looking finger and toe nails which generally persist. It's an insignificant problem.

Hair either is or isn't there. If it is there, it usually, but not always, falls off. New hair grows to replace it.

Jaundice of the Newborn

A yellow tint to the skin is visible in at least half of all newborns by the third day. This is usually a normal, or "physiologic," jaundice. Your doctor will watch the jaundice, and if it occurs too early or becomes too acute he will test the level of blood bilirubin. If the bilirubin level becomes too high, there is a possibility of brain damage to the baby, and steps must be taken to lower the bilirubin level. This is usually accomplished by exposing the baby's skin to a light, which breaks the bilirubin into a harmless substance. If the jaundice is too severe, an exchange transfusion may have to be done.

Jaundice in the newborn occurs because babies are born with an excess of red blood cells which break down, releasing bilirubin. Bilirubin is changed into bile by liver enzymes and excreted into the bowel. The liver enzymes don't work well enough at birth to handle the extra load of broken down red cells, so the bilirubin level rises in the blood and stains the skin yellow. In most babies, the liver is able to handle the bile by the fourth day and the jaundice fades away within a week. The livers of premature infants are very immature, so there is a greater likelihood of prolonged high bilirubin levels.

Severe jaundice is often due to Rh disease, which occurs when the mother is Rh negative and has developed antibodies to the baby's Rh positive blood. The antibodies started forming during a prior pregnancy when some Rh positive red cells from the fetus leaked into the mother's blood stream, or if she had a transfusion of Rh positive blood. No antibodies are formed if both mother and baby are Rh negative. The antibodies to Rh positive blood which have formed in an Rh negative mother pass through the placenta and destroy the infant's red cells. Formation of such antibodies is now largely preventable by injecting a substance called RhoGam into the mother right after the birth of the first baby: The injection neutralizes the baby's red cells and prevents the formation of antibodies, thus sparing the next baby the possibility of Rh disease.—*Thomas J. Conway, M.D.*

Torso and Extremities

The baby's chest, abdomen, back, arms, and legs rarely show any significant effects from labor and delivery. However, because of the crowding that occurs in the uterus during the final months of pregnancy, a newborn's legs and feet may be rotated inward or outward to a significant degree. Almost all infants appear bow-legged; and, in some, the front part of the feet will curve inward. In most cases, time, growth, and the normal use of the legs in kicking (and later on in walking) will correct these conditions without any need for corrective shoes, braces, or other mechanical devices. Occasionally, an infant with wide shoulders will fracture his collarbone (clavicle) during the birth process. This heals within a few weeks and requires little or no special treatment.

Umbilical Cord

At birth, the umbilical cord may vary in size from one-half to almost an inch in diameter. If kept dry, it quickly shrivels; and by the third or fourth day it resembles a hard dry scab over the navel, and usually falls off from about the seventh to the fourteenth day. Then it sometimes oozes blood for several days. This is nothing to be concerned about, and no special care is necessary unless the bleeding is truly excessive—if it is, call your physician.

Clean the base of the cord daily with a cotton-tipped applicator and alcohol to help keep it dry and uninfected. Sometimes the cord oozes a little blood for a few days. Unless there is a foul odor or a truly excessive amount of blood, this requires no special care.

Genitalia

The external genitalia of girls, particularly the clitoris and the vaginal lips, are noticeably larger at birth than one might expect. This is due to the effect of the mother's adult female hormones, which are passed through the placenta to the infant during the later months of pregnancy. These hormones also cause a thick milky-white mucus discharge from the vagina of a baby girl, and, occasionally, a small amount of menstrual-like vaginal bleeding a few days after birth. For the same hormonal reason, the breasts of the newborn male or female become swollen and may secrete a little milk. This is normal and should be left alone; do not squeeze the breasts.

In baby boys, one or both testicles are occasionally not in the scrotal sac. During fetal life, the testicles develop in the abdominal cavity and ordinarily descend into the scrotum at birth; they sometimes can be felt in the groin area, but occasionally they are still high in the abdomen. Usually they will descend at a later age.

Circumcision

At birth, the male baby's glans, or reddish end of the penis, is covered by a tube of skin called the foreskin. Circumcision is an operation which cuts off the foreskin, leaving the glans uncovered. This is done primarily in order to reduce the possibility of infection occurring under the foreskin in the future. However, there is controversy among physicians about the desirability of circumcision.

Representing the advocates of routinely circumcising all male infants, Dr. Robert Polley says: "There is little to be gained from letting the opportunity pass to have a simple, safe, and economical circumcision done in the nursery. A significant number of male babies will need circumcision sooner or later anyway because of hygiene and infection problems and will then have to have the discomfort and risk of any surgical procedure requiring the use of an anesthetic." However, Dr. Ed Shaw believes that "the operation should be reserved for very rare cases of infection under the foreskin, for there is a risk of hemorrhage and infection from the procedure." He points out that "circumcision is almost routine in the United States, but this is not true in many other modern nations, such as England and Germany." There is no middle ground in the circumcision controversy. Either you cut off the foreskin or you don't. Either way, there are very few problems. He is your child and it is your money, so the choice should be yours. But circumcised or not, some baby boys do develop problems, says pediatrician A.S. Hashim who points out:

> If an ammonia diaper rash occurs, the uncircumcised tip of the foreskin may become red, slightly swollen, ulcerated, and sore. If circumcised, then the opening of the penis becomes red, slightly swollen, and ulcerated. Naturally, with the ammonia—which can be strong enough to burn your eyes—the bottom may look "scalded." Note that this may interfere with sleep.
>
> This sort of ulceration at the tip of the penis may scar as it heals and create a pin hole opening and a very narrow stream of urine. A small operation is needed to enlarge the hole to the normal size; the matter is usually handled in the office or the out-patient department of the hospital.

Reflexes and Responses

Most babies spend much of the time sleeping during the first few days after birth. At feeding time, they will suck for a few minutes and then doze off. A newborn may seem completely disinterested in eating when wrapped in a warm blanket and held comfortably in his mother's arms. But then you wouldn't be very interested if someone awoke you out of a sound sleep at 3:00 A.M. and said, "Let's go eat!" Short periods of crying after eating and between feedings are normal and rarely need any special attention. Within a few days, sucking becomes more vigorous, continues for a longer time, and allows the baby to complete a feeding more quickly.

The term "reflex" refers to reactions in the nervous system leading to muscle action and behavior patterns which are not under the conscious control of the individual. An example of this is breathing, which occurs regularly, without any conscious thought. In the newborn, almost all muscle action and behavior is reflexive in nature. A reflex, such as crying, is purposeful and necessary in order for the baby to signal his discomfort when hungry, wet, cold, or lonely. Other reflexes, such as the grasp reflex, the startle reflex (moro response), and the step reflex are of no significance except to indicate that the nervous system is intact. As the baby matures, self-willed behavior develops, and the immature reflexes gradually disappear.

Breathing and Crying

The first reflex one observes after delivery is breathing; the second is crying. Except when crying, the newborn does not breathe through the mouth, only through the nose. For this reason, it is essential to insure that the nasal airway is open and clear of mucus, amniotic fluid, blood, or any other substance which can obstruct breathing. At birth, the nose, mouth, and throat may be filled with these substances; and even after the doctor or nurse has removed most of it by gentle suction, noisy "rattling" breathing sometimes continues. As long as the baby seems to be breathing comfortably and maintains a pink color, such noisy breathing is not a cause for concern and it usually clears up within a short time. Breathing during the newborn period is usually irregular, with short periods of rapid, shallow respirations and occasional three to five second episodes of breath holding.

Crying should not be interpreted as always being a sign of pain, discomfort, or hunger. Nor should the volume of noise put out by a new baby be used as a means for judging degrees of discomfort. In time, parents learn to interpret the meaning of various kinds of crying used by the baby. At first, it all just seems like a lot of noise.

Newborn babies sneeze a lot. Their nostrils are rather small, so a small amount of mucus can make a lot of rattle. If the nose is really blocked, it is difficult for the baby to nurse and breathe at the same time. The resulting frustration interferes with eating and causes hungry, unhappy babies. This should be reported to your doctor.

Hiccoughs are caused by air swallowed when the baby is fed. This irritates and causes spasm of the diaphragm, the muscle which separates the chest from the abdomen. Although hiccoughs are annoying, they are harmless and should be ignored. Quivering around the chin is common for the first few years of life just before or during crying.

The Feeding Reflexes

The second important group of reflexes observed in the newborn are those which are necessary for taking nourishment. "Rooting," "sucking," and "swallowing" reflexes are the principal ones in this group. The "rooting" or "searching" reflex refers to the reaction one observes when pressure is applied to the baby's cheek near the corner of the mouth. When this is done, the baby turns the head toward the side which is pressed and then opens the mouth, looking for something to suck. It is because of this reflex that a newborn, when placed with his cheek against the mother's breast, will turn his head towards the breast while searching for the nipple. Sucking and swallowing are instinctive reflex behavior patterns in the newborn. During the first weeks after birth, they have little relationship to real hunger. Unless a baby is sleepy, he will usually suck on anything he gets into his mouth, whether it is a nipple, a fist, or a blanket. Do not interpret vigorous sucking to always mean that the baby is hungry.

Awareness Reflexes

The "startle" reflex is a newborn's total body response to a sudden movement or loud noise. The infant reacts first by stiffening the body. The arms and legs extend outward and then become slightly flexed and rigid with general trembling, followed by crying. It is because of the startle reflex that many babies act frightened and cry when placed on their backs.

Walking Reflex

A stepping action will be observed when an infant is held in a standing position with the feet touching the ground. Similar rhythmic crawling movements are initiated by pressure on the soles of the feet when the baby lies face down in bed with the legs pulled up under the body. It is for this reason that a baby will creep to the head of the crib; and, if left alone on a bed or table, he may push himself off the end. *Never* leave a baby unattended on a high unprotected surface.

Vision and Hearing

The color of a newborn's eyes is usually an indistinct slate gray. (The true eye color may not be apparent until a year has passed.) Some swelling and streaks of blood may be apparent, caused by the strenuous trip through the birth canal. The many pressures result in some injury to superficial tissues; but the swelling soon disappears. Some of the pressures exerted break the tiny capillaries in the "whites" of the eyes, causing little blood clots, which disappear after several weeks without any damage to the eyes. The eyelids are often puffy, making it difficult to open them for several days. Once the eyes are open, the baby can see, contends pediatrician David Sparling:

> For years, we believed that babies don't really see during their early months. Although there are babies who at first do nothing but eat and sleep, one has only to observe an alert newborn who stares wide-eyed and studies everything in its environment to discover how important eyesight is in the process of learning for the small infant. Children born at term may start following large objects with their eyes anywhere from two to six weeks of age. At this age, a "mobile" is a real pleasure. Studying the motion of a speaker's lips and recognizing Mother by sight comes soon after. Even before two months of age, they may be attracted to certain colors and patterns. Soon they will recognize many objects in their environment. By four or five months of age, they will differentiate strangers from family and friends. Parents, by the way, do not need to fear taking flash photos. It will not harm a baby's eyes.

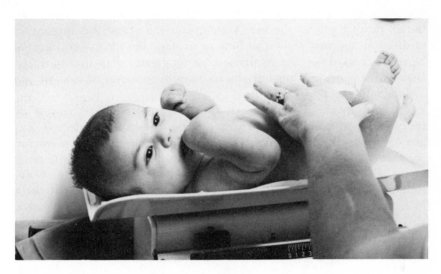

Figure 7   *Babies see!*

I don't know how much they see, and I suspect newborns have as much difficulty focusing as they do with other controlled fine muscle movements. It is not uncommon for their eyes to cross intermittently at first. If they are crossed a lot of the time, tell the doctor. But if you move into a newborn's focal plane, I suspect that they can recognize some details of your face. Others are still skeptical of vision in the first month, but all agree that visual stimulation is essential. It certainly doesn't take too long for most of them to respond, and, very obviously, to look at things.

Eye Problems in Newborns

Gonorrheal conjunctivitis is an infection caused by the venereal disease bacteria, the gonococcus, caught when the baby passes through an infected birth canal. The eyes become red and pussy, and, if the disease is not treated, blindness may result. To prevent this, a silver nitrate solution is put into the eyes of every newborn baby as a standard practice. Although very effective in preventing infection, it is nevertheless irritating to the eyes and causes formation of pus. This usually clears by itself; and the eyelids may be wiped with some sterile water on some soft cotton. If the discharge is profuse or lasts for more than a few days, notify your doctor.

In some newborns, the tear ducts are blocked, causing the tears to spill over rather than to pass through the tear duct (the tiny opening in the lower eye lid close to the nose.) Sometimes the ducts become infected, causing pus in the eye. Your doctor may prescribe appropriate medication and may show you how to massage the duct. The duct can be easily blocked because its diameter is no greater than that of a hair. Usually it opens spontaneously by six months to a year, if not, an ophthalmologist may probe the duct.

Your baby may have required extra oxygen after birth because the lungs were not open enough to keep him pink and supply adequate oxygen to prevent brain damage. This is more common in the premature baby. If too much oxygen is given, the extra oxygen damages the retina in the back of the eye and this can cause blindness. Your doctor would have given only the smallest amount of oxygen needed, but it is better to have eye damage than brain damage and at times it is difficult to strike the exact balance. If there is a question, the doctor will have an eye specialist check the baby's eyes.

Your Baby's Hearing

Hearing impairments are among the physical disabilities most difficult to detect because you cannot "see" deafness. The only way to be completely sure how well a baby hears is to have him tested by an experienced audiologist. You and your doctor can work together to check your child's hearing. However, *your* careful observation is the crucial step in the early months of life. Use the following check list, created by the California Association of Parents of Deaf and Hard of Hearing Children, at home and report the results to your doctor.[2]

From two weeks to ten weeks old, does baby:
1. Seem aware of your voice?
2. Stop crying when you talk to him when you are out of sight?
3. Waken when there is a noise?
4. Cry at sudden loud noises?
5. Blink or jerk at sudden loud noises?

From two and one-half to six months old, does baby:
1. Turn his eyes to the speaker when speaker is not visible?
2. Cry when exposed to sudden loud, unexpected noises?
3. Stop movements when a new sound is introduced: for example, the ringing of the telephone or doorbell?
4. Show interest in a music box or noise making toy when he cannot see it?

At one year, does baby:
1. Babble, using consonant sounds?
2. Use some words, such as "mama?"
3. Pay attention to a softly playing radio, a telephone ringing, or a knock at the door?

By two years, does baby:
1. Pay attention to speech?
2. Begin to mind when told "no?"
3. Try to sing or dance?
4. Start to talk with recognizable words?

If there is any significant question as to whether a child can hear *soft* as well as loud sounds, your doctor will refer him for an examination by an audiologist or otologist. Seek further services *early* so that better speech will result.

Bodily Functions

Bowel movements usually are passed shortly after a feeding has ended. The first stools of the newborn consist of meconium, a greenish-black sticky material which has accumulated in the digestive tract during fetal life. As soon as some milk has been taken, the stools become greenish-yellow. One or two days after breast feeding begins, stools are yellow in color and somewhat watery, but with no offensive odor. Stools with a pale green tint are not uncommon.

The urine of a newborn is at first clear and almost colorless, but after the second or third day, due to the excretion of excess bile pigment, many infants will have dark yellow urine. This normally clears by one week of age.

THE CARE OF THE NEWBORN

That overwhelming feeling of panic and self-doubt felt by a new parent with a new baby on the first day home from the hospital cannot be described—it can only be experienced. The advice found in this section is directed mainly to new parents, but you may want a short refresher course for your second, or third—or even your fourth baby.

Babies are people. He or she is not an "it," nor a fragile piece of china which can fall apart if slightly mishandled. Babies are tough. In coming through the birth canal during a normal delivery, an infant sustains, with no significant after-effects, enough pressures to completely immobilize an average adult for several days. So don't worry that you might injure your baby because of clumsiness or inexperience.

There Are Many Ways

There are as many good ways to provide care for babies as there are good parents. A little knowledge combined with a lot of love and common sense are the essential ingredients of parenthood. Inexperienced parents must depend, in part, upon the experiences of others. Often they are bombarded with what seem to be conflicting "expert" opinions from friends, relatives, physicians, and books on child care. The resulting confusion leads to self-doubt. Consequently, many new parents will question their own ability to make common sense decisions.

Dr. John Richards offers the following advice:

> To each new parent facing this dilemma, one can only say: "Listen to the advice of others." Every experienced mother will have definite opinions on infant care and usually loves to give advice—some of it good. Physicians who regularly supervise the care of infants can offer many good tips. Nurses, grandparents, and even the mailman may have some good ideas. Listen to what others say, and then *do what makes sense to you*. What works for one parent doesn't necessarily work for another, or even for the same parent with a different child.
>
> And finally, don't worry unnecessarily over your mistakes. No parent does the right thing at the right time, every time. Yet babies usually manage to survive and thrive.

On the following pages, experienced pediatricians, with help from countless mothers, will offer commonsense answers to questions asked by parents. Associate editor John C. Richards, M.D. reminds you that "each expert describes '*a* way,' not '*the* way' to manage many common problems; but keep in mind that each infant, each family, and each situation is unique. Therefore, no 'pat' answer will completely apply to each specific problem. When in doubt, use your own good common sense."

The "Proper" Sleeping Position for the Baby

One would think that the experts could easily tell you the proper sleeping position for baby. They do, but their advice often conflicts. Grandmothers can tell you, too. So can American Indians or a famous orthopedist. Even the Indians disagreed: The Flathead tribe kept their babies' heads strapped to papoose boards—flattening the back of them to an acceptable (to Flatheads) social shape. The orthopedist decided that a major reason for turned-in feet was because infants slept on their stomachs. However, a lot of babies simply won't sleep on their stomachs in spite of the good doctor's admonitions. I haven't found any correlation between sleeping position and toeing-in in my practice; on the other hand, Dr. Richards, my partner, believes that if toeing-in exists, it may get worse with belly sleeping. Pediatrician Neil Henderson believes that babies should sleep on their stomachs. And Dr. Polley believes they should sleep on their sides.

Although we were in some disagreement about whether a baby should sleep on its stomach, back, or side, all of us have noted that infants, as well as children and adults, often sleep better and have fewer complications when they have colds if the head of the bed is elevated. Sleeping propped up helps by allowing mucus in the nose and throat to drain away rather than puddling, thus often tending to harbor infection, and making it difficult to get air through the nose. There is also less swelling of the face and membranes in the nose because the extra edema fluid in the body (which causes swelling of the feet when you stand up all day) doesn't settle out in the head as it does if you sleep flat. Two other practicing pediatricians, Harvey Kravitz and Robert Scherz, compared experiences and found that they had never heard of an infant dying from "Crib Death," the Sudden Infant Death Syndrome (S.I.D.S.), when they slept propped up. They checked with over 600 other pediatricians and none knew of S.I.D.S. occurring when the baby was propped at a 10° to 30° angle. Considering that around 10,000 infants die from S.I.D.S. each year in the United States, it seems reasonable, then, to prop the baby up in the crib—either by putting blocks under the legs at the head or a wedge of newspapers between the mattress and springs. Time and future study may demonstrate the worth of this simple procedure.

As to the disagreement on whether a baby should sleep on his stomach, back, or side, we asked three experienced pediatricians to give their advice—and we offer the varying opinions for your choice. Regardless of which of the experts you follow, their advice is only good if the baby tolerates it. As the baby grows older, he quits complaining anyway, and moves into the position he wants.

My advice is to let the baby sleep any way he wishes as long as he doesn't start flattening his head. My own special prejudice is for "natural" shaped heads.

It is better for the baby to sleep on his stomach. That way, if he should vomit, he will not aspirate food into his lungs. Also, the head is relatively heavy. Constant pressure on the back of the head from its own weight might make the head fairly flat or lopsided. The baby who sleeps on his stomach seems to have a more symmetrical head, as he rests his head first on one side and then the other.—*Neil C. Henderson, M.D.*

A baby should not be put to sleep in the same position all the time, either on his back or abdomen. When sleeping on his abdomen, a normal active baby will never smother as long as the pad or mattress under the baby is firm. On the other hand, I have never heard of a normal baby (other than a premature baby) having serious problems develop because of vomiting that occurred while sleeping on the back. Lying on the abdomen will usually aggravate the twisted hips or knees that occur in some babies.—*John C. Richards, M.D.*

There's no general agreement on this important question at the present because it has not been studied sufficiently. However, I am

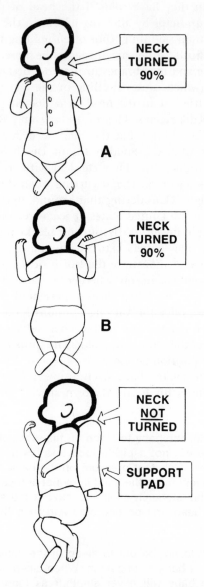

Figure 8   *Dr. Polley believes sleeping on the side is best.*

firmly of the opinion that the newborn infant should be neither flat on
his back nor on his abdomen when he is sleeping. When he is placed
on his back his head usually flops over in one direction because it
is flatter on the sides and quite heavy. This twists his neck 70 to 90
degrees to the right or left. In fact, babies who begin life sleeping flat
on their backs often become creatures of habit and will tolerate no

other position. The constant turning of the head to the same side can cause enough pressure that the child may develop a very prominent and unattractive flattened-out area on one side of the back of the head.

When the child is placed on his abdomen, his head and neck are likewise turned sharply at 90 degrees, with the face and chin pointed toward one shoulder or the other.

I feel that it is best to have the infant sleep on the side of his head—ear down against the mattress. He should be lying on the side of his chest so that his neck will not be turned and so that his body will be facing in the same direction as his head. It is more comfortable for him to sleep in this position.

During the first few days, the infant will stay on his side fairly easily. But after he is two or three weeks old, he will become active enough to slip himself from his side to his back if he is not supported with a pillow or some kind of pad. Many mothers pin a small pillow or rolled up blanket to the sleeping garment so the baby won't slide away from the positioning pad.

Small premature infants receive this special attention with regard to their sleeping posture because of the greater risk of breathing difficulties. And I feel that the practice of sleeping on the side should be followed for all babies during their first few months.—*Robert F. L. Polley, M.D.*

Holding and Handling

Holding and handling a baby come naturally to most parents. New parents, however, may be a bit anxious and awkward. For them, Dr. Polley offers a mini course with illustrations from his book, *Call the Doctor*.[3]

Figure 9 *Put your left hand under the chest.*

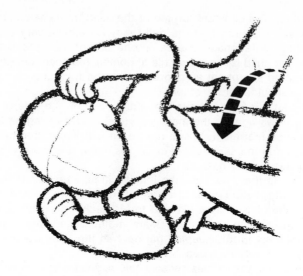

Figure 10 *Roll the infant into the palm of your other hand.*

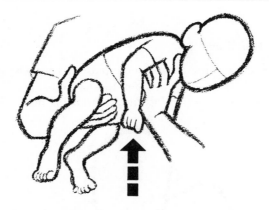

Figure 11 *Infant held "Bottoms Up." (Note: right hand should be holding chest if possible.)*

Figures 9 and 10 illustrate how a newborn infant is rolled from his back onto the palm of the adult's hand when being lifted up. Holding an infant *Bottoms Up* (Figure 11) or *Bottoms Down* (Figures 12 and 13) provides security and comfort during visiting periods, exercise sessions, and when the child is being carried. These positions are ideal for infants from the first few days of life until they are able to crawl on their own, do push-ups, roll over, and support themselves in a jump seat.

The "Ankle Hold" (Figures 14 and 15) permits safe handling of infants who are very active at diaper changing and bathing times.

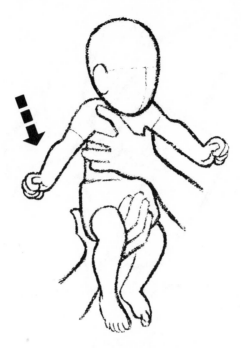

Figure 12   *Infant held "Bottoms Down."*

Figure 13   *Infant sitting "Bottoms Down."*

Figure 14 *Ankle hold when changing diapers.*

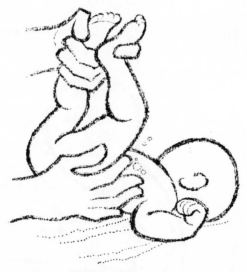

Figure 15 *Ankle hold for bathing.*

Holding an infant "Face Up" is unsafe and uncomfortable for him, because the muscles along the front of the baby's neck and body are weak. He cannot control his neck and back when he is "Sunny Side Up." The adult has great difficulty trying to support his head, shoulders, back, and pelvis all at the same time. The infant is uneasy and wants to wiggle out of this position. Holding an infant in the "Face Up" position is particularly risky when his skin is moist and slippery after bathing.

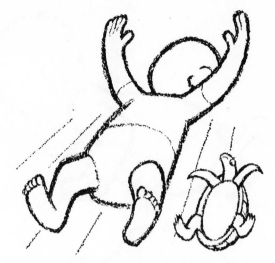

Figure 16 *Restless and frustrated on his back.*

Figure 17 *Some babies are frustrated when confined on their backs in a reclining seat.*

Figure 16 provides a demonstration of the helpless frustration experienced by an infant when he is laid flat on his back. It's a frustration rather similar to that of an overturned turtle. The arms, legs, and necks of newborns are not strong enough at the very first, but by two or three months of age babies enjoy the freedom of being placed on their abdomens, "Bottoms Up." The baby is free to practice moving his head, shoulders, and extremities.

Figure 18 *"Right side up turtle." Happier with the freedom to try crawling and swimming.*

Skin Care

How should a baby be bathed? Until the umbilical cord falls off (5 to 14 days), you can sponge bathe the baby using a mild soap and water. Rinse well. After the cord is off, tub baths are indicated. The handiest and most convenient place for bathing is in a plastic dishpan in the kitchen sink. This usually offers the best height, is easiest on your back, and is quite safe until the baby is able to turn the handles on the tap.

If Baby Cries During the Bath

First make certain that water is not too hot or too cold. Some babies feel they are falling and cry from fear. One mother developed a very helpful large tub sponge (called a Pansy-ette Bath Aid) which conforms to the baby's body. The sponge makes the baby feel more secure when being bathed; and both of mother's hands are free to wash the baby.

Care of the Umbilical Cord

After the umbilical cord has fallen off, a scab of dried blood is usually left on the navel. It is important that the navel and scab be bathed. The dried blood can be cleansed away gently with a cotton tipped applicator dunked in rubbing alcohol. Be careful to go to the base of the "belly button"—you won't poke through anything. Before the cord falls off there is an occasional discharge of pus. This too should be cleansed with a cotton tipped applicator wet with alcohol or smeared with a little antibiotic ointment or painted with Merthiolate or Mercurochrome, easily obtained over the counter. If the skin around the base of the cord turns red or if there is a foul odor or yellow, green, or brown pus, call the doctor.

Washing Baby
When you wash the baby, remember that both ends get dirty. Don't be afraid to use soap and water and a wash rag on the baby's face and on the soft spot on the top of the head. Wash whatever hair the baby has each time you wash the face. Use one plain soap; if you switch brands, sooner or later you are likely to find a soap that creates a rash. Rinse well, since soap left on the skin is damaging.

Dry Skin
After the bath, if the skin is too dry it is better to use a baby lotion than baby oils. When cleaning the skin after urination, the use of a little baby powder is helpful to absorb the moisture in the creases of the skin. After a stool, cleansing with soap and water and an application of lotion is helpful in keeping the skin soft. There are, however, many precautions you should take in using lotions and ointments.

At birth, a baby has "lived in a lake" all his life. The constant wetness in the uterus keeps the horny outer layer of skin from peeling off, but exposure to air after birth causes this excess layer to shed, making many people think that the skin is dry. Consequently, people put oil on the skin, thinking that it will stop the "peeling." It doesn't stop it, but it does hide it as well as hold dirt to the skin. Oil certainly doesn't clean the skin.

Tender Skin
Once the excess horny layer has peeled off, the baby's skin is thinner and less resistant than an adult's skin. One result is that it absorbs chemicals more easily than an adult's skin. This may be dangerous, especially when the parental instinct seems to be to put something on the skin just because "the skin is there." A good rule is to treat the skin only if there is a good reason to treat it. Don't treat it just because you have a shower gift of oil or a sample the drugstore gave you. Sooner or later you may use something that will damage the skin or poison the baby.

Stanford dermatologist Dr. Alvin Jacobs gives several reasons for not applying ointments without good reason:

1. The material may cause damage.
2. It may treat the wrong thing.
3. It may sensitize the skin, preventing later use of a good drug.
4. Most people don't know what they are using.

There are some baby skin problems you *should* treat, such as urine or stool burns. In the diaper area you may use a barrier ointment, one that protects the skin from external moisture, such as an inexpensive petroleum jelly product. However, don't use barrier ointments all over the skin, as they may block the small pores of the sweat glands, thus causing a prickly rash, misnamed "heat rash." Do not use a barrier ointment if the infant *already* has a rash.

Diapers and Diaper Rash

Diapers
Both cloth and disposable diapers are acceptable, but I prefer cloth. Neither should be so tight that air cannot circulate through. If applied too tightly (as on the T.V. ads for form fitting diapers), diaper rash often follows, particularly if plastic disposables or rubber pants are used. Pediatrician A. S. Hashim agrees:

> Changing diapers, washing diapers, and buying disposable diapers command a significant amount of time. You will have to change diapers often, and if you fail, the baby may suffer from rash. Disposable diapers ought to be used mainly for special purposes. If you want to shop, or to go here or there, or if you want to go to the doctor, you can use the disposable diapers. My unhappy experience with them is that using them routinely at home is too expensive and that they are more likely to give the baby diaper rash.

Diapers serve two purposes. One is to keep the baby's bottom warm; the other is to keep the bed or the parent dry. The use of disposable plastic covered diapers keeps the parent dry and the baby's bottom wet. Cloth diapers, without a plastic cover, induces a quicker diaper change. I guess it depends on your sense of values—certainly there are some of our clothes that deserve protection. And it is certainly handy to use disposables when you are away from home.

Diaper Rash
There are many kinds of diaper rash, each with a specific cause or causes. The most important general cause of diaper rash is "the tropical effect" of chronically moist hot skin. The humidity inside a plastic diaper cover is the same as that of an orchid hot house. Warm moist skin

becomes soggy like "dishpan hands," and the outer horny layer of skin loses its resistance.

To prevent this, you should "air condition" the diaper area.

1. Don't pull the diapers tight against the skin. Leave them loose, with room for air to circulate.
2. Do not use plastic diaper pants.
3. Keep and use a large supply of dry diapers.
4. Protective ointments can be used to help prevent moisture diaper rashes *if* they form a barrier between the moisture and the skin and *if* they are used just at night (zinc ointments are satisfactory).
5. The skin should be dried out during the day time and therefore should be free of ointment.
6. Most of the baby ointments on the market will work on the residual rashes that remain after the skin has dried.

Diaper rashes may occur even with dry skin. Allergic or contact diaper rash may be caused from detergent in the diaper, from a diaper ointment, or from the diaper fiber itself, especially with some of the form fitting plastic coated diapers. Such contact rashes usually spare the creases in the groin and buttocks. Another type of rash in the diaper area is the fine bumpy "heat rash" of plugged-off sweat glands. It is frequently due to oils or ointments that mechanically plug the fine skin pores. At times, the small bumps may blister and spread, indicating a possible staphylococcal impetigo infection starting in the irritated skin.

Rashes in the creases of the groin, buttocks, and the skin folds may be due to seborrhea or yeast infection. Seborrhea is an inflammation of the oil glands of the skin. Yeast infections are related to thrush in a baby's mouth. Occasionally, alkaline feces can scald the area around the anus, burning the skin.

A major cause of diaper rash in babies older than two or three months is ammonia. Urine in the diaper is broken down into ammonia by a bacteria which uses the urine as food. The by-product of the bacteria is ammonia. You can easily identify the smell of ammonia—it is the same compound and has the same smell as the ammonia water you use for cleaning. The longer ammonia is on the baby's skin the greater is the resulting burn and rash. These ammonia germs don't wash out of the diaper easily. They go into a spore state within the threads of cloth, waiting for the next bath of urine so they can grow again. The spores can be killed by boiling the diapers for twenty minutes:

1. Wash with your usual detergent.
2. Spin dry.
3. Simmer in a large pan of boiling water for twenty minutes.
4. Spin dry.
5. Hang on the clothes line in the sun to dry.

Sunshine also kills the spores, so hanging the diapers out on a good sunny day may do the trick. Your doctor can tell you how to treat the baby's ammonia burn. Of course, there are many, many other causes of diaper rash. Dr. Alvin Jacobs mentions a few:

> Sogginess of the skin from wetness and irritation from rubbing against the diapers reduce diaper area resistance, making it more susceptible to other skin diseases. Viral diseases that may concentrate in the diaper area include chicken pox and the coxsacki virus rash of hand, foot, and mouth disease. There are many other diseases that cause diaper rash, such as syphilis, psoriasis, and atopic dermatitis. Any rash may become secondarily infected with staphylococci or other germs causing impetigo and even boils. If pus appears in diaper rash sores, you should certainly check with your doctor. Any rash that becomes progressively worse or doesn't respond after a week or so deserves a check by a physician.

Treatments for Diaper Rash

Below, several doctors give their thoughts on how to treat diaper rash.

My wife used corn starch on our children's bottoms, and she says it works well as long as the diapers are changed often and the starch washed off with each change. Dr. Jacobs, however, notes that cornstarch serves as a food for yeast and can make a yeast diaper rash worse. He believes it is preferable to use a simple baby powder. If you do use talcum powder, rub it on in a thin coat with your hand so it won't cake. Don't shake it on the baby, for even simple talcum powder can be inhaled if too much gets into the air—resulting in talcum powder pneumonia.

Pediatrician John C. Richards notes that detergent used in the laundry frequently causes red and inflamed skin in the diaper area resembling a severe sunburn. This is most noticeable in front, from the navel down to the upper thighs where the diaper is the wettest. The redness is not present in the deep creases of the groin area. As the rash heals, the skin peels off like a sunburn, but then the new skin again becomes red and burned if exposed again to detergent left in the diaper.

Treatment for detergent burn is simple. Either change to a mild soap when washing diapers, or put diapers through at least two extra rinses after washing. A change to disposable diapers is a more expensive but equally satisfactory solution to this problem.

Dr. A.S. Hashim says that many cases of moisture diaper rash will respond to Vitamin A and D ointment. But before you put baby to bed, double diaper him and leave off the rubber pants. Before you go to bed "be cruel," wake him up, and double diaper him again.

Dr. Lendon Smith strongly advises against a treatment you should *not* use even if it works—boric acid ointment. Boric acid is absorbed from inflamed skin, and enough used over a period of time may poison the kidneys and can cause death.

Regarding plastic diapers and diaper liners, one of our contributing mothers, Nancy Cookson, notes she had a problem with two of her foster babies due to plastic pants or plastic covered disposable diapers. Once she had taken *all* plastics away from these particular babies but used the same cloth diapers with the same laundry care, the diaper rash problems cleared up. Diaper liners are a big help to her, not only in preventing diaper rashes but in changing dirty diapers. A lot of liners are wasted, but the money is well spent.

A final and perhaps often overlooked preventive and treatment step is given by Omaha pediatrician Hobart Wallace: "Leave the diaper off and allow the area to air dry. Sometimes changing diapers hourly, even though they are not soiled, makes a difference, because this keeps the skin area dry by reducing the humidity effect of perspiration and moisture."

What About Dandruff and Cradle Cap?

On this subject, dermatologist Jacobs tells us:

> Most dandruff or cradle cap is actually caused by a poorly understood condition called seborrheic dermatitis, an inflammation of the oil glands. The outer or horny layer of skin peels off faster than usual, forming dry-looking flakes of dandruff. These flakes are not really dry—they are greasy—and oil or grease on the hair or scalp will aggravate the condition. Hair gels are a good substitute for oils, although for a short time you may use warm oil or vaseline to soften thick crusts of cradle cap or dandruff, as long as the area is thoroughly washed and scrubbed off with soap and water soon after, and the oil or vaseline not reapplied.
>
> There are many good non-prescription antidandruff shampoos that are also effective against cradle cap. I would, however, avoid Selinium-containing shampoos for babies, as they are extremely poisonous if swallowed.

Pediatrician Leo Bell points out that "cradle cap is a common occurrence in the newborn, usually because the new mother is afraid to hurt the 'soft spot.' Adequate daily cleansing and washing of the scalp helps prevent it. Scrubbing with a soft brush or wash cloth and the gentle use of a fine-toothed comb or even your fingernails will clear it. You will not hurt the soft spot when you massage vigorously to clean the scalp."

Everyone has his or her own cradle cap remedy. Personally, I take my information where I can get it, and see good results. A mother in my practice tried Bactine for cradle cap and says it worked. I have had others try it with success. All treatments share two common principles: Soften and loosen the crusts and then scrub them off well.

FEEDING YOUR BABY

During the first three months, the baby is primarily interested in eating, sleeping, and being held. Aside from changing diapers, most of a mother's time is occupied by feeding the baby. Feeding the baby what? how? when? how much? I feel somewhat sorry for new parents who are barraged with conflicting advice about feeding. But before you read this section, you should be aware that it *also* contains conflicting advice. If you cannot stand some uncertainty, you should ask your physician to suggest one method. Stick with it, and ignore this part of *The Parents' Guide*. Similarly, don't read this section if your mind is already firmly made up. Relax, and be confident that your decision is the right one.

Breast or Bottle

One of our consulting mothers commented: "It is a mother's *right* to make up her own mind as to whether or not to breast feed. She really should not be advised, but should do what comes instinctively and naturally." We agree that only the parents themselves can and should make this very personal decision. However, no matter how hard you try, you probably cannot escape advice or the influence of neighbors, friends, and family. Since you can't escape advice, you may want to read ours. It is deliberately balanced in such a way that the decision will still be left where it belongs—up to you. And "you" definitely means "both husband and wife," since the father's support is usually essential to a happy nursing experience.

Until the turn of this century, a baby was either breast fed or he perished. Today, a mother enjoys the chance to weigh many factors before making either of two viable, sound choices. If you do read this chapter, concentrate on your own attitudes and don't try to read "between the lines." Your ideas are the ones that really matter. After reading the various opinions, you will have to "put it all together." In doing so, you will probably discover that our contributors are not all that very far apart on the important principles.

A Case for Breastfeeding

Dr. J.W. Gerrard, D.M., F.R.C.P., has prepared this section. (Dr. Gerrard is a Canadian professor of pediatrics and a specialist in allergies).

In countries where foods are not packaged with the care that they are in the United States, breast milk is essential for a baby's survival. If a mother is unable to feed her baby, she has to loan him out to a mother who can. In countries where standards of cleanliness are high, milk substitutes and formulas are safe. They are so safe, in fact, that many mothers prefer to give these to their babies rather than breast milk.

Most formulas are made by modifying cow's milk. The proportions of protein fat and milk sugar (lactose) are usually altered to some extent so that they resemble those found in breast milk; and sterilization alters the proteins, making them less allergenic than ordinary cow's milk.

In spite of the care which goes into making cow's milk formulas, they still upset some babies with eczema, colic, vomiting, or diarrhea. One or more of these reactions occur in about ten percent of all babies. When they occur, the baby has to be offered a hypo-allergenic formula made from soya, lamb, beef, or hydrolysed casein. Babies allergic to, or upset by, cow's milk are often allergic to or upset by other foods. If no formula suits the baby, a search may have to be made for breast milk, for this is the one "formula" that suits most babies. The composition of breast milk has been designed and developed over millions of years by an evolutionary process to ensure for the human infant the optimum chance of survival. It suits baby's digestion, and, of all foods, is the one least likely to upset him or to cause allergic reactions. If allergies run in the family, or if the baby is to be spared allergic problems, breast feed him.
However, occasionally babies develop allergic reactions to foods that the mother eats: shell fish, chocolate, cow's milk, and so forth.

Another reason why "breast milk is the best milk" is that it provides the baby with ammunition to fight off infections. Breast fed infants have fewer respiratory and fewer gastrointestinal infections. Part of the reason is that the acidity of the intestinal tract of a baby fed breast milk alone suppresses the growth of bacteria such as pathogenic E. coli and salmonella. If cow's milk or solids are added to the diet, this acidity is lost, and the baby will be more susceptible. Therefore, the best protection is from breast feeding alone for the first six months of life. At birth, the intestinal tract of babies is free from germs; but following one or two feedings, even though the formula itself contains no germs, the bowel becomes colonized with bacteria. One of the reasons these bacteria live harmlessly in children and grownups is because the cells lining the bowel make a special sort of antibody called "Secretory Immunoglobulin A," which keeps these germs at bay. The bowel of the newborn baby has none of this special antibody; but if the baby is breast fed, it receives a liberal supply of it, first in colostrum, (a rather thick yellowish pre-milk substance) and then in milk itself—thus breast milk is not only safer, it also provides important defenses.

Breast feeding insures not only that the baby will receive all the essential nutrients for normal growth and development, but also that he will be provided with the best ammunition to fight off germs and with protection from exposure to harmful allergens. If you want your baby to grow up with all the cards in his favor—breast feed him.

Breastfeeding Is Elating

Mrs. Nancy Cookson has this to say:

For me, breast feeding is the most rewarding way to feed a newborn baby. Breastfeeding is not only good emotionally, but it also helps my uterus contract to normal size faster than if I did not nurse. It is good for a baby who needs a lot of sucking, and it relaxes both mother and child. Nursing does take longer; but, if you have the time and the patience, it is well worth the extra effort. I nursed two of my own children, and I would like to have nursed my four foster babies.

And Mrs. "Tommie" Austin adds: "I noticed a real feeling of elation when breastfeeding my second baby that I hadn't noticed when bottle feeding my first one."

Breast Milk Is Best Milk

Betty Ann Countryman, R.N., M.N., says it this way:

Since the beginning of the twentieth century, the popularity of breastfeeding has declined alarmingly, despite evidence in favor of mother's milk as the ideal. Its immediate readiness, correct temperature, and freshness, coupled with rapid and easy digestibility, make mother's milk the obvious choice for the newborn.
The ease and convenience of night feedings at breast, and its advantages to both parents, is evident; and the psychological advantages to mother and baby are many.

If in Doubt—Try It!

Over the years, I have seen many mothers make their decisions about whether to feed by breast or by bottle on a social basis. If they are in a predominately bottle-feeding neighborhood, they often feed by bottle, largely because of the real or imagined social pressures. If they have a lot of breastfeeding family, friends, or neighbors, they almost automatically breastfeed. The social pressures, real and unreal, arise from the herd instinct as well as from the implication that the majority way is the best way. Mothers can become quite aggressive or quite defensive about their stands; and they welcome others to their respective camps almost as though baby feeding is a political issue. Keep firmly in mind that it is *your individual choice* to do what is best for the baby and for you and your husband. It is no one else's business except your doctor's— and with his help you can make up your mind. There may be times when some mothers will be advised to feed in a way they don't desire. It is fine to follow your natural feelings to make up your mind—with exceptions! If there is a family history of milk allergy or infant feeding problems, you probably owe it to yourself and to the baby to try the breast. And regardless of how intense your desire to breastfeed may be, switch to the bottle if the baby does poorly on breast. An important aside for the determined breastfeeding mother is that if you feel you must "breastfeed or bust," you may "bust." The greatest single reason for a mother's inability to breastfeed her child successfully is nervous tension. So go at it loosely. If you can breastfeed, great! If not, things will still work out well.

If there is any doubt at all, I urge you to *try* to breastfeed. If you change your mind, you can easily quit—and it's harder to start once you have quit. Most of us believe that mother's milk is, without doubt, the best food for the majority of babies. So try it—your baby will probably like it, and so will you. If he doesn't, or if you don't, then quit with the satisfaction that you tried.

Summary of the Advantages of Breastfeeding
- Ideal food for human infants, possibly lacking only enough iron and vitamins A, D, and C. (These partial deficiencies conceivably may be altered if the mother's diet is high in iron and vitamins.)
- Helps the infant fight infections.
- Fewer bowel upsets and infections, and less chance of eczema or other skin diseases and allergies.
- Ensures a lot of holding and cuddling, essential if the baby is to thrive.
- Easier on the mother, who doesn't have to fix or warm formula in the middle of the night.
- Milk is always fresh and available when traveling.
- Immediately available—the baby needn't wait for hunger to be satisfied.
- Mother derives many emotional and physical benefits from nursing.
- Satisfies the mother's urge to mother in a "natural" way.
- More economical than bottle feeding.
- Anti-obesity measure—breast fed babies are well nourished but less heavy than formula-fed babies.

Summary of Disadvantages of Bottle Feeding
- Formula feeding leads to a temptation to leave infants propped with the bottle rather than holding them.
- Preparing formula takes mother's energy and time.
- Formula should be sterilized for the first three months.
- Unsterile formula can cause bowel disease and diarrhea.
- Formula, if not made to resemble human milk closely, may cause many ad-

verse reactions, including: dehydration, constipation, diarrhea, intestinal cramps, skin disease, and excessively fat babies.
• Formula, no matter how well prepared, will cause cow's milk allergy in some infants with symptoms of fussiness, anemia, skin rashes, and diarrhea.
• Formula is expensive.

Breastfeeding Is Not the *Only* Way!

In spite of all of the listed advantages, for some mothers, there are valid reasons *not* to breastfeed. The first and most important reason is the mother's feelings. If, for whatever reason, a mother is uncomfortable or unhappy breastfeeding, she should stop. It is better to have a happy mother and a bottle-fed baby than an unhappy mother with a breastfed baby. Unfortunately, some people push so hard for breastfeeding that some mothers feel guilty if they don't breastfeed. A guilt-ridden mother is an unhappy mother. Don't let the fact that you don't nurse make you feel inadequate. Breastfeeding may be great for most mothers and for most babies, but not for all. Most important, is it for *you?* Even ardent breastfeeding advocate Betty Ann Countryman says: "The happy bottle feeding mother who holds and cuddles her baby has a more secure and loved baby than the unhappy breastfeeding mother who neglects him except to feed, and vice versa." And pediatrician Neil Henderson states: "Breastfeeding is not a test of a woman's femininity. Further, there is absolutely no proof that breastfed babies are happier than bottle babies. Tender loving care is given in many ways."

Associate Editor John C. Richards sums it up well:

> A mother who wants to nurse her infant should be given every possible encouragement; but the mother who prefers formula should be allowed to follow her wishes, rather than being urged to "try" nursing because of an obligation to give her child "the best possible start in life." Breastfeeding, in order to be successful, should be a pleasant experience for the child, for the mother, and for the father as well. Most mothers who want to breastfeed will do so successfully. Most who have been talked into trying it against their real wishes will switch the baby to the bottle within a week or two after leaving the hospital.

Sometimes there are medical reasons not to breastfeed. The anatomy of the nipples occasionally prevents it, as do serious maternal disease and maternal fatigue. A few mothers don't produce enough milk to make it worthwhile. On rare occasions, I have seen babies who do poorly on their mother's milk, even though there was an adequate milk supply.

Most physicians, aware of all of the good reasons to breastfeed, offer mothers the choice of the bottle. Breastfeeding is not for all mothers.

Occasional mothers who have bottlefed their first one or two babies will get the urge to breastfeed the next one. They usually succeed, and then express regret that they hadn't breastfed the prior babies. Often they "blame" this on non-cooperative doctors, forgetting that it is the mother, not the doctor, who breastfeeds and that therefore she must be the one to make the decision.

Physicians see mothers who feel they have failed their babies when they are unable to continue breastfeeding; they are perfectly excellent mothers whose sense of guilt, however unjustified, makes them a little less effective and perhaps a little less loving of the child. To breastfeed or not should be—must be—the mother's decision based on how she feels. How she feels is, to a degree, based upon how the father feels. On the one hand, a husband can encourage breastfeeding, but he should not push a reluctant wife into it. On the other hand, if a husband has a serious emotional aversion against breastfeeding, to try breastfeeding might do more damage to the marriage than good to the baby. In either case, a man must recognize that his wife is up at night feeding the baby and is home twenty four hours a day every day of the week. She needs help, including relief from some night feedings; assistance with dinner, dishes, and housekeeping, or diaper changes. Even more vital is the need of both husband and wife for a bit of babying themselves.

What it all boils down to is that you, as a potential breastfeeding mother, have a choice. This sort of advice leaves some mothers dissatisfied. Bambi Scofield, after reviewing our attempt to present the facts yet to stay neutral, protested:

> In their anxiety not to jump on one side or the other of the breastfeeding question, some doctors tend to offer no help or advice at all—which tends to make them seem to be pro-formula. This is further complicated by our specialization system where the mother finds one doctor (an obstetrician) in charge of her aching nipples and another (a pediatrician) in charge of whether the baby is gaining properly. It's all very confusing and discouraging.

She was answered by pediatrician Merrit Low, who replied: "It is not for the La Leche League or for doctors to decide, but to support the decisions parents make. Decision-making is a badge of maturity, and mature parents help the baby most. Maturity and self-esteem are also foes of guilt and anxiety."

Advantages of Bottle Feeding
- Modern formulas are well designed and closely resemble mother's milk.
- Good formulas can adequately nourish around 90% of all infants during the first several months of life.
- Modern formulas are easy to prepare and to give with a minimum of work.

- Father can hold the baby and share directly in bottle feeding but not in breast-feeding.
- Mother can get out of the house more easily, leaving the baby with a sitter.

Summary of the Disadvantages of Breastfeeding
- Some mothers feel distaste or revulsion about breastfeeding.
- Mother cannot always be relieved from feeding to catch up on sleep.
- It is more difficult to get away from home for a needed break.
- Some breasts and nipples become too painful to breastfeed comfortably.
- Some mothers just don't give enough milk.
- It may be difficult or embarrassing, yet impossible, to avoid breastfeeding in front of family or friends.
- The mother's own health may make it difficult or impossible. (In special cases, it is safer for a tubercular mother to bottle feed.
- Working mothers' schedules may present many problems.
- Many mothers fear weight gain and loss of their firm, youthful figure.
- Certain babies with rare, inborn errors of metabolism may have to be brought up on special formulas.

How to Breastfeed

In the first few days after birth, very little milk is produced. Considering that the entire human race was raised this way until the turn of this century—there was no formula or sterilized milk available before —you can be certain you are well endowed. And you can also be sure that babies are designed to go without significant intake for those first few days. Some colostrum comes out when the baby sucks. Colostrum is a thick yellow milk-like substance that contains some energy and a lot of antibodies.

When they bring the baby out at first, he may be too sleepy or tired to suck. If he is hungry, just touch your nipple to his cheek and he will turn and take it. Don't try to push him toward the nipple or his rooting reflex will cause him to turn toward your fingers—toward the pressure. If he isn't hungry, just open his mouth and put the nipple in—usually he will suck then.

There is no "Red Cross Approved Position" in which to hold your infant for feeding. Most mothers hold the baby across their upper abdomen; some sit, and some lie down to feed. But you can hold your baby any way that works well for the two of you. Don't hesitate to experiment with positions. The best position for any baby depends on the shape of the breast, the tilt of the nipple, and the shape of the baby's mouth.

Don't let him nurse over a few minutes on each breast at first. If your nipples tolerate this well, then gradually increase the nursing time with each feeding. When your milk comes in, the breasts often become swollen and a little tender. This only lasts a day or so, so continue to breastfeed.

Once the milk comes in, it is a light bluish color and almost looks watery. That is normal for human milk, so don't worry. The milk is so thoroughly digested and absorbed by the baby that there isn't a lot left over for bowel movements. These are usually of small volume, and they are watery, with little yellow curds. For the first few days, there may be a greenish tinge to the bowel movement, but that should soon pass.

As a rule of thumb, don't go over one half an hour for total feeding time. I advise that you empty one breast fairly thoroughly at each feeding and thus alternate breasts. As a rule of thumb, wait at least two hours after you have finished the last feeding before you start another. It takes about two hours for the baby's stomach to digest the milk and to become empty.

Details About Breastfeeding

For details about breastfeeding, and for a more sophisticated approach, we turn to the real experts—experienced breastfeeding mothers. Specifically, we have asked the Nursing Mothers Counsel to offer you their help. This is a group of volunteer California mothers who, along with an advisory board of pediatricians, encourage breastfeeding and help mothers who have problems with breastfeeding.

One reason I like them and their advice is that they will accept it as reasonable that many mothers don't want to breastfeed, and that they don't push breastfeeding as a way of life. Because of this low key attitude, they are quite effective in encouraging breastfeeding.

BREASTFEEDING *

Breastfeeding may be natural, but it doesn't come easily to all mothers or babies. If you want to be successful at breastfeeding, set out ahead of time to inform yourself as completely as possible about how to position baby properly at the breast, about methods of building up a good supply of milk, about how to prevent sore nipples, and so forth. Read some books on nursing, and, if possible, find a group in your area from whom you can get good advice about breastfeeding.

Some say that breastfeeding keeps a mother more tied down to her baby. That's not necessarily true, since you can always supplement with bottles when you go out. But it usually does result in more time being spent holding the baby. The temptation to prop a bottle in bed with baby is obviously eliminated. We feel that this is a positive aspect of breastfeeding. The period of time when a baby wants to be

* Nursing Mothers Counsel, Inc.

held passes quickly; by the time he's one and a half years old, your child won't hold still long enough to be rocked. It's gratifying to know that during the time when touch and feel and taste are all important, you are able to fulfill your child's needs in such a direct way.

Get Help
Get some current books on breastfeeding from your library, such as Karen Pryor's *Nursing Your Baby*.[4] Find a group in your area that is close to your ideas about breastfeeding. Try to meet a member. She may have some good suggestions. If you do have problems, doubt, or questions once your baby has arrived, you will feel more comfortable talking to a woman whom you have already met.

Nipples, Nipple Shields, and Bras
Check yourself for inverted nipples. With the thumb above the areola (the dark circle around the nipple) and the index finger below it, gently squeeze together behind the brown part. If your nipple fails to move outward (forward) or if it moves in, then you have inverted or flat nipples. One or both nipples may show this characteristic. Flat or inverted nipples can be corrected during pregnancy by wearing Swedish Mild Cups, Netsy Breast shields or Woolwich shields. At first, wear them until they become uncomfortable (as little as five minutes). Gradually increase the time until you can wear them for two or three hours or even all day. After the baby arrives, wear them for at least half an hour before each feeding. If you are leaking milk, throw away any milk collected in the shields. The warm, wet plastic is a great place to breed bacteria. Your nipples need fresh air. Don't wear the shields all the time. Wash your nipples with clear water only. Soap and alcohol are very drying and should be avoided. You may wish to toughen your nipples up a little by scrubbing gently with a wash cloth. [Some pediatricians disagree, and believe that the use of soap and water reduces the chance of infection. What counts the most is the way each mother's nipples respond. If soap doesn't bother you, use it—if it does bother, just use water.]

Purchase one or two nursing bras, no more. Try them on for fit. You are looking for firm, comfortable support. The cup should not be too tight, as your breast may be larger with milk in it. Cotton bras keep the nipple drier and let air circulate better. Nylon tends to keep the nipples damper and doesn't breathe as well. However, nylon dries faster, so the bra can be washed and changed more often. Some bras come with a pocket to slip nursing pads into. Others have a plastic lining sewn into them in order to keep milk from leaking out onto your clothing. This plastic should be *removed,* and used only on very, very special occasions. The plastic doesn't allow air to circulate and can make your nipples sore from sitting in a warm damp bra. You may want to purchase nursing pads to absorb leaking milk. There are washable cloth ones as well as disposable paper ones available.

You can make your own from old diapers cut in a four inch circle and sewn around the edges. For dresses, you will want outfits that pull up from the waist or unbutton in the front. A-line dresses are definitely out.

Get the Right Doctor

Before you go into the hospital for delivery, find out if it offers rooming-in, where the baby can stay in the room with you rather than in the nursery. This allows you to feed the baby when he or she cries rather than just feeding on schedule. Remember that you will only be in the hospital a few days and that you can be your own boss once you get home. Tell your doctors (both your obstetrician and pediatrician) that you plan to breastfeed, and ask how they feel about nursing. Try to find a pediatrician who is supportive of breastfeeding, and one who encourages mothers to keep nursing when the baby is over five months old. You may not want to nurse that long, but the doctor is supportive of breastfeeding if he doesn't encourage mothers to wean early.

Expressing Colostrum

The value of expressing colostrum pre-natally is controversial. Some claim it does no harm; others claim that it is not replaced by the body and may cause premature uterine cramping. If you wish to express colostrum, a few drops every few days is plenty. Some women are not able to express colostrum pre-natally. This does not mean that they will not be able to breastfeed.

The Techniques of Breastfeeding

From almost every standpoint of successful breastfeeding, *the earlier you start the better!* Finding the right position for early nursings is important: Some mothers find it most comfortable to sit upright while nursing. A straight-backed chair with armrests or pillows to prop mother's arms and shoulders from being strained works well. A bed may be cranked up so that mother can lean forward a little. The mother's legs should be propped on a stool whenever possible; the arms may be propped with armrests or pillows. The less muscle effort Mother has to put into supporting herself and the baby, the more relaxed she will be. Lying down on bed may be more comfortable for mothers whose perineums are sore; however, it takes some women a while to learn to nurse lying down. We recommend lying on the side, with the baby lying on the bed and nursing from the breast closest to the bed. A pillow under the mother's head will keep her neck from being strained. The lower arm should be under the pillow, not under the baby; while the free arm guides the baby to a comfortable nursing position and places the nipple in the baby's mouth. The "upside down" position often works—mother and baby lie with the baby positioned so that his feet extend beyond mother's head. In the "football hold," the baby is held under mother's arm, at her side. The baby must be raised to the level of the breast by supporting his body with pillows. Mother's arm goes over the baby. Mother should be propped slightly forward, with pillows behind her back; and her arm goes over the baby in order to lift his head to the breast.

Getting the Baby to Take the Breast

When the baby is first put to breast, his rooting reflex should be stimulated by stroking the cheek nearest the nipple to make him turn toward it. *Pushing* his head toward the nipple will make him turn away from it. The nipple and areola should be placed well back in the baby's mouth. Mother may have to compress the areola, or first express milk to soften it; and then compress the areola so that the nipple will project—and then place the nipple in the mouth properly. During the nursing period, mother may need to continue to press on the areola in order to keep the nipple far back in the baby's mouth. To be sure that the baby can breathe easily while nursing, mother should push in the area on her breast below the baby's nose.

Nursing Time

Nursing time should be limited at first to about five minutes on each breast. Sucking time should be increased steadily so that, by the time milk comes in, in two or three days, the baby should be able to nurse for ten minutes on each side, or longer if mother experiences no discomfort. Nursing times will be variable; efficiency of sucking changes as baby gets accustomed to the breast. Mother should not time each feeding exactly, but should aim to lengthen the feeding times rapidly.

Each feeding should be started on the side last used, and both sides should be used at each feeding. If the hospital or obstetrician definitely prohibit using both breasts, or if baby won't take the second side, some colostrum should be expressed from the side not nursed on in order to help prevent engorgement.

Burping

The baby should be given the chance to burp between nursing at each breast and after feeding. If the baby is fussy after feeding and difficult to burp, mother may try burping him earlier—after two or three minutes—and then return him to the same breast. A few babies never burp.

Encouraging the Baby to Suck

If the baby has to be encouraged to suck, awaken him by loosening the covers, and prop him in a sitting position, having tickled his feet and stroked his chin. Express a few drops of colostrum or milk into the baby's mouth to help him to begin sucking; or, if he is extremely reluctant, put honey or corn syrup on the nipple.

Not all babies will respond and nurse when offered the breast. Some will sleep through part or all of the early feedings. Newborns may simply not have developed appetites yet, or they may be being given sugar water and/or formula in the nursery, which reduces their appetites. If rooming-in is not possible, mother can ask the pediatrician to leave special orders to eliminate water and/or formula and to have the baby brought to her every three hours, or on demand. If the baby doesn't nurse, colostrum should be released to stimulate milk production and prevent clogging of the nipple.

After Feeding

To break suction when the baby is to be removed from the breast, insert a finger in the corner of his mouth, or depress the breast slightly with the finger tip. After nursing, nipples should be blotted and air-dried for ten minutes or more by leaving the bra flaps down under the nightgown or robe. If the nipples are even slightly tender, a goose neck or high intensity reading lamp or low wattage light bulb can be used on them. After air drying, if leaking is a problem, mother should use nursing pads and change them frequently.

Avoid Water

You may be concerned about the lack of wet diapers on a newborn. Even if baby is nursing early and well, normal urinary output for the first day or two may be a *total* of an ounce or two, or less. Thereafter, the amount of urine should increase steadily. Many hospitals routinely advise mother to offer baby some water after each feeding. It is more important that mother and baby concentrate on learning to nurse than on giving the water—if it is needed, it can be given to the baby in the nursery.

If Baby Is Not Interested

An overtired baby may not be interested in nursing even if he is screaming. Calming him down first will make it easier to get him onto the breast. A lazy baby may need encouragement and short, frequent nursing sessions. If awakened from a sound sleep for a meal, the baby may at first not suck well. The hospital staff may be well intentioned but ill informed about breastfeeding. Mother should ask to be alone with baby at nursing time if she feels that suggestions, or even just the presence of others, are making things more difficult. Demand feeding and rooming-in, whenever possible, help to assure that the baby can be put to breast when he is hungry, not when the hospital time tables say he ought to be hungry. Difficulty nursing while in the hospital doesn't mean that the problem will continue when you get home.

If an older baby won't nurse, it may be due to:
1. Illness
2. Teething

3. Too much supplement or solid food
4. Low milk supply
5. Over-tired or over-stimulated baby
6. Delayed let-down
7. Getting ready to wean: Be cautious about forcing a baby who is seeking more independence to nurse.
8. He may want to socialize rather than nurse.
9. Or it may be time to stop!

Fussiness after Nursing

Fussiness after nursing may mean that the baby needs to be burped, rather than that he is still hungry. Some large, eager babies who are fed on four hour schedules may not be satisfied by nursing alone during the hospital stay. If it is impossible to arrange that they be fed on demand, a little water given after feedings may be helpful.

The Let-down Reflex

"Let-down" is the process during which the breasts' milk-secreting glands release milk through the ducts into the sinuses behind the areola and nipple. Uually the baby's sucking begins the process by signaling the pituitary gland in the brain to release a hormone—oxytocin—which, in turn, makes the milk glands contract to release the milk. Let-down can occur, however, without sucking stimulation, when other factors, usually emotional, trigger the process.

Some mothers are aware of a tenseness or tingling of the breasts when let-down occurs; others have no conscious feeling of it. Most new mothers do not recognize let-down until the baby is several weeks old, even though it is functioning normally. Milk may flow from the unoccupied breast (or from both breasts if the baby isn't nursing). A change in the suck-swallow rhythm may be evident. Before let-down, the baby will suck four to six times before he swallows; after let-down occurs, enough milk is released that he must swallow after each suck.

Let-down may be inhibited by tension, worry, and fatigue. The baby can receive only a small portion of the milk his mother produces if let-down does not proceed normally. Mother should try to relax to assure that the let-down does occur: You should be undisturbed during nursing. Take the phone off the hook and put a "do not disturb" sign on the front door. A favorite drink helps induce relaxation. Many mothers find that intense thirst accompanies let-down; have water or another drink at hand while nursing. Hot bouillon may be better than too much coffee or tea—they act as stimulants and also have some diuretic effect. Relaxation and breathing exercises may help by easing muscle tension. Systematic exercises are good: Deliberately contract all the muscles in the face and neck and then relax them, proceeding to the chest, arms, abdomen, legs, and so on. If you have taken preparation-for-childbirth classes, you may find some of the labor-relaxation exercises helpful. Other aids to relaxation, such as music,

TV, dim lighting, and reading while nursing, may be tried. You can try to condition the let-down reflex by nursing at relatively regular intervals, always nursing in the same place and having all "props" such as drinks, pillows, books, and so forth at hand before beginning the feeding. If let-down is noticed between feeding times, you should nurse baby immediately so that let-down and nursing are associated. But don't become unduly concerned about let-down. It will occur automatically. If you really don't have a let-down and don't want to breast feed, go ahead and wean the baby. It may be harder to feed in the late afternoon or early evening if you are tired or if the baby is especially fussy. Try gently pulling out the nipple before a feeding to help stimulate let-down; letting the baby nuzzle at the breast beforehand may work, too.

Cardinal Rules for Establishing a Good Supply of Milk

1. *Frequent nursing.* You should probably try to nurse seven to ten times in twenty-four hours during the first two weeks, allowing around two to three hours between feeds. The amount of milk produced is directly related to the amount of sucking stimulation the breasts receive.
2. *Adequate fluid intake.* Drink two to two and a half quarts of fluids per day. (Tea and coffee should not be counted in with the total, since they are rapidly excreted by the body.) Drink lots of fluids early in the day. Have the fluid beside you when you nurse.
3. *Adequate rest.* Try to catnap while baby sleeps until the night feedings are over. Get out of the house, even if just for a walk around the block.
4. *Adequate and balanced diet.* You require an additional 500 to 1,000 calories per day while breast feeding. Vitamins and minerals prescribed during pregnancy should be continued.
5. *Relaxation during feedings.* In order for let-down reflex to function best, you should get comfortable, relax, and enjoy your baby.
6. *Almost empty the breasts.* Emptying your breast (they never *completely* empty) is important. Usually this takes about ten to fifteen minutes a breast. Both breasts should be used at each feeding, beginning with the breast last used at the previous feeding time, in order to empty it thoroughly. To tell when a breast is empty, listen to the baby's suck-swallow rhythm. When the breast is nearly empty, the baby swallows only occasionally, as opposed to the regular suck-swallow, suck-swallow pattern that can be heard when milk is flowing freely.

The milk supply is well established by six weeks if the baby is totally breast fed (e.g., not relying on bottles or solids for any regular part of his nourishment) and is gaining steadily (i.e., regaining birth weight by two weeks of age and then gaining approximately one ounce per day until three months old).

The Problems of Breast Engorgement

Engorgement is a temporary problem which arises at the time the milk comes in. It is due to enlarged or swollen tissues of the breast and to increase blood and lymph supply—all of which tend to pinch the milk ducts closed, thus increasing the problem. If the baby can nurse frequently, the problem will probably be alleviated in forty-eight hours. If, however, the baby cannot grasp the breast because of the hardness of the areola and flatness of the nipple, any or all of the following may be tried.

1. Sitz baths for the breasts. Fill a clean pan or basin with hot water and lean over it so the breasts can be rinsed or submerged in the water. This should be followed by massage and, if necessary, by manual expression of the milk.
2. Hot packing. Using two towels (or washcloths) and a basin of hot water, wring out towel, and apply over breasts from neck down and from armpit to armpit. As soon as towel begins to cool, apply second towel, putting first towel back into basin to reheat. This should be done as often as possible, for about thirty minutes before each nursing, and can be followed by massage and, if necessary, by manual expression of the milk.
3. Hot showers. Massage and expression of milk can be done in the shower, or immediately after.
4. Massage the breasts with a lubricant, such as cocoa butter or cold cream. With both hands open and flat, push from the collar bone down, from armpit and cleavage in, and from the underside up—all toward areola. Then hand-express milk with the thumb and forefinger, or use a breast pump to soften the areola and pull out the nipple.
5. A nipple shield can be tried when beginning nursing, in order to pull out the nipple, but a breast pump will do just as well. (Baby may become used to the shield and later refuse to take nipple.)
6. Ask your doctor for permission to have the baby brought in either on demand or more frequently—or at least for the 2 a.m. feeding skipped in most hospitals.
7. Let the baby suck long enough that he doesn't stop just as let-down has occurred; or express the milk manually until the let-down occurs, and then put the baby to breast. It is important to let the baby withdraw the milk. Limit the sucking on the first side to be sure that the baby gets to the second breast.
8. If baby has slept or nursed lazily each time, milk should be expressed to keep it flowing and to provide some comfort. A breast pump can be used if manual expression is too difficult.
9. Sit up while nursing, leaning forward slightly to allow gravity to assist flow, and support the breast from underneath with one hand. If distinct lumps are present, massage them toward the nipple with one hand as the baby nurses.

10. The use of Woolwich shields or Swedish milk cups between feedings may stimulate flow and help to pull out the nipples.
11. Ice packs can be used between sessions of hot packs. Hot packs stimulate the circulation, whereas cold packs relieve pain.
12. If the mother has considerable pain and fever, a small dose of aspirin will help relieve these symptoms.
13. A well-fitting bra must support engorged breasts so that tissues don't become over-stretched. The bra may be kept on during sleep and even in the shower—and changed afterwards.
14. If engorgement is severe, limiting fluid intake somewhat may be helpful.
15. After nursing is well established, mild engorgement or fullness can occur if your bra is binding, or if the baby misses regular feedings. This engorgement should be treated as above.

Prevention of Sore Nipples

There are a number of things you can do to prevent sore nipples. It is easier to prevent them than to treat them. During the last few weeks of pregnancy, it is a good idea to rub the nipples briskly with a towel after your bath or shower, and then to roll nipples and gently pull them out. In the beginning, nursing time should be limited to a few minutes on each side at each feeding, increasing fairly quickly (up to five minutes on each side during the first twenty-four hours, five to ten minutes the second twenty-four hours, and ten to fifteen minutes during the third twenty-four hours, provided that there is no nipple tenderness).

1. It is important to get the nipple and as much areola as possible well back in the baby's mouth. In order to manage this, compress the areola; if it is hard, soften it first by expressing a few drops of milk.
2. Short, frequent feedings are better than long, infrequent ones. Baby should nurse only as long as the "suck-swallow" rhythm persists.
3. Between nursings, the bra and/or padding must be kept as dry as possible. "Modella" type fabrics, which conduct moisture away from skin and into absorbent padding, can be used inside the bra. ("Modella" diaper liners, by Kleinerts, can be cut up for this purpose.)
4. The following items may irritate nipples:
   a. Any soap.
   b. Phisohex or other antiseptic preparations.
   c. A nursing bra or pad with plastic lining.
   d. Any substance used next to the skin that may cause allergic skin reactions.
   e. Certain creams *may* cause skin allergies. Discontinue them entirely or substitute another brand if necessary.

What to Do About Sore Nipples

Sore nipples early in nursing are a frequent, but usually transitory, problem, one which generally disappears within two weeks or so with adequate treatment. Below are some measures you can take to relieve the pain.

1. Baby should nurse first on the least sore side until let-down occurs —this prevents early, vigorous sucking from irritating the sore nipple further. If both nipples are sore, mother may wish to try hand-expressing until let-down occurs.
2. Changing either baby's or your position will enable baby's jaws to exert pressure on other, less tender, spots. It may be easier to control nursing positions if you sit upright and use pillows for propping the baby at various angles.
3. You may use vitamin A and D cream or hydrous lanolin (from the drug store, non-prescription) if your nipples and areola are chapped. Apply only to the areolae and sides of the nipple, for cream on the tip of nipple may cause plugging, and should be applied lightly, if at all.
4. Warm dry heat can be used for ten to fifteen minutes after nursing: a lamp with an ordinary 25 watt bulb, placed six to eight inches away from the breast after nursing, or a 40 watt bulb placed twelve to eighteen inches away.
5. If soreness is severe, and if other measures haven't worked, it may be necessary to rest the nipple and to express milk into a cup.

Be sure to report any fissure or crack in your breasts to your doctor immediately. A bumpy, scaly redness on the areola could be eczema or a fungal infection. A blister on the end of the nipple sometimes appears. It may be no more than skin sloughing off, but if it is blocking the duct, it should be opened by the doctor.

Questions and Answers About Nursing

How can a nursing mother know if her baby is getting enough milk?

If extra water is needed between most feedings, if the baby's urine output is less than usual, if the bowel movements are small and infrequent, or if the baby just seems hungry too often, it is wise to check with the doctor. Although regular weighing is the most accurate way to tell if the baby is growing satisfactorily, it is usually not recommended that parents use a home scale to determine how much milk the baby takes at a feeding or how much weight he has gained daily. Since weight varies by several ounces at different times a day, weighing the baby too frequently only causes confusion and unnecessary anxiety for the parents—*John C. Richards, M.D.*

What about breast infections?

Breast infections usually start with a local soreness and, sometimes, redness. Antibiotics and hot packs help, but it has proven important to continue to nurse and to keep the breast as empty of milk as possible. It takes far less time for infections or abscesses to heal when nursing is continued, and it will not harm the baby.—*Betty Ann Countryman, R.N., M.N.*

Is your breast milk "rich" enough for you to feed successfully?

Two reasons for apprehension on the part of a mother who is breastfeeding for the first time are:

1. The two-to-four-day delay in milk production that almost always occurs after delivery.
2. The "thin" appearance of the milk when it does come in.

Because of these, a mother may question her adequacy or fear for her baby's health. However, this natural delay happens to everyone. Human breast milk does not look like rich cow's milk. It is blue-white in color when compared with the rich yellow colostrum, or with the rich creamy appearance of cow's milk. In spite of its appearance, breast milk is always rich enough to satisfy the baby's nutritional requirements.—*John C. Richards, M.D.*

How can a nursing mother empty her breasts?

One method of improving milk flow is to make certain that the breasts are drained during or after feedings. This clears the lacteal ducts, relieving inflammation, congestion, and pain. In addition, complete emptying of the breasts stimulates better milk production. By encouraging full production, at least ninety percent of women can successfully breastfeed.

Colostrum and excess milk can be removed with the hands. Use the following "exercise" during the last six weeks of pregnancy and at the onset of breastfeeding. There are two distinct maneuvers. The first starts with the hands encircling the base of the breast—one above, one below—exerting firm pressure as they are moved from the base of the breast to the areola about five times, squeezing the milk from the base toward the areola. Then, with the flat of one hand below and the other above on the pendulous portion of the breast, milk toward the areola. Finally, milk the breast with the forefinger and thumb, starting behind the areola where the milk is stored.—*Glenn Austin, M.D.*

What can be done when a baby still seems hungry after emptying both breasts?

First, be sure his fussiness is not caused by something other than hunger. This could be teething, illness, boredom, or many other things. By the time you figure it out, the baby will probably have forgotten it. Every baby, hungry or not, will suck on anything that comes near the mouth. It may be that he needs to be held, or to have a short period of play before going to sleep. Or he may be kept awake by intestinal contractions which soon result in a bowel movement or in passing air, normally started by reflex actions as food passes into the upper end of the intestine from the stomach so bowel movements occur towards the end of a feeding or within a few minutes after eating. He will probably fall asleep as soon as the contractions have ended. To help him, you may use a pacifier, rock him in a cradle, or just hold him for a few minutes. When these techniques work to relax him, then you can be assured that he's probably not hungry.

Sometimes, nothing works. In that case, a small bottle of sugar water may be offered. If, now and then, it's obvious that he just won't settle down without more to eat, offer a little formula. Don't be too quick to give formula, or soon he'll learn to expect a bottle after every nursing. He'll spit out his mother's nipple as soon as her milk slows down a little, and before long the lack of adequate sucking stimulus will cause her breasts to dry up.—*John C. Richards, M.D.*

Many breastfed babies customarily nurse about every two hours, with occasional sleep spans of four or more hours each day. The small easily digested curd of breast milk and the relative indigestibility of some components of cow's milk account for the shorter time span between feedings in a breastfed baby. Don't offer formula to the breastfed baby who awakens two hours after the last feeding; just nurse him again—which both satisfies him and provides an increase in your own milk-making ability. Any introduction of formula at this point is a step toward weaning.—*Betty Ann Countryman, R.N., M.N.*

As an enthusiastic nursing mother, I find a bottle of water a great help and a relief at times; I'm glad to have it at my fingertips for those times I call "impossible" to offer the breast—*Alicia Herman, consulting mother*

Does the size of a mother's breasts make any difference in her milk supply?

Usually not. One cannot use breast size alone as a means of predicting success or failure in nursing. In general, small-breasted women can breastfeed their babies better than other women with large pendulous and fatty breasts because of better milk-producing tissue with less interference with extra gland tissues.—*Bruce Valentine, M.D.*

Does blood swallowed by a baby while nursing do any harm?

Sometimes the nipples become irritated and bleed a bit when the baby sucks. No harm is done. If more than a few drops are swallowed, however, it will cause a black tarry color in the baby's stools. When this persists, it may be necessary to discontinue nursing from the affected breast for a few days in order to be sure that the baby has no internal bleeding which has caused black stools.—*John C. Richards, M.D.*

Can twins be breastfed?

They certainly can be—triplets, too! Often, they, even more than the single child, need the advantages which mother's milk offers. Twins are frequently premature or of lower birth weight than the baby who is born alone. For such infants, the ease of digestibility and the immunity factors in human milk are especially desirable.

It is not much more difficult to produce sufficient milk for twins than for the single baby. The techniques for managing the nursing, however, may initially be harder, so the mother of twins is put to a rapid test. An inexperienced mother may find it difficult to nurse two babies at once, or she may think that all she will ever do is nurse if she attemtps to nurse each child.

Ideally, learning to handle the breastfeeding of twins will begin in the hospital. Rooming-in will make it much easier for the mother, since she will be able to nurse each child on demand. But even if the hospital has not yet modernized to include rooming-in, it is still possible, with a helpful nursery staff, to begin to learn with minimal difficulty.

The mother who has breastfed a previous child will often find it easy to nurse both babies simultaneously from the start. For the inexperienced mother, the best approach may be for the mother to nurse one baby first, and the second one shortly thereafter, alternating the breast used by each baby at successive feedings. If both babies are nursed every two to three hours, the mother will have sufficient milk for them, just as she would for a lone baby. As the mother becomes more comfortable with each separate child, little by little she should begin to nurse the two together whenever the babies are willing. The basic management of nursing twins is the same as that for one child: Neither baby should miss a single feeding; no bottles of formula or water need be offered between nursings as long as both mother and babies are normal and well; and the babies should be fed upon demand whenever possible.

Sometimes one baby may be in an isolette temporarily until he attains sufficient weight. When this happens, the mother may nurse the larger twin regularly, and pump or express milk for the smaller one mid-way between feedings. The pumped milk should be given to the little one and the mother should have no difficulty building and maintaining a sufficient supply for both babies.

If both twins are too small to nurse initially, the mother should begin to pump or express her colostrum, and later her milk, about every two hours, to be given to both babies until she is able to nurse them directly at breast.

Isn't this a lot of trouble? Yes and no. It does take time—but babies, especially two at a time, require a lot of time and attention, whatever the method of feeding.—*Betty Ann Countryman, R.N., M.N.*

Talking with another mother who has successfully nursed twins is especially helpful. In the early weeks, keeping records is important: for example, feeding time, side used for which baby, how long, and so forth. Mother must be particularly careful about the prevention of sore nipples. A little manipulation of schedules may be necessary for for mother's needs. She may use a modified demand schedule, feeding the first baby awake and then awakening the second baby, or waking the second baby and feeding them simultaneously. Mother needs extra nourishing food, and extra fluids.—*Nursing Mothers Counsel, Inc.*

What foods are needed and which should be avoided?

A well-balanced diet is necessary for the nursing mother's health, but usually what she eats or drinks does not affect the infant. If certain foods disagree with you, then skip those foods. You may find that of you eat too much candy or too much fruit, the baby may have looser stools. It is not essential to drink milk, if you don't like it. You should have adequate fluid intake and be sure of an adequate calcium supply. —*Leo Bell, M.D.*

Muscle cramps and weakness can result from calcium depletion when a mother nurses for many months without an adequate dietary calcium intake. Calcium can be given in tablet form or in milk substitutes such as cheese, yogurt, and ice cream. See *The Parent's Medical Manual* for a thorough list of calcium containing foods.—*John C. Richards, M.D.*

Can a nursing mother take medicines, smoke, or drink alcoholic beverages?

Certain drugs do enter a mother's milk but usually not in sufficient quantity to affect the baby. Too many cigarettes may cause an excess of nicotine in the milk, and I recommend that you not exceed ten a day. If you wish, a little wine or a beer or two is permissible. It is not true that if you drink a lot of beer, you'll have lots of milk. Alcohol in moderation may be o.k.; but taken in excess or chronically, it is potentially harmful to the baby.—*Leo Bell, M.D.*

As far as I am concerned, most drugs pass through mother's milk, and I advocate that mothers take very few drugs while nursing —*Norman Kendall, M.D.*

Two common drugs have no adverse effect on the baby but will affect your milk supply. Birth control pills, even the newer low dosage types, can dramatically decrease and even dry up your milk supply. We do not recommend that you plan to use birth control pills while nursing. Antihistamines also *may* lower your milk production. They dry the sinuses in the body, and milk sacs are sinuses. However, not all women are affected by antihistamines. If you do use them, watch your milk supply carefully.—*Nursing Mothers Counsel, Inc.*

Drinking beer does not increase the milk supply, but it's a pleasant way for a mother who likes beer to ensure an adequate fluid intake. The tranquilizing effect of beer can help a mother to relax at the end of a trying day.—*John C. Richards, M.D.*

It is the brewer's yeast in beer that has given beer a reputation of being beneficial to nursing mothers. Unfortunately, brewer's yeast is no longer used in beer. You can, however, buy it in powdered form at health food stores and drug stores. You can stir it into juice if you care to try it. It does appear to increase some women's milk supply. —*Nursing Mothers Counsel, Inc.*

Perhaps you believe it is the yeast, but I vote for relaxation.

Does menstruation affect mother's milk?

Maybe a little, but rarely enough to interfere with nursing. An occasional mother will report that her baby did not nurse as well, or seemed uncomfortable during the first day or two of her menstrual period. I don't know whether this is due to a change in the amount of milk, in the character of the milk, or in the mother's feeling of well being. Menstrual periods are usally infrequent or absent while nursing; and when they do occur, no change in the milk or the baby's behavior can be seen.—*John C. Richards, M.D.*

Must a nursing mother stop breastfeeding when she has an infection?

Not necessarily. Of course, if she is seriously ill, breastfeeding may be out of the question. Most infections, such as the common cold and mild flu-like illnesses, as well as bladder infections, are of relatively short duration and will only temporarily slow down the milk supply. Although an occasional supplemental bottle, using formula, may be needed for a few days, nursing may continue without fear of passing the infection to the infant through the milk. When she has a fever, a mother must increase her intake of fluids in order to make up for what is lost through perspiring and by an increased rate of breathing. Early treatment is essential if a breast infection develops. This is sometimes an indication to discontinue nursing.

Both viral and bacterial infections are easily passed to the baby through direct skin contact as well as by the air-borne route. For this reason, whether nursing at breast or bottle feeding her baby, an ill mother must take extra precautions in order to avoid the transmission of her germs to her baby. Wash hands thoroughly before handling the child: don't breathe toward the baby; and never kiss on the baby's face or hands. Face masks help only for about five minutes, and then the droplets and their germs are blown right through the mask.—*John C. Richards, M.D.*

What methods of contraception are safe for the nursing mother?

Nursing may reduce your chances of becoming pregnant, but don't assume that because you are nursing, you don't need other means of birth control.

The birth control pill is definitely not recommended for the nursing mother, as it usually decreases or totally dries up the milk supply. Intrauterine devices are 97% effective. Most doctors will insert an I.U.D. six weeks after delivery, but some won't insert one in a nursing mother because they feel that during nursing the uterus is small and more apt to be damaged by an I.U.D. Vaginal foam and condoms used *together* are an effective means of birth control, but foam alone is not a guarantee against pregnancy. The rhythm method is not applicable, because nursing mothers either don't menstruate or have irregular periods until the baby is weaned. It is even possible to get pregnant before your first period starts after the delivery.

Will nursing affect the mother's sex life?

After a normal delivery, many doctors recommend waiting six weeks before resuming intercourse in order to allow episiotomies and stretching to heal. The first experience of intercourse after childbirth may be rather painful. A warm sitz bath will help relieve the pain. The estrogen drop that accompanies breast feeding may result in dry vaginal walls and therefore in painful intercourse in some nursing mothers. This can be alleviated by use of a non-prescription K-Y jelly, or your doctor may prescribe an estrogen cream.

Other causes of painful intercourse are directly related to the birth process: inadequate healing of episiotomies, or trauma to the vaginal walls from the delivery itself. The vagina may be particularly susceptible to infections during the early post-partum period, and these infections can make intercourse painful, if not impossible.

Most couples are under stress as they enlarge their roles from wife/husband to those of wife–mother/husband–father. The stress of learning new roles and of being responsible for a new baby may be reflected in the couple's enjoyment of or displeasure with intercourse. Fatigue, particularly on the part of the mother, is a notorious cause of sexual problems after delivery. One way to cope with fatigue: Mother can go to bed early and get a few hours sleep before her husband comes to bed, she may then feel more relaxed about the idea of having intercourse at that time.—*The Nursing Mothers Counsel, Inc.*

Painful intercourse that accompanies breastfeeding is not described in the medical literature. It does occur, however, in some women, and may last a few months. The degree of dryness of the vaginal walls is usually mild and gradually it corrects itself. If there is severe pain on intercourse, it may represent an infection and should be checked by a doctor.

Supplements, Solids and Weaning

Hard line breastfeeding advocates argue against giving the baby a supplemental bottle of formula. They also are against the early introduction of solids and early weaning. Are they right or can a nursing mother give her baby an occasional bottle of formula?

Many nursing mothers will find that their milk supply decreases late in the day. Toward evening, the baby isn't satisfied with his feeding; or he awakens hungry one or two hours after nursing. What does one do? Here are two views, one presented by Betty Ann Countryman, R.N., M.N., a nursing mother and La Leche League expert, the other by Dr. John C. Richards, an experienced pediatrician with a good record in helping mothers to nurse successfully. This exchange brings into focus the differences in general approach to breastfeeding between La Leche League and most pediatricians. Perhaps we can learn from both.

At this point, the mother may be tempted to offer a bottle of formula. It is far better if she will attempt to get a litle more rest, slow down on home and outside activities, and take a late afternoon nap. Generally, increased rest and more frequent nursing of the baby in late afternoon and evening, for a few days, will increase the mother's milk supply and the apparent need for a formula supplement will disappear. Some mothers assume they have to leave a formula for the breastfed baby when they plan to go out. If you can't take the baby along, collect some of your milk with a breast pump and put it in a sterile bottle in your refrigerator so that your sitter can give it later. You may even freeze it for later use. If you really wish to nurse your baby, the use of a bottle is best kept to an absolute minimum; even better, it is best not used at all except in an emergency.

A final consideration may be that the baby is not really hungry for food. He may, however, be "hungry" for social stimulation. Play with him and see how he enjoys it!—*Betty Ann Countryman, R.N., M.N.*

Formula may be given as a "relief" bottle, without nursing. When a bottle is given at the 5–6 p.m. feeding time, it allows mother to relax or to prepare dinner for the family while father feeds the baby. At the next feeding, usually before bedtime, the breasts will have a large quantity of milk—which will satisfy the baby and, hopefully, will lead to a longer nighttime sleep. Mother will also sleep more comfortably if her breasts are relieved. If formula is regularly offered immediately after nursing, the baby often begins to reject the breast as soon as the mother's milk slows down its rate of flow. Before long, the lessened sucking results in a lessening in the mother's production of milk. For this reason, formula should seldom be offered after nursing, but it may be given once a day, routinely, as a complete feeding.

A baby who never receives a bottle during the first three or four weeks will often then reject it completely. Thus, it is a good practice to offer an occasional bottle during the first month in order to teach the baby how to suck from a rubber nipple. If her milk supply is adequate, a mother may prefer to pump her breast and put the milk in a bottle to feed the baby.

More time can be devoted to a baby if there are no other children in the home whose needs and demands interfere. Every nursing mother just can't feed her baby every two or three hours and regularly give between meal snacks, at breast, when the baby fusses. That is, she can't do it without neglecting other responsibilities.

In fairness to those who object to a daily bottle feeding, I must agree that this does occasionally lead to an earlier discontinuance of breastfeeding than might otherwise have occurred. But isn't this as it should be, if it suits the needs of the baby and his parents?—*John C. Richards, M.D.*

A simpler way to handle the problem of low milk supply in the later part of the day and to avoid the bother of making a formula (as well as the inevitable decrease in milk supply) is for the mother to prepare dinner earlier in the day, so that little need be done at the last minute. Then, in the late afternoon or early evening, you can sit down and relax, drink some fluids, visit with Dad and nurse the baby. After a few days or so, you'll find that your late day milk supply will increase to meet your baby's need.—*Betty Ann Countryman, R.N., M.N.*

An Evening Out
We all need to leave our baby at home some time or another. When you need to have a babysitter feed your baby, you have several choices. If you have been expressing milk into boiled jars and freezing it, you can let it thaw at room temperature for your babysitter to give to the baby. Some breastfed babies will refuse bottles. If you know this to be the case with your baby, then use an eye-dropper (plastic) to feed the baby. You may also wish to experiment with different shapes of bottle nipples.

If you haven't frozen any breast milk, then a powdered formula is probably the best buy and the most convenient method for occasional bottles. Liquid formula must be thrown away after twenty-four hours, and chances are that you will not use a whole container of liquid formula in one day. The powder is always ready to be added to warm or cool tap water or boiled water, and you can make as little as two ounces.

If you are gone more than three hours, you will begin to feel some discomfort shortly after the time that the baby would have emptied your breasts. If possible, you can express milk and discard it. Take along extra nursing pads to keep your bra dry. If a let-down should spontaneously occur, simply apply firm pressure, with the palm of your hand or with the crook of your elbow (as you inconspicuously scratch your shoulder) directly to the nipple and areola.—*Nursing Mothers Counsel, Inc.*

I believe it is essential for most mothers to have an occasional evening out away from the baby. And no matter how good a producer of milk a mother is, she may not always have enough. If there is no family history of milk allergy, most babies tolerate regular formula. If there is a history of suspicion of milk allergy, frozen breast milk or a soy formula may be safely used. Regardless of the advice of the experts, the decision, mother, remains yours.

When Do You Start Solid Foods?

You will get a lot of different answers to this question. Betty Ann Countryman says: I have seen nursing come to a halt because of early introduction of solids—and quite soon. I believe that early solids tend to confuse the normal physiology and psychology of breast feeding." On the other hand, pediatrician A.S. Hashim tells his mothers: "When the baby acts hungry and is not satisfied on milk alone, start cereal. Many so-called colicky babies are just hungry. But some babies will take milk and refuse solids, while others will take solids well and refuse milk in spite of heroic efforts by the pediatrician or the mother. Some babies are just geared differently."

Personally, I see no valid reason to start solid foods before a month with a normal baby, and I don't argue very strongly for starting then. It is doubtful that an infant's digestive system is able to digest or absorb much cereal in the first weeks of life. Some mothers give solids early in the hope of getting the baby to sleep through the night. But whether they are fed beef steak or cereal, most infants don't store enough to go through the night until around six weeks of age. Other mothers, in an effort to show good mothering, take pride in being the first on the block to start solids or to try new foods on the baby. But there really is no hurry. And when you do start solids, introduce only one new food at a time, and give the baby a week or two on that food before you try another. Restrain yourself from buying everything on the babyfood shelf. Baby is not yet ready to be a gourmet.

For most babies, solid foods aren't absolutely required until about six months. As Dr. Gerrard has noted, giving foods too early may increase the infant's chances of an intestinal infection. Giving foods too early also seems to be associated with the development of allergies later in life for some children. This is especially true of such highly allergenic foods as eggs and citrus juices.

I advise most mothers with bottle fed babies to start experimenting with solid foods around a month of life and for breastfed babies, around three months. I have never seen well-established and *desired* breastfeeding stop because of starting solids at this time. Further, it conditions the baby to take the spoon and to start building up needed iron supplies. In practices where solids are started early, we see good overall nutrition and healthy babies. On the other hand, babies fed only by breast till six months seem to do just as well.

Weaning

Associate Editor Dr. John C. Richards feels that a mother should nurse her baby until she's ready to quit.

> When the advantages of nursing no longer seem important, and when nursing interferes with other more pressing needs of a mother, she is usually ready to start the weaning process.
>
> Some mothers will switch to the bottle after three or four months. At that age, the baby often accepts solids quite willingly, and sleeps longer at night. His mother finds that his decreasing interest in nursing causes her breasts either to become painfully engorged or gradually to cease producing much milk.
>
> Those who continue nursing regularly past six or seven months can usually teach their babies to drink cow's milk from a cup. By nine or ten months the baby can go from the breast to the cup without ever needing bottles.
>
> Some mothers and babies enjoy nursing once or twice a day until twelve to fifteen months. If that is what suits her best, and if her baby's efforts to grab a snack in public causes no concern, more power to her.

Nurse Countryman concurs with Dr. Richards:

> There is no "best" age to discontinue breastfeeding. When both mother and baby are ready to stop is time enough. Let your baby be your guide and accept happily his need for you—or his indication that he is ready for you to help him take a step toward independence.

Don't force him off the breast. Guide and encourage your little one toward independence as he shows his readiness; but remember that the mother who "manages" her baby's life activities as if he is a pet to be trained or a toy to be played with will have to face the negative results in later life.

Many nursing mothers continue past the age of two and occasionally let a toddler continue to breastfeed after the birth of a younger sibling. I believe nursing should cease between nine months and a year, at the time when the child is developing some independence. As Dr. Merritt Low says: "Some children need a bit of nudging into the next developmental stage, and some parents, unwittingly, put a brake on the development of their child, perhaps for their own psychological needs. Don't try to keep your baby a baby; let him grow up. That's the fun of it all!"

Can You Switch to a Bottle Without Taking Pills?

If a mother wants to switch to a bottle in a short period of time, she can do so without getting pills from her obstetrician to dry her breasts:

First: Reduce the intake of liquids.
Second: Nurse the baby just enough to relieve any engorgement that causes discomfort. Finish the feeding with a bottle or cup, using formula or cow's milk.
Third: Don't nurse the baby unless the breasts are likely to become engorged before the next feeding time.

Most mothers can discontinue breastfeeding completely within a few days. Some breast milk will continue to be produced for several weeks, but there should be no significant discomfort.

More gradual weaning to a cup can usually be accomplished between six and nine months of age. Offer milk from a cup once or twice a day, at mealtimes, starting at about six months of age. Continue nursing several times a day, but, as the baby learns to drink from a cup more easily, he will want fewer breast feedings. Feedings at the breast will gradually be refused, and within two or three months the baby will usually stop nursing completely with no objections, and with no discomfort to you.

The Father's Role in Breastfeeding

Whenever there is a discussion of the possible use of supplementary bottles, we automatically think of father. Certainly it is helpful for father to give a bottle in the middle of the night, thus allowing mother to catch up on some very much needed sleep. But father is more than an occasional substitute says the Nursing Mothers Counsel, Inc.:

The father might be the only adult that the new mother will see regularly. She will turn to him to fill many of her emotional needs. Many of these needs will be new ones, both to the mother and to the father. At times, the new mother will need to just drop out, to forget the parent role. She may feel depressed and frustrated. She will need "mothering" herself. In the old days, a house was full of aunts, grandmothers, and mothers who could "mother" the new mother and guide her along. Today, in our isolated families, the father is left, by default, with the role of "mothering" the new mother. The father is very important, not so much as a father at first, but as a husband. His continual support, understanding, and protection of his wife from unnecessary stresses—deciding what to have for dinner on the first night home from the hospital; nosy neighbors asking, "What is she bothering with breastfeeding for?"—all are very, very important. He, too, of course is adjusting to being a father; but it is the continuation of the couple relationship that is important. A new mother needs to feel that her husband still accepts her, even though she may have a slightly baggy stomach for a few weeks, even though she forgot to do the laundry, even though she feels depressed. A new father must be extra aware of his wife's emotional needs, and accept the quick changes in his wife's moods. It is very difficult for many new mothers to fill their husband's emotional needs at first; but gradually, as the new mother becomes more confident in herself as a mother, she can return to her normal role as a wife.

Fathers can also help in the more traditional ways by helping to prepare dinner, changing diapers, burping the baby, and playing with him.

Bottle Feeding

Breastfeeding advocate Canadian professor John Gerrard has this to say about formula feeding:

Formula feeding is safe, easy, and satisfying; and the majority of babies will tolerate the majority of formulas. What formula should *you* use? Ask your doctor. In general the best formula for your baby is the one which provides the needed calories, fluid, vitamins, and minerals, and which, at the same time, suits and agrees with baby. This formula will probably be derived from cow's milk; but if the latter does not agree with your baby, it may be derived from soya, or even from goat's milk. Your doctor will tell you that we all mean sterilized formula, not just milk. There are many reasons why straight milk should not be used for infants: The first and most important is that unsterilized milk has the potential of making your baby quite ill. Until partial sterilization was developed around the turn of this century, babies who were not breastfed often perished from infections due to bacteria growing in the milk. Even pasteurized milk can cause trouble for some little babies, loading their intestines with unfriendly (if not terribly bad) germs.

Facts about Cow's Milk are Detailed

Raw or unpasteurized milk is highly dangerous and may infect the user with tuberculosis, brucellosis, diphtheria, streptococcus, and other diseases. Careful measurements show that it contains no more vitamins or nutrients than pasteurized milk.

Pasteurized whole milk and whole homogenized milk contain unaltered cream and protein and a higher load of salts than human milk.

Pasteurized low fat milk has most of the cream removed.

Pasteurized skimmed milk has all the cream removed.

Pasteurized dry powdered skimmed (or low fat) milk. The dehydrating process alters the milk protein, possibly reducing the risk of allergy.

What it all boils down to is that modern formulas have been carefully developed over the years to assure the greatest safety and best nutrition possible.

Why Use Formula?

Cow's milk is not bad for calves, but it can be damaging for some babies. Excessive cow's milk results in an imbalanced diet and iron deficiency because not enough iron-containing solid foods are taken. Dr. Gerrard has this to say about the controversy:

When it first became fashionable to bottlefeed, rather than to breastfeed babies, many babies were brought up on whole boiled cow's milk. The majority thrived, but some did not. Among the latter were babies who had extensive eczema and troublesome diarrhea. We now know that breast milk contains factors that prevent the growth of harmful bacteria in the bowel. Breast milk is so effective in this respect that it has been found to halt troublesome outbreaks of gastroenteritis in babies.

The factor in breast milk that indirectly interferes with the growth of harmful organisms is called lactose. It leads to acid stools, a process that slows the growth of harmful germs. Once a baby has been given cow's milk, which contains less lactose than breast milk, the harmful germs can thrive. If these germs cause diarrhea, they may damage the lining of the small bowel which produces the enzymes that digest lactose. If lactose cannot be digested, the lactose itself may cause diarrhea. This means that cow's milk may cause diarrhea. A similar problem also occurs in adults, more commonly in blacks, who, until a few generations ago, never drank milk once they had been weaned. They may find that if they drink cow's milk they may be troubled by wind, abdominal discomfort, and diarrhea.

It has been shown that in some babies, homogenized cow's milk will cause an undetectable blood loss into the bowel, with resulting anemia. In one research project, infants were randomly selected and one half were fed homogenized cow's milk while the others received a standard commercial formula. At a year of age, those infants on cow's milk had significantly lower average hemoglobin than those fed formula. It is thought that unmodified cow's milk may damage the intestinal lining in a way that will lead to iron loss. There was less iron lost with evaporated milk than with fresh milk, and no loss with soy bean formulas. Furthermore, forty-five percent of those infants on fresh milk had developed antibodies, possibly indicating a hidden or low grade allergy to milk at one year of age, while only eight percent of the infants on formula had cow's milk antibody. However, Dr. Gerrard cautions that, the fact that forty percent of all infants have antibodies to cow's milk in their blood does not necessarily mean that they are allergic to milk.

In commercial formulas, milk fat is replaced with vegetable oils; and the protein has been changed to resemble mothers' milk. These do not seem to cause as much iron loss or milk allergy as does unmodified milk. Other studies suggest that infants on whole cow's milk may have cholesterol deposits in the arteries of the heart as early as a year of age. It could be that the high rate of heart attacks in American adults was instituted by the swing from human breast milk to cow's milk formulas forty to fifty years ago. All of these facts and speculations add up to some good reasons to keep cow's milk for calves. If you feed the baby cow's milk, use a commercial formula with less tendency to cause anemia, milk allergy, and later heart attacks. Some physicians advocate formula until the age of two years. I believe that formula should be continued for at least a year. Then switch to low fat milk (powdered will do well) and start extra vitamins. If you use skimmed or low fat milk, make certain that the baby gets an adequate supply of meat to furnish needed fatty acids.

It should be pointed out that these negative factors about whole milk do not apply to everybody. Evidently the Nordic races are genetically able to tolerate cow's milk better than many other ethnic-genetic groups such as blacks and Mexicans. In America, where the population is so mixed, who knows what is "best"?

Regardless of the negative factors about cow's milk, pediatrician Thomas J. Conway comments: "Cow's milk will continue to be part of the diet of the American child. It is an excellent source of protein and calcium. You can offer undiluted, pasteurized, unsterilized cow's milk by cup when the baby accepts the cup. The cow's milk problem tends to be quantitive; large amounts are more likely to cause disturbances. The amount offered by cup with meals is not damaging to most children." So, for most babies, unmodified pasteurized cow's milk is acceptable when they have a good intake of solids and are getting close to a year in age. Formulas, however, are generally recommended by pediatricians

Formulas

There are three basic types of formulas:

1. Modified commercial cow's milk formulas which contain all the scientifically proven requirements for protein, fats, carbohydrates, water, and vitamins. Some have added iron. Your doctor will tell you whether your baby may need a formula with added iron. Extra vitamins are not necessary: Required vitamins are contained in commercial formulas. These formulas are designed to resemble human milk as closely as possible, so the major brands are almost all alike. Yet a minor difference in formulas, even between the concentrated liquid and dry powdered varieties of the same formula, may make a difference to some babies. Overall, these are quite satisfactory.
2. Commercial soy bean formulas are also well-balanced preparations containing all of the known required nutrients except iron. Extra vitamins are unncessary. Soy formulas are usually used when an infant will not tolerate modified cow's milk formulas.
3. Canned milk, sugar, and water formulas are more economical than the others. However, extra vitamins must be added, thus increasing the cost. This milk is less modified than that in commercial formulas, so some babies do not tolerate it as well. Yet others tolerate it better.

These formulas are put up in a variety of ways, starting with the most easily used pre-mixed, ready-to-feed type. Ready-to-feed formulas should have twenty calories per ounce of formula, and must not be confused with the concentrated formulas which require dilution with water. Ready-to-feed formulas may be available in disposable bottles or in economy sized thirty-two ounce cans. For the cans, only a bottle and nipples are needed. The required quantity of formula is poured into the bottle, the sterile nipple is applied, and you are ready to feed your infant. Be sure to discard the contents of unfinished formula and rinse any bottle you wish to save with cool water. Cover the bottle with its plastic cap and refrigerate until the next feeding. Ready-to-feed formulas are not economical. You pay for the weight of all that water they have to ship around the country when a formula isn't concentrated. But it is cheaper than a maid and is often a real boon to mother and father. For traveling, ready-to-feed formula can't be beat. Most babies will take formula at either room or refrigerator temperature, although some small infants and a few larger ones do better with warm formula.

Prepared concentrated formula is the most commonly used variety. It is cheaper than the prediluted ready-to-use variety and usually has to be diluted with at least equal parts of water. Powdered concentrated formulas are economical when used to supplement breastfeedings because you don't have to discard as much milk as you do with the concentrate. As a routine method of feeding, concentrated formulas are expensive. Powdered formula weighs less and takes up less space when traveling; and if you can add boiled water, it is safe almost wherever you are.

Family practitioner Bruce Valentine prefers evaporated milk to commercial formulas: "A case of evaporated milk is cheap; and most young mothers have only one working member of the family for income, and are just starting out with big expenses and/or mortgage payments and need to watch their pennies. The current fad of readily prepared foods, including baby formulas, is fine; but the total cost exceeds the convenience achieved when you are on a tight budget."

Preparing Formula: Bottles and Nipples

The method used to prepare an infant's formula depends upon the type of formula recommended by your doctor. You will need the following equipment:

Bottle and nipple brushes
Bottles (wide-mouthed), preferably eight
Can opener
Graduated pitcher (marked in ounces)
Mixing bowl
Mixing spoon or egg beater
Nipples, preferably eight, and caps
Tablespoon
Tongs (for handling bottles)

Sterilizing

There are two basic methods of sterilizing formula. In the terminal heating method, everything is mixed and put into glass bottles, which are loosely capped and are then kept in boiling water for twenty minutes. This is the safest, and, in the opinion of most parents who use the technique, the easiest. The aseptic method requires presterilized or disposable bottles, nipples, and water and careful mixing in order to avoid contamination. Neonatologist Dr. Norman Kendall offers careful instructions to cover the various methods used to sterilize different types of formulas.

Terminal Heating Method

Pre-sterilization of utensils and bottles is not necessary and there is little opportunity for contamination.

Mixing:

Concentrated liquid formula. This formula contains forty calories per ounce and requires dilution. Mix equal quantities (one can of formula and one can of water) in a bowl. Do not prepare the formula with less than equal parts of water or your baby may become dehydrated.

Prepared powdered formula. Put the required amount of water into the bottle. Add one scoopful or one level tablespoon of the powder to each two ounces of water. Cap and shake well until mixed. Do not strengthen the formula by using less water or your baby may become dehydrated.

Evaporated milk. Combine the required amounts of canned milk and water (at least an equal amount) into a mixing bowl and add the required amount of sugar.

(There are many different sugars that can be used in varying amounts, depending on the individual infant. Check with your physician for the type and amount.)

Whole milk. Combine the required amount of milk and water in a mixing bowl; add the prescribed sugar. Mix by stirring.

Sterilizing:
Pour the prescribed ounces of formula, mixed as described above, into the previously cleaned bottles, and place the nipples and caps loosely on the bottles. Place the bottles on a wire rack or towel in the sterilizer or in a deep pot. Add water until it covers about half of the bottles. Cover the pan and boil for twenty-five minutes. If an automatic sterilizer is used, follow the manufacturer's directions. Allow to cool slowly, remove the bottles with the tongs, tighten the caps when cool, and refrigerate until ready to use. With this procedure, formula can be kept for forty-eight hours in the refrigerator.

Following a feeding, the bottle and nipple should be thoroughly rinsed with cool water and washed with a detergent in order to avoid clogging of the nipples and coating of the bottles.

[On heating the formula, Bruce Valentine, M.D. disagrees with the above, saying: "When using the terminal heating method, try *not* to make caramel of the sugar by exceeding the heat necessary to pasteurize milk. I suggest only three to five minutes of heating in a sterilizer after being brought to a boil. Try the taste of twenty-five minute boiled formula yourself sometime. Pasteurization occurs at 154–155 degrees F° for only a few seconds." Although formulas can be overcooked, it rarely seems to happen. I would use a *low* boil for 25 minutes.]

Aseptic Method
This method is not universally recommended because the formula may be contaminated by improper techniques. However, it is the only method that can be used for the disposable plastic bag nursers.

Place the bottles and the utensils used to prepare the formula in a large pot or sterilizer. Add a small amount of water, usually enough to cover about the bottom three inches of the bottles, and boil for five to ten minutes.

For concentrated prepared formulas. Empty a thirteen-ounce can into a pan containing thirteen ounces of previously boiled water which has cooled to room temperature.

For evaporated milk. Wash the top of the can with soap and water and dry, shake can well, punch two holes in the top, and add the required quantity to the previously boiled water (cooled to room temperature). Then add the prescribed amount of sugar and mix well by stirring.

For whole milk. Wash the bottle top with hot water. Turn the bottle several times so that the contents are mixed. Place the required amount of water in a pan, bring to a boil, add the required amount of whole milk, and boil for five minutes, stirring constantly. When the mixture is lukewarm or cool, add the sugar. Pour the amount of freshly prepared formula the baby will take into the sterilized nursing bottles. Put the nipples and caps on with tongs in order to avoid touching them with the hands, and store the bottles in the refrigerator until feeding time. These formulas can be used for up to twenty-four hours if they are properly refrigerated.

Single Bottle Method

Preparing a single bottle of formula at a time is recommended when a breastfed baby needs a supplemental bottle or when you are away from home with a bottlefed baby. You may also consider employing this method for the baby who is completely formula fed. It has advantages (providing the infant is fed immediately following the preparation of the bottle, the remains are discarded, and the bottle is rinsed with cold water). You avoid overcrowding the refrigerator with bottles of formula; you can use unboiled hot water straight from spigot or tap, *providing the water supply is known to be clean and free of contamination;* and you may not need to sterilize bottles. providing they are cleansed with a brush immediately after a feeding and washed in a household dishwasher. The nipples and caps should be sterilized as previously described above.

Prepared Concentrated Liquid Formula. Wash the top of the can with soap and water, and dry. Punch two holes in the top. Pour the desired amount of concentrate into the bottle and add equal parts of hot tap water. After feeding the infant, discard the remainder of the formula. Rinse the bottle and nipple in cold water, and later wash thoroughly. Keep the formula can in the refrigerator.

Powdered Prepared Formula. Use one level tablespoon or scoopful of the formula for each two ounces of water. Add the required amount of the powdered formula to a bottle containing the water, cap with the nipple, and shake until mixed. Check the instructions on the can. If the baby requires eight ounces of formula, add four tablespoons or scoops of the powder to eight ounces of water.

Standard Powdered Milk. Follow the directions on the package or can for proper dilution.

Selecting Bottles and Nipples

Ninety percent of babies can tolerate ninety percent of all bottles and nipples. I usually recommend glass bottles; but disposable plastic bag types seem to work as well, although you have to be careful to use aseptic sterilization—and they are more expensive. However, there are babies who have problems with some nipples, partly because of the shape, which may not match their particular mouth. At times, you may have to experiment with various types of nipples. Make certain that the nipple hole is open adequately—the milk should come out with a short squirt and then with a fairly rapid drip. New nipples and small holes can wear a baby out. To open the holes, it is best to use a small red-hot needle (hold with pliers) and burn a larger hole in the nipple rather than simply to poke a cold needle through the nipple.

Dr. John Richards has found that a baby usually adjusts quickly to whatever is used regularly; but a baby who has nursed at the breast for several weeks often does best if given the plastic disposable nurser, which has a nipple more like mother's.

Bottle Feeding Techniques

First, you and the baby must be comfortable and relaxed. If you are sitting in an awkward, uncomfortable position, your muscle tension and frequent shifting of position can interfere with the baby's ability to relax and enjoy the feeding. Dr. Richards feels that most babies do best when held in a semi-sitting position. This allows the milk to fall by gravity into the lower part of the stomach. The swallowed air rises up to the opening of the esophagus where it can easily be "burped." The baby's head should be extended slightly back so that the chin is at a right angle to the chest. (Try swallowing a drink of water with your neck bent forward, and you'll understand the need for this position.)

The tip of the nipple should go over the tongue into the back of the mouth as far as the baby can take it. Don't push the nipple into the throat, just let the baby pull it in, and there will be no gagging and choking. Other doctors feel you should hold the baby any way that works well for you and for the baby. This may vary with the shape of the baby's mouth and the mother's breast or the type of nipple on the bottle. You shouldn't hesitate to experiment.

Dr. Polley believes that the popular way to hold the newborn during bottle feeding is incorrect: Figures 19 and 20. According to Polley:

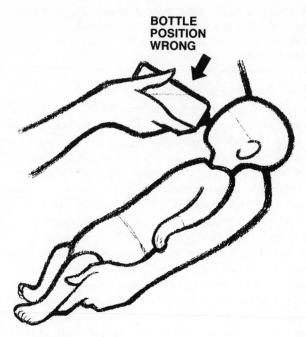

Figure 19 *Dr. Polley believes that holding the baby face up, head and neck cradled in the bend of the elbow, is wrong.*

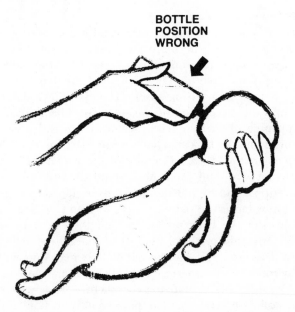

Figure 20 *Wrong position. Held semi-upright, neck flexed forward.*

The custom of cradling the infant in the adult's arms, face up, with the bottle pointed straight down into the infant's mouth, has unfortunately become common, probably for two reasons:

1. Photographers preparing illustrations of bottle feedings like to have the face of both the mother and infant show in the pictures. This necessitates the positions in Figures 19 and 20. These pictures then find their way into books and pamphlets for instruction in the care of the newborn.
2. There is a popular belief that a bottle fed infant should be held close and cuddled at feeding time.

Neither reason is valid. The face-up position, with the infant's head tilted forward, places its chin down on its chest, preventing freedom of motion in case of choking. Also, the infant's head and neck are stuck, so to speak, in the bend of the parent's elbow, making it all the more difficult for the infant to shake loose from the nipple if too much milk floods the back of his mouth. Choking and gagging are very common and also very risky when this face-up bottle feeding position is used. Excess milk tends to puddle in the back of the infant's throat and can easily "go down the wrong way."

The need to provide "security" by squeezing and cuddling the infant at feeding time is also a misconception. Infants do need lots of holding, loving, and visiting. However, they do not really need them at feeding time. As a matter of fact, perhaps the worst time to choose for cuddling, patting, stroking, and squeezing an infant is when he is trying to take his bottle. Many newborn infants are very easily distracted while nursing, and eat very poorly if other things are going on.

Breastfeeding mothers learn to "back away" from the baby and not disturb him, so that he can concentrate on nursing without the distractions of head pattings, squeezing, and tender loving care when he is trying to concentrate on nursing. A safer and more efficient way to give the infant his bottle is to hold him on one's lap, head toward the knees, his shoulders and head turned to the side. The bottle should be horizontal, tilted a little downhill (Figures 21 and 22).

Feeding problem infants who are temperamental and easily distracted goes much better if they are lying on their side on a table or in a crib with the bottle propped or held in this horizontal position. Understandably, the adult must closely supervise the infant during every minute of the feeding period, whether the bottle is propped or held.

Freely flowing nipples, such as the Playtex nipple, permit an infant to receive the formula easily; and the horizontal bottle position allows him to stop and rest without having the milk flow over the back of his tongue and choke him. If he pulls too hard and gets more in his mouth than he can handle, the excess milk runs out of the corner of his mouth when his head and body are turned to the side.[6]

Whether you hold your baby during feedings as is recommended by most, or whether you follow Dr. Polley's advice and prop the baby—hold the baby and play with him a lot anyway, and anytime, you can. If you learn to "listen" to your baby, he may tell you whether he prefers being held or being propped. Try both and see which works best. Your expert on this is your baby—not one of us!

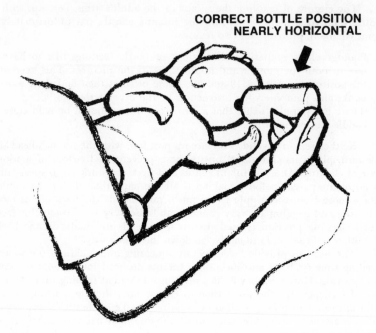

**CORRECT BOTTLE POSITION
NEARLY HORIZONTAL**

Figure 21   *A good position. Lying on side on parent's lap.*

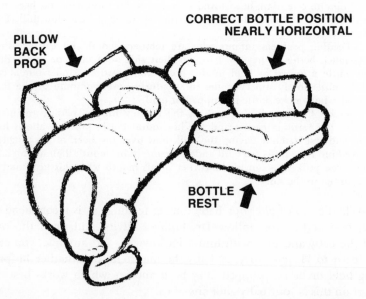

**PILLOW
BACK
PROP**

**CORRECT BOTTLE POSITION
NEARLY HORIZONTAL**

**BOTTLE
REST**

Figure 22   *A "good" position. Taking bottle lying on side.*

Questions and Answers on Bottle Feeding

What can be done if the baby wakens and seems hungry between feedings?

A little baby, when awake, will suck on anything he can get into his mouth, whether hungry or not. If the previous feeding was taken well and seemed to satisfy him completely, it's best to try other things to comfort him. Often a baby stops crying and goes back to sleep when picked up and cuddled. Some infants will relax and will soon become sleepy again if given a pacifier. Occasionally, a small bottle of water is all that is needed.—*J.C. Richards, M.D.*

We should avoid the notion that all infants should be quiet at all times.—*Thomas J. Conway, M.D.*

How do you burp a baby, and what is a belch?

Burping and belching, especially when done early in the feeding, help avoid colic. There are two processes: first, burping the baby by sitting him up and patting him on the back; and second, belching, when the baby passes the air from the stomach to the outside. A belch is not necessary every time the mother burps the baby.

Sit the baby erect or hold him over one shoulder and pat him on the back to burp him. Rubbing the baby's back or patting the bottom does nothing. Rather forceful pats on the back are needed to jar the air loose so it will rise to the top of the liquid in the stomach. Eight to twelve pats is all that can be done in one attempt at "burping." Pounding the baby endlessly achieves nothing except to aggravate the baby and waste the parent's time.

A baby's stomach empties most quickly in the early part of any feeding, and least quickly of all at the end of the feeding. Therefore, burping should be done mostly in the beginning of the feeding, when the stomach is emptying quickly, a little bit in the middle when the stomach is emptying less rapidly, and least of all at the end, when the stomach is probably not emptying at all.—*Marvin McClellan, M.D.*

During the first few weeks, I prefer holding the baby on the lap, not over the shoulder. Put the baby in a kneeling position, face forward across the knee, with one hand holding the chin so the head extends slightly. Don't spend more than a minute or two trying to get the air up. Put him back on the bottle or to breast before he falls asleep or starts crying much. After a month or two, the shoulder position for burps is usually satisfactory.—*John C. Richards, M.D.*

Do babies on the breast or the collapsible containers have to be burped?

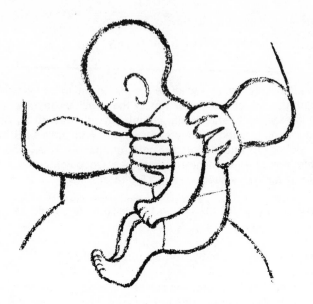

Figure 23   *Seated for burping—a good position.*

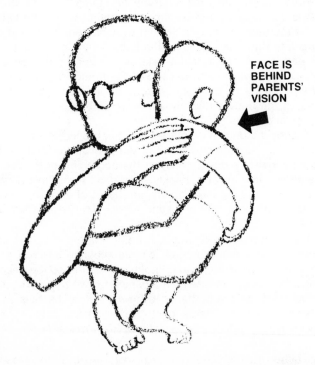

FACE IS
BEHIND
PARENTS'
VISION

Figure 24   *Over the shoulder burping—less desirable.*

No other animal burps its babies, why should we? I think burping, like circumcision, is a custom and not a necessity.—*John Gerrard, D.M., F.R.C.P.* [Look, mother, you do it your way!]

How can a new baby be kept awake during feedings?

1. Be sure he is wide awake and ready to eat before starting the feeding. Until two or three weeks of age, it often takes ten to fifteen minutes after the baby first comes awake before he is ready to eat. Later on, he'll waken and be ready immediately.
2. Don't wrap him in a snug blanket while feeding. Let him move his arms and kick his legs freely.
3. If falling asleep is a problem during the first week or two, don't cuddle him too closely or comfortably, or rock him in your arms while he's eating.
4. When his sucking slows down, slowly move the nipple back and forth in his mouth to stimulate his sucking reflex.
5. Holding the baby against the shoulder when burping and spending too much time trying to get up the burp will sometimes put a baby to sleep. Try the lap method, and put him back on the nipple after two or three minutes, even if he hasn't burped.—*John C. Richards, M.D.*

If the baby is on a demand schedule, he usually is hungry and you don't have to bother with all these things.—*Leo Bell, M.D.*

When all else fails, snapping the soles of the feet has a remarkable effect for a few minutes. It really does help.—*Alicia Herman, Reviewing Mother*

How long should sterilization continue?

When the baby is three months old and his immune system is working well, I believe you can stop sterilizing as long as all the family members are healthy. An easy way to prepare the formula then is:

1. Wash the bottles and nipples, dry them, and store them with the dishes.
2. Punch two holes in the formula can and keep it in the refrigerator.
3. When you want to feed the baby, pour the formula in the bottle and add an equal amount of hot tap water. It will be just right to feed immediately.—*Glenn Austin, M.D.*

How often should a new baby be fed?

In general, feed your baby whenever he is hungry, usually between two to six hours. It doesn't really matter whether or not you decide to feed on schedule or demand—you end up compromising either way. Most babies eat around every three hours during the first two weeks, and once or twice a night for the first six weeks.—*Glenn Austin, M.D.*

It is a good general rule to feed your baby when he's hungry and let him sleep when he wants to. If you must have a schedule, don't try to be strict about it, because there is no synchronizing mechanism inside the baby's stomach.—*Leo Bell, M.D.*

How much should a baby be fed?

A good rule of thumb in the newborn period is that the baby will go "about an hour an ounce." If he eats one or two ounces he'll go about one or two hours. If he takes four or more ounces, he'll go about four hours. If, after a good feeding, he wakes in an hour or two, it's likely he'll be fussy. A little "burping," placing him on his abdomen over a warm (not too hot) water bottle, or a little sugar water in a bottle is usually sufficient to quiet him.—*Leo Bell, M.D.*

These rules are oversimplified, as newborns vary so in size. "Rules" may be fine if your baby is an average baby. Unfortunately babies can't read and don't always follow all such advice. I would rather let the baby's appetite be the guide for an individual feeding as long as he doesn't take over thirty-two ounces in twenty-four hours. If he wants more than that, put him on solids.—*Glenn Austin, M.D.*

How fast should a baby take the bottle?

In order to be satisfied before he tires, a new baby needs to take his bottle as rapidly as he is able. Milk shouldn't run out of the sides of his mouth, nor should he be made to gag or choke on milk passing too rapidly into the throat.—*John C. Richards, M.D.*

How long should a baby take to finish a feeding?

After one or two weeks of age, a baby who sucks vigorously should usually complete a feeding within a half hour. This includes time for "burps" and for changing the diaper.—*John C. Richards, M.D.*

Can a baby ever be overfed?

Yes. When I hear mothers complain about constant crying, spitting up, or watery bowel movements, I suspect overfeeding. This doesn't seem like a very important question, especially since grandmothers have been telling young mothers for years to feed babies all the milk they want. Mothers get lots of compliments about big, healthy babies, and about roly-poly babies that look so cute! But if it is not healthy for adults to be big and plump, then why is it good for babies?

Think about the size of a baby's stomach when you wonder about the amount of food a baby can take. It isn't very big—imagine a small balloon. In fact, you may want to do a little experiment. Partially fill the balloon from a water tap. Empty it, remove the water, and refill it till you get about three ounces in the balloon. Then hold the balloon over the baby's middle—just below the ribs. Looks big, doesn't it? Now imagine some air in the balloon with the fluid. Doesn't it seem logical that a little stretching by overfilling may cause some discomfort? Baby doesn't know why—so he cries and may be eager to suck some more milk. This overload may or may not cause more fussing. But the fluid that goes in must come out—either up or down—thus, the spitting-up or squirting. But unfortunately, some of the excess doesn't get squirted or spit out; it just adds unnecessary fat.

What is "unnecessary"? Most babies about double their weight by five months, and just about triple their weight by their first birthday. When a baby is gaining so fast that the doubling occurs much before five months, there's a good probability that the baby is getting too much milk.

How much milk does a baby need? Of course, this depends on the size and age of the baby—but keep in mind that there are more overfed than underfed babies in our country today. Twenty-four ounces a day is plenty for the first few months, and twenty-six to thirty ounces is about as much milk as any infant needs. (A new baby may only want an ounce and a half or two ounces per feeding—and that may be just fine.)

And what about a schedule? "Should I wake my baby up every three hours to feed him?" Of course not. How would you like to be awakened to be fed a hamburger at 3:00 a.m.? Let baby work out his own schedule. Relax—and enjoy things.

Most things about caring for baby are fun—and simple. It's a lot simpler than most people think. But this doesn't mean pushing a nipple in baby's mouth every time it opens. Ranchers feed calves for maximum weight gain—every pound is a bonus. The same is not true for babies.—*Glen Griffin, M.D.*

It is best to let the baby decide when he has had enough. His system is unique, and may not go "according to the book." About the only time I have seen babies overeating on their own is at the evening "colic time" during the first three months. Then there are the mothers who stick a bottle in the mouth just to shut a baby up, but I don't see them often. A wakeful baby does the only thing he can for comfort: Get something into his mouth. He will often settle for a fist or pacifier, or for being held, as well as for a bottle or breast. The important "rule" is to limit the amount of milk per day to less than a quart (32 oz.)—*Glenn Austin, M.D.*

SLEEP

Sleep is critical for the baby and for the parents. Generally, you know how much sleep you need, whether you get it or not, but how about the baby? Dr. Neil Henderson says it is rather simple: "As long as the baby is healthy, growing, and developing normally, he is getting enough sleep. The daily amount needed decreases with age. Don't use your own sleep need as a guide. Generally, the amount of sleep needed varies from baby to baby—from ten to twenty hours a day." That sort of variation can be really bothersome to parents who want to know the "proper" amount of time a baby should sleep. But the wide variation is a fact of life. What counts is, as Dr. Henderson said, if your baby is healthy.

What can be done if a baby doesn't sleep? Dr. Charles Hoffman puts it bluntly: "You are just stuck if you have a 'short sleeper,' and it is easiest to accept his pattern of sleep and adjust your schedule to his. The factor controlling a baby's sleep is the baby—who must be tired and want to sleep. The parents have little to say about it except to provide a quiet environment." However, he adds: "Sometimes you can help convert a nightwatchman to a night sleeper. If he gets up every hour at night to be fed and then sleeps twelve hours during the day, keep him awake during the daytime: Play with him, wash him, feed him. If he is tired enough, he will put in his long stretches at night." Perhaps some of this can be prevented, says Dr. John Richards: "An infant who is allowed to nurse in the mother's arms until falling asleep before being put to bed will often wake up and cry to get back to mother. This can be prevented if parents put the baby to bed when he is still awake, right from the start. A short period of crying should be tolerated." The small infant who turns night into day should have direction and discipline in the literal sense of "showing the way" rather than punishment. This involves more attention and care during the day and delayed and lesser feeding and handling at night.

Prevent Sleep Problems

Parents can sometimes prevent sleep problems, says Dr. Merritt Low. To do this it helps to know about the development of sleep:

To start with, each newborn infant has a temperament of his own, and responds in his own way to noise and variations in living patterns. Some babies sleep all the time; others are awake most of the day. These general patterns are due to the temperament of each baby. If the baby seems unable to sleep, try a few simple steps: rocking, comforting, warmth, food, a change of diapers, a quieter or darker room. Don't fuss around too much; it just aggravates everything and everybody. And avoid sleeping pills, drugs, and other aids that, at the best, provide only temporary crutches. Give your baby a chance to sleep. Beyond that you cannot force things.

It is normal for an infant to have short sleep periods, plus one or two long ones of five to six hours or more. The average baby begins to sleep through one night feeding by six to eight weeks of age, and through the whole night by twelve weeks. It is all right to "encourage" this when the time comes by avoiding pampering and undue night attention, and by substituting a quick diaper change and drink of water for the midnight feeding ritual observed in the past.—*Merritt Low, M.D.*

Also be sure your infant has enough room. Small bassinettes bother even a two-week-old infant.—*Robert F. L. Polley, M.D.*

Why won't the three-to-six month old child sleep?

By three to four months the baby sleeps right through the night. For a number of reasons, some infants restart night-time feedings, playing, and yelling:

1. He still may need changes in positioning.
2. He is more aware of the activities of others.
3. His teeth may bother him.
4. Circumcised boys may have some crusting and diaper irritation at the very end of the penis (meatus). A dab of vaseline at bedtime may prevent the discomfort and awakening caused by the discharge of "strong" urine in the night through this tender irritated spot.
5. He may be sick.—*Merritt Low, M.D.*

Why won't the six-to-twelve month old sleep?

Poor sleep habits at this age stem from several causes: no separate room for the baby, increasing awareness of what's going on (or what isn't!), overstimulation during the day, and disturbing nighttime happenings which have not heretofore been bothersome. Children can be "very light sleepers" or "heavy" ones, and need differing approaches by parents.

Nap patterns which have been established are beginning to change. Most babies take two naps a day till ten to fourteen months. Then put the child on a one nap per day schedule: Make it a long one after an early lunch.—*Merritt Low, M.D.*

Avoid too many toys, lights, and gadgets in the room. They provide another excuse for staying awake. Fatigue is the best sedative. A stroller ride in the evening, followed by a late evening bath, is helpful. It also helps to be put to bed with father's firm hand and voice. The infant or child whose *father* puts him to bed is more likely to stay in bed.—*Robert F. L. Polley, M.D.*

Should a new baby sleep in his parents' room?

Leo Bell, M.D. believes that an infant belongs in his own room in his own bed. Bassinets and cradles are usable but not necessary, and result in double expenditure. Many infants who sleep in the parents' bedroom continue to wake at night long past the normal time (2–3 months). They instinctively recognize their parents' presence and wake and cry at night knowing full well they'll get the attention they desire.

An important reason to put the baby in his own room, says Dr. John Richards, is that everyone then rests better. Every baby makes odd noises: breathing irregularly, squeaks, grunts, hiccoughs, sucks, burps, and passing air rectally. When all is quiet in the house, these sounds can keep parents awake if the baby is sleeping in the same room. At first you think: "If he doesn't shut-up, I'll never fall asleep." And then, suddenly all is quiet and you wonder: "Has he stopped breathing?" Then begins the routine of jumping up out of bed every few minutes to see if he's all right.

Mothers are tuned in to their baby's wave length. When your baby sleeps close by, but in a separate room, never fear: if he's hungry, you'll hear; but you will not be disturbed by the normal sounds made when sleeping.

Neil Henderson, M.D., prefers to see children in their own rooms and says: "A baby certainly should not sleep in his parents' room after six months of age. The baby who sleeps in his parents' room too long becomes too dependent upon the arrangement. The older he is, the harder it is to break the habit. After waking, many babies fuss for a few minutes, but if left alone they develop the habit of amusing themselves."

Should a premature infant sleep in the parents' bedroom? Dr. Ed Shaw says yes.

When the baby first comes home, I believe his crib should be very close to the mother for the first five months; and I certainly disapprove of the idea of placing him in a distant room where nobody sees him until morning. Mother shouldn't hover over him, but she should be close enough to be alerted if he vomits or chokes. Irregular breathing and short periods of stopping breathing, unless these are quite severe and prolonged, are not especially alarming and certainly do not point to the possibility of later trouble.

How should a newborn's room be prepared?

If possible, a large sunny, well-ventilated room with screened windows should be selected. Fresh air is important, but the baby should never be in a draft. Good ventilation can be maintained in winter by opening the window slightly. In hot weather, an electric fan may be used but not directed toward the baby. Walls, floors, floor coverings, furniture, and all furnishings should be simple and easy to wash or clean. The nursery should be cleaned frequently, taking precautions not to stir up dust while baby is in the room. The temperature should not be subjected to large fluctuations. Ideally, the temperature should be 72 to 74 degrees in the daytime, and around 68 degrees at night. If necessary, use supplementary heating apparatus in the nursery to control the temperature.—*Charles Hoffman, M.D.*

I prefer 70 degrees F° during the day and 60–65 degrees at night, with appropriate clothing.—*Leo Bell, M.D.*

CRYING, COLIC AND SPOILING

Why Babies Cry

Crying can be due to a whole host of things, both physical and emotional. Wet diapers, hunger, and colic are the most common causes. Pyloric stenosis (a constriction of the bowel where it leaves the stomach) or other partial obstructions further down the bowel can cause pain and vomiting. Infants can get urinary infections, various viral infections, and almost anything that adults can get. Some infants have terrible tempers and are mad at the world. Others have a deep need to be carried around by mother. This need is worth consideration, as failure to meet it is a common cause of crying; and, as you will see in the following discussions, it creates considerable differences of opinion among pediatricians.

Colic means spasms of abdominal pain. If a baby cries as if in pain, pulls up his legs, and you can hear the bowels "roar," it seems reasonable to call this "infant colic." When physicians talk about colic they usually mean the "Three Month Colic," a common complex of symptoms of crying that starts after the baby is a few weeks old and is largely confined to the late afternoon and evening. It is more common in the first baby, but can occur in infants of experienced parents. Most colic "burns itself out" at around three months.

Regardless of the starting cause, once the crying starts, the crying itself seems to make the colic worse. It is self-perpetuating, because the baby's crying makes the parents nervous and tense. Nervous and tense parents seem to make the baby cry more. Not that you can blame parents for becoming tense when their baby cries and screams, and is seem-

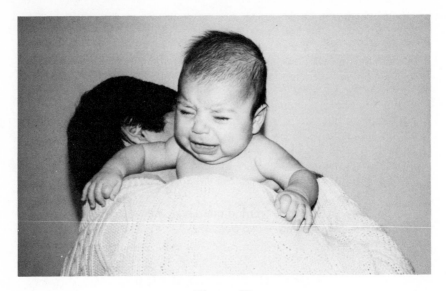

Figure 25

ingly desperate and inconsolable. We will discuss several aspects of colic
in this section; but if your baby has colic, you don't just have to wait
for him to outgrow it. Talk to your physician.

What Causes Colic?

Dr. Sid Rosin describes some of the intricacies of colic—its causes
and treatment:

A small number of infants will have intestinal discomfort as a
result of food intolerance or allergy. Most often, however, babies who
cry a great deal do so as a manifestation of their personalities. The
rapid changing of formulas and the use of sedatives do little to help
these children. These are usually infants who are high strung, alert, and
responsive and who over-react to any stimulus. What is needed in
these cases is that the parents understand the type of infant they have.
Parents must give love, warmth, and affection to this baby. But, after
first insuring that the infant is well fed, clean, warm, and comfortable,
they must learn to walk away for at least twenty minutes. These babies
often do well with pacifiers, the early introduction of solid foods, and
the use of background music. A baby should not be fed again before
two and a half hours have elapsed, but water is permissible prior to
that time. Many times, such a baby will feed every two and a half
hours for three or four times and then sleep six or eight hours.
Success in stopping the turmoil and achieving peace and quiet in

the home often takes a great deal of time, and counseling by the pediatrician. Actually, with such steps, "colic" is seldom a major problem. It is comforting for parents to know that in the majority of cases, these infants turn into "doers," leaders, and early achievers.

See Your Doctor

Further light is shed on "colic" and crying by Dr. A.S. Hashim.

Your baby may cry a lot in the evening: His stomach gurgles; he passes gas; he is difficult to burp; and you are irritated and dismayed. The lovable sweet baby you were expecting has turned out to be a terror. Your tired husband is back from work wanting rest and relaxation; but instead he is confronted with a "noisy session" that frills his nerves.

Intestinal discomfort or pain can have many causes. One cause is formula intolerance, especially from cow's milk allergy. These infants scream and cry after finishing their formula; and they may have diarrhea, a stuffy nose, or a skin rash. This sort of formula intolerance usually produces a different pattern than the "three month colic," where the crying occurs just in the evening. With milk allergy, they usually cry whenever they eat.

I recommend that you see your doctor first. So many cases of the so-called "colic" turn out to be something else. Let your doctor analyze the situation. Let him see if it is only hunger in a hyper-alert baby; or if it is a "tight rectum," in which case all that your baby needs is a dilation of the anal ring; or if it is a faulty technique in feeding, which can be corrected with proper advice and handling; or perhaps, if it is an allergy to the food or even an infection somewhere!

If your baby screams constantly, he may have an earache. Many mothers think that the baby is crying because of teething or colic and patiently tolerate the screaming and crying. By waiting, precious time is lost, and the middle ear will bulge with pus and rupture the ear drum. It is easier to treat ear infections if you take the baby to the doctor early. There may be symptoms other than crying—such as colds, cough, and lack of appetite. Often the first sign is pus in the ear canal.

Usually a colicky baby has his troubles from the first three weeks to the end of the third month. It is really not too common to see a colicky baby, especially if the mother is calm, confident and is bent on enjoying her baby. A colicky baby is usually a tense easily bothered baby who doesn't tolerate minor annoyances.

On rare occasions, I have seen "colic" which turned out to be due to such odd things as bootie strings on too tight, a hair band around the penis, or a scratch on the cornea of the eye. Babies have many reasons for crying. Even a wet diaper is liable to bother him—he demands comfort.

If other causes of colicky pains are ruled out, a medicine can be prescribed by your doctor which will help to relieve the pain.

What can *you* do for a colicky baby? Once you have determined that colic is the cause of wails and tears, try some of the following to comfort the child:

1. Bundle the baby tightly.
2. Rock him in a rocking chair or cradle.
3. Go for a ride with the baby.
4. One parent should sleep while the other suffers with the baby. Then you can switch, and not both be exhausted.
5. Use a pacifier—if it pacifies.

What can be done when the baby cries?

A baby who cries is not necessarily colicky, sick, hungry, or uncomfortable. It is the only vocal sound he knows how to make for the first six to eight weeks. If he is awake and wants to be heard, he will cry. You do not have to feel that you are a horrible mother if you do not jump up and run to him the minute he cries; he will not injure himself by crying. The average baby will cry for a few minutes and fall asleep. Ninety percent of all babies will be sound asleep within ten minutes. Therefore, one of the easiest ways of not overhandling the baby is to put a clock where it can be seen. After checking him to be sure that he is in no acute difficulty, try to steel yourself against handling the baby for ten minutes by the clock. With relatively rare exceptions, the baby will be soundly asleep without your handling him.

A baby who demands constant attention from a parent can be conditioned to accept substitute attention. Unless the mother can accept these constant demands, they will not be met anyway. You should fulfill any and all basic needs; and when you are busy or are too tired to meet the demand, it will do no harm to let him cry a while. This demand is frequently no more than a temper tantrum because he is not getting what he wants. The best treatment for a temper trantrum is to give the baby plenty of love and attention where there is no demand but to show complete indifference to the temper tantrum. If this tantrum does not get response, it is frequently abandoned as an ineffective mechanism to attract attention.—*Charles Hoffman, M.D.*

Crying and Spoiling

Many babies cry simply because they want to be held—even twenty-four hours a day. This shouldn't be surprising. After all, the infant has been held tightly and warmly in the uterus for his entire life, with all sorts of constant motion and noise. Suddenly he is cast out into a "hurricane" of air and peculiar sensations. An infant flat on his back in bed probably feel that he is twenty thousand feet in the air without a parachute. No wonder he howls! A real need to be held exists. In fact, if a baby isn't held enough he may not thrive well at all. In my opinion you can't "spoil" a *little* baby by holding him too much, in spite of some of the disagreements that follow.

Born Spoiled

Actually, a baby is "born spoiled" by adult definition. If an older child or adult acts like a baby we don't like it. In fact we sometimes seem to dislike babies acting like babies! Don't worry about spoiling your baby; actually, over a period of time you gradually can civilize your child. Start the process around six months, when a thinking brain is better developed, rather than earlier, when a baby is just a "bundle of reflexes." It takes a while to unspoil a human—probably only a hundred years. Meanwhile, give the baby what he needs when you can. And don't forget to pick him up when he is happy as well as when he cries.

When You Can't Hold the Baby

Since you can't hold a baby twenty-four hours a day, lay him down and do what you must. But don't let him "cry it out" any more than you have to. Some sort of Indian-style papoose basket is often worthwhile. So is an "infant seat." Some babies are content if they are in the same room with you so they can see and hear you. Some babies can be pacified with a pacifier, others with a transistor radio. (Not to chew on, but to have in or near the crib, turned on.) Their choices vary. Some like music. Many like talk. And some scream their heads off at the whole idea. But it may be worth a try.

Are You Insecure?

Dr. Leo Bell says one of the reasons for seeming unaccountable crying is a lack of confidence in the parents:

> Babies perceive instinctively and react when parents are insecure. This causes the baby to feel insecure with resulting anxiety, restlessness, and crying. It is not easy for new parents to gain confidence, but a parent's self-confident reaction calms the baby. This is best demonstrated when the fussy baby who has been up all night and driven the family to distraction quiets down almost immediately after the physician has been called. The doctor says, "Bring him in and we'll check him over to be sure everything's O.K." The mother is suddenly relieved to think she's going to be helped, and the baby recognizes the self-confidence re-instilled in the mother.

One of the rules I've given over the years to mother is: "If the baby is fussy, but not hungry, has been checked and is neither soiled nor wet, and is not being pricked by an open safety pin, pick him up and love him a little bit—it's good for both of you."

Won't It Spoil the Baby to Hold Him?

In answer to the question, "Won't it 'spoil' a baby to be held too much of the time?" Dr. John Richards says:

During the first three months, a baby, when awake, soon starts to cry. If he is picked up and held, his crying usually stops. When the fussy baby becomes content when held, his parents receive the reassurance they need. To me, this is much more important than worrying about "spoiling." After reaching three months of age, an infant can learn to entertain himself. Make certain the baby is well fed, dry, warm, and otherwise comfortable; then a busy mother should finish whatever household chore she's started without stopping to "entertain" the baby each time he cries. No amount of attention will spoil a baby if it does not interfere with other needs of the parents.

Teach the Baby Patience

One contributing mother, Bambi Scofield, has the following comments about teaching a baby patience:

For a self-entertaining baby, start right away. When your baby cries for a feeding, go in, turn him over, and talk to him. Then put the bottle on or get out clean clothes, and so on. When he begins to fuss again, change him, talk to him, play with him, and so forth. Finally, there will be nothing left but to feed him; and after he eats, he'll be ready for sleep. As he grows older, the periods of lying in a new position and viewing his environment grow longer and he comes to expect not being picked up immediately. A patient baby is a great thing!

Will Letting a Baby Cry Tend to Make Him Schizophrenic?

That may sound like a silly question, but Dr. Lee Salk, in his book, *What Every Child Wants His Parents To Know*, implies that letting an infant cry may set a pattern of withdrawal that will carry over into childhood. He says you should never let him cry it out.[7]

Under extreme conditions there might be some substance to such a theory, but don't feel that you must not ever let a baby cry it out. The experienced physicians contributing to *The Guide all* advise you that you should let a baby cry it out on occasions. They also all advise that you hold, play with, and socialize with the baby as much as possible. Picking babies up when they are *not* crying will do more to reduce the incidence of schizophrenia for both baby and parent. Picking a baby up for every whimper will probably cause some parents to withdraw from reality if they can; and such a practice is unnecessary busy-bodying. It is more important to follow positive advice of pediatrician Glenn R. Stoutt, Jr., in his book, *The First Month of Life,* "Write these words somewhere: TOUCH, LOOK, TALK. They are the synopsis of the entire field of infant psychology and probably the most significant concept I have learned in practicing both pediatrics and fatherhood." [8]

SAFETY IN THE FIRST FOUR MONTHS

Safety in the home is the first place to start in adjusting to a baby. Check the following list. (See Chapter One of *The Parents' Medical Manual* for a detailed review of safety.)

- Crib. Make certain the head cannot be caught between the springs, rails, or between the slats.
- Bath. Avoid scalding. Check the bath water with your elbow. Keep a hand on the baby.
- Falls. The baby's bed and playpen are the only safe places for the baby to be alone. You never know when he will roll over.
- Toys. These should be too large to swallow and too tough to break, and all should have no sharp points or edges.
- Sharp objects. Keep pins and other sharp objects out of the baby's reach.
- Smothering. Filmy plastics, harnesses, zippered bags, and pillows can smother or strangle. A firm mattress and a loose covering for the baby are safest.
- Auto safety. Use of a good car bed is essential for safety.

ADJUSTING TO THE BABY

Having a baby in the house, whether he is your first or fourth, requires adjustments in your household by your spouse, by your other children, and by you. Regarding your adjustment as a mother, the best thing a baby can have is a happy mother. Happy mothers find it easy to love their babies. So take care of yourself, mother! If you don't watch out, you will find that your twenty-four-hour-a-day, seven-day week with your new baby will catch up with you. You will get "cabin fever" and begin to wonder what happened to the rest of the world. Discipline yourself to get out once or twice a week without the baby. Tell your husband that if he wants his wife and his child's mother to be reasonable to live with he had better get you out occasionally. A night on the town and a baby sitter are cheaper than a psychiatrist!

YOUR OLDER CHILDREN AND THE NEW BABY

Many people advise that a child should be allowed to handle and "help" with the new baby as soon as the baby comes home. Some "authorities" even suggest that the child should come to the hospital and see mother and baby, saying that the germ problem is "nonsense." Unfortunately, however, the pre-schooler is a walking "bug factory" who has two to six times more infections than an older child or adult. This can amount to almost one infection a month. Parents with several children observe that the first baby rarely had infections in the first year of life; succeeding children have many more infections during their first year, given to them by their drippy nosed brothers and sisters.

Concern is expressed that keeping the toddler away from baby for the first few months will make the toddler resentful and jealous. This, I believe, is nonsense. Our first task is to look at what is best for the new baby.

What Can the Older Sibling Do for Baby?

1. He can make baby wake up.
2. He can drop him.
3. He can give him germs.
4. On top of that, baby couldn't care less about brother or sister (and vice versa).

After the first three months, however, things are different. The baby now has a fairly good immune system working. He has awakened, and wants to look around at this world he is in. He is no longer just a warm puppy, and, he may even impress his personality on his older sister or brother.

Jealousy Is Natural

Jealousy of the new baby is a feeling very common in older brothers and sisters. Put yourself in your child's shoes: Mother vanishes for several days and then returns home with a new baby who seems to take up ninety percent of her time. What if your spouse brought home a new mate and said: "Move over honey, there are three of us now." You know how you would react. Yet, in the case of your child, it is a *fait accompli.* My wife's mother, who raised ten children, used to say: "They all get a 'broken nose'!"—meaning that all of the children had hurt feelings and had to adjust to the succession of new babies.

Reducing Jealousy

It is important to recognize that, although the baby may be the focus of attention, the resentment is usually against mother for not giving as much time, attention, or love as she had in the past. That, of course, is no wonder; mother simply can't physically stretch far enough to meet all the demands. Still, there are ways of reassuring the child and of reducing the problem.

First, have other people who come over to visit and see the newborn give their attention to the older children rather than to the baby. People coming over to see the new baby want to show pleasure and enthusiasm, so they frequently come in not even saying "Hello" but rather "Where is that new baby?"—thus completely ignoring the other children.

It is better that visitors give the children the attention and a little gift rather than give the mother or the baby a gift. The baby couldn't "care less" about the visitor anyway. The toddler or older child might ordinarily not have been interested, but under the circumstances they can be now. This is also a good time for an active father. Fathers are often much better at entertaining a toddler or child than at handling the baby.

Second, when mothers are handling, feeding, or washing a baby, they usually concentrate completely on the baby, to the exclusion of the rest of the world. So when the toddler comes in from the yard to check on mother, he can't even get her attention. Then panic or anger may follow, and if he has to he will "tear down the house" in order to get attention. Avoid this by being aware of your older ones; and as you handle the baby, look at your child, smile or talk to him. Let him know that you are well aware of him and that he isn't excluded from your world. Try to do only the most necessary things for the baby when the older child is around. Playing with and bathing the baby can usually be held off until you are alone with the baby.

Third, as you now can't possibly give your child as much attention as you have in the past, make the attention you do give count the most. One good way is to look for times when the child is doing something that is neither particularly good nor particularly bad—*when he isn't looking for attention*—and give him attention at that time. Drop your mop, put the baby down, and give him a minute, free—just because you like him. You don't have to make a "federal case" out of it: Just a smile, a few words, a quick hug, or a friendly swat on the bottom will do. Then go on about your business, because you must. A minute of time given spontaneously is probably worth a half hour of time that he "drags" out of you by demand.

Of course he may still be insecure or jealous. But he will get over it. Do what you reasonably can and leave it up to him. It is, after all, his problem. And don't forget that mothers and fathers can have the same feelings and needs for reassurance, too!

The Jealousy Response

Any child will react to some degree when the new baby comes home, says pediatrician Charles Hoffman—especially those between the ages of two and five years.

The older child becomes aware that the new baby gets a lot of mother's attention which used to be his. The jealousy responses are usually not hitting or hollering at the baby but are indirect: temper tantrums, disobedience, destructiveness, aggression in the street, or wanting a bottle if he has been weaned.

Don't Give Attention

The child looks for attention, and he cares not if it is pleasant or unpleasant—as long as he gets attention. There is only one effective way to stop such obnoxious behavior, and that is to ignore it completely. For example: The child has a temper tantrum in the living room, kicking and screaming at the top of his lungs. Don't say anything to him. Lie down. Read a book. Do your dishes. He will try the temper tantrum a few times and then quit doing it. It is an inefficient mechanism when it does not get the attention he wants. He may think of something worse next time, but at least this one stops. Of course, you don't ignore him if he tries to tear the house down—stop him. But don't give him a *lot* of negative attention for his efforts.

The positive approach to this problem is to know that he is looking for attention. Give it to him *before* he looks for it. This does not mean an expensive toy. The toy is interesting for a couple of hours, and then he will be back to his old routine again. Rather, make the child aware that you are interested in him. Watch his favorite television program so that you can talk to him about it. Participate in a game he likes. Take him along shopping if he wants to go, and if it is not too inconvenient. Insist that he help each time you take care of the baby. Make him responsible for a job—it can be as simple or as complex as the child's age and intelligence warrant. Examples are: folding the diapers, holding the powder box, and feeding the baby.

There are three purposes served by such positive approaches. First, such tactics are the fastest way to get him to leave the baby alone. If you say no to something, that "no" is the first thing he will want to do, since it will insure attention, even if negative. Second, it gives him a sense of possession and participation which allows him to accept the baby more readily. It is "his baby" and he is taking care of him. Third, it gives you a defense weapon. If you are handling the baby and the child yells "tie my shoe," he is asking you to drop the baby and take care of his needs only. If you yell at him instead to get his own job done, he will probably be quiet while you take care of the baby because he is afraid that if he attracts your attention you will make him come in to help you.

People remark about the cute baby and do not remember to praise the older child. The child is not worried about what they say about the baby, but he *is* concerned that he not be left out. Mother and father can help by including the child in the picture by saying things like "I hope the baby is as cute as his older brother."

Graduate Him from the Crib

Dr. Neil Henderson suggests another way you can help to avoid jealousy: "If a young child is to graduate from a crib to a bed in order to make room for the baby, move him a few months ahead of time. There will be more jealousy if the change of beds is delayed until the baby is born, because the child gives up his crib for someone else. This same principle applies to a change of rooms or to the starting of nursery school."

Get Him Out of the House

Dr. Henderson also feels that it is important to have the other children away at first:

> When the baby arrives home, it is wise to have your other children out of the house for a few hours with a friend they like until the hustle and bustle of getting baby and mother settled has subsided. That way, no child will be standing about being ignored. Try not to act too excited about the infant in front of his brothers or sisters. Many things can be done for the baby while the other children are occupied or are outside playing. The normal jealousy exhibited toward a new addition to the family will usually disappear in six months. Try to set aside a certain amount of time each day for every child so that each child will feel part of the family group. Help the situation by suggesting how your older children may help mother care for the baby. This puts them in the role of substitute parents. Of course, they will want to hold the baby; and if they do it sitting down, I see no danger of dropping the baby. Children can feed the baby occasionally, and it is all right to let them watch mother breastfeed.

Play with Dolls

Playing with dolls is a good way to let children act out what is happening to them and the baby. Many parents tell me that their children only show love towards the new infant and are not jealous at all. I don't believe it. Your children may help with the baby and not hit him; but if you are observant you will see jealousy expressed in more subtle ways. One example I have seen is angry and impossible requests by the child for dinner.

Let Them Express Their Feelings

Encourage your children to express their feelings of jealousy with the understanding that you will not permit any harm to come to the baby. A frank discussion of the child's feelings initiated by the parents can be helpful; tell him you understand how he feels: "It is no fun to have a baby around the house. There is less time for you. We cannot go to the store together as much as we did before. Come and tell me if you are angry." The child can then realize that his mother accepts him even when he has angry feelings. This is the greatest assurance of love possible.

RELATIVES AND THEIR ADVICE

Mothers, mothers-in-law, friends, neighbors, and all are loaded with unasked-for advice. It is natural and it is human. A.S. Hashim, M.D. advises:

Be patient and be considerate and listen to what they say—smile and agree as if you will do all they suggest. This way they will feel appreciated. But, of course, you don't do anything they say, you simply follow the advice of your doctor or some of the advice in *The Guide*, if applicable. In such a way you will not have antagonized anybody, you will not have hurt anyone's feelings, and you will not have argued —yet you have not hurt your baby.

WHEN CAN YOU TAKE THE BABY OUTDOORS?

By three months, the baby may enjoy a stroll outside in good weather; but don't take him out excessively and unnecessarily, especially in the first few months of life. Covering his face to protect him from the wind may be of some help, but don't smother him. Too many clothes are as bad as too few. Dress him just well enough, and according to the weather. Don't expose him to direct sunlight for the first three months because he can easily sunburn, even in winter time. Outdoor air doesn't hurt babies but avoid sudden temperature changes. Also avoid crowded stores, churches, and the like for the first six months.

"Taking the baby from home to a warmed-up car during winter time, and then from the car to another warm place, is not 'taking him out,'" Dr. A.S. Hashim says. "You really are not exposing him to the fresh air or to the outside atmospheric condition. So, if you want to take him to visit Grandma, you should feel free to do so regardless of his age."

TOYS FOR THE ONE-YEAR-OLD

Learning to walk is a wonderful accomplishment which makes obsolete many of the rattles and rubber animals infants tend to collect. But before then, David Sparling, M.D. recommends push toys with long handles, like toy lawn mowers, vacuum cleaners, and "corn poppers." Wheeled animals are interesting if they are large enough to ride; and before long the child will be able to manage toy tractors and other kiddy-cars which are pushed with the heel. Before then, the Crawlegator (Creative Playthings) is interesting, if a bit expensive. More than anything, however, the one-year-old enjoys exploring. The insides of cartons are wonderful caves, and a blanket over a chair is better than a tent in the woods. There are many stacking toys on the market, but nesting tin cans and pots and pans are as much fun and make a much more exciting noise. And do go outdoors regularly. Indoors or out, don't forget the hazards of steps, sharp cornered walls or tables, and small objects which can be placed in the mouth.

A large number of "learning toys" have been advertised in such a way that many parents feel guilty if they don't have them for their children. Such unscientific claims provoke unnecessary expenditures, worry, and guilt. Playthings are important, but common household objects may be as adequate for use as developmental toys. Although such toys may be fine, the American Academy of Pediatrics states: "There is no evidence to suggest that any specific set of toys, systems, or environments is necessary, sufficient, or desirable to learning." [9]

HEALTH PROBLEMS PECULIAR TO INFANTS: QUESTIONS AND ANSWERS

What about "colds" in babies?

Colds in infants may be of more significance than in an older child or adult. A cold in the nose can obstruct breathing because a baby breathes poorly through the mouth. A cold settling around the narrow larynx or small bronchial tubes can reduce the baby's air space, making it difficult for him to get enough air. This can be true whether there is a fever or not, or whether the baby seems sick or not.

There are several steps you can take that may prevent some of the complications of colds in infants. (For details see *The Parent's Medical Manual.*)

1. Prop the head of the crib or bassinet up so there is better drainage. If the nose is very stuffy, it may be best to sleep the baby in an "Infant Seat."
2. Moisten the air to keep the mucus loose and draining.
3. Use a nasal suction bulb if the nose has a lot of visible mucus.
4. Check with your doctor. He may advise a decongestant to be taken by mouth and/or baby nose drops.
5. If the respiratory rate is rapid, or the small infant has a fever, or if the baby is listless or in pain, call your doctor.

Why does a baby hold his head to the side?

A baby who is two to three weeks old may develop a lump on the neck in the muscle which runs from behind the ear to the breast bone. It gradually becomes as big as a walnut with "rubbery firm consistency," but it doesn't bother the baby. Yet the baby will gradually hold his head more and more towards that side, and will have increasing difficulty turning his head to the other side. If you let it go and the baby keeps holding his head towards one side, then a "wry neck" will develop. The face will gradually shape itself to the new position and will gradually lose its symmetry. Your doctor may tell you how to massage the lump, how to turn the head, and will talk to you about sleeping position. It takes a few weeks before the lump disappears, but the wry neck may linger and require longer term treatment.—*A.S. Hashim, M.D.*

What is the difference between spitting and vomiting?

After or during a feeding, milk may run out of the baby's mouth. Occasionally, food or milk will shoot out two or three inches. This is "spitting up," and is of no consequence aside from being annoying. If the baby continues to grow and gain weight, you needn't worry. Chronic spitting does not mean that the baby is sick, just that he is messy.

Spitting is usually caused by a weak muscle in the esophagus, the tube that goes from the mouth to the stomach. Where the esophagus joins the stomach, there is a ring of muscle which opens to let food in and then closes so that the food doesn't flow back up when the stomach churns. In a large number of babies, this muscle ring is weak; and whenever the stomach contracts or pressure is put on it, the food flows back up the esophagus. It is like a bottle without a cork. The spitting occurs when the baby is moved, held over the shoulder with the weight on the stomach, or laid down.

Vomiting is a different problem. There are three types: mechanical, formula intolerance, and from illness. Mechanical vomiting is usually due to pyloric stenosis, and the milk may shoot out of the mouth for over a foot or two like a projectile. Babies will eat hungrily right after vomiting. Although they are not ill, they can become quite dehydrated and lethargic after several days, so check with your doctor if the baby vomits.

Formula intolerance or allergy causes different symptoms in different infants, varying from skin rash to cramps, vomiting, or diarrhea.

Vomiting with illness is a different sort of problem altogether. Usually the baby is fretful and lethargic, and often he isn't taking food well. There may by symptoms of a cold, cough, fast breathing, fever, a swollen tense soft spot on the scalp, or just an ill-looking baby. Don't wait: Call your doctor.

The following suggestions by A.S. Hashim, M.D. may help prevent spitting:

1. After feeding him his solid meal, don't give more than two ounces of milk to wash it down with.
2. Put the baby in an infant seat after finishing off his meal; even let him sleep upright.
3. Occasionally, using skim milk will stop the "spitting up." Try it for a few days; and if it works, then fine and good—use skim milk. However, if it does not work, go back to the previous formula.
4. Patience, please. It is a virtue.

What is a normal stool for infants?

There is great variability. Some babies have one or two bowel movements with each feeding. Breast-fed babies have less stool, and it consists of small yellow curds in a slightly watery base. Formula-fed babies have a more pasty yellow curdy stool. Babies fed whole or homogenized milk usually have large formed stools. In the first few weeks of life, their stools are occasionally greenish.

Usually, after a month, stools diminish in number. An occasional infant may have a stool every three or four days without problems. If the baby has to grunt or strain with bowel movements, and if there is blood or much mucus, then there may be a problem. Diarrhea stools are often green, and may contain a lot of mucus. If there is a very water fluid stool that looks like somebody spilled coffee on the diaper, call the doctor.—*Charles Hoffman, M.D.*

What if your baby is constipated?

Constipation does not occur often in babies. Actually, some infants can go for two or three days without a bowel movement—yet not be constipated. Signs of constipation are:

1. Large firm stools.
2. Pain and grunting on passing a stool.
3. Distended stomach.
4. Blood streaks on the stool.

If there is any question, your doctor will want to check the baby's rectum to see if it is large enough. However, every grunt, strain, or pain does not indicate constipation. It is not necessary to have a bowel movement every day. Breast-fed babies sometimes seem to use up almost all of the breast milk, leaving very small amounts of material left for stools. The bowels of some babies are so immature that they cramp when they contract to expel the stool rather than smoothly pushing it out; thus, such a bowel movement hurts. Usually babies outgrow these symptoms, which are unrelated to constipation.

Streaks of blood can occur on the stool, especially if it is hard and large. This may be due to an anal fissure, a crack in the rectum caused by passing an overlarge hard stool. Blood can also occur on the stool from diaper rashes around the anus; but whatever the cause, blood in a bowel movement deserves a call to the doctor. Stool softeners should be used. Locally, an infant glycerin suppository helps to lubricate and protect the fissure. If there is much discomfort, a bit of anesthetic ointment put on the crack with the finger, or a warm sitz bath, will help. Don't use laxatives unless they are ordered by your doctor.

What is an umbilical hernia?

An umbilical hernia is not a rare thing, but it can be frightening. The "belly-button" seems to pop out, more when the baby cries, grunts, squirms, or exerts any effort. Push it back, and you may feel the gurgles of the intestine and a small ring, which is the "neck" of the hernia. The size of this ring varies. The smaller it is, the faster the hernia is likely to go away. It may become bigger by five months, and then slowly become smaller and disappear at around a year. However, if the hernia is big, it will take up to three or four years to go away.

The umbilical hernia doesn't need your help to go away. Some people advocate taping a big coin over the hernia. I believe this is useless in practically all cases. The baby may end up with a rash caused by the sensitivity of the skin to the adhesive tape or the coin. Surgery may be advisable in rare cases which persist beyond the expected age.—*A.S. Hashim, M.D.*

3

THE GROWTH AND DEVELOPMENT
OF CHILDREN

One of the things I enjoy most about pediatrics is watching the children in my practice grow and develop. Each is so unique, and each offers his parents joy, companionship, fulfillment, and a link with the future. Of course, children also present problems: health problems, emotional problems, behavior problems. Books such as this one often seem to emphasize a negative aspect of raising children because parents so often ask about problems they have with their children. The question parents so frequently ask is: "Where can I find a book that will tell me how the normal child acts at this age?" There are two things wrong with this universal question. *First* is the unspoken assumption that a specific type of behavior is limited to a certain age group. It isn't. At times, we can all act childish. *Second,* as to normal behavior, this *Guide* is dedicated to the principle that "normal doesn't count."

NORMAL DOESN'T COUNT

Personalities differ right from the moment of birth, and a newborn's basic reactive pattern may vary from "high strung" to placid and from tough to timid. The innate personality differences between individuals of any age preclude all being normal. We will describe some patterns of "normal" behavior for different ages. However, there is less value in looking for age-typical behavior patterns than one might think, even though they represent hallmarks of obvious emotional steps toward maturity. Rather, look for the emotions themselves, and for the understanding of

Figure 26   *Kids, like people, are all different. Some will always be small and some will always be big. What is normal for an individual child can be statistically abnormal for the group.*

the principles and the motivations involved. Concentrate on helping your child develop his or her best potential. The same is true for physical growth. Don't take our normal age groupings too literally, for the concept of normal is of relatively little value on an individual basis. If you measure everything about almost any person, the odds are that he will be abnormal in some way. In fact, one of the outstanding characteristics of humans is their variability.

Understanding "Normal": The Bell Curve

One way of understanding "normal" and "abnormal" is to study the concept of the bell curve. The bell curve is a graphic illustration of variability. It serves as an indicator for the majority (the normal), and also, equally as important, of the minority (the abnormal). To form a "bell curve," we might select the first hundred five-year-old girls to enroll in kindergarten, and chart the weight of each of them. Then we line the children up in order, from the lightest to the heaviest, count the number of children in each weight group, and form columns for each group. If we draw a line over the tops of the columns, it would form a curve shaped rather like a bell. It is obvious that the greatest number of children are in the center of the curve. The group in the center is defined *statistically* as "normal." Those at the ends of the curve would be defined as statistically "abnormal."

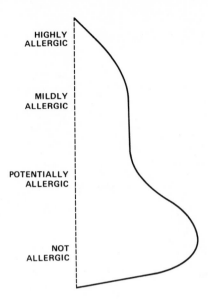

Figure 27   *Allergy to milk.*

Not all measurements of people form a perfect bell curve. For example, the majority of people are not allergic to milk. An attempt to graph the accurrence of allergy to milk in the general population would produce what is called a skewed bell curve, one which is lopsided in one direction:

Most advice on the need for milk in one's diet ("everybody" needs milk; it is an essential part of a balanced diet) is aimed at the majority. If you happen to belong to the group in the "abnormal" end of the curve, such advice is literally poison for you.

Normal or Not, Children Grow

There is continuous change in children as they grow and develop. Physically they mature; and as they do, their brain power increases, along with their control of their impulses, emotions, nerves, and muscles. Each child, and each of the various aspects of growth in an individual child, is different. The major thrust in this chapter is emotional and social growth—maturing. Such a process is not smooth; in fact, it seems that there is one step backward for every two steps forward.

Blossoms and Thorns

In discussing the blossoming of a child, it may seem at times that there are more thorns than blossoms. There *are* thorny stages of behavior

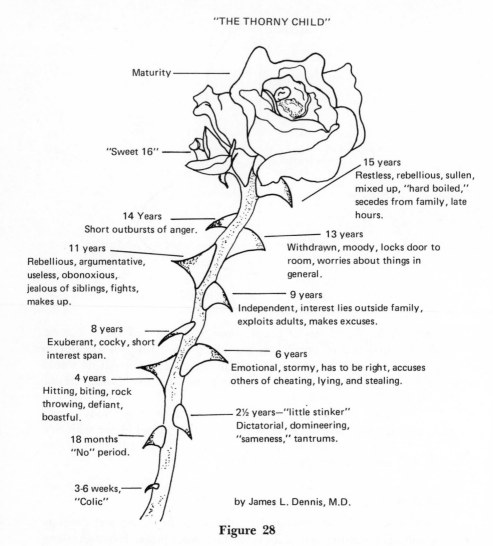

"THE THORNY CHILD"

Maturity

"Sweet 16"

15 years
Restless, rebellious, sullen,
mixed up, "hard boiled,"
secedes from family, late
hours.

14 Years
Short outbursts of anger.

13 years
Withdrawn, moody, locks door to
room, worries about things in
general.

11 years
Rebellious, argumentative,
useless, obonoxious,
jealous of siblings, fights,
makes up.

9 years
Independent, interest lies outside family,
exploits adults, makes excuses.

8 years
Exuberant, cocky, short
interest span.

6 years
Emotional, stormy, has to be right, accuses
others of cheating, lying, and stealing.

4 years
Hitting, biting, rock
throwing, defiant,
boastful.

2½ years—"little stinker"
Dictatorial, domineering,
"sameness," tantrums.

18 months
"No" period.

3-6 weeks,
"Colic"

by James L. Dennis, M.D.

Figure 28

that children go through, and it is best for parents to be forewarned.
Pediatrician Dr. James Dennis observed that about every other year of
childhood seems to be a problem year. The thorns can often be predicted
in a general sort of way. One of our tasks as parents is to *modify* such
thorny behavior. This requires a reasonably adult approach and some
knowledge about the needs of children as well as about the various
stages they hopefully "go through" in growing up. Keep in mind the
great variability of children as you study their "normal" stages of development.

FROM BIRTH TO ADOLESCENCE

Age 0 to One Year

Newborns are exciting gifts to the family, and the first one, especially, represents an unsurpassed change in life style for the parents. (We discuss newborns in detail in Chapter 2.) Infants are helpless and have many needs. Considering that they have had their needs met 100% in utero, and that they have been held closely *all* the time until birth, it is reasonable to expect that they have a great need to be held, fondled, and stimulated in the first few months after birth. Their development is helped if the parents learn to differentiate between the cry of hunger and the many other cries. Keep in mind that the open mouth isn't just something to be filled with breast, bottle, or pacifier, even though that usually quiets the baby down. Holding and loving are as important as feedings.

The baby gradually learns to trust mother and father by being held and fed, and he begins the process of recognizing himself as an individual. The first few weeks are consumed with eating, sleeping, and growing at a tremendous rate. By six weeks, and for some few a bit earlier, most babies don't have to eat through the night; and by two to three months they become interested in looking at the world around them and in studying their hands, their parents, and trying it all out. You can't spoil them at this stage, although we discuss how to teach them some patience by around six months. It is around this time of life that the long, slow process of civilizing a child starts. It only takes a hundred years or so to complete the process, so don't try to hurry it too much.

By six months, I believe that most babies have begun to think and are something more than a bundle of reflexes. They usually have recognized mother's voice and face for some time, and they respond to smiles of parents with smiles of their own. (And this is a very important milestone.) They should be able to hear someone talking and turn their head toward the person. Some of the thinner ones can sit with help, but many of the heavier babies just don't have the necessary strength or balance yet. The six monther has great fun learning to use his hands: Generally, he grabs everything in reach and stuffs it in his mouth for a taste. Mostly, at this age, infants need people to play with. Colic and fretfulness should be over, and they aren't old enough to get into things yet. Be sure to pick the baby up when he is happy as well as when he cries—in order to avoid convincing him that the best way to deal with the world is to cry.

As babies become more aware of the world and of the people in it, they begin to recognize strangers. Each infant, being different, responds in a different manner to people. Some hold out their hands to almost anyone; others develop stranger fears. These instinctive fears often peak at around nine months, and can be embarrassing to the mother and somewhat bothersome to grandparents: It is a time when infants should be mothered mostly by one person. Changes in caretakers may create severe problems in some babies.

As the baby starts to crawl and pull himself up and take those first steps, his self-esteem shoots up. These first solo excursions often show a lot about the baby's personality. Some crawl fearlessly away, convinced that they can soon fly. Others dart away, only to find that it is a big scary world; and then they get homesick for mother, and cry to get back in her arms.

Once a baby begins to crawl, the possibility of accidents and poisons rises drastically. You should accident-proof and baby-proof your house. Keep some syrup of ipecac on hand to use promptly in case they eat some poisonous substance (see Chapter 1 in *The Parents' Medical Manual*). Most babies have an unbounded curiosity, and they should be allowed a world that they can explore freely as well as protection from a world that can harm them. They get into so many things that if you aren't careful you may find yourself going around saying "No!" all day. I have seen fifteen month olds come into the office actually singing, "No, no, no. . . ." Discipline should begin at this age, although there is considerable disagreement as to how it should be accomplished. If an infant does something "bad," it is just because he hasn't yet had the ability or the teaching to understand that it is bad.

From One to Two Years of Age

Life with a toddler is, at the least, a consuming experience. They vacillate between trying to become completely independent to clinging and insisting on being held "all the time." One trap you can avoid is that of giving him time and picking him up *only* when he demands it. The one thing that makes your child's separation fears worse is the feeling that he is not wanted—that you pick him up because you *have* to, not because you want to. His curiosity continues, and this is a vital time to teach him that the world is conquerable and that learning is fun. The parent should be around as much of the time as possible in order to respond to the child's questions and stimulate his play. Play is a very serious thing for infants and children; it is their way of learning.

It is important that your baby hears you, and that you talk to him a lot and encourage speech. Some talk by a year, and others don't start until two. But all infants should be stimulated by company, play, and speech. They love to look at pictures in story books, but they learn even more from following you around. A child needs to hear praise for effort as well as accomplishments. This makes the effort more worthwhile. Given a chance, babies will listen to adults and study them in their own way, so they should be around adults a good part of the day.

"A one year old is always on the go . . . all over the house and into everything," writes pediatrician Glen Griffin:

> In fact, it's a full time job to keep up with this curious little creature. Some one-year-olds walk alone, while others quite normally hang onto things for a while before soloing. Other intriguing talents to be watching for include opening boxes, poking fingers into holes, and marking with a pencil or crayon on a book, wall, or any handy surface. He may also begin the sport of climbing—noteworthy because it's easier getting up than down—which may mean some tumbles. Baby may say something that resembles "Mommy" or "Daddy" or maybe another word or two. Don't expect too much but it's fun to repeat words clearly for baby to learn. (Note that when other children are around to answer a baby's needs, talking usually does not occur quite as early.)
>
> As they develop new skills and self-esteem during the second year, they want to do things for themselves. For one thing, this means messy eating. If you try to force them to eat, it can lead to problems. They usually eat less at this age than they did before, and they don't grow as fast as during the first year. For another, this often means that they have a need to test their powers and to see if they can't push the world around a bit. They can become bossy and a bit tyrannical for a while, using any behavior required to get their way, from screaming to whining, and from temper tantrums to pure charm. If one or another of these techniques doesn't work, some babies actually will hit you. Often a child finds that the only real power he has lies in a refusal to cooperate. Thus two of the most common problems arise from parents trying, albeit unsuccessfully, to insist that the child eat or go to the toilet. (You can lead a horse to water. . . .) Your response to your child's methods of "getting his way" will teach him much about how to deal with the world in the future.

From Two to Three Years

At two years old, a child should be able to talk. Some will pick out letters on blocks and words under pictures. They love new experiences, and they love to go places with Mom and Dad. They must explore the things we take for granted—the cracks in the sidewalks, the weeds in the cracks, the bugs under the weeds, and, if you are not careful, the toilet cleaner under the kitchen sink.

As you've sown in the preceding years, you harvest in this year. The terrible two's and the child's stubborn "No!" come not only from innate stubbornness but sometimes from prior overemphasis on parental power.

If a child finds that he can satisfy his overwhelming need to explore without being "No'd" to death at the age of one, he isn't usually as much of a problem at the age of two. The child should hear "yes" at least as often as "no." Keep a count for a while—it can be embarrassing. Set up his environment so he can be free to explore and so you can say "yes!"

Even when a two year old says "No!" it is positive behavior. He tries to assert his independence to show that he has a mind of his own; and he must test the limits of his world repeatedly in order to find which limits stay intact and which disappear when mother is busy or tired. He is brave and goes outside, and then gets homesick and rushes back inside. He begins to imitate and admire the important adults in his life and to identify with the parent of the same sex. It is interesting, if not alarming, that he tries to act like us—as he sees us. His coordination allows easy toilet training, although his sense of self-esteem may interfere.

From Three to Four Years

A preschooler is usually more social, and, having proven his independence, makes less fuss about it. He is ready for increased limits, and the world is his oyster. Not only does physical coordination increase, but so does mental coordination and his ability to understand some abstract concepts. He usually talks your ears off and asks endless questions. If he doesn't, you perhaps should spend more time with him and try to bring him out. Generally, three-year-olds can learn at a phenomenal rate. We should take advantage of this and start teaching him neatness, how to dress himself—and even bravery, compassion, and manners. Most of this is best done at home, although some can be accomplished by a good nursery school or day care center.

The sense of possession becomes well developed and the world gets divided into "mine" and somebody else's. At this age, children often become acutely aware of differences in the genitalia: They learn, to their fascination, that boys have penises and girls don't. Some three- and four-year-old boys are afraid they will lose their penis "like the girls did." Illogical? Not from a three- or four-year-old's standpoint. If half of the population lost theirs, maybe he is next! And I have seen three-year-old girls who, because of admiration of an "older" boy, announce that when "I grow up and go to school I am going to be a boy."

The sense of possession applies toward parents, too; and, along with the fears of separation (which often peak at age four), this sense may be the reason a child will announce that he is "going to marry mother" or that she is "going to marry father." A child often hates to see his parents "wasting" a lot of time on each other. So he often makes an effort to get between parents—physically and psychologically. Children must learn that they cannot marry mother or father. It helps the child to overcome this desire and to develop healthy emotions at this stage if mother and father do not allow the child to be the center of attention most of the time.

Many three- and four-year-olds insist that they should always be center stage. They reach the height of their omnipotence complex: They want to be God, to run the world. Some find they can run their world (mother and father); and if they are not taught to take their turn and recognize the rights of other people, then they may become proverbial spoiled brats. Or maybe they will have to go into politics for a living.

Three-year-olds are ready for more indirect discipline than two-year-olds, and it is vital that they be brought under control. In the discipline process, they learn that they aren't God, and that the world doesn't often mind them. They should also learn that they are very important little people. Depending on their individual personalities and the perceptiveness of their parents, they react to discipline in differing ways. Some become fighters against the establishment, feeling that is the only way to retain their self-esteem. Others retreat to a magic make-believe world where things are always as they want them to be. But magic and fairy tales aside, at this age, you should begin teaching them to protect themselves against accidents and poisons. You should also help them build (or keep) their self-esteem by increasing their responsibilities and sense of self-importance. They should be "required" to help around the house; and you should start conditioning them to stay alone a while at home and to go alone to a neighbor's house a short and safe distance away.

We usually enjoy watching three-year-olds, with their boundless energy, unlimited egos, and uninhibited approach to life. This is partially because we get a vicarious satisfaction from their behavior. The behavior of the three-year-old is worthy of study by all of us, whether we have children or not. If we look at them closely, we see us—without our veneer. Look at the daily newspaper and analyze the actions of many adults in terms of the stages of emotional growth. Much of the behavior reported could be by three-year-olds. This is no reason to despair over humanity. The news media tends to accentuate the immature and negative behavior of the rest of the world. Maybe it makes us feel better to know that others act even sillier than we do. Another reason for guarded optimism is that emotional growth need never cease. We can all have remarkable spurts of emotional growth, and the development of healthy control, even as grandparents. So think of your own inner child of the past. Don't, then, expect too much in the way of good behavior from small children; rather, count your blessings that they behave as well as they do. And keep in mind that some of their child-like qualities aren't so bad anyway.

Figure 29

From Four to Five

With an increasing comprehension of the scope of the world and of his relative impotency, the four-year-old often becomes rather fearful. Children at this age go from the bandaid stage of realizing that they are vulnerable and can be hurt, through the monster stage, to the biggest fear of all—fear of separation from home and mother and father. It becomes apparent to the child that he will finally grow up, that childhood has an end, and that he will someday have to go into the world like all those other people without mothers or fathers to take care of them. There are several ways a child may deal with this problem. Some decide that, as marriage seems to persist, their best bet is to marry mother or father. Others decide that being brash, tough, and strong is the best way to handle the world. Often there is considerable hostility at this age, coming from the realization of all the problems they will ultimately face— the necessity to partially abandon their make-believe worlds; the realization that they must mind their parents and respect other adults; the knowledge that they cannot always get their own way.

The greatest separation fear of all is the fear of death. At this age, it is emotionally unacceptable; and they either worry about it, bury it (often with resulting nightmares and odd fears that are suppressed death fears), or they will protect themselves from it by deciding that they will never grow up, get old, and die. It is the Peter Pan in all of us—eternal childhood sounds attractive. In any case, I believe children should not be taken to funerals, especially those of people they were close to, including immediate relatives. Some adult psychiatrists advise that children *should* go to funerals, but I have seen severe and long-lasting problems from exposure to death under the age of ten. If it is all right for children to believe in Santa Claus or other myths, then it is all right to let them remain children a while longer and avoid much exposure to the death–separation concept.

Learning goes on at a great rate, although not much is necessarily academic, nor need it be. The more important lessons are self-control, self-respect, and how to deal with other people. Children at this age are enthusiastic; they tend to mimic other people; and often their perceptions of adults are such that they become bossy and bombastic, and strut around. It gives one pause to think that they see and copy much of this from adult behavior. They don't have much social polish, and many of them are more likely to fight than to love. Parenting, by the parents and in preschool, is essential. Children's behavior can become very positive, and their personalities can be effectively modified by proper handling at this age.

Careful teamwork with discipline is essential; and mother and father should spend at least a few minutes each week working out a unified approach to discipline and love. Self-esteem and confidence need to be carefully encouraged. The parents should insist that the child must learn to accept responsibility for himself, to help with chores around the house, and to earn respect for himself and give respect to other people.

Age Five to Ten

Children ages five to ten are usually delightful. They have acquired enough varnish during the first five years to control the uncivilized portion of their make-up. The drive towards independence is accelerated; an urge to be big and important usually overshadows their fears and uncertainties of the adult world. Although they suppress their fears, the fears still linger. Five-year-olds face many things, including enforced schooling and the prospect of venturing away from the homeplace. This is not an easy age for all children, and this is attested to by the high incidence of stomach ulcers in five-year-olds as compared to children of other ages. There are "gut wrenching" decisions to be made by that kindergartener "happily" trudging off to school.

Tasks for the Growing School-age Child
- To develop greater physical strength and coordination.
- To develop a firmer sense of identity and self-respect.
- To become comfortable and assured in one's sex role.
- To become aware of one's potential places in the world.
- To learn to relate successfully to and to deal with all sorts of people.
- To obtain knowledge and develop skills.
- To develop a sense of moral guidance and responsibility to self and to society.

The most significant underlying drive of children between the ages of five and ten years is preparation for independence and separation from mother and father. This major step in emotional growth does not always come easily. It is the root of many of the "psychological" problems that beset families. The full fruits of these years usually are reaped during adolescence.

Although most five-year-olds may have had some valuable preschool experience, all of them are faced with the necessity of academic learning and the need for discipline. They generally enjoy the challenge of school and of growing up—but growing up has implications. Grown-ups don't have mothers and fathers to take care of them. And few five-year-olds feel capable of taking care of themselves. Childhood's end becomes visible. Meanwhile, the child is in school with thirty other "wild ones" who may do bad things like not like him or make faces. Then there are teachers who make him do terrible things like "sit down and be still." So most children become somewhat homesick, and when school is out they rush home wanting more love, more attention, and more security. This, they know, comes from mother and father, and mother and father "waste" a lot of time on each other—time and attention that the child wants for himself. So to get some extra attention and become center stage and "noticed," the child will do almost anything. He will be very bad—a clown—or, if he has to, even very very good. But he makes an effort to get one or the other parent under control; in a sense, he hasn't given up the idea of marrying a parent.

If the child, especially the "good" child, manages to dominate his mother, say, then he has effectively taken her from father. The child believes (whether true or not) that if mother *had* to make a choice that she would take the child's side. This, of course, means he has won a mother (of *the* greatest value) from father. In effect, then, the child has wronged and hurt a father whom he loves. This leads to guilt feelings—

and no one likes feeling guilty. Even as adults, we usually find a way to blame things on someone else. For a child, it is natural to blame his guilt feeling on the person who made him feel guilty—in this case, father. And, if it is father's fault, then the child would like to get even. But Dad is too big to hit; and if he did hit Dad, the child would feel even worse because he *does* love him. So the child is left with a big bundle of feelings: love, fear, guilt, anger—confusion. What can he do with all these emotions?

What usually happens is that the child does something, usually in innocence the first time, that really gets the parent mad. When the parent "goes up the wall," the child realizes that here, finally, is a way for him to get even, to win and punish the parent for making him feel bad. So when the child's tensions increase, he can misbehave again with telling effect. In fact, if the parent becomes angry enough to holler or to spank the child, it proves that the child wins—even if by doing the "wrong" thing. Thus the child learns to "win" psychological battles by misbehavior. As we discuss discipline in Chapter 7, it becomes apparent that a form of discipline must be established which teaches the child to win by the correct behavior that is in the child's best long term interest rather than by "bugging" his parents.

All children, however, don't follow this model. They usually go through these feelings, each in a different degree and in an individual manner. But the instinctive drive to become big and important as well as secure and loved dominates at this age.

So, five- to ten-year-olds can be beset with problems. Toward parents they feel love, respect, and dependence mixed with anger, impatience, and rebellion. Toward themselves they have the need to establish feelings of self-worth in the face of self-doubt and fears. With children of their own age, they must adapt and identify, suppress or succumb, lead or follow. In school they must learn to obey others, to control themselves, and to produce on command. Most do these things easily and with contentment. But not all. Part of the problem is that children want their cake, yet they would eat it too. They need complete security, yet they want complete independence. Few of us ever thoroughly resolve the freedom versus security issue—we compromise—and even adults can be a bit homesick while making their way in the world.

It is little wonder that children deal with the world by escaping it when they can. They escape to comic books, to incessant all-consuming bursts of interest and activity; and they escape from the adult world by tuning us out. They become so preoccupied with their own feelings that they simply and selectively don't hear Mom or Dad—they develop protective "parent deafness." During this stage of development, some children may act and talk "tough," and "bug" their parents. A certain amount of this is normal testing in an attempt to establish the reality of parentally imposed limitations. Some of it represents a trial of outside values on the parents. Some represents a deeper guilt/hostility feeling toward an unsuspecting parent. Most children, however, have enough love and respect for their parents so that there are few problems. And a child's needs for parental affection and security are often so great at this age that severe misbehavior is rare.

The child prepares for adolescence by developing physical and intellectual skills, by gathering experience on how to deal with varying types of people, and by improving emotional and physical control. Five-to ten-year-olds will identify strongly with their parents; but at the same time other children become more important, while adults other than parents also begin to serve as models and friends. It becomes important to a child to be one of the gang, to talk and dress like others his age. "At this age," says Dr. Neil Henderson:

> Neighborhood children form clubs with rules and regulations. There is a great deal of secrecy, with pledges and rituals. This is an important time when children prove to themselves that they can establish and abide by their own rules and regulations without interference from the parents. Most children of this age become more concerned about what other children say and do than about what parents say and do. He wants to talk, to dress, and to be like kids his own age. During this time he will probably develop a few bad manners. He may no longer hold his fork as he was taught, hold the door open for ladies, or pick up his clothes from the floor. However, he avoids doing anything that is morally wrong, so that he still can live with himself while asserting his right to be more independent of his parents. Such a child has not forgotten what he has been taught before: Otherwise, there would be no rebellion. His good manners will return, and his good training will reassert itself when he has established his independence in his own mind.

During this time of conflicting and usually suppressed turmoil, a lot of emotional pressure can develop. The price of self-control is not cheap. As Dr. Henderson points out:

> Around the age of eight to ten, it is not uncommon for compulsions to begin, such as not stepping on cracks in the sidewalk. There is no logical reason for this, but the child has a superstitious feeling about it: "Step on a crack, break your grandmother's back." These habits should be considered normal unless they become excessive.
> An example of an excessive compulsion is when a child wipes off the seat of the toilet each time he sits down, in order to prevent contact with germs. If an excessive compulsion involves a lot of your child's time, ask your doctor if a psychiatrist needs to be consulted.
> Like behavioral compulsions, tics and nervous habits are common

around the age of nine. The child may constantly clear his throat, play with his identification bracelet, or adjust his glasses. Don't bring the tics to his attention. They will usually go away by themselves, providing that no great psychological tensions exist. If the parents notice a tic, they should review in their own minds how things are going, in order to make sure that the child is not under too much pressure.

Your parenting duties will involve helping the child develop independence and self-control while offering yourself and others as acceptable models for behavior.

Your parenting art may help your child develop both independence and self-control without too many compulsions. This art involves perceiving the child's internal struggles, listening to him, and offering support and encouragement in his efforts to mature. Avoid criticism of his efforts—rather, praise them. Parental models of behavior will be closely examined by the grammar school child, and will be compared to those of current heroes, including those in comic books, movies, and rock bands. It should be realized that a child's view of the world may come largely through the newspapers and television, which tend to emphasize the negative and undesirable actions of humanity.

Perhaps the greatest impact from the media for the five- to ten-year-old comes from comic books. This starts, writes Henderson, around the age of six:

Independence needs are often expressed by imagining great deeds and accomplishments of super-human feats. The future adult becomes super-human, and might and right always win at the last minute. This happens in comic books, which fulfill the need of the child to play a role. Don't worry, children realize that they are fiction.

Comic books may not be very literary, but they are of value to the growing child, who finds it necessary to control many of his hostile impulses. The comic book provides a socially acceptable "superman" outlet.

Comic books, movies, radio, and television do not encourage your child to become a juvenile delinquent if heroes do the right thing and always win. However, media that frighten the child will have adverse affects on him, and should be avoided. Parents should review the material in current use and decide for themselves if it is suitable. This judgment cannot always be left to the producers.

There is little question but that television violence has an effect on people, including children. The awesome amount of murder and mayhem on television seen in one night is more than most of us saw in our total growing years. Parental control of television becomes vital. Some social control of television at those times when children are usually watching now exists. How effective it is remains to be seen; but there is evidence that the television industry is responding to social necessity as well as to public pressure. Although we hope that television news commentators and program directors will recognize some of the bad effects of their electronically inflated negative view of life, we as parents should be carefully selective about what television programs our children are allowed to view.

Although children need protection and positive images to emulate, they also have a vital need to become truly competent and independent. This requires, as Georgia pediatrician Martin Smith so nicely puts it, that mother must "loosen those apron strings"—even to the point of allowing the child to make a few mistakes. Dr. Smith advises:

> The process of beginning to free the child to make some of his own decisions and some of his own mistakes can and should begin before the teen years. Perhaps at this age it is just a matter of allowing him to camp out overnight in the back yard with a friend, or of allowing him to go to a real camp, or of allowing him to undertake a money-making chore in the neighborhood. These are steps in the process of freeing himself from constant parental guidance, and they should be allowed—within the range of his capabilities at that time.
>
> Our toughest job as parents is trying to determine what are the reasonable capabilities of our child at that time. We have to try to judge as best we can when it is appropriate for each apron string to be loosened. It is a shame to loosen them all too soon and send our ten-year-old in pursuit of something that really represents a frustration of the parent. It is also tragic to keep all of the apron strings in tight grasp, and to deny the eight-year-old the first opportunity to feel some independence and to do some growing up. If we could all succeed in letting loose of our children judiciously and gracefully and at just the right time we would be completely successful parents.

Learning is doing. And as children grow toward adolescence, they usually become easier to live with: they consciously try to do good and be good. It is a time when the conscience develops at a great rate, and when children should be able to respect their parents. They will honor their parents if they can. If they don't, then it may herald more serious problems during adolescence. It pays to spend enough time with your children at this age to establish constructive relationships and help avoid future problems.

4

BASIC TRAINING: SLEEPING, EATING, AND TOILETS

A good portion of parental time and concern in taking care of infants and children revolves around the three inescapable basics: eating, sleeping, and going to the toilet. From the parents' standpoint, it might be better put as *how* to feed them, *how* to get them to sleep; and *how* to get them to go to the toilet. As you will see, there are many ways to accomplish these tasks. But regardless of the way you choose, you can rest assured that your child *will* eat, sleep, and eliminate. So try to approach this basic training course with confidence, a light heart, and as much faith in your prejudices as ours. It really isn't very hard to accomplish this training, or, in fact, to feed, bed, and clean your child's rear end. Admittedly, some people make it hard, but that isn't necessary. The one thing that is necessary is to carefully look at what effects your attitudes and techniques have on your particular child.

EATING AND FEEDING

It is impossible to completely separate nutritional "facts" from the more emotionally complex issues of eating and feeding. Because they are intense experiences which carry so many emotional overtones, they quite often stand at the center of many family confrontations. When you think of it, "Food is more than calories and nutrients, it is the sum of a person's culture and traditions, an emotional outlet, gratification of pleasure and relief from stress, a means of communication, security, status, personal experiences—all interwoven in the fabric of life and unconsciously expressed in food likes and dislikes. There are days when love is measured by the amount of food you eat." [1]

If the way to a man's heart is through his stomach, the way to gray in a parent's hair is often through worrying about how, when, and what their children eat. Very few parents manage to avoid completely the proverbial "battle of the strained peas." Each of us, whatever our age, enters the battle armed with our particular food fixations and with time-honored cliches entangled with emotion, memories, rules, guilt, and sense of duty. Before we know it, the act of eating has taken second place to a series of indigestion-producing directives: "No turnip—no dessert," "Elbows off the table," or "No wonder you're skinny as a rail; I never saw a pickier eater!"

When such interchange become the rule rather than the exception, dinner hour becomes the arsenic hour—whining children, a harassed mother, an angry father, and a thick blanket of tension. The table becomes a place to fight and complain rather than a place to eat and relax. Often the child is the focus of the problem. He won't use proper table manners, he won't eat what he should, he complains or sasses, or he does things he knows full well will get his parents' goat.

Why? To start with, *everyone* sometimes has a "hard day at the office." The preschooler has played hard, and he is just about exhausted— and very hungry. Mother has been busy getting dinner and trying to keep the preschooler out of her hair while she cooks. The school age child did poorly on a test, had a bully heckle him, and is tired. Father *did* have a hard day at the office, and mother may have had one, too! Everyone wants to relax and have *someone* take care of him or her. Everyone has demands—sometimes just to be left alone. Mother is the usual focus of these demands, and at times she feels like turning in her mother's badge. Johnny wants Dad to play before dinner, and Dad would rather get lost with a drink and the paper. So what to do?

Mealtime should be relaxing. Make a pact with the family that all of the problems will wait until after the meal is over, the table cleared, and the dishes washed. Then sit down and discuss the problems of the day. Next, don't force your children to eat with you. Eating with the family and as a grown-up should be a privilege, not a duty. If a child is unable to sit and eat properly without a hassle, tell him he is too young to eat with the family. Feed him before the others. If he persists in coming into the dining room and bugging you, send him to his bedroom and lock the door if you must. Once he finds that he has to use a fork instead of fingers, manners instead of surliness, or occasional restraint instead of constant showing off, he may decide to cooperate. On the other hand, don't be in the habit of bugging the child. Serve a reasonable portion and let him alone. If he doesn't eat, just forget dessert. If he complains, send him away from the table, firmly but without anger.

Adopting a more relaxed attitude at mealtimes may require you to examine some of the expectations you hold concerning how, what, and how much your children eat. The following guidelines by associate editor Julie Oliver may help you take a new look at some of your standards—and perhaps to decide that their nutritional (or social) value is not worth the emotional upset required to maintain them. In other words, how much are you really willing to pay to get Johnny outside of five spoonfuls of strained peas?

- Try to keep your worry about the whole subject to an absolute minimum. Ulcers aren't healthy, either!
- Maintain an open but questioning attitude towards all nutritional advice, including ours. A lot of it may have some merit, but none of it carved in stone.
- "You are what you eat": Yes; but consider all the differences among people. One diet can't be right for all of us.
- Think "plain." Fancy gourmet meals look like you're really trying, but children are usually very suspicious of them.
- Try to avoid camouflage unless you're sure you can get away with it. The teen who discovers wheat germ in the chocolate pudding may never eat another dish of it.
- Don't expect your children to enjoy everything you cook. The noodle dish that reminds you of cozy days in the old farmhouse may look and taste like mush to your child.
- Set mealtimes to suit your family needs, not social custom. Dinner at four o'clock is fine if that works for all of you.
- There are no laws governing what food should be eaten when. If your family thinks chicken noodle soup is a fine breakfast food, your only problem is keeping plenty of soup on hand. Certain foods for certain times of the day is a rut, not a commandment.
- If you must hold a "kangaroo court" at the dinner table, do it when you're not eating a meal.
- Treat your children at the table with the same courtesy that you would use for guests. You wouldn't point out to Aunt Hilda, right in the middle of her scrambled eggs, that she obviously hadn't cleaned her nails in three weeks.
- Think about the things you say to your children about eating. Put yourself in their shoes. How would you feel if someone suddenly lunged at you yelling, "No matter how long it takes, you can just sit there until all those peas are gone."
- Don't give your whole family heartburn over a ten-year-old and two ounces of that green leafy vegetable.
- Be slow to banish any foods from your home. "NO SOFT DRINKS EVER" could turn cola into a forbidden fruit and your child into an insatiable cola sneak. Sometimes it's better to encourage moderation.
- Keep your responsibilities firmly in mind. It's your responsibility to provide the food; which and how much of it to eat is your child's responsibility.

FEEDING YOUR OLDER INFANT

Before children reach the age at which they "eat," they go through ages at which they have "feedings." Each age presents its own challenges to the parent.

The First Five Months

In the beginning, there is a hungry mouth and milk; but sooner or later your baby needs other foods as well. The two major questions facing mothers are: "Is baby ready for solids?" and, perhaps even more important, "Are *you* ready?" When your baby is two to three months old is usually a good time to start preparing yourself. If you're convinced that three months is too late to begin, and if you aren't a very allergic family, simply move your preparations up accordingly. By the time you're ready, your baby probably will be too.

Before you get into what the "experts" say on when to introduce other foods (their opinions vary tremendously), try to adopt a relaxed perspective on the whole issue. Julie Oliver's suggestions may help:

- Cultivate a casual, devil-may-care attitude about the whole process.
- Don't advertise your doubts about your ability to feed your baby successfully to your family and friends; only your pediatrician needs to know that you are not completely in control of the situation at hand.
- Either pick your most relaxed time of the day as "feeding time," or decide to forget a schedule and handle each day as it comes.
- Pick a location that's easy to clean and aimed away from your new carpet or unwashable wallpaper.
- Steadfastly refuse to join the highly competitive sport of baby feeding. Convince yourself that it is totally irrelevant to you and your baby that six-month-old Horace down the block eats corn on the cob.
- Repeat to yourself frequently: "All rules are made to be broken, especially rules about feeding children."
- Remember that there are very few absolutes when it comes to the food your baby must eat. And the need for strained peas is not one of those absolutes.
- Provide yourself with a large apron and a small spoon, a large amount of patience and a small number of rules and expectations.

When Should You Start Your Baby on Solid Foods?

By "solid" foods we mean, of course, pureed or homogenized foods at this age. Ask any three experts when to start your baby on solid foods and you are likely to get three different answers. Our first expert is a highly regarded and experienced mother of six who starts her babies on solid foods very early:

I start my babies on a little rice cereal when they are seven to ten days old, just for the experience of eating solid foods—even if they get only a little nutrition out of it. Of my six children, three were put on rice cereal at ten days and they were very good eaters later. The other three, for a variety of reasons, were not started on cereal until they were between one to two months old, and they were very poor eaters. Even when I offered them new foods all they wanted was a bottle.

Dr. William Foster disagrees strongly: "To subject the infant's relatively immature digestive tract to a large number of foreign proteins in the form of early solids seems illogical, time consuming, and often inconvenient." The reason Dr. Foster objects is that as a pediatric allergist he sees a large number of children who may have had their allergies made worse by a too early an introduction of solids, especially from highly allergenic eggs and citrus juice.

If you have a family history of food allergy, you may want to heed Dr. Foster. If you have a bunch of hungry babies, you may decide to go with the mother of six. I usually suggest that bottle-fed babies be started on solids with the spoon at about one month, and breastfed babies at about three months. The trouble is that the babies sometimes ignore our advice! So the best time to start is when your baby is ready.

Teaching Baby to Eat Solids

Do babies have to be taught how to feed themselves? Some do and some don't; many babies let parents know when they're ready to eat solid food by feeding themselves. If your baby needs a little assistance, Dr. Charles Hoffman advocates teaching by example:

Take a few pieces of food from your baby's tray and eat them. Your baby will soon begin to imitate you and eat, rather than play. Most babies have a problem with a spoon. When they get it about two inches from the mouth, the tension in the wrist often turns it over. The best approach is to sit behind him with your arm around him and near his hand so he won't pull away. You can then help him keep from spilling the food during those last two inches—and in a short time he'll be able to do it himself.

At this age, some foods are good, others are best avoided. Good foods for initial self-feeding are arrowroot cookies, graham crackers, and soft teething biscuits. Even though a large piece may seem to choke the baby when it falls into the throat, a soft crumbly cookie will quickly break apart, becoming smooth and easy to swallow. Crisp toast, hard teething biscuits, and soda crackers should be withheld until the baby can chew more efficiently. Soft bread should never be given to a baby, because it may form a large wad which could obstruct breathing if it should fall into the throat.

Five months is a good age at which to offer juice—in a small cup rather than in a bottle. Some pediatricians advise that fresh, frozen, or canned juices are as good as "baby" juices. They are usually less expensive. For an allergic baby, you may want to avoid most juices anyway. If the baby has never associated the taste of juice with a bottle, there will be less rejection of the cup when you offer juice rather than milk. And, as one mother said, "I prefer to give my babies juice from a cup. Once they have teeth, juice (if put into a bottle the child is given when he goes to bed) can contribute to tooth decay."

Five to Twelve Months

Just about the time you get the hang of heating up little drabs of smooth food and adjust to all those tiny bottles in your refrigerator, it's time to advance to the next stage: food with hunks. This stage is followed, sometimes quite quickly, by full graduation to table food. If you observe "chewing" motions of the jaws from five months on, the baby is probably ready for a trial of canned junior foods or small tastes of soft vegetables and fruits which have been mashed with a fork rather than completely pureed. If the baby enjoys the taste and accepts the food, even though it's not as smooth as usual, you may gradually substitute table food for baby food. (Foods need not be bland. Most babies show a decided preference for seasoned table food as soon as they learn to handle the coarser textures and small lumps.) The appearance of teeth has nothing to do with a baby's ability to swallow small tender pieces of food, so don't wait for teeth to come in. Most babies, after five months, can digest anything edible they can swallow. Dr. Richards cautions: "A little gagging should cause no concern as long as you avoid hard and crisp things such as celery, raw carrots, raw apple, nuts, crisp bacon, and large tough pieces of meat."

Preparing Your Own Baby Food

If you have the time and energy to prepare your own baby food, fine. Although in rare cases some commercial food additives may bother a baby, the major advantage to home-prepared baby food is economy—and whatever security you may get from knowing you made the food yourself. Leftover vegetables and fruits from your family meal can be put through the blender or a baby food grinder and then frozen in an ice-cube tray. Later, you can thaw out one or two cubes at a time, as you need them. A blender is invaluable in preparing baby foods of high quality and relatively low cost, if you follow these basic principles:

• Use the minimum amount of water needed for cooking the food. Minerals and vitamins can be lost if the cooking liquid is thrown out, so incorporate as much of the cooking liquid in the preparation of the food as possible in order to insure maximum retention of nutrients.

• Always add some of the liquid to your blender before adding any of the food This will enable the blender to work at its maximum performance with less need to stop, mix, or stir, in order to get the material moving in the blender.

• Meats require more liquid and a longer blending period (four to eight minutes) than fruits and vegetables. To get them smooth and creamy, add liquid gradually and blend well. Stop the machine several times, and with a spoon or spatula make a "pocket" in the bottom of the mixture and pour your liquid into it, then blend some more. Blending time and the amount of extra liquid needed will depend on how much liquid is absorbed by the food, and upon how well it was drained.

• When following a recipe, start out with the amount of liquid suggested, although more or less liquid may be required, depending on the particular food used. Add it gradually, alternating the addition of liquid with the addition of food. If you accidentally get it too thin or runny, it can easily be thickened with dry baby cereal.

• Once prepared, the foods can be placed in baby food jars, or in any small refrigerator container, and stored in the freezer. It is best to defrost them on a rack in the refrigerator rather than out at room temperature in order to prevent possible spoilage. In the refrigerator, they will defrost in a day. Once defrosted, they should be kept refrigerated, and will usually last a few days before they will spoil.

BABY FOOD RECIPES

These examples may help you begin to develop your own recipes:

Lamb

1½ lb. ground lamb   1½ cup water
1 pinch of salt

Thoroughly cook the lamb, by browning, in a fry pan. Drain off excess fat. Place ⅓ of the lamb and ½ cup water into a blender. Blend well. Add second ⅓ portion of lamb, a pinch of salt, and ½ cup of water to blended lamb. Blend again. Add last ⅓ portion of lamb and ½ cup water and blend, thoroughly, until creamy. Makes 3½ cups of prepared lamb.

Egg Yolks (after six months of age)

6 hard cooked egg yolks   7 tablespoons water

Add half the water and half the eggs to the blender. Blend for a minute. Then add remaining water and liquid to blender and complete the blending. Makes 1 cup.

Carrots

1 lb. fresh carrots   1¼ cups water with a pinch of salt

Brush carrots clean with a vegetable brush. Cut into half-inch pieces and bring to a boil in salted water. Simmer tightly covered for 11–15 minutes or until tender. Drain water from carrots by pouring through a colander, with a bowl underneath to collect liquid. There will be approximately 1 cup of liquid. Place half the water in the blender and add half the carrots and blend. Add the remaining water and carrots; blend again. Makes 3 cups.

Peas

1 16-ounce can of peas

Pour *entire* can into blender. Blend for 1–3 minutes, or until consistency is creamy. Makes approximately 2 cups.

Applesauce

For very small babies, it is simplest to take the commercially prepared cans of applesauce and blend them briefly in the blender. Dump contents of the entire can into the blender and smooth out the lumps. Older babies can probably take it straight from the can. This is much less expensive than buying the small jars of commercially prepared baby food.

The most convenient blender for preparing baby food is the type that has small blender jars in which the food can be both blended and stored. But you don't have to have an expensive blender; a baby food grinder works very well and can be purchased inexpensively.

Is Homemade Baby Food Harmful?

A baby food company questioned the safety of homemade baby food, citing the danger of nitrates from the water. The company also noted that homemade baby foods contain less vitamin C—because the commercial products have vitamin C added. However, the Committee on Nutrition for the American Academy of Pediatrics pointed out that only very young infants under two and one-half months old might be damaged by nitrates, and that no nutritional advantage or disadvantage has been demonstrated for supplementary solids at this age. They urged care in preparation and storage of fresh foods, and were not eager to feed small infants fresh spinach, beets, or carrots because of the innately high nitrate content in such fresh vegetables—although no harm from them has been reported. There have been cases of nitrate poisoning from well water on farms where nitrates are used as fertilizer. Enough nitrate combines with the blood to give the individual a bluish cast. However, carefully prepared homemade baby foods are generally nutritious and safe and may contain less unneeded salt, sugar, and food additives than commercial products.

Questions and Answers

The *Guide* editors asked a number of pediatricians and mothers to respond to the most asked questions about feeding an infant. Here are the responses (including some from *The Guide*'s editors), untainted by any hint of consensus!

How much food variety, and how many daily meals, does a baby need?

Small infants are often content with only one or two meals a day. By seven months, most babies are well satisfied to eat just three times a day, having learned quickly the diet patterns already established in their households. Let your baby tell you how many meals are enough. More than three meals a day of solid food is seldom desirable— *Thomas J. Conway, M.D.*

Many babies—and even some adults—eat five or six times a day if you include mid-afternoon and bedtime snacks. I don't take the three meals a day advice too literally. Some babies may need to eat more often—*Glenn Austin, M.D.*

How much variety should you serve?

Many foods are acquired tastes; and when new foods are presented, the baby will balk until he has become used to the taste. You can train him to accept new foods by offering a taste of the new food at breakfast—if he cries, quit. Repeat it at lunch until he objects, and again at supper. Within a week, most children will acquire a taste for the new food and accept it readily. Start a new food every week or so to expand his range of tastes—*Charles Hoffman, M.D.*

When a baby rejects the taste or texture of a new food, mix it with a favored fruit or cereal rather than discard the whole jar. When disguising doesn't work, just don't give it again. There is nothing a baby "must" eat, nor is there any essential nutrient which cannot be provided by substituting something different.—*John C. Richards, M.D.*

When should I feed my baby?

What time of day you feed a baby solids doesn't matter except to you, so pick a time when there are few distractions in the house. Avoid those times when the baby is ravenous for milk. There is no need to offer food more than once a day until the baby accepts it willingly. Some babies learn to eat quickly, some slowly. An experienced mother will usually have less difficulty than a new mother, but even the most resistant babies eventually learn to enjoy food if they are encouraged but not forced to eat it during the early months.—*John C. Richards, M.D.*

Small infants are often easier to spoon-feed immediately after a good sleep. They are relaxed, pleasant, and eager to please.—*Robert F.L. Polley, M.D.*

At this stage, the idea is to get baby used to eating solids, not to provide three solid meals a day. Don't worry about keeping to a schedule, skipping days, or waiting a week or two before letting the baby try again.—*Julie Stone Oliver*

I prefer a schedule of 10:00 a.m., 2:00 p.m., and 6:00 p.m., later changed to 8:00 a.m., 12:00 Noon, and 6:00 p.m. That way you don't have to vacillate—just do it and get it over with.—*Charles Hoffmann, M.D.*

What is the best way to get food into my baby?

Since babies aren't born with silver or any other kind of spoons in their mouths, they don't know what to do with that thing in their mouths except to suck on it. As you will quickly learn, sucking is *not* the way to get the cereal in, but it is a dandy way to have it spewed back out. You will soon develop your own techniques, but some tips may help avoid frustration in your first tries.—*Julie Stone Oliver*

Prepare a thin mixture of rice and oatmeal, using one teaspoon of dry cereal and one-half ounce of formula, breast milk, or water with a little honey or sugar. Hold the baby's head back, looking almost straight up, so that gravity will help carry the cereal mixture into the throat. Using a narrow spoon, put a small amount of cereal on the tip; and then touch the lips with the spoon. This will cause the mouth to open. Gently, but quickly, push the spoon over the tongue into the back of the mouth where the baby can suck on the spoon to swallow the food. Have the spoon far enough into the mouth so that when the tongue comes forward to suck, the food won't all be pushed back out. If he takes the first bite without difficulty, continue with more until, by fussing or spitting, the baby tells you to stop. If the baby is unhappy with the whole process, stop for now, and try it another day.—*John C. Richards, M.D.*

Another trick is to place the spoon on the upper lip so that when the tongue comes up and out the food can be dropped on the middle of the tongue. It will then be carried to the back of the throat when the tongue is retracted. If the baby refuses to eat from the spoon, try to calm him with an ounce of milk, and then try the spoon again. If unsuccessful today, try tomorrow. Trying to force the feeding may cause vomiting, or the process may create a "cheek holder" who stores the food in the cheek and doesn't swallow it. Forcing a baby to eat can sometimes lead to overeating and obesity at a later age, as the child associates eating with pleasing his parents.—*Isaac Reid, Jr., M.D.*

Are there any foods I should not feed my baby?

It is worth repeating that you should not give babies or toddlers hard raw vegetables or fruit, nuts, or large pieces of meat before they are two years old, for they may cause choking. Another important factor in deciding what to feed your baby is his possible allergic reactions. Your decisions on when and how many solids you will offer should reflect your family history. If there is a food allergy on either side of the family tree, there is a greater chance that an early introduction of solids will lead to development of allergies in your baby—and in that case you should proceed with caution. If not, you still have to ask, "What will the baby gain by a big variety?" The answer is: "Little or nothing." I feel it is unwise to offer highly allergenic foods like eggs or citrus juices before a baby is six months old. Avoid mixed foods until the baby has had all of the component foods separately. If he doesn't tolerate a mixed food, you have no idea of which food it was that caused the reaction—and there can be over thirty different substances in some of those cans! (One point about the meat and vegetable mixes: There isn't enough meat mixed with the vegetables to do much good. It is best to use the all meat variety, or, when the child is older, high-meat-dinners.)—*Glenn Austin, M.D.*

On the possible relationship between allergies in later life and the easy introduction of solid foods, doctors disagree. Pediatrician Sid Rosin contends:

Although allergy occurs in infants, it is a relatively infrequent problem in the first six months of life. The anxieties created over newborn allergies are unwarranted, and the preventative regimes suggested by allergy enthusiasts are usually unnecessary. There are very few families that do not have some history of allergy, and yet their infants are seldom allergic.

I recommend that breastfeeding mothers not eat shell fish or chocolate. Still, even with a strong family history of allergy, I find very few babies who react with rash, upset stomach, diarrhea, or colic. I suggest parents start solid foods—usually cereal or banana—at the age of one or two months. Orange juice I recommend at one month: one teaspoon per ounce of water, and increased gradually until there are equal parts of juice and water. About one-third of my patients don't tolerate this mixture very well; but this itself is important information for parents to have. Vegetables should be introduced at three months, fruits at four months. At five or six months, parents should introduce hard boiled egg yolk, even in an allergic family—but I avoid egg white products until ten to twelve months. I recommend cereal feeding, and the early introduction of egg yolk to increase iron input. For the same reason, meat and meat soups should be started at five months.

Pediatric allergist William Foster is more cautious. He says: "Egg yolk is highly allergenic and doesn't need to be given as an iron source if cereal and meat are part of a baby's diet. Why offer orange juice if so many babies can't tolerate it? Vitamin C is either in the formula or in a vitamin supplement. Some allergies induced by a hasty introduction of solids may not show up until much later, so the fact that there are no immediate symptoms is not a good argument for the early introduction of egg or citrus."

Until infants are over six months of age, their intestines absorb almost undigested foods. It has been found that breastfed babies from highly allergenic families have fewer allergies by age two than those fed cow's milk and early solids.

For a full list of foods high in iron, see *The Parents' Medical Manual*. For a summary of when, how, and if to introduce solid foods at this age, the rule of thumb seems to be: smooth texture, not too hot, not too cold, and not too many.

Feeding the Toddler and Preschooler

This is the age when many children present their parents with eating problems. Rumors are bandied about from time to time concerning toddlers who sit down three times a day; eat everything on their plates in a quiet, mannerly fashion; and never, ever beg for snacks between meals. Many believe these rumors to be myths. Actually, such toddlers aren't myths—although they are very rare. Such "chowhounds" sometimes seem like bottomless pits, and the satisfaction of seeing them "eat well" soon pales. Whether your toddler is a "chowhound" or a finicky eater, the toddler stage is a good time to start some mealtime house rules. Make up your own list and use it as a foundation to build on and modify as your child matures:

- Allow nothing between meals except a little fruit or milk.
- Limit milk to twenty-four ounces per day. Half this much is enough.
- Limit juice to four ounces per day (real juice, no "juice drinks").
- Serve small portions: allow seconds.
- Keep desserts (except for special occasions) to small portions of fruit. Pudding or custard are really not needed.
- Permit meal-skipping, but then don't allow any eating until the next meal.
- Make no *comments* about your child's eating habits.

• Offer food at regular times—up to three regular meals and three between-meal snacks: midmorning, midafternoon, bedtime.

Questions About Eating Habits of Toddlers

How can I make sure my children get three well-balanced meals a day?

It is unfortunate that so much emphasis has been placed by nutritionists upon the need for a "daily balanced diet," or for a "hearty breakfast" and a "good hot dinner." Children under five years grow slowly and gain only three or four pounds a year. They need to balance their diets over a two-to-three month period—not daily, or even weekly. What they need daily are some carbohydrates (sugar and starches) for energy, and most parents will agree that it's seldom difficult to get a child to eat sweets and starches.

Most small children prefer the "same old things" rather than accepting or even tasting new and unfamiliar foods. Furthermore, children are "streak eaters." That is, they will eat large amounts of a particular food for a few days and then suddenly refuse to touch the food which has previously been a favorite. Offer a small child small portions of whatever has been prepared. Don't expect him to eat each food served. When fixing a meal for the child alone, offer a choice and let him decide, within reasonable limits, what he'd like. Nutritionists urge a variety in the diet, but children rarely listen to nutritionists. Still, a variety should be offered; and most children will balance their diet over a week or so if given a reasonable choice.—*John C. Richards, M.D.*

It should not be your concern whether or how much your child eats. It is up to you to provide the right foods; and then, within reason, to allow the child to eat whatever he wishes. If he refuses to eat because he doesn't want something you feel should be part of the meal, then you can merely stop the meal whenever he chooses to stop eating. Provide small servings so that the child can have a sense of accomplishment. Allow him to come back for more, rather than to take too much and then refuse to eat it all. Above all, make no comment about whether the child eats or doesn't eat. There should be no bribing, no begging, and no coercing about eating. You don't have to appease, play games, or use undue force.—*Marvin McClellan, M.D.*

Don't use dessert as a reward for eating, or refuse dessert as a punishment for not eating. When he eats, he's not "good," he's merely hungry; and when he doesn't eat, he's not "bad," he's just not hungry enough to want what was served.—*John C. Richards, M.D.*

Why has our toddler changed from having such a big appetite to having such a small appetite?

Babies under six months gain two pounds and grow one inch each month. In the second year, they only gain five pounds or so and grow three to four inches—compared with fifteen pounds and ten inches the first year. Therefore, since they grow one-third as much, they eat one-third as much. The appetite of a two-year-old is very small indeed compared to that of a four-month-old baby. By the age of three or four, the child's appetite picks up again somewhat. It is normal for a two-year-old to eat only one decent meal each day—they just pick at the other two meals. Remember to allow your child to get hungry.—*William Misbach, M.D.*

Our mealtimes have turned into the "screaming hour." How can we have some peace and still do something about our child's awful manners?

Until three or four years of age, table manners are relatively unimportant. When children are constantly corrected for messy eating habits, the tension, anxiety, and fear which result can destroy their appetite. Your child may become so negatively conditioned that, even when hungry, he loses any interest in food as soon as he reaches the dinner table, and then regains it soon after the tension of the dinner hour is over. He then starts the begging for snacks—a practice parents find annoying but difficult to refuse. In teaching desirable eating habits, be reasonable in your expectations, but be firm when necessary. Establish rules which you can live with; but do your best to avoid nagging and scolding at the dinner table. Mealtime can and should be a pleasant experience for the entire family.—*John C. Richards, M.D.*

My toddler just plays with the food after the first few bites. Should I take over the feeding?

No! As growth slows down, a child's appetite decreases and changes, and he will refuse previously accepted foods. His independence and stubbornness will doom to failure your efforts to make him eat more. Avoid distractions at mealtime, and take the child down from the highchair when it is obvious that playing with the food is more interesting to him than eating. Don't worry when your child eats little, or nothing, at some meals. He probably just isn't hungry; and if left alone, he will make it up at the next meal or during the next day. If a child is hungry, he will feed himself. Your efforts to feed him simply slow down his self-feeding desire. Try not to make him dependent on you.—*John C. Richards, M.D.*

How important is it to insist our children eat three meals a day?

Since we usually serve meals three times a day, children must learn eventually to adapt to this routine. Some do so easily; some stubbornly resist routines and want to eat only whenever they are hungry. Establish what you consider is a reasonable mealtime schedule, but don't expect your children to always finish every meal.—*John C. Richards, M.D.*

Our children beg for snacks at all hours of the day. Should we forbid all snacking?

If snacking is permitted, children quickly learn to get their own and can be found eating at all hours of the day except, of course, at mealtime. It is best to stop this habit before it gets out of hand. A small mid-morning and mid-afternoon snack may be offered, but that is all. Don't insist that a snack be given only if the meal is eaten well, for this makes the snack a reward. Requests for extra milk or juice between meals should be refused just as firmly as when the request is for cookies or candy.—*John C. Richards, M.D.*

Our child is unable to sit through a meal. What should we do?

Give such children smaller feedings, and feed them more frequently. Each meal should consist of two or three bites and a small drink. Children get some solids this way, learn to eat, and can gradually be brought back to more complete meals.—*Charles Hoffman, M.D.*

I know my toddler can't be hungry all the time. Why is he always asking for food?

Small children, when bored, will frequently beg for or demand snacks as a means of getting attention. When you're busy, you may often give in to these persistent demands just to keep your child occupied and quiet. This frequently sets up a pattern which can lead to poor eating habits and potentially poor nutrition in later childhood and adult life. If a child snacks within an hour or two of the next meal, he will spoil his appetite. On the other hand, he may need a mid-afternoon snack. If a friend drops in and you offer a cold drink or a cup of coffee, it would be unfair to refuse to allow your child to snack while you sit there having yours. When a friend offers a cookie, it's unreasonable to expect your child to turn it down. Don't use food treats, such as candy and cookies, to reward good behavior too much of the time. Furthermore, don't tell your child how much he has pleased you or how "good" he is when he finishes his whole meal. Compulsive overeating and craving for sweet foods usually result from early childhood experiences. A child who has been made to believe either that he must eat to gain your love, or that candy and other sweets represent the rewards he receives for being a good person, will often use food to later compensate for feelings of insecurity, inadequacy, or failure.—*John C. Richards, M.D.*

Nutrition experts say a good breakfast is essential, but our children rarely have even a glass of juice. How harmful is this?

Breakfast is often ignored by older children and teenagers because they sleep late and then rush out of the house to reach school before the first bell rings. A small morning meal to help prevent mid-morning let-down is desirable. On the other hand, I know of no concrete evidence to support the belief that a hearty balanced breakfast is essential for good school performance or for adequate nutrition. Obviously, it is wise to encourage children to eat something before leaving for school, but to insist upon a large breakfast is unnecessary. The teenager who refuses even a glass of juice is probably best left alone. He'll get his own snack when hunger strikes later in the morning. —*John C. Richards, M.D.*

KEY POINTS ABOUTS FEEDING, EATING, NUTRITION, AND OBESITY

- Eating comes naturally to people, though you might not think so when you hear the hassle at some dinner tables. So relax and don't try to force it; you rarely can and really shouldn't.
- Most children, given an adequate choice and no pressure, end up eating enough of the right kind of foods to insure good health.
- Happy people eat what they need for their bodies. They don't eat just for emotional satisfaction—or refuse to eat to oppose a parent's power. Keep mealtimes happy events.
- One person's food is another poison. It isn't simply a matter of taste; it may be a matter of digestion or allergy. Don't insist on treating your children as if they are assembly-line products. Give them choices whenever you can, and respect their idiosyncracies—just as you hope people will respect yours.
- If you are concerned about your child's nutrition, keep a list of what he or she actually eats and drinks for a week or two. Then check out the nutritional contents in *The Parents' Medical Manual*. Take your list and your child to your child's doctor and let him help you decide if the child's diet is adequate.
- Relax a bit. Remember that the human is about the most viable and adaptable organism ever to inhabit this earth. We have a penchant for survival. Think of how hungry some Chinese must have been when they started eating soup made out of birds' nests. They survived—and left a gourmet food as a heritage.

TOILET TRAINING

There are many ways of "skinning a cat"—and just as many ways for toilet training a child. We present several techniques that have generally worked well for the patients of the authors. You will find conflicts in the various methods—but also some agreed-upon principles. We hope one of these methods works well for your child. If not, check with your doctor—sometimes it takes very individual assessment, thought, and advice to come up with an answer.

Principles for Toilet Training

- Regardless of the child's age, don't force the issue. This is one situation in which the child can and should successfully control his own actions for himself. "You can lead a horse to water but you can't make him drink."
- Do not punish or scold a child who does not use the toilet.
- Conscious control of urine and bowel movements is often not developed until near the end of the second year of life. "Catching" excretions in the toilet at an earlier age is merely a conditioning process.
- All children eventually learn to use the toilet, so don't let early training become a status symbol.
- Never force a child to stay on the toilet.
- If he refuses or is afraid to use the toilet, stop trying for a few weeks and then try again.

If your child resists or is late in learning to use the toilet, don't become upset. Keep in mind this thought from Dr. Robert Burnett: "Everybody learns to go to the toilet; it is not much of an accomplishment. A good deal of needless time and parental anxiety are spent over this. It *is* an accomplishment to teach the child good behavior; a parent's concern is better directed toward that aspect of child raising."

The Old Fashioned Method

Dr. Sid Rosin recommends an "old fashioned" but casual approach to conditioning a baby to the toilet:

When the infant is able to sit well at approximately seven months, he is placed on a small toilet seat for five minutes after breakfast. If he rejects sitting at this time, stop the procedure and forget it for one or two months, at which time it can be tried again. If he does not wish to sit for the entire five minutes, do not make strenuous efforts to restrain him, although you can entertain him if you wish with talk, rattles, or musical toys. After five minutes, and no longer, remove him without any emotion. At no time, applaud or reprimand him. I specifically forbid "good boy" and "bad boy."

It is amazing how many infants seem to enjoy this interlude, actually cooperate, and in a few months have a daily evacuation after breakfast. Increased attempts at training are not recommended until well into the second year, when those children who have reacted favorably are encouraged to sit on the toilet after each meal. I must reiterate and reemphasize that all attempts at training must be casual, that achievement is not important, and that with any rejection

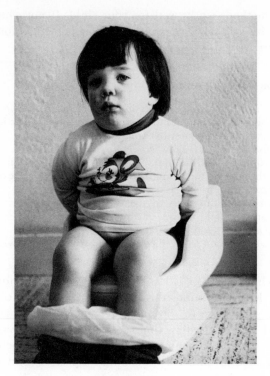

Figure 30

by the child, all attempts are stopped. I suggest my plan only when there is complete acceptance of this attitude by the parents.

The "Positive" Approach

The early conditioning advocated by Dr. Rosin can be time-consuming and frustrating when the infant has no regular pattern for emptying the bowel. Others advocate waiting until near two years and using a positive approach to teach the child to use the toilet, as outlined by Dr. Marvin McClellan:

> Parents don't really train their children to go to the toilet; rather, they convince children that this is the way it should be. Start by catching the child when he shows telltale signs, such as a red face and grunting, that indicate he is about to have a bowel movement or to urinate, and put him on the toilet right away. Also, try to "catch him" by putting him on the toilet several times a day—such as on arising, after meals, or at bedtime. As his attention span is short, don't keep him on the toilet for over two minutes. While he is on the toilet, don't

give him books, food or toys; the toilet is a place for elimination, not for socialization and entertainment.

To teach the child that going to the toilet is desirable, you can't be altogether permissive. Let him know that it pleases you "You went to the toilet, thank you." A more effective soft selling technique is to say: "If I were you, I'd like to go to the toilet," or "I'd like to stay dry." Soon the child forgets the phrase "If I were you" and remembers the last part—"I'd like to go to the toilet." Then, having convinced himself concerning this, he'll go willingly one day.

Wait Until They're Older

Mother Ruth Poarch waits until her children consistently wake up in the morning with dry diapers before she tries to toilet train them. She advises: "It requires a lot of patience to wait; but stay in there, for they do grow up." Some pediatric gastroenterologists (a specialist on the intestines) believe you should never make the child feel you want him to go to the toilet, for that is a subconscious demand rather than a request.

That a parent demanding performance can lead to problems is documented by a case of Dr. John Richards:

Don't be too insistent that your child sit on the toilet regularly after eating. I know of a twelve-year-old boy who had to strain to have a bowel movement every time and the results were small and stringy. Diet changes, stool softeners, and bulk producers didn't help; and I was about to order x-rays of the bowel when his mother casually wondered out loud how he could have a bowel problem when she still faithfully followed her previous doctor's instructions—given when the child was eight months old—and put him on the "potty" after each meal! She still sent him to the bathroom after each meal with firm instructions to stay on the toilet until he had a bowel movement. It is amazing what can happen when people take instructions too literally.

A New Way to Toilet Train

I believe there is a better way to toilet train a toddler rationally. To understand the feelings involved, it helps to look at things from the child's standpoint. Put yourself in his shoes. You are a midget in a world of giants. Everyone in your world can do anything you can do better. Life is full of frustrations. The giants run your life, interfere with your freedom, and are aggravatingly patronizing. Suddenly "your" giant swoops down, picks you up, lays you on the bed, takes your pants off, sets you on a toilet which looks five feet high, and then stands there watching you. Can you think of a more constipating experience? Because of this, the methods offered don't always work. When they don't, this one may be of help.

I feel that several things are required before a child can be taught or induced to use the toilet:

* He must be able to control his urine and stool.
* He must be able to get his pants down for himself, by himself.
* He must be able to get on a toilet for himself, by himself.
* Finally, but most important, he must *want* to go.

What all this means is that a child must go to the toilet for himself, not for his mother. After all, who does mother go to the toilet for? Self-motivation is the key. It must be the toddler's problem, not the parents' (or grandparents' or babysitters'!). Therefore, try to make going to the toilet a privilege, not a duty. Dress the child so he can get his clothes off without help. Put him in "big boy" training pants and show him how to get them off himself. Have a toddler potty or a step stool so he can get on the toilet by himself without help. Avoid interfering "duck heads" or deflectors on the front of the seat. Show him once or twice how to get there. Allow him some other privilege such as playing in an area not allowed previously or doing something which is new and exciting to him. Turn him loose. Yes, he will mess his pants. When he does, pick him up, casually and sympathetically, put him on the bed, take off his pants, clean him up, and put him back in diapers. Tell him it's all right; he is just a baby, not big enough for "big boy" pants. In diapers, he is not allowed on the toilet or allowed the "big boy" pants or the other play privilege. Be relaxed: Don't do it as if you are disgusted. Make it *his* problem, not yours. Be neutral. Just follow the rules. In a few days, re-offer the privileges: "Do you want to be a big boy today?" If so—training pants and privileges. If not, diapers. But stick to your rules and only offer privileges that you can and will withdraw if he doesn't use the toilet. And don't worry: He won't go to college with diapers.

Train Them at Three Months

Just when I thought I had heard every conceivable way of toilet training, two contributors and a mother in my practice added to my education. First, psychiatrist Irving Philips, in writing for us about permissiveness, quoted from Holt's pediatric text of the 1920 era showing that the idea of toilet training at age three months by routinely sitting infants on the toilet after meals was advocated by pediatricians. So grandmother is simply passing on advice that started with the professionals. It still is a form of conditioning rather than training, and a parent would certainly have to hate dirty diapers with a passion to go to all of that trouble.

Train Them With Candy in Four Hours

Then, a mother in my practice asked if I knew about a new method of toilet training in four hours. I hadn't, and was skeptical; so she brought me a book by psychologists Nathan Azrin and Richard Foxx that claims almost complete success in toilet training twenty-month-old children in half a day.[2] Their venture into the "down with diapers" field started by developing methods that work on a lot of retarded children. In fact, it worked so well that they decided to apply it to normal children. It is an interesting technique that our baby sitter used on one of my children years ago. She gave him candy when he would go. Admittedly her technique wasn't as sophisticated as that of the psychologists, who utilize "psychoanalytic emphasis," "Pavlovian learning," and "operant learning with reinforcers." In spite of this, to my surprise, I found their technique of some worth.

If you are really concerned, at least this method is better than spanking your child to get him to go to the toilet. I know of one pediatrician who advocates spanking for toilet training if it is needed. But we have seen failures from the spanking method leading to severe constipation, hostility, and physically ill children: I would rather have you try candy. The four hour method is an intense exercise in parenting and discipline that has broader application than a dry bottom. The technique requires a concentrated four hours of absolute attention to modifying the child's behavior. In that it can succeed, it offers an opportunity for the parent to learn some basic psychological skills and shows what can be done with a reasonable approach and determination.

Like all techniques reported as successful, it eliminates from its series those children on whom the technique isn't likely to work. The child has to be able to stay dry for a while, be able to control urination physically, and the child must not be stubborn. He or she must decide to carry out your instructions. And if you have blown it before and tried to force your child to stay on the toilet unsuccessfully, you may not be the right one to try this technique.

The technique utilizes a wetting doll to show the child how it all works, treats of candy and drinks, great praise, and an offer to please "friends who care." Our old baby sitter told our child that his mother and father would be very pleased. However, when our child found that we didn't give candy, he decided we weren't pleased enough, and quit for awhile until he decided it was more comfortable for him to stay dry. Still, there is worth in the many techniques: intense education with great attention to details; such as using a shirt that allows the small child to be able to get to the pants to take them off and put them on; the elimination of distractions; scolding the child when he is wet; praising him when he is dry; helping him teach his doll how to use the potty; teaching him how to take the pants off; sitting and watching for the child to urinate; teaching the child the concept of practice and dry runs; using the child's name before giving each instruction; waxing enthusiastic when he produces good results; having the child clean up the floor if he wets it; and then giving a diploma of potty training when success is achieved and followed up with later reinforcement. It is a lot of work and effort. The lesson is that it *can* take a lot of work and effort to get a child to behave; and that it *can* pay off.

I would like the technique better if they hadn't quoted a mother's reaction to her little boy saying, "Pee-pee, potty!" as "The sweetest sound she had ever heard." The mother in my practice who brought Azrin's book to me said it took her ten hours to succeed, and that the problems she encountered were: (1) Getting her child's full attention (like trying to lasso a butterfly); (2) The child was jealous of the doll on her potty; (3) She lost interest in the snacks after an hour, and they consequently lost their value as a reward. The mother said: "Dina is really proud of being dry. I must say, I think she was just plain ready—and that any method would have worked!"

Actually, the "four hour" method is somewhat similar in principle to mine as well as to that of my old baby sitter. You reward success and punish failure. Yes, there are 1,001 ways of raising children!

Lessons From Toilet Training

As you can see, the methods used to help or hinder a child muster the art of using a toilet vary considerably. Nevertheless, we all agree on some general principles which apply, whatever method you use:

1. Some children can be "conditioned" to the toilet before a year if the parent has the patience and drive and doesn't try to force the issue. Some of us question the worth of such early efforts.
2. Most babies seem unable to control bowel movements or urination consciously until around one and a half to two years of age; boys generally acquire this control later than girls.
3. There should be no social prestige or neighborhood sweepstakes for the mother of the baby who is trained earliest.
4. "Forcing" the issue with a baby gives him his first inkling that finally here is an issue *he* can win, for it requires *his* cooperation.
5. You probably shouldn't punish or reprimand a child for not going to the toilet, or react with disgust or anger when accidents occur.
6. Mothers with several children do not have the time to spend training their children to go to the toilet, and they find that their children toilet train themselves sooner or later.

If the parent does try to force the issue, the end result is likely to be constipation. To put the whole area of toilet training in perspective, ask yourself one basic question: Who do *you* go to the toilet for?

Problems

Many problems besides "how" may arise as you toilet train your child. A few are described below.

Constipation

It is not necessary to have a bowel movement once a day. Some people can go normally once a week without problems. Constipation exists if the stools are large and hard and if they hurt the child when he goes. Sometimes there will be blood on the bowel movement from a large stool splitting the anus and causing a fissure. Not infrequently, constipation exists when a child continually dirties his pants. Severe constipation can cause cramps, a distended stomach, and even a vague illness. Constipation, however, does not cause fever or vomiting. See *The Parents' Medical Manual* for further causes and treatment, including how to give an enema.

Fear of the Toilet

Some toddlers have great fear while sitting on the toilet seat because they have seen you flush it, and have seen that the contents are flushed away. Some are terribly afraid that they, too, will be flushed away, so they never flush the toilet while they are on it. This is a very real fear in some, and causes tenseness and constipation as a result. —*Bruce Valentine, M.D.*

Does Your Child Mess His Pants?

Sometimes children have bowel movements in their pants because they are deeply disturbed emotionally. Help may be required by a doctor or a child psychiatrist. However, most children who mess their pants are, in fact, suffering from constipation as the result of a long-standing failure to empty the rectum properly. The rectum, the end portion of the bowel, is not meant to contain feces all the time. Ordinarily, it becomes filled once or twice a day, when a wave of muscle action (peristalsis) forces food residues into it. This entry of bowel content into the previously empty rectum stretches it, giving the person a desire to empty the bowels. If he obeys this "call to stool" and empties the bowel, the rectum is again empty, waiting for a wave of peristaltic action, perhaps on the next day, to bring further bowel content into the rectum which will again cause the desire to defecate.

But if a child is too busy playing to obey the call when it comes, or if he is afraid of hurting himself because of a previous painful experience with a large, hard, constipated stool, or if he doesn't like to use the school lavatories, or if he holds off for any other reason, including fighting toilet training, the feeling that he wants to go to the toilet soon passes, leaving him with contents in his rectum which should have been evacuated. This soon leads to a chronically stretched, insensitive rectum that neither sends messages when it wants to be emptied nor has sufficient muscle power left to empty itself without external aid. The stage is then set for soiling the pants, which is simply an overflow of liquid feces that leaks around the chronic, firm accumulation of hard stool in the rectum. The child can honestly say that he doesn't really know when he wants to go to the toilet; and he can't do anything about it without help anyway. The parents usually don't believe him when he says this: and they often handle the situation with anger or punishment, all to no avail.

If you can understand how the situation has developed and can appreciate the need for a regularly emptied rectum, you will be able, in most cases, to help your child to regain normal regular habits. Seek the guidance of your doctor, who will probably arrange for the rectum to be emptied with enemas or suppositories and who may prescribe regular bowel softening agents to be given by mouth. It may take some time for the ill effects of such long-standing faulty habits to be corrected, but if you understand why it happened in the first place, and if you adopt a helpful attitude, you will be amazed at the improvement.—*Eric Sims, M.D.*

Playing With Bowel Movement

Sometimes a two-year-old will be very proud of his bowel movement, and will eat it or smear it on the wall. Disliking this activity is a learned response. Correct the child, but try not to be upset by it. The young child has control over very few things, but he controls his bowel movements. If you try to force him into toilet training, it will become next to impossible. It is not worth fighting over.—*Neil Henderson, M.D.*

SLEEP

Sleep seems most important when you don't have it. One of the first questions a parent asks is "How much sleep does my child need?" For school children, Dr. Merritt B. Low proposes the following schedule:

7:00 to 7:30 P.M.	First two grades
8:00 P.M.	Third and fourth grades
8:30 P.M.	Fifth and sixth grades
9:00 P.M.	Seventh and eighth grades
9:30 P.M.	Ninth and tenth grades

Dr. Low says:

> Variable needs must make his timing flexible: One half-hour
> to an hour later on weekends works well and provides a reward for the
> child. Of course, the schedule should be modified to suit the
> individual child and family. Infants usually sleep unless they are
> eating for the first few months and then gradually stay awake longer
> and longer. Toddlers usually should go down for two naps a day, and
> preschoolers for one nap a day. However, there are rare individuals
> who can get by with only a few hours sleep, even at the toddler
> age.
> A handy rule of thumb for both children and adults is that the
> individual has had enough sleep if he has no daytime sleepiness,
> jitteriness, fatigue, or impaired performance. It is interesting to see
> a sleepy parent who fits this description nicely, complaining that his
> or her bright-eyed alert child "won't sleep." Children often have sleep
> problems, but I suspect they are most often important only because
> they create interference with the parents' own sleep. The parents lie
> awake worrying about it while the child, usually not troubled by
> conscience and responsibility, catches productive cat naps. Some
> children, of course, have real sleep problems.

If one doesn't sleep enough, then a good medical examination or even a psychiatric examination may be in order. Children may awake because they have problems breathing due to plugged off noses or large tonsils; or they may wake up crying with headaches, earaches, stomach aches, leg aches, and other ailments—including nightmares. Others can't sleep because of fears or overexcitement. Then there are rare individuals who just don't need much sleep.

Problems With Sleep

Sleep itself is rarely a problem. Lack of sleep can be a problem—both to children and to their parents. If the child doesn't sleep or nap when he should, is this misbehavior? Not necessarily, says pediatrician Henry Richanbach:

> Variations in sleep patterns are normal, and are not caused by
> bad or malicious, developmentally aberrant children. Daytime naps
> and a continuous night sleep time are culturally imposed, and are,
> to me and to most parents, quite desirable. Nap times should be
> preserved, anyway—people don't learn to be alone if they are not
> asked and trained to be alone. They can sit and sing to the birds, if
> they wish, but both infant and mother need the time to recharge their
> batteries.

Of course, it may just be impossible to sleep because your home is too noisy. But assuming your home is quiet as a mausoleum, you may still have children who won't sleep. Dr. Merritt Low describes the problem for the one-to three-year-old:

> At around one year of age, the baby becomes aware of his individuality. He begins to talk, to run, and to manipulate people. He may become a night prowler, climbing into his parents' bed. Scolding, spanking, and "giving in" seem to aggravate such situations—and vacillating between several approaches is even worse. "Isolation" combined with calm firmness usually works well on most misbehavior at this age.
>
> It is a good idea, at this time, to insist on an after lunch rest period when you place the child in his own room. Let him play in his room if he wishes; if he is tired, he will go to bed.
>
> It is not really that important for the child to go to sleep—you can't force it anyway. But the "rest time" habit is important. In these years, there will be periods when sleep will be customary, alternating with several weeks or months of play, rest, and quiet without sleep.

But what if your child is a night prowler? How do you keep him or her in bed? The advice offered by Dr. John Richards has one sterling feature. It usually works!

> Mothers complain: "My child won't stay in his bed at naptime and at night. If I put him back, he won't stay. Spanking doesn't help, and the only way he'll sleep is for me to lie down with him or to bring him into my bed at night. I know this is wrong, but what else can I do?"
>
> Many children between the ages of one and two years will learn to climb out of the crib, a practice which is potentially both dangerous and disruptive to the rest of the family. The child might hurt himself in a fall. His roaming around when the parents are sleeping exposes him to many potentially dangerous situations both in and outside of the home. If he climbs into bed with the parents, this should be stopped immediately.
>
> A few simple rules will do much to prevent this troublesome problem. First, have the child sleep in the crib until at least two and one-half years of age. Second, always keep the crib mattress at its lowest level and the crib side all the way up after six months of age. Third, don't leave large stuffed animals and pillows in the crib for the child to climb on. The child may learn to go over the top in spite of these precautions. Buy or make a crib net which can be securely tied to cover the top of the crib. Not only does a net keep the child safely in bed, but it also has the effect of making it uncomfortable to stand up in the crib. As a result, the child will usually lie down and go back to sleep quickly. In spite of the objection sometimes raised that this sort of "caging in" may do drastic psychological damage, I

have always found good results when a net is used properly, particularly if the parents don't let the first two or three nights of listening to a screaming child wear them down. Almost all children accept the net within three nights. In some cases, they won't go to bed without it from then on.

Physical restraints, such as harnesses, bed straps, and restraining blankets, are potentially dangerous because of the risk that a child could strangle in a loose strap.

One of the bedtime issues is who controls whom at bedtime, says pediatrician Blackburn S. Joslin:

Many children will use sleep problems to "work" a parent. They play a game at bedtime of arguing for the fun and attention of the game rather than from a real need to be up.

The child should be put to bed when it is the proper time. Do not tell him he must go to sleep, for he may not be sleepy. If he is sleepy enough, he will go to sleep without your having to say so. But leave him alone, and do not allow him back out of his room once he is in bed. Chain lock the door if you must. Three simple principles help get the child to bed with fewer problems.

- Avoid a direct argument.
- Set up good basic rules and stick to them.
- Don't try to control those things the child controls himself (like going to sleep).

Another method of value is for you as parents to insist on time for yourselves. Specify a time period when the child must remain in his room so that the parents can have some time to themselves. There are fewer arguments if you give several alternatives to consider rather than giving a simple command. Instead of saying, "Go to bed," say: "Now is the time for Mother and Dad to have some time to themselves. You go to your room where you can read, color, rest quietly, or go to sleep." Whatever the decision the child makes, he ends up in his bedroom, away from the parents. He will go to sleep if he is sleepy unless he is receiving his parents' attention.

Dr. Merritt Low suggests:

A good way to stop a child from hurting himself when he crawls out of bed is to put the mattress on the floor. Let him sleep there. Then place a gate across the child's doorway, or, if he can circumvent that, use a hotel-type chain or "hook-and-eye" closure, out of reach, but with enough space to see out. Usually the child will accept such gadgetry at face value as proof of meaning business.

Locking a child in the bedroom with a net or a chain lock on the outside of the bedroom door doesn't sit well with some. Mother Ruth Poarch objected, commenting: "I don't believe a child should be locked in his room, terrified and caged; it is better to establish and stick to good basic rules." Although I admit I don't like locking children in their rooms either, I have seen more children physically and psychologically traumatized by parental anger and ineffective discipline than by being locked in the safe bedroom. Parents can get so mad that they either hate the child or hit the child or both. A chain lock is not the same as locking the door—the door is left open, and it does force the child to recognize that the parents mean business.

Bedtime Fears and Sleeping With Parents

Two frequent sleep problems are a child's fear of the dark and his desire to sleep with his parents. As in other areas of parenting, they evoke a variety of opinions. Dr. Neil Henderson offers his view on the child who is afraid to go to bed:

> Fear of separation is great, particularly if the mother is starting to work. This fear is most acute at bedtime, when he may cry or scream for hours, and be quiet only when mother is sitting next to him. The best treatment is prevention. Don't accept excuses which are used to avoid going to bed, such as asking for a drink of water. Tell him where Mom and Dad will be in the house in case he really does need anything. A two-year-old child will frequently climb out of bed by himself and go wherever the rest of the family is. At this time, he will be particularly cute, because he realizes that he must perform if he is to stay up with his parents. However, once the child is put to bed, make him stay there.
>
> If parents already have a two-year-old fearful about going to bed at night, ask your doctor for a sedative. Although phenobarbital is commonly used, it causes excitation in some children. Some children, by sheer will alone, may counteract any sedative. If this is the case, it may be necessary to sit at the child's side until he is fully asleep.
>
> You can also plan ahead for the times you will have to be out at night. Begin by going out for an hour, and then returning. This allows the child to become adjusted to a babysitter. Mother's quick return reassures him that she will always return. Then the time can gradually be increased.

Dr. John Richards says:

> I agree with most of this advice, but two of the techniques should only be used in extreme circumstances. Sedatives can only be a temporary relief to the harassed parents in need of a decent night's

sleep. Sitting at the child's bedside may pacify him, but if he later wakens to find his parent gone, he may feel he has been deserted. Furthermore, if the parent stays with the child, it may mean to the child that there really is something to fear.

Should you let your child sleep with you? "Yes!" argues Dr. A.S. Hashim:

> I believe that a child *should* be allowed to sleep with his parents. If you are hungry, you will eat. If you are frightened, you will need assurance and love. Occasionally, one child is more frightened than others at his age, because of this separation at night. To be "isolated" in a cell, with darkness or long shadows, can stir the poor child's imagination. He will surely holler and scream. If assurance by the parents (reading stories, and so on) doesn't work, and if the child seems to be very upset, I tell my patients to let the child sleep with them—for one to two hours—in order to give him psychological support. If such a child is denied his right, he will make life miserable for himself and for his parents; and it will take much longer until the "dust settles." It is not a matter of seeing if the parents or the child is the winner in this contest—there is no contest. It is a matter of a child who is scared stiff and shaking in his boots; and he wants his parents' love and understanding.

"No!" argues Dr. Henderson:

> A child should *never* be allowed to sleep in his parent's bed. It may seem the simplest solution at the time, particularly if the child is anxious and nervous, but it is difficult to get him to give up this security. The child should be brought back to his own bed and reassured. Talk with him and try to figure out what is bothering him. It is not necessary to keep children's doors open. If he is afraid, put a night light in the room, but do not let him become overly dependent on it. The parents must look for the underlying reason. A child's fear of the dark could persist into adult life.

A mother reviewing this argument commented that it isn't a contest, it is just showing him that his place isn't in bed with his parents. I have to support Dr. Henderson's position: Children should not sleep with their parents. I have, at times, seen psychological problems, usually competition by the child against the father for the possession of the mother. On the other hand, bedding with the parents surely happens without harm at times. Dr. Merritt Low suggests that "if a child is allowed to sleep with you for a specific reason—usually because of overwhelming fears—it should only be done if there is a built-in plan to terminate it. The plan adds to the child's security."

Prevention of Sleep Problems in the Three- to Four-Year-Olds

A child of three to four years is somewhat insecure and divisive, explains Dr. Low:

> He tries to play one parent against another. This phase of his development calls for carefully planned parental "togetherness" in handling many situations, including sleep problems which arise from:
>
> • Family arguments
> • Overstimulation from play
> • Excitement late in the day
> • Too much play with older children
> • Fears
>
> The three- to four-year-old is easily scared. A horror movie on television or an older youngster's surprising shout of "Boo!" may prevent the child from sleeping well at night. In fact, scare "play" should not be employed by anyone living with the child.
>
> Avoid unnecessary tension around the child, but let him learn gradually that there *are* surprises and shocks in life. Do not expect him always to tell you what's bothering him. Often, he may not know. Overfatigue at this age may contribute both to disturbed sleep and to the over-heavy sleep often associated with bed-wetting (enuresis).

Dr. Robert F.L. Polley recommends: "Take the child for a routine trip to the bathroom to empty the bladder at the parents' bedtime. This is a custom up to even seven years of age. There will be less bedwetting, fewer nightmares, and the child will sleep better."

Sleep Problems in the School Age Child

In the school age child, there are many factors which affect a child's sleep. Recognizing that his guidelines for the amount of sleep needed are only guidelines, and that some people need more and others less sleep, Dr. Low says you can help when problems occur:

> The school age ushers in the era of identification with the parent of the same sex, as well as the struggle for the development of conscience and values. This is an age associated with fantasy problems, dreams, nightmares, sleep walking, and delirium with febrile illnesses. Parents should give their child support by focusing on his strengths and abilities during this stage.
>
> As the child's conscience develops and life becomes harder, busier, and more hectic, he may run into the problem of not being able to get to sleep at night, which in turn may make it harder to get up

in the morning. Paradoxically, the child needs rest in order to sleep. Overfatigue is often a villain. This phase will usually pass if the parents do not become overanxious. Suggest that your child develop techniques—like counting sheep, or a similar device of his own—to fall asleep. Examine his daily routine and eliminate excess activities. If the sleep problem seems to have a known or unknown fear at its base, suggest to the child that he think of some nice experience he has had or a pretty place he has visited. Do not use tranquilizers and sedatives, which merely smother the problem and cause problems of their own, such as dependence. It is important to examine the causes of general anxiety rather than to give undue attention to specific fears. A specific fear may mask a more basic problem. One can get rid of one fear only to have a new one "rear its head."

Dr. Robert F.L. Polley elaborates on the problem of overactivity as a problem preventing good sleep: "A real plague these days is the 'conscientious kid fatigue syndromes.' The life of these intelligent, alert, and conscious school children include work, play, athletics, scouts, studies—and more. They usually need eight to twelve hours *more* sleep a week than they get. Use weekends and after school naps in order to prevent this fatigue."

Yet another cause of pre-adolescent sleep problems may be rooted in poor family relations which require psychological help—as outlined in the case of J.G., a manipulative eleven-year-old boy who was brought to the pediatrician with the complaint by the mother that he couldn't go to sleep at night. He continually went into his parents' bedroom complaining. The child domineered the mother in the office. Counseling unearthed that the boy was very hostile toward the father and was a "very good boy" for his mother. Father and mother were instructed to become a team, to exclude the boy from some of their activities and to involve him in more outside activities. Mother withdrew somewhat from the boy and backed father in needed discipline. The boy was told by both parents to stay out of their bedroom after the lights were out or he would be grounded and not allowed out of the house after school. This was followed rapidly by improvement in his behavior and mood.

Sleeping Medicines

Avoid sleeping medicines. Most adult insomnia is due to drug dependence. Children can develop the same problem. Sleeping medicine can also make some children overactive and agitated. The most restful portion of deep sleep is reduced by drugs, so sleep in a drugged state may not have as much "rest" value as normal sleep. Furthermore, the individual soon becomes tolerant to the drug and has to take greater and greater doses in order to achieve sleep. Withdrawal becomes a real problem, as he may go sleepless for a considerable time and lose his sleep rhythm. Chronic use of the following drugs may lead to drug dependences: barbiturates, antihistamines, and alcohol—as well as across the counter and prescription sedatives.

5

SOME NEEDS OF CHILDREN

The needs of children are many and varied. Not the least are food, clothing, shelter, and good health care. They are as basic as that intangible commitment called love that each of us has for our children. There are many other basic needs; and some of these are occasionally swept under the rug by busy parents. Others are not completely understood by most of us. But whether we meet them well or not, they deserve our study and thought. Each child's needs are somewhat different. Parents must first be able to know and understand their particular child if his needs are to be met. To some of you, these needs may seem so commonplace that they don't deserve to be said. But, as with any successful human endeavor, we must continually review the basics. The first basic is that individual needs aren't met nor are they always recognized from reading a book; the first requirement is that the parents spend enough time with the child to enable them to know their child.

YOUR CHILD'S NEED FOR YOUR TIME

Parental love, to be of value to the child, requires parental time. A lot of parents have so many demands on their time that their children may be short changed. In an effort to make busy or unsatisfied parents feel better about themselves, and less guilty, most of us have said, "It is the quality of time that counts." That is certainly true—ten minutes of listening to the child, playing with him, guiding him, is worth an hour of ignoring him or scolding him or being bored with him. But that is only true *if* you give the ten minutes. Certainly ten minutes a day (and that is all a lot of children get) is not enough time for even minimal parenting. It would be different if the children could be around you when you work, and better still if they can help you. Or, if they could be with you when you golf, or around you at a meeting (why not?). They would learn a lot more than they do when they spend their time watching television. They could observe you and model after you. One way or another, you have to allot time to parent. But some of you may object: "I go bananas if I am around children all the time!" However, people like Captain Kangaroo of television fame, who *is* around children, replies: "Why? We never make that statement about teachers and they work with children constantly. The trouble is we don't take children seriously. The first thing that goes when a city gets into financial trouble is the school budget." [1]

It isn't so much setting aside a half hour an evening for the child, it is being around the child enough to take advantage of those times when the two of you can share your lives with each other. A mother can get to know her child better, for example, if the child routinely wipes the dishes as she washes. Father can take the child shopping for groceries, and make an effort to listen to the child on the way. Of course, there are more direct amounts of time required: time to wash behind the ears, time to teach the child how to behave, time to feed, to hold, to love. But usually these functions require relatively little time. Another important type of time is when you are available to the child, although not actively involved with him. You may be busy with housework, television, hobbies, exercise, or office work, but you are still readily accessible to the child when he needs you. Immediate physical availability is required for certain stages of the child's life, but at other times quick telephone availability suffices.

For the newborn, a lot of time is needed. Up to twelve hours a day are spent directly doing something for, with, or to the baby. And mother or father or a good substitute must be immediately available during the other twelve hours. The amount of time required decreases gradually after the first six weeks. You may then find that you spend more time playing with your infant. Babies are extraordinarily attractive—and they are fun. But the amount of direct time spent *can* be reduced to a few hours a day as he learns to entertain himself.

From three to nine months is the time when the infant learns to trust. It has been found that infants who experience a lot of changes in their caretakers during this time can become psychologically maladjusted. Some*one* has to mother the infant. Some*one* is lucky enough to get to really know the baby, and allow the baby to have time to really know the parent. Yet it doesn't take a phenomenal amount of time, as compared to the first few months.

As the infant becomes a crawler and toddler, the amount of direct time required may increase. This is because of the toddler's separation fears (they cling), educational needs (following you around and learning from watching you work), and safety (they are always exploring something). Still, parents can do all sorts of work if the infant is allowed to be with them and watch. A minute or two every ten to fifteen minutes given directly to the baby when he needs help, comforting, stimulation, or discipline is frequent enough. Time is critical at the toddler stage, for it is here that the baby learns to learn; and here, too, you have the best chance to affect his personality by your attitudes and actions.

By around three years of age, the child is usually ready to be left alone for short periods of time in a safety proofed house, and should develop the ability to entertain himself for longer periods of time. Good half-day nursery schools are valuable; and parents will then have even more time to pursue other interests.

Most school age children are so busy with school and play that they appear to need relatively little time. But a child coming home from school needs a parent—just as when a parent comes home from a day's work, he or she needs a spouse. An awful lot of critical attitudes are being formed from ages five to eighteen. Parents have a lot of guidance to offer their children both directly and by example. To put your imprint on your child requires time. For your child to put his imprint on you requires time. And generally these are enjoyable times. Kids are fun, interesting, and challenging. They grow up so fast—and before you know it, they are gone. Don't let time pass you by. At the least, put in time so that you know your child.

THE NEED TO KNOW YOUR CHILD

Often it is the little things in life that make life worthwhile. These little things, as well as the big ones, depend more on our attitudes and feelings than on our physical or social circumstances. There will be fewer problems if you enjoy your children. But not all parents enjoy their children; and this may be especially true when the children are at certain thorny stages of development. In an effort to improve parental enjoyment of children, many experts advise an early and very close physical association of mother, father, and baby right after birth. If, as a parent, you didn't have early and close association with your child when he or she was an infant, you overcome this by spending an extra amount of physical time together. Even just holding your child in your lap helps. I see wonderful devoted parents who were rarely able to even see or touch their baby for months because of prematurity or illness. So, while early association is helpful, you needn't feel lost because it didn't occur.

With or without an early imprint, all parents have a deep commitment to their children to one degree or another. But there are times when some parents find it hard to really see, hear, and understand their child as a separate person. Beyond recognizing symptoms of physical illness and glaring signals of emotional distress, some parents simply do not observe their children carefully. They are so intent on what their children "should" be thinking, feeling, and doing that they fail to see what is actually going on. Others are so insecure and guilt-ridden that they translate any problem their child experiences as something they did wrong—and so they stop listening. You need to try to see your child as he is, not simply as a reflection of your own ambitions or fears. Because it sometimes isn't easy to be objective, you may want to get objective opinions from friends, relatives, or teachers. Observing and listening may come naturally to you. If not, there are a raft of books from psychologists illustrating the positive philosophy of communicating with children as a way of solving problems. Haim Ginott wrote fascinating books which show parents how to avoid confrontations with children.[2] He believed that the fewer confrontations and the less punishment, the greater the chance that children would grow into less hostile, less brutal adults. His techniques of answering children's questions, of sensing their feelings and helping them express them, are all derived from a basic principle of therapeutic psychology: Ventilation of feelings helps relieve tension.

Psychologist Thomas Gordon offers a penetrating and practical look at the techniques of "how to listen so kids will talk to you" and "how to talk so kids will listen to you." [3] Behind his Parent Effectiveness Training techniques lies a very valid principle: Be as thoughtful and polite to your child as you are to anyone else. Respect your children enough to understand their feelings. You rarely will achieve that understanding by simply giving orders. Still, it is also vital that you talk with the child in a manner which encourages the child to really listen—and you should tell him *your* feelings, too. I have found the following principles of active listening to be of value in getting to really know a child:

- Active listening involves letting the child know you understand what he is saying:
    Repeating what you feel the child meant.
    Accepting negative feelings from the child.
    Indicating understanding and empathy for the child's feelings.
    Encouraging the child to make the decisions.
- Advantages of active listening by parents:
    Gains the confidence of their children.
    Allows children to express their feelings.
    Increases insight about the child's problems.
    Gives children a chance to solve their own problems.
    Shows that parents care about and want to understand their children.

- Active listening doesn't work if:
    You try to guide the child's behavior or thinking.
    You moralize, advise, or offer solutions.
    You feed back the words but not the meaning.
    You do not respond directly to the child's requests.

These principles of communication, developed by psychologists over a period of years, represent a method you can use to get to know your child better. In this way, you can start to meet your commitment to your child, as well as your commitment to parent. You can begin to help your child fill his needs.

THE NEED FOR YOUR CHILD TO KNOW YOUR VALUES

Whether you listen to your children and get to know them or not, you still have a profound effect on them. Your children learn how to act from being around you. If you aren't around, they learn how to act from others. They learn not only from what you do and say but also from what you don't say and do. So you are a teacher for your children whether or not you wish to be. If you are going to teach them, why not make the effort to impart some worthwhile values and goals in a conscious way? If you succeed, you may be able to spare them a lot of uncertainty. And there are a lot of uncertainties facing our children. Of these, Walter Lippman wrote: "No mariner ever enters upon a more uncharted sea than does the average human being born in the twentieth century. Our ancestors knew their way from birth through eternity; we are puzzled about the day after tomorrow." Much of this uncertainty is unnecessary. As a parent, you can help your children by offering them values and goals—a compass and a map of sorts for the future. Others, however, argue that specific values must be picked by the child.

Opinions on Teaching Values and Goals

We Create Our Children
Although it has been fashionable for some time to pretend that children are not, or at least should not be, their parents' creations, both research findings and common sense demonstrate that, with varying degrees of consciousness and conscientiousness, parents do in many ways create their children psychologically as well as physically.—*Diana Baumrind* [4]

Their Values Should Be Theirs
We don't select the "right" values and pass them out to our children. The "right" values for us are the ones we believe in and use. They may be power, status, academic achievement, and material wealth as well as the ones we usually think of as "good," such as

patriotism, kindness, honesty, and reverence. We all have to decide individually what qualities we feel are worthwhile as personal goals.

Our ancestors' value systems were well known to them—clear and specific, and accompanied by plenty of reinforcement and reassurance. Their problem was not finding the right path, but following it. Our problem is more complicated: It means more choices, more decisions, and maybe even more chances to fall flat on our faces. But it also means the freedom to be ourselves.—*Julie Stone Oliver, B.A.*

We Should Indoctrinate Our Children

There is a critical period when certain kinds of instruction are possible in the life of the child. . . . Their concepts of right and wrong are formulated during this time. . . . Permanent attitudes can be instilled during the first seven years of life. When parents say they are going to withhold "indoctrination" from their small child, allowing him to "decide for himself," they are almost guaranteeing that he will decide in the negative. . . . The child listens closely to discover just how much his parent believes what he or she is preaching; any indecision or ethical confusion from the parent is likely to be magnified in the child.—*James C. Dobson, Ph.D.*[5]

I believe our children have a need to be protected during their formative years from having to make choices for which they are unprepared. We should encourage them toward goals we believe are worthwhile and offer them a firm value structure. We all agree that ultimately each individual makes his own personal value selection. But that is "ultimately." Pediatrician Merritt Low offers a compromise: We should expose children to the concept of having values and pass on the idea of having values, not the values themselves. However, in this age of future shock, I believe children and adolescents desperately need specific values and goals to try to live up to. There is good evidence that religious and traditional values are helpful in developing the best in children.

It has been shown by psychologist Richard Blum that children brought up by families who have strong religious beliefs have fewer drug abuse problems and are more apt to adopt parental values.[6] It has been found that youth raised within the traditional family structure in a traditional community may circumvent the adolescent crisis and its attendant suffering altogether. In fact, psychiatrists in the prestigious American Association for the Advancement of Psychiatry come out strongly for offering specific religious values. The following paragraph was condensed from their excellent book, *The Joys and Sorrows of Parenthood.*

Many parents feel that they are doing the child a favor in not presenting specific religious beliefs; or they will expose him to a number of different beliefs in the hope that he will, as he matures, pick out the ones he wants to keep. But it may well be that obscurity or permissiveness in matters of religion gives the adolescent nothing to rebel against or to depend upon. It is as though he wanted something crisp and exciting to chew on and was given vanilla pudding instead. We are proud, in our society, of our great tolerance and of the fact that we permit many different kinds of religious values and beliefs to co-exist. But in such a society, the adolescent's religious conflicts may not be so easy to resolve, as they are in a society with a much more structured set of values and points of view. In a more dogmatic society, at least, he knows what he is fighting. . . . Often, the child's rebellion is against what he *thought* was taught him, not what he was actually taught. Sometimes, however, his rebellion is directed against what he was taught as it differed from what was practiced. In general, he is basically rejecting not a mature religious belief but his own childhood conceptions. Many years may pass before he realizes that his rebellion was not so much against parents, church, or culture as against his own immaturity.[7]

Many parents rebel at the idea of teaching values. But most teach them whether they know it or not, even if they object to the Biblical commands of "Thou shalt and thou shalt not." It is interesting that a parent who will not insist that his child memorize the Ten Commandments will insist that the child learn good manners and will discipline the child for refusal to obey. Perhaps this reflects the reality of our adult conflict between partial or free acceptance of ideal "commandments" and our rebellion at being forced to obey such "commandments." When we solve these issues, our society will undoubtedly have made some major social advances. Meanwhile, children need values and ideals; and if they don't get them from parents they will get them somewhere—values they learn and accept from "somewhere," for example, from crime shows on television. To counter values which are completely unacceptable to you means that you, or someone you pick, will have to teach your child. Whether this is done by command or reward is largely up to you.

THE NEED FOR A BALANCE OF LOVE AND FREEDOM

Love is easier to feel than to define, but as parents we ought to know something about our feeling of love for our children. An oft neglected fact about love is that it can start as a very personal emotion. In fact, love can be quite selfish. My love for you may be meaningful to me, but it may mean very little to you. In parenting, our love for our children is a personal reward we receive as parents. Obviously, love can have a real effect upon the loved one; usually it is shown by commitment. Pediatric author and columnist Robert F.L. Polley says that most of us love our children even though we go through periods when we don't feel the least bit loving. He finds the term "love" too vague; and suggests that we use the word "loyal" instead. If we think of "love" more in terms of "caring for" than of "my feeling," it may be easier to focus on what our children need, instead of on our own emotional reactions or our own needs.

Loyalty means that to care *about* your children is to care *for* your children. Keep them fed and clothed, warm and happy, learning and growing. Most important, as you do these things for your children you must help them to become self-sufficient. Perhaps one of the greatest things a loyal and loving parent can give children is freedom—freedom to try, succeed, and even to make their own mistakes, within limits.

Love is more than words, kisses, and hugs. Love may be patience and restraint from *unnecessary criticism.* Love may be letting toddlers learn about the law of gravity by picking them up and dusting them off when they stumble. Love may be removing the coffee table from the living room when they are learning to walk so they won't split their scalps when they fall. It may be taking the time to listen when children really need your attention. Conversely, it may be swatting them with the back of your hand if they try to monopolize your time when the telephone rings or when company comes. Love may be appreciating your son the mechanic when you had your heart set on your son the lawyer, or your daughter the architect when you'd planned on her becoming a housewife.

But words, kisses, and hugs matter, too! Don't be afraid to react emotionally with your children. Parents and children need affection. Our lives would be very dry and cold if we did nothing but look upon caring for our children as a duty. Most children are open, spontaneous, warm, little people who know much that we've forgotten about living. Our responsibility is not just to learn to show our children honest affection, but to learn to receive the affection they will return to us.

It is neither necessary, desirable, nor possible for us to be 100% perfect parents. And even if you are a perfect parent, keep in mind that a significant principle in child rearing is that many of your child's problems and needs are his, not yours. If you make them your problems, why should the child bother solving them? Naturally this is not the case when the child is very young, but he should be allowed to try as soon as there appears to be any prospect at all that he can succeed. If he fails to solve the problem or meet his needs, *then* show him how. Remember that many problems and some needs vanish with time. If you make a big thing about problems, the child will believe they are serious—and this may make them harder for him to solve. Of course, some problem solving requires parental help, and some needs can only be met by the parents.

Psychologist Diana Baumrind brings up the issue in a different perspective. She agrees that parents must love—be responsible for—their children. She also believes that children must have responsibilities, including that of loving—respecting and obeying—their parents. She points out that responsibilities—certainly a sort of manifestation of love—are based on the fulfillment of the other's needs:

> At each age, the duties and rights of adults and children differ, finally approximating the balance which characterizes adult relations. During the period when children are dependent on their parents, the parents have a social and moral duty to commit themselves to the children's welfare, while the children have a duty to conform to parental standards. This relationship of mutual responsibility between parents and children is the origin of the social contract.[8]

THE NEED FOR SELF-ESTEEM AND SELF-CONFIDENCE

Two basic needs of children are self-esteem and self-confidence. Self-esteem and the confidence it engenders are built or destroyed in many ways. One of the most important factors is the way children measure themselves, using parental and social values. However, few of us as parents (or citizens) have ever taken the time or energy to study our personal priority list of values and to look at their effects upon our children. Although there are many values we espouse, it often seems that the most popular are beauty, brains, and money. The concept of beauty, for example, has become so standardized that the first screening, of girls for example, seems to be on the size of the bust, waist, and hips, and the color of the skin. Because most girls do not physically fit the artificial standards we tend to follow like sheep, many feel that they are not and cannot be beautiful.

It is, of course, reasonable to value the intellect, yet we cannot all be intellectuals. The problem is that some teaching seems designed to screen out all who don't have natural talent, rather than helping "inferior" students to develop that talent. Math instruction is a case in point. The "figure it out yourself" techniques can be devastating to many grammar school children and adolescents. The net result is that a large percentage of high school graduates give up on math before they become even reasonably proficient. Thus, instead of having some self-esteem for partially mastering a difficult subject, students are set up for failure.

Money is something we value, seek, envy, and curse; we begrudgingly admire the wealthy while our own esteem requires that, if possible, we cut them down to our size. Fame we value and admire. Yet, for instance in sports, we rarely seem satisfied to let a winner stay a winner. Post-season games go on interminably until only one winner is left. (The Little League has even imported international teams to compete!) Many of these values can put people down. The net effect, contends child psychologist James Dobson in his book *Hide or Seek*, is an epidemic of inferiority:

The current epidemic of self-doubt has resulted from a totally unjust and unnecessary system of evaluating human worth, now prevalent in our society. Not everyone is seen as worthy; not everyone is accepted. Instead, we reserve our praise and admiration for a select few who have been blessed from birth with the characteristics we value most highly. It is a vicious system, and we, as parents, must counterbalance its impact. . . All children are created worthy and must be given the right to personal respect and dignity. It can be done! [9]

Dobson offers a series of strategies for building self-esteem. His first suggestion is that you remain very sensitive to your child's feelings of self-worth. These fragile feelings are easily damaged. Parental displeasure and resultant damage to the child's self-esteem are more likely to occur when the parent is tired or pressured. We should guard against excessive pressures on ourselves and against taking our frustrations out on the children. Dobson, too, is concerned about the effects of parental guilt feelings upon the children. He says: "Parenting is a very guilt-producing affair, even for the dedicated professional." He recommends facing guilt feelings squarely, writing them down, and then objectively assessing the validity of the feelings and what we can do about them. Another cause of self-doubt in a family is when a new baby comes along who is a rival for parental love. Dobson suggests that you help children verbalize these feelings so they can openly ask for more love and attention.

What Can You Do?

Dobson suggests that you teach your children to respect themselves and not to dwell on their weaknesses. Teach them that we are all different and all vulnerable to criticism. When they are weak in one area, help them compensate in another. Support them in all possible ways of improving themselves—their looks, their intellect, their charm, their physical abilities. Help them cope with school without defeat. Watch the child's intellectual and emotional development carefully and intercede early enough to offer help. If he has low academic potential, help can be given by tutoring and by showing as much respect for factory workers as people as you do for professors or teachers. Avoid overprotecting children so they can feel more confident about facing the world and have more experience. All in all, be positive, and think about how to build your children up. Throughout *The Parents' Guide to Child Raising* many suggestions are offered by many people. If you use them, think about their possible effects on the child and try to use them in a way that will build confidence rather than decrease it.

One of the most significant sources of self-esteem and confidence comes from being esteemed and valued by parents. Although specific praise counts, the most effective tool parents have is a positive and accepting attitude toward each child. You can build children's self-esteem by loving in the "right" way. There are two distinct ways of loving a person. One is for what they are, and another is for what they do. When you love children for what they are, you love them for themselves—the way they look, smile, talk, or whatever. Loving them for what they are is a more valuable personal judgment, and usually increases confidence more than loving them for what they produce or do. Both ways of love are important, but we often forget to emphasize, or even to acknowledge, the first. Ask *yourself:* Would I rather hear that I am a great housekeeper or a great person?

However, confidence building really starts at a very early age when you make it a habit to pick up your baby when he is happy as well as when he cries. Spontaneously given attention bolsters confidence and trust. So does letting your child crawl around exploring everything he can get his hands on. Baby-proof your home so he can try out most of the things he sees without the need for reprimands. It is vital to teach children that there are limits; it is also vital to give them some freedom outside of a playpen.

Another way of helping a child build self-esteem is your attitude toward your child's successes or failures. First, be realistic: Help him to accept the *facts.* Then try to help him see that a failure doesn't mean that *he* is a success or *he* is a failure, but that what he *did* produced certain results. Assure him that you, as a *parent*, don't measure him by the results of his actions. The world may, but that is another ball of wax. Let him know you *know* he is great. He should be loved and given security, just for himself. So listen to him, and accept him. Perhaps try gently to bring him down to earth.

Avoid becoming too involved with his successes and failures. They are *his* successes and failures, not yours. So moderate your pride and hurt. Recognize that he is a good person, passing or failing aside. Avoid warnings that will make him feel that he is likely to fail. Part of life is trying, honestly, "on your own." Don't rob him of the chance to succeed or fail —all on his own. The world won't fall apart in either case if you remain a supporting, helpful parent.

Self-esteem must also be based on social realities. A child must learn many skills to function well in the world. Some of these skills are taught in school and college, but many of the important ones are taught at home. Children respond to stimulation and stress; love and loyalty are demonstrated by preparing a child for life, not simply by protecting him from harm by filling his current needs. Some Apaches helped prepare children to meet life by a rigorous course in self-control taught by tribal elders. As part of the puberty ceremony, the adolescent brave had to hold a hot coal in his hand. If the boy cried or dropped it, he was not yet accepted as a brave. This method taught manhood and enabled survival in the wilderness. It was undoubtedly done with love. Today, we have no need for such extreme conditioning, but we err if we don't allow our children to face life. Today, the "wilderness" is one of a different kind. Children should develop emotional and physical skills as well as work-a-day and learning skills.

There are many skills we must teach our children, and there are specific tasks we have as parents. Some basic parental tasks are to prepare the child for eventual independence. Parents need to teach their children how to:

- Overcome fears and develop confidence
- Develop good social relationships
- Achieve the needed basic skills and strengths to function as a citizen and as a possible future parent
- Develop an adequate base for a future vocation and career
- Establish a sense of responsibility to self and society

You may have other goals, and, of course, more tasks for you and your child. In planning, you have to recognize the child's needs for increased freedom and independence, which are required to build self-confidence. You also have to recognize the individuality of your child. Your goals for your child have to be modified as his personality, talents, strengths, and weaknesses unfold. They may be further modified, depending on whether your child accepts your values as his own.

One social reality is the high value placed on the ability to earn a living and to contribute to the community. Society must want the blossoming adult and value the labor and productivity as well as the person. However, it is often very hard for youth to find a place in society in these turbulent and rapidly changing times. Our colleges turn out more graduates than needed; and our high schools turn out too many youths who go to college because there is little else to do. One major cause of the identity crisis and lack of self-esteem in our youth is because children are not prepared for productive jobs, or, when they are, there aren't enough jobs to go around. This is a critical problem that must be solved if our culture is to survive. Parents, family, church, and local community must join forces with business and government to assure that each youth is wanted, has a place, has a role, and thus has a healthy sense of identity and self-esteem. The basic responsibility for this rests upon each child's parents—but society must help with proper social organization. While helping youth find meaningful roles in life, we must emphasize the value of basic productive jobs as well as the responsibility to see that these necessary jobs are completed. In other words, youth usually has to start at the bottom of the ladder; and our attitude should make them proud to be on that first rung of the ladder. In American society there exists a marked amount of flexibility and unparalleled opportunities to be free to try new things, to step higher, or to change ladders.

As with values, job roles at least give young people something to rebel against or a base to build from. One of the basic human needs is the opportunity to dream and to try to turn those dreams into reality. In this, parents can only be permissive and try to be helpful.

THE NEED FOR SEX IDENTITY

Self-esteem depends on many factors: Among them is the security one has from a sense of knowing who you are, that you have a role in life, and that you are wanted and needed by somebody. As a start, a child needs to know if he is a boy or if she is a girl. There was never much of a question about it in the past; but efforts to enhance sexual identity may have caused an over-stereotyping of sexual roles, which in turn has created artificial barriers unnecessarily barring some men and women from certain occupations and opportunities. In the opinion of some thoughtful pediatricians like Dr. Merritt Low, many children don't fit the stereotyping we set up for them, and therefore children question their masculinity or femininity—they fear that they are not "normal" if they don't fit a pattern. Dr. Low and Sandra Price write:

> Why can't we love our children for themselves and guide them toward humanness, not just assumed or falsely defined maleness or femaleness? In the process of old-fashioned male–female molding, our children's natural abilities and temperaments can be suppressed. A girl who enjoys trucks may wonder if she is "more boy than girl." It is wrong to instill these fears in our children, continually making them prove their sex. We should be assured, and we should assure them, too, that they are boys or girls according to their anatomy and hormones, and that nothing changes that. It is true that there are different kinds of males and females. Within each sex there are varying physiques, abilities, interests, temperaments, and even hormones. Specific characteristics shouldn't be singled out and accentuated as being more masculine or more feminine than others. Nature has created these variations and heredity passes them on, in spite of a culture's antagonistic selectivities and preferences.

Some women's movement advocates feel that there is overemphasis on sex roles and that sex identification and differentiation, which starts in childhood, should be reduced. Dr. Spock has been criticized for advocating in the past that boys play with boy toys and girls with girl toys. Now many believe that there should be no difference in how boys and girls are treated. Psychiatrist John Money of Johns Hopkins believes that the basic and openly recognized genital difference between boys and girls is sufficient to develop sex identification, and that the abolition of sex stereotyping will help rather than hinder a child's fullest develop-ment.[10] On the other hand, it is quite possible that adult intervention in children's sex roles may be less important than some believe. Even ex-perts like Eleanor Maccoby and Carol Jacklin, who researched sex dif-ference and who challenge many aspects of the traditional sex role as socially defined, note that children stereotype themselves. Children's sex-typed behavior does not closely resemble that of adult models. Boys select an all-male play group, but they do not observe their fathers avoid-ing the company of females. Boys choose to play with trucks and cars, even though they may have seen their mothers driving the family car more frequently than their fathers; girls play hopscotch and jacks al-though these games are totally absent from their mothers' observable behavior.[11]

On the other hand, few boys follow in their father's vocational foot-steps anymore. Girls who have followed in mother's footsteps in the past now have questions raised about the value of the roles of wife and mother. Psychiatrists like Arthur Kornhaber of New York blame some mothers for robbing their daughters of their sexual identities and many fathers for teaching their boys to retreat from male responsibilities. Child psychiatrist Thomas Johnson of San Diego reports: "I'm seeing more and more children concerned and confused with sexual roles." [12] All of this re-emphasizes that the long-term implications of many new child-rearing and social practices may turn out to have effects yet un-studied or unrecognized. It is this lack of knowledge which can worry parents, whose short-term actions are geared towards long-term results.

The Need for Sex Education

Education about sex starts when babies find that they have a penis or vagina and that it often feels good to play with it. What starts as curiosity can become a habit, and almost all parents find it necessary to make genital play taboo. Some psychologists may differ; but sooner or later, control of sexual impulses must be established. Probably the best way to teach infants control is to diaper them and to distract them. Later a non-emotional "We don't do that" may be added, and if a child per-sists in playing with himself or herself around the family or other people after two years of age, you should talk it over with the doctor. Genital play could be caused by anything from pinworms to natural curiosity or anxiety, or when older, exposure to pornography.

Sex Education for the Three-Year-Old

The next step in sex education usually comes at around the age of three years. Overall, most children are far too busy exploring the world to get hung up exploring sex. But around this age they discover new concepts, including the concept of possession. This leads many three-year-olds to examine the phenomena of sex. Possession is that wonderful feeling that comes from knowing, "It's mine!" And the world gets divided into "mine" and "yours." And if one is lucky, or quick, or strong, "yours" can be converted to "mine." So children take toys from each other and squabble over ownership. And around this age they become acutely aware that there are differences in plumbing between the sexes. One has and one hasn't a penis. Why? Each child comes up with his own answer. Remember that they have neither the experience or background to use in judging this phenomenon. For all they know, Daddy may have taken Mommy's! Some of their explanations are really funny. "Who took her penis?" is not an uncommon question from little boys. One little boy suggested to his Dad that they go buy one for Mother! But how about little girls? I have never heard one ask, "Who took mine?" To do so would be admitting a loss, a defeat. We don't trumpet our defeats—only our victories and our hopes. So little girls may say instead, "When I grow up and go to school I am going to be a boy." Why not? Maybe a penis is issued with the equipment? Or grows? If a little sister greatly admires big brother, she may decide he is her model in life—not mother. It is "cute" at this age. But what happens if the child grows up feeling this way? Then it is not so "cute." It can be a catastrophe—one as bad as polio or diphtheria.

So in a way, a three-year-old needs a sex education. He should know that he is going to grow up to be like Dad. And that is good. She needs to know that she will grow up to be like mother. And that is good. This means that a boy needs a happy father and a girl needs a happy mother. So tell her or him a couple of times casually, that she or he will grow into a wonderful woman or man. Then go and be happy.

I don't believe that it is usually necessary or even wise to give a preschooler very much sex education. Certainly if they are young enough to believe in Santa Claus they don't need *all* the sexual facts of life. In any case, we should not tell them more than they want to know or more than they can meaningfully absorb. On the other hand, pediatrician Glen Griffin, in his sex education book for young children, called *You Were Smaller Than a Dot,* has this to say about three-year-olds:

> Now, supposing you were a three-year-old—and you wanted to know something about babies—and you asked a very special somebody (like your Mommy or Daddy) a question. How would you feel if that special somebody acted shocked or upset? What if you were told "sh–h–h?" What if you heard: "Don't talk about that." What if the answer was "Never use that word again!" Or what would you think if the answer was ". . . ah . . . later . . . I'll tell you about it later." Could "later" ever be as good a time as right now? Could anything be more important than a few words of explanation—right now?

"Now" answers are usually the ones best learned and most appreciated. If you were a youngster and received a good "now" answer, it's quite likely that you would come back to the same source for more information.

But what if you got hushed up or put off? You might just register a negative attitude about the subject—and remember not to bring it up again. You might proceed more cautiously about asking things. Or you might look for a better source for answers—maybe the kid next door—or someone in the school restroom—or just anybody else.

It's hard to find better people than parents to answer these important questions. And it's really not so difficult anyway. But how? With the truth! It's that simple. Just answer whatever a youngster asks.

But what if a child learns what intercourse is and then asks, "Can I watch?" Dr. Griffin advises that you reply, "No, this is a very private time between a mommy and daddy." [13]

This brings up some other thoughts about modesty. Should parents intentionally allow children to see themselves without clothing? How much privacy should exist in the home about bathing, dressing, and in regard to the toilet? And how about modesty around brothers and sisters? Certainly, children have a great learning opportunity when there is a baby to bathe and change. Then, up to around four years, children are not very concerned about modesty and privacy. When they become concerned, their wishes should be respected.

Most children over four years old become concerned about modesty. Parents should not roam around nude—it can be upsetting to many children. However, should an accidental intrusion occur into a dressing or bathing situation, calm is far better than anger and upset. There is no reason to make the youngster feel as though he has done something terribly wrong. He hasn't.

Of course, learning about sex doesn't come only from books. Pediatrician Maxine Sehring points out:

> Sex education occurs when the six year old laboriously reads "R–A–P–E" in the morning paper and asks, "What does that mean, Daddy?" If the term sex education means learning about relationships between males and females—and understanding one's own sexual male or female identity—then an alert and normally curious toddler learns a great deal by simple observation—long before parent or school teacher considers "formal or specific" sex education appropriate. Sex education comes from many sources, some constructive and factual, some destructive and very inaccurate. The process of "sex education" is lifelong—especially if one includes the on-going development of attitudes.
>
> Accepting the fact that we give our children a "sex" education by the example of our daily living and interpersonal relationships, then we should look at ourselves and decide, "Am I a good example?" Do

I have hang-ups relative to the opposite sex which I would like my child to avoid? Is it flattering or threatening to me if my spouse seems to enjoy the company of members of the opposite sex? Do I have warm relationships with my parents, neighbors, and friends? All of these attitudes and actions are part of parental education of the young; and, in a sense, they are the background that sex education rests upon.

When children go to school, many parents automatically expect the school to do all of the educating—including educating about sex. Other parents are concerned that the school will teach the wrong things, or that they will teach too much too early. And who decides what children should be told about homosexuality, bisexuality, child sex freaks, transvestites, prostitutes, free sex, masturbation, and oral and anal sex—and should love or morals be mentioned? Pediatrician Robert Black believes that sex education should include:

> Not only the sexual act and its product, the child, but all aspects of male and female relationships, including the future role and self-esteem of the young person. These represent several levels of sex education:
>
> 1. The biological "facts of life."
> 2. The emotional–social aspects of dating, courting, love-making, marriage, and child-bearing.
> 3. The general area of family life and individual responsibility to society.
> 4. The problems associated with sexual behavior, venereal disease, unwanted pregnancy, homosexuality, and divorce.
>
> Learning about the "facts of life" should precede learning about the social, moral, and family life aspects of sexual relationships. The exact age to tell children about intercourse varies with the child. Learning is usually best in small bits, and the young child learning about and from his body acquires sexual information. Questions should be answered honestly and correctly. For example: "The baby is in mother's uterus." A child must have a knowledge about himself and his genital equipment and functions in order to be able to cope with the social, moral, and interpersonal relationship problems of adolescence.
>
> Few families are comfortable in satisfactorily teaching the biology of reproduction. It is my strong opinion that a well-taught course in school is far superior. Junior high schools should offer courses with information on dating, morality, and the social problems of sex. The morality aspects, however, vary from family to family; and the school must make it clear that there are varying patterns of allowable behavior. The family or church should reinforce the areas of their concerns.

At the same time, there is a need for education into problems of sexual behavior such as venereal disease, unwanted pregnancy, and divorce—and this education should occur early enough so that the young person has adequate information to protect himself from the "seductive" friend who uses friendship as a way to obtain sex.

Although I agree with most of Bob Black's approach to sex education, I am bothered by the idea that public school should teach that there are varying patterns of allowable normal behavior. The effect is to pull all values down to the "lowest" in the community. This creates a need for baseline community standards and all the problems which that entails, making sex education in public school a difficult problem even if the community agrees to "adequate" values. Associate editor Julie Oliver objects:

Children are ultimately going to learn to "drive" with or without "rules of the road." Statements by teachers on varying patterns of "acceptable behavior" don't pull all values down to those of the community's lowest. The teacher simply makes the only possible *general* statement—and a perfectly factual one. Our moral values do differ quite widely. Our communities *will* not, probably *could* not, and very possibly *should* not agree on "adequate" values. This is the responsibility of parents—to determine and to live (as well as we're able) our moral values—and to expose our children to them by word and example. We cannot place this responsibility on our schools.

On the other hand, psychologist James Dobson writes:

I am not opposed to sex education in the public schools—provided both elements of the subject [morals and facts] are presented properly. Simply stated, I don't want my children taught sex technology by a teacher who is either neutral or misinformed about the consequences of immorality. It would be preferable that Junior learn his concepts in the streets rather than from a teacher standing before his class, having all the dignity and authority invested in him by the school and society, and telling his impressionable students that traditional morality is either unnecessary or unhealthy. Unless the schools are prepared to take a definite position in favor of sexual responsibility (and perhaps the social climate prevents their doing so), some other agency should assist concerned parents in the provision of sex education for their children. The churches could easily provide this service for society. The YMCA, YWCA, or other social institutions might also be helpful at this point. Perhaps there is no objective that is more important to the future of our nation than the teaching of moral discipline to the most recent generation of Americans.[14]

If you are going to give your child an early sex education, I recommend Dr. Griffin's book. Dr. Sehring also recommends, "How to Raise Children at Home In Your Spare Time," [15] or "Mothers are Funnier than Children" [16] and "Communion With Young Saints." [17] However, I question the need and the results of early sex education. Children have enough growing and developing to accomplish without bothering about sex. Most children under age twelve ask very little about sex. They are not usually very interested in it and have very few sex hormones or little sex drive until puberty. It is the "sleeping dog" age of psychological latency. Children are usually very modest during these years, and many become upset at exposure to sexual knowledge, or at exposing their bodies to the view of others. They haven't yet mastered their emotional separation from parents; and adding sex to such unresolved conflicts can be just "too much" for some.

For example, a nine-year-old boy in my practice saw a television sex education series in school. The series was done by a psychiatrist for grammar school children, but it was inadvertently stimulating. Following this, the boy became quite upset whenever his parents went to bed, hammering on the door, crying, "Stop that, don't do that!" As a rule, I believe that most sex education should be put off until around puberty —the junior high school age. For some, it is well tolerated earlier; but for others it creates problems. As a parent, you will have to make the choice. But I don't think you should hesitate to let your children know that they are not ready for some things. Nor is it necessary to go into detail when answering a child's questions on sex. That often just leads to more questions. Five-year-olds do not need details about intercourse. An adult who is in good standing with his children can reply to questions honestly and say, "That's enough for now," without damaging the child's psyche. This may not hold true for some adults, who seem to think they can blurt out "the facts" as if it were a chore well done.

When a child of around ten to twelve years asks a question, offer him sex education, but don't make a federal case out of it. More often than not the child won't ask. In this case, you can introduce the subject by taking advantage of an article in a current newspaper or by discussing some sex-related happening about someone the child knows. Have a book on sex education around. If you are too embarrassed or uncertain, ask your doctor to give your child sex education.

If the purpose of sex education is to reduce unwanted pregnancy and venereal disease, then much sex education has failed. In fact, family physician Dr. Murray Elkins writes:

> Money spent for sex education has as much chance of stopping V.D. as a boy on a tricycle has to ride it to the moon. Our social atmosphere is completely sexual—from pornographic movies to smut aimed at teenagers. Clothing is "hot," tight, and as form-fitting as shortness of breath and painful constriction will allow. Some educators

Figure 31

encourage mixed rooming-in of the sexes in dormitories. Lack of protest by the public, and permissive parents who won't say no, give silent sanction to unlimited sex. Schools are prohibited from enforcing student standards of decency and behavior. With teenagers and young adults sexually stimulated every waking hour, the incidence of V.D. will continue its rapid increase.

Human sexuality agencies promote and disseminate erotic guidance as though sex is a new discovery. But the unfortunate gonorrheal infections of the fallopian tubes, of the heart, prostate, or joints, and the syphilitic damage to the brain are frequently omitted or de-emphasized. The spectacular triumph of the gonococcus and the spirochete of syphilis is directly proportional to the acceptance of the new sexual liberality. Some semblance of morality in our society must be restored before the overwhelming epidemic of V.D. becomes irreversible. (For more information on venereal disease, see *The Parents' Medical Manual.*)

How Do You Raise a Child Not To Be "Hung Up" Sexually?

Early sex education is given with an underlying assumption that it will change attitudes so that sex educated children will be sexually healthy adults. Actually, the emotional attitudes an adult takes into sex may have nothing to do at all with early sex education. Sexual performance depends largely on a healthy self-esteem. Self-esteem is unhealthy if it is too little or if it is too great. Children develop low self-esteem from chronic belittling by parents who criticize excessively in an attempt to get the child to function "better." This self-doubt as an adult can make for unrealistic self-sexual demands, with a resulting disappointment which reinforces the low self-esteem, and makes good sexual adjustment even less likely. Other children develop a too great and unrealistic self-esteem if they are overindulged as children. The "prince and princess" methods of raising children leads to the expectations that some one will produce for "me" without any reciprocation. The adult who was raised in this manner is often disappointed and bored sexually, regardless of the efforts of the spouse, who then gets the blame. However, the authoritarian method of child raising gets the most blame for sexual malfunction. Children who are constantly and rigidly directed during growth develop a "super conscience," always telling themselves they should do better. They may end up rebelling against these parentally instilled overkills and refusing to do the things their conscience tells them to do. Thus, the woman who continually tells herself she "should be a good wife" actually rebels, especially in bed, and becomes a poor lover. A few children are taught by attitude to fear their own sexual impulses. Some few fear sex because they are brought up by mothers or fathers who distrust the opposite sex. Adult emotional reactions based on such past conditioning are hardly inducive to a happy love life.

Another troubled group of adults spent much of their childhood in a situation where they almost replaced one parent. For example, the boy who is mother's favorite, who is able continually to take her attention away from father and feels he has displaced his father in mother's affection, may be in for trouble when he develops a sex urge. So is the girl who is the apple of Daddy's eye to the virtual exclusion of Mother. These children love and possess their parents so closely that when they become adolescents the anti-incest instinct may force them to reject the favored parent. This may spill over to the point where all women (for a man), or all men (for a woman), remind them of the intensely loved parent. The resulting anti-incest instinct then makes it difficult, if not impossible, to function very well sexually with the opposite sex.

Another cause of sexual hangups is lack of modesty. Most children become very modest by the age of five years or so. From that age on, there is a gradual build-up of sex hormones and sexual feelings. Most children deal with these feelings by repressing them. One reason is that some children really don't want to grow up, and sexual impulse indicates growth. Another reason is that children between the age of five to twelve can be stimulated or threatened by the sight of parental genitalia. One may argue that increasing nudism makes such "theories" invalid. However, the most prudish and modest children I have ever seen were from nudist families. One required psychotherapy for guilt feelings resulting from his sexual urge, which was stimulated by seeing mother nude. Members of even the most primitive societies, where clothes are not needed, wear covering for the genitalia. Nudism may be fine for little children and mature adults; but for children from five through adolescence and independence, it is a highly questionable practice.

THE NEED FOR MOTIVATION

We know little about motivation, even if the carrot and the stick are basic. The motivation to learn and to explore is natural in all children. Great efforts are expended by parents and society to encourage this vital trait. From "creative" toys to teaching the two-year-old to read, to the governmentally sponsored Head Start Programs, we show our concern. Unfortunately we don't always show good results, as evidenced by the high drop-out rate in high schools, the passive hedonism of segments of youth, and, on occasions, the depression and aimlessness with which many face the future. Actually, studies have shown that parents can have a far more positive effect than teachers. Head start programs, where the preschooler was exposed to teachers, were ineffective. On the other hand, where programs encouraged each parent to parent and showed them how, the children seemed to become and to stay far more motivated.

Studying highly motivated achieving and creative young people offers some clues. One factor seems to be the result of family affluence and values. Psychologist Harvey Blum, in a study of Stanford University students, found that many of the satisfied, achieving, drug-free group came largely from conservative blue-collar working-class families, while the alienated, frustrated, and drug-abusing group largely came from the sophisticated liberal upper-class families.[18] This is not dissimilar to the widespread legend of the past that it was the minister's or banker's sons that went wrong. A lot of Americans don't know how to handle affluence—either of time or money.

Another source of motivation is self-esteem. Varying psychological studies relate this to family structure and parenting practices, especially to the type of discipline. In a large group of normal boys, those with the highest sense of self-esteem came from homes where discipline was strict. They were honestly loved and appreciated, and were allowed freedom, with limits, to develop their own personalities. The group with the lowest self-esteem were insecure, and were generally from permissive homes. A study of dinner table discipline revealed parallel findings. Children who weren't permitted to speak at the dinner table had low self-esteem, but those who were allowed to dominate the dinner table had the lowest. Children with the best self-esteem were allowed to speak and were listened to *when their turns came.*

Early Parenting Practices and Motivation

Motivation to learn and drive to succeed probably start in early childhood. Statistical differences in developmental I.Q. levels have been shown between toddlers who were raised by a mother at home or by a single mother substitute, and other toddlers whose mothers worked and whose caretakers changed several times, especially during the age of six and nine months. Children whose parents responded to them in their infancy when they cried seemed more motivated and confident than children who, when infants, were picked up only on schedule or on the parents' desire. Evidently the ability to improve the environment (be held) on demand as an infant gives a child the feeling that he can succeed in altering things for the better later in life.

This ties in with psychologist Burton White's findings about maternal availability and response to the infant when he starts moving around and exploring the world from eight months of age on. According to White's results, children became more socially and intellectually competent and curious if they were allowed a safety-proofed home to explore freely and mess up; if the mother would respond when the child was frustrated, bored, or asked for help; and if the mother offered a lot of conversation and played with the child. Children turned out to be more negative and less intellectually competent if they were raised in more orderly homes, spent a good amount of time in playpens or in front of the television set, and were given organized teaching sessions and educational toys rather than having mother readily available and responsive. In White's study, high school educated mothers were more likely to give the child the time, freedom, and companionship and to respond on demand than college educated mothers. Others rush to the

Figure 32   *Learning!*

defense of college mothers, pointing out that most college students come from college educated parents. This may not be so in the future. It is a hard pill to swallow for some college mothers who, with the best of intentions, offered the "ideal" environment for toddlers, modeled on adult sophisticated standards, only to hear that perhaps it wasn't so ideal.[19]

Love and Discipline

Motivation may be suppressed by parents who love the child so much that they do everything for him. It can also be suppressed by the constantly critical parent. Perversely, motivation may be increased in some by rebellion against domineering parents—although an unsuccessful rebellion may crush it. It has long been recognized that the carrot and the stick are both powerful motivators. But the motivation we usually value most in our children is self-motivation. Self-motivation can spring from several sources. One of these is guilt—a reaction to conscience. Another is pride—an outgrowth of self-esteem. For some, it is curiosity and the need to explore new frontiers.

I believe one of the best ways to teach children self-motivation is

Figure 33   *Their world!*

by dispassionate discipline. This is a method in which the parent acts as a neutral enforcer of reality—and lets the child make his own choice of how he will behave—and then makes certain that he takes the consequences. When the child does the right thing, he wins—not the parent. When he does the wrong thing, he loses—not the parent. This can occur only if the parent remains an unemotional though warm teacher and enforcer. Freedom of choice is offered, but responsibility for behavior is enforced. If the child acts immaturely, he receives the limitations of a young child; if he acts maturely, he receives the privilege of age.

CHILDREN'S NEED TO BE CHILDREN

Through intent or frustration, or because to some there seems no other choice, many adult problems are foisted off on children. In the schools, children are faced with problems adults haven't solved, like how to integrate, how to avoid adult sexual problems, how to deal with teachers who are often poorly paid, how, in some areas, to live under the threat of street gangs, and how to live with the temptation of drug pushers. Children are bombarded with the negative aspects of society via the newspapers and television and often in the classrooms; nuclear warfare, inflation, corruption, and so forth. Few of these problems are new in principle, and when we were children they were the province of adults. Especially today, children need to be protected from the problems of the adult world; they need to be allowed to be children. Of course, many of them protect themselves.

Before adolescence, children live in a very magic world. This magic can protect them from adult pressures and from the realities of the world, and can give them the security and faith needed for healthy, emotional growth. Such needs have been recognized by people for ages, and have been met by a wide variety of customs, fairy tales, and myths. By passing along customs about Santa Claus and the Easter Bunny, and about the tooth fairy and Halloween goblins, adults protect, educate, and shape the attitudes of children. These imaginary figures can have a very positive role in shaping childlike attitudes toward life.

We don't give up our myths easily. As we change from accepting Santa Claus as a person to recognizing the fine spirit behind the myth, we move into Superman and Paul Bunyan. Our modern society needs current writers of fairy tales to point the way to a better life and to allow an escape from our technological society. Some of this is being done for adults by science fiction writers. But who writes for the children— and allows them to be children? We should cease debunking heroes and start, again, to emphasize their positive virtues. Heroes, myths, and fairy tales all meet vital human needs for security and positive thinking.

HOW YOU MEET THOSE NEEDS

All of the various needs of children are important. Your method of meeting their needs depends upon many factors, including the realities of your life and your personality and principles. Make your decisions on meeting these needs in your way. My way, *The Guide*'s way, or even your own parents' way may not always be right for you and for your children. In order to decide if your methods are correct, look at the results—as measured by the behavior, growth, development, and happiness of each of your children. This way, you will develop that bit of professionalism that all parents need.

6

UNDERSTANDING YOUR CHILD'S
BEHAVIOR

For most of us, raising children is relatively problem free and enjoyable. Not so for all, nor all the time for any of us. Problems do occur. Many are normal in the sense that they occur in almost every child. Others are abnormal in that they are exaggerated or do not resolve with time. Here, we discuss some of the most common problems—recognizing that problems are normal. Our emphasis is on understanding the behavior pattern and adopting a course of action designed to lead to long-term improvement. Of course, this implies that we as parents can be rational. That isn't always easy. Sometimes it is difficult to understand a particular child or even to understand our own reactions to a child's behavior. Most emotional problems (and the child involved in such problems) just require some thoughtful attention from you. Almost all children can suffer through one of the problems described here—or through one of many other problems we haven't covered. If the problem doesn't last too long or isn't too intense, perhaps you can apply some of your own simple, practical, time tested philosophies to prevent or correct the situation. Most problems are soluble, but some do require the help of an objective and knowledgeable individual who understands parents and children. It doesn't hurt to get advice from respected friends, neighbors, or members of your family—as long as you end up making your own decisions. Don't "cop out" by following "their" instructions and then blaming them. Parenting is your job—your role—and most of you know more about you and your child than anyone, even more than most amateur or professional "super-parents." And super-parents, or books like this by people like us will never replace the instinctive good sense of parents. Our book can only humbly hope to increase your general knowledge so that *you* can make the specific decision.

But what if the problems still exist? You may be able to find help from teachers, ministers, rabbis, or priests. Or maybe you need the help of a psychologist or psychiatrist. At the end of the chapter is a section on deciding whether professional help is necessary and what you can expect from it.

If you find yourself usually facing your child's problems with anger, you may need some professional help, because the anger itself will create greater problems. If you can face your child's problems with the recognition that they are normal, you will have less cause for anger. So keep in mind that, reasonably enough, children are childish.

THE CURIOUS CHILD

Humans, especially babies, are characterized by marked curiosity. They have to try out this wonderful world: see, feel, handle, taste, smell, and hear *everything*. They have to experience the law of gravity by dropping a dish on the floor, and to experience the limits of matter by the exciting observation that the dish can break. When this sort of behavior starts, it is usually time to start to teach your baby that there are limits in this world aside from gravity. While you are teaching—disciplining—it is equally important that you allow your child a chance to explore the world, and that you don't try to inhibit those exploring hands and that curious brain too much. This is especially true for the fearful child. To discipline a child to be cautious while developing self-confidence and self-esteem requires a subtle grip on the reins.

Figure 34 *Curiosity is finding out what makes a heater go on!*

Is the way out to completely child-proof your house? Certainly we are all aware that accidents and poisonings are common to this age group, so a toddler needs protection, and the house must be examined from top to bottom for sources of danger. However, that can be overdone, contends pediatrician Martin H. Smith:

> I have been in homes that are virtually stripped to the state of an army barracks ready for inspection. The adults and the older children in the household have some rights and deserve some pleasures. All efforts cannot be focused on the toddler. I do not believe that the toddler is too young to be taught that certain objects in the household belong to others. He can learn that he can play with his toys, but not with the clock in the bookcase. This does not require a constant succession of "No–No." Most of the time, diversion to another object or the substitution of a toy will work better.

On the other hand, don't put a baby down among attractive objects and expect him not to go for them, any more than you would set food before a starving man and expect him not to eat. Baby-proof your house. Put the ashtrays (and their poisonous cigarette butts) up and out of the way. Don't fight with the baby over everything. Freedom to explore unhampered is as vital as is discipline. As your discipline becomes effective, you can begin to put things down and normalize the house. Hopefully, this stage of getting into everything peaks at around one and a half years of age.

TEMPER TANTRUMS

Toddlers are midgets in a world of giants, and it is a frustrating world for them. The frustrations may reach a point where the best they can do is lie on the floor, bang their heads in frustration, and kick and scream. If they find that such actions really upset "the" giant, that what they do makes mother mad, then wow! What a way to strike back at the establishment. And the feeling "I showed her!" is a very valuable one! So it is worth the child's while to take the scoldings and spankings—in fact the parental anger he created *makes it worth his while.* He has finally found a way to manipulate the giants in his world!

The best way to handle temper tantrums is to ignore them. Act as if they aren't even there. If the child throws things, or hits or bites, simply and casually take him to his room. Unceremoniously dump him gently into his crib, go out, and quietly shut the door. If you are talking to someone, keep talking as if nothing is happening. Children will give up sooner, and will have fewer tantrums if you don't make their tantrums your problem.

A mother told me that it is best to avoid temper tantrums by avoiding the reason for having a tantrum in the first place. For many children this will work, but other children are built differently, and they will end up having some tantrums no matter how hard you try to please. Dr. John Richards cautions: "Ignore the tantrum but not the child. To refuse to help children when they need help, because they are behaving badly, is unreasonable." Another approach is advocated by pediatrician A.S. Hashim, who says, "He is trying to 'show you for once and for all' by his tantrums. Every once in a while you may have to respond in a positive manner by using your hand on his bottom if he is too unruly. Show him that the tantrum leads neither to leniency nor to love."

WHAT SHOULD YOU DO WHEN YOUR BABY BITES OR HITS?

We offer many views here, starting with one a mother gave me:

"Biting is one of the worst behavior problems for a mother to take. Other mothers view the child as a cannibal. It leads to many gray hairs and little relaxation in the presence of other children." What do you do? Others disagree (see below); but I advise that you bite him back about as hard as he bit you! Do it through the clothes, not on open skin. But don't make a "big thing" about it, just continue with what you were doing and ignore your toothy biter. If children get the idea that it is a "big thing," they will be far more tempted to bite again in order to get your attention. If big sister gets bitten, tell her to bite back, with the same precautions you observe: Don't bite too hard. If your baby bites your neighbor's smaller baby, it would be wise for you to pick your biter up and bite back yourself before your angry neighbor mother decides to spank. It will help to use a casual "no" just before you bite. This will put more "bite" into your "no's."

Dr. William Foster disagrees. He advises: "Don't bite him back. This is negative reinforcement. I would do nothing except the methods you ordinarily use for other important items, such as exclusion to his room, spanking, or firm 'NO'S.' "

Dr. Henry Richanbach is a bit more social. Instead of this sort of approach, he advises:

Biting and hitting are certainly undesirable and antisocial behavior and should never be disregarded or approved of, but both are sometimes best handled by attacking the child's reasons for indulging

in such behaviors, not by attacking the children themselves. Perhaps they need a little extra attention in order to avoid resorting to hostility. Social amenities are things they must learn. If they want to play with another child or get the attention of someone else, they can try less hostile introductions, such as "My name is Johnny, what's yours?" instead of biting or hitting.

Biting back reminds me of the often repeated remark, "No matter how often I spank him for it, he won't stop hitting other children." Chew on that—instead of on the child—for a minute.

Dr. A.S. Hashim agrees with the "bite back" technique, but points out that "there are two kinds of biting. Defensive biting is used by children to defend themselves against bigger and stronger people who hurt or frustrate them. Aggressive biters are the ones who use biting as an expression of their aggression; and the parent should have a stronger bite than theirs to give them a taste of their 'nasty means.' "

When children hit you, hit them back reflexively but mildly. Don't scold. Don't say it's "bad, you shouldn't hurt mother." Just casually return the blow a bit harder than you were hit and go about your business. Don't laugh or make a game of it. Don't reward this type of behavior with a lot of attention. If you do, your child will take the belts in order to enjoy the bows. Babies are "hams." They like to be center stage, whatever the cost. Needless to say, the same "action–reaction" response can apply for pulling hair or for other playful, or angry, damaging behavior. You should be a reflex "law of gravity" in teaching that such behavior results in being hurt. If you are persistent and consistent, and if you have the needed nerve to hurt them back, they will soon learn.

WHY DO CHILDREN HOLD THEIR BREATH?

Breath holding usually starts during the second year, and occurs most often in strong-willed, aggressive, determined personalities. It starts from frustration, particularly after being disciplined. Children will take a deep breath in the midst of crying, and, instead of continuing to cry, will hold the breath, often to the point of becoming blue, or, occasionally, even until losing consciousness. However, these things are important to remember:

1. The vast majority of these episodes are harmless, and, if given time, the child will breathe normally again.
2. Although frightening to witness, it is essential not to react in a way which demonstrates to the children that they can use breath holding as a means of getting their own way.

Dr. Sid Rosin writes: "Breath-holding children would control their parents, the household, and the world if allowed. They need a critical balance of discipline and love. Above all, parents must not acquiesce to the children's demands or retract threats about discipline which may have triggered the breath holding. Sometimes the startling effect of a sharp slap to the cheek with two fingers will help stop the episode."

Associate editor Dr. John Richards objects:

> Since breath holding is harmless, why resort to a slap on the cheek? I don't condone face slapping for any reason. Sometimes crying three-or four-year-old children who have sustained a relatively minor injury will take a deep breath, hold it for a few seconds, and then fall to the ground unconscious. Most often this happens *after* children have looked up to see mother rushing to the scene to learn what the crying is all about. This kind of fainting from breath holding can be mistaken for a convulsion, but is easily recognized as harmless by the fact that upon regaining consciousness children are fully alert and often start crying again to gain mother's sympathy. The only real risk is that, when they faint, they may injure themselves in a fall to the ground.

HOW CAN YOU TEACH YOUR THREE-YEAR-OLD TO LIVE WITH THE WORLD?

It's not easy. Three-year-olds would rather *run* the world. Their sense of self-confidence and feeling of self-esteem now have to be modified. Three-year-olds would like the world to mind when they snap their fingers, to jump when they stamp their feet. At this age, they reach what we fervently hope will be the peak of their godlike feeling—the omnipotence complex. They can rather easily become tyrants.

Sooner or later, they must make the discovery that they are not God. So it is reasonable to begin a new step in the civilizing process. We may not want to eliminate that feeling entirely, but we certainly had better modify it some. The first person in the child's life is mother. And a question she must answer when she has a child of this age (and older) is "to be or not to be—a slave." Some mothers respond—literally jump—to the child's every whim for whatever ill-founded reason. So the poor misguided child grows up expecting the world to do the same.

The way to help a child control these feelings is by demonstrating that we *all* feel a bit that way. Mothers must not become slaves. When their demands are unreasonable, children should be "put in their place" as they were in past generations. There are times when a child should "be seen and not heard." They must be taught to "respect their elders."

Of course, you should listen and show respect toward your child. That, too, is part of discipline, a means to show a way by example to deal with people. It does mean that you should not allow the child to be center stage all the time, and that you should insist that he respect the rights of others.

If mother teaches her child to respect and value her, and if she lets him know that she also has needs and must leave the child to face life alone at times, then much of the problem is solved. So don't do all the things your child wants. If he wants something badly enough, let him try it himself. Let him start living his own life and taking some responsibility for it himself. To be his slave is to set him up for a life of unreal desires, with resultant frustrations and heartaches.

IMAGINARY FRIENDS

"Make believe" is probably vital for young children. The three-year-old's omnipotence complex or godlike feeling leads him to demand a lot of the world. The world rarely responds. The resulting frustrations, added to the frustrations of trying to live with the other uncivilized children around him, may force him to tantrums. Hopefully, by now, he has found that these do not work. So what next? Retreat. Retreat to a make-believe world where things can be as he wishes them to be, as he *needs* them to be. This make-believe world isn't a cop out, it is a safety valve. It is a spot to which he can retreat and heal his bruised ego.

A child who spends too much time in his make-believe world probably needs a few more successes in his real world. Perhaps you should try to make it nicer for him. You don't need to be his slave; but we can all be each others' servants temporarily. Too much make believe may indicate that he needs a hand—so don't hesitate to help him into our real world. But a little make believe—we never outgrow the need for that!

Dr. John Richards writes:

> A bright, well-adjusted, imaginative preschool age child will often have an imaginary friend—a friend who never talks back, who is willing and constantly available to listen when a sympathetic ear is needed, and who uncomplainingly takes the blame for many of the little "accidents" that just "happen" in the everyday life of a small child.
>
> Fantasy can be both fun and therapy. After the age of five or six, make-believe play is usually at the "let's pretend" level, and, as such, should cause no concern whatsoever. On the other hand, an older child who uses this means as an escape from the stresses of home, neighborhood, and school responsibilities may need professional help.

DIRTY WORDS

As children get older, usually around four, they often learn dirty four letter words from older children and repeat them at the most unexpected and embarrassing times and places. The observation given here by Dr. Henderson is also applicable to other problems:

The child really does not know what the words mean, but he knows they are bad. He is often secretly delighted to shock his parents and is pleased because he looks on these words as "grown up" words.

These four letter words have a place in a child's vocabulary, and forbidding their use will not solve the problem. The parents should state that some words are not used in their home. Mother can say, "I know children use them, but I don't like them."

The principle involved is to label unacceptable behavior as immature, which it is. Then it becomes the child's problem to control it, not yours. And the great urge of these children is to grow up and be "big" and "important."

SHARING AND STEALING

It is amazing to me to see how intent most adults are in teaching children to share their prized possessions while the adult so rarely shares prized possessions. How often do we share our car, our house, our golf clubs? We should recognize that stealing is a natural trait of small children. If they want an object, they take it. I have found it of some value to point this out to older children who steal. When stealing is accepted as immature behavior, then it loses some of its luster. Another help is to develop something in children besides the fear of being caught as a detriment to stealing. Moral values must have a reward to the individual—in this case, it can be the recognition that respect of others' property is a trait of a civilized mature individual.

Nearly all children go through periods when they take things which are not theirs, explains Tacoma pediatrician David Sparling:

At four or five years of age, this is a normal exploration of the difference between "mine" and "not mine." Their understanding will be helped by encouraging them to value their own possessions and to respect the possessions of others. Do not, at this time, insist too forcefully that they share.

If they do steal at the grocery store or at a neighbor's, insist that they return the object themselves. Talk to the owner ahead of time to be certain that your child will get an impressive but not damaging lecture, not an offhand, "It's all right." If the object cannot be returned, arrange to have it repaid by deducting portions of their allowance for a sufficient number of weeks, or by having them work it off.

If theft occurs, see if children are being pressured to keep up with or brag to their playmates. Help them to maintain their self-confidence and prestige with their peers. If their friends seem to be displaying more of their affluence than is appropriate, a discussion of this in the family or the neighborhood may be necessary. Be friendly but firm in dealing with stealing. If it becomes habitual, your physician should be consulted.

THE LITTLE TOUGH GUY

How humans handle the emotion of fear has taken up much of history and literature. How children handle their fears takes up much of their time and effort. At one extreme of the bell curve of human variability, there are preschoolers who are afraid of their shadows. At the other extreme, there are preschoolers who would fight the devil himself, and would probably win. These are the ones who get into more things; who are hard to discipline; who may be hyperactive; and who are stubborn and refuse to eat, toilet train, get dressed, or get undressed. They get angry; they have temper tantrums and breath holding spells. Later,

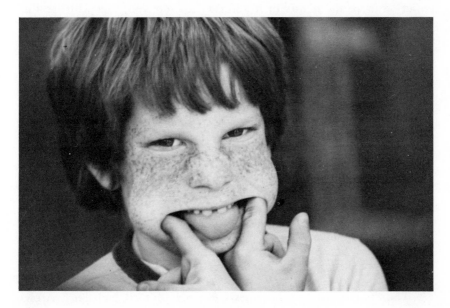

Figure 35

they bring home grubby friends and dirty words. Many are defiant and aggressive with both adults and children. They insist upon center stage and are uncowed by the world. One way or another, they try to run the world. All told, they can be a handful; and if you have a child like this, you need all the help and advice you can get in raising him.

All of us have a bit of the "tough guy" in us. Even as adults, we are apt to display temper tantrums, to try to be center stage, or to push at our world aggressively. If our omnipotence complex is "in hand" and our aggressions properly channeled, we may have a modicum of success without incurring anger from the world. Our aim with the little tough guys is to help them develop enough control of their aggressions so that they, also, are able to achieve such success.

The child who is difficult and defiant needs love as well as discipline, the carrot as well as the switch. Teaching a child discipline begins with a parent's own self-discipline. You do not want to feed a child's anger with your own anger; rather, you should "show the way" to self-control by example.

Because "defiant" children are not "good" for the adults in their world, the adults frequently respond by coldness, if not anger. When mother has a chance to avoid contact or to escape her "bad" child, she understandably does just that. This engenders insecurity underneath the child's bravado. The vacillation of the preschooler between wanting to rule the world and needing tender loving care tends to drive some parents to distraction. Unfortunately, if the child finds that he has the power to drive the giants in his world "up the wall," he will use this power uninhibitedly. From temper tantrums to dirty words he becomes, albeit innocently at first, a manipulator.

In the process of control and discipline of their "bad" children, we should heed the experience of child psychiatrist Dr. Robert Herman:

> This reminds me of the tough little guys we often see in the psychiatry clinic. I call them the "Tom Sawyers" and "Huck Finns" of this world: independent, resourceful, tough, and determined to survive come what may. No amount of schooling or spanking by parents seems to daunt their determination to stand up to the world, to be seen and heard. Yet after treating these children, I am amazed to see how frightened and sad they are inside after they finally are able to express their feelings openly.
>
> It is important that parents learn to understand these children, and to know that they often hide their true feelings. They need to be helped to come out honestly with what is hurting, rather than being labeled "bad," "stupid," or "stubborn."

The "tough guy" stubbornness certainly isn't all bad. Such strong spirit, if properly channeled, can be a boon to the child and to the world. Still, two cautions are in order. If not properly channeled, such spirit can represent a threat to the child and to his world. And remember that early in life, as well as later, little tough guys are great explorers: Their life expectancy is threatened by the things they get into. If you have one of these children, you will want to read Chapter 7 on Ways To Raise Children.

THE FEARFUL CHILD

Fear is a necessary part of humanity—a "survival-imperative." Those children with an excessive amount of fear instinctively overreact to hurts, physical or psychological, real or imagined, by clinging, crying, and withdrawing; and they can be truly crippled in many circumstances by their excess fear and their lack of confidence. A child's fears are real whether he is in danger or not; and whatever the hurt, crying is a natural reaction, even for boys. It takes a lot of time to develop control. The parents' reactions to the child can make these traits worse or better. For a child to learn to control and modify his fear requires careful conditioning, education, and positive parenting—by example and reaction, and by logic and discipline.

To modify the clinging, crying behavior requires as much forbearance and self-control from the parents as it does for the little tough guy. That isn't easy, for the behavior is both exasperating and guilt-producing. There is the added problem of deciding how much shielding such a child needs: A balance must be struck between realistic protection, parental overprotection, and exposing the child to life.

Normal Fear Times

There are several age levels at which children are normally fearful. The first is usually from six to nine months, when many infants become afraid of strangers. Some may even become afraid of father or grandmother—creating no end of ruffled feelings! At this age especially, most infants seem to need one mother.

Then, around nine months babies often become anxious when mother leaves for a short period. This fear may be helped by peek-a-boo games that demonstrate that mother does come back. It is usually important that between nine to twelve months the baby be handled and loved occasionally by at least one or two people besides mother, thus giving the child company to help lessen the initial anxieties until mother returns. It also allows mother some often much needed time away from the child.

The next normal fear time is usually when the baby starts to walk.

Figure 36   *"It's a big scary world. Mom come get me!"*

Up until this time, the baby has regarded mother as a fixed part of his life—as if mother and baby are one. When baby begins to walk, however, his impression of himself goes up immensely. Now he is an individual! He can even choose to run away from others. And then what? Suddenly he discovers that the world is big, and he becomes homesick for mother. Without her he is very vulnerable. So the next time mother sets him down, he doesn't want to let go. And mother may become impatient and force the baby away from her. This really panics some babies, and they react by desperate clinging. Such "illogical" behavior, by adult standards, often makes mother angry, which further compounds the problem. The only way I know of to deal with this problem is to condition toddlers, gradually and unemotionally, to being left "alone." However, the problem frequently can hang on or even rekindle itself at a later age in a common syndrome we call the "clinging two-year-old."

When the two-year-old goes out into the back yard, he is king of his domain. But things happen. The sun is hot, the sticks hurt, the noises scare. It is safer inside. So he goes back into the house to check on home base; he asks, without the words, "Is everything all right, Mom, do you still love me?" Mother is usually only partly aware of the fears and insecurity, and is acutely aware that he is tracking up the floor that she is mopping, so she replies, "Go outside and play!" The child perceives this as rejection; and underneath, he may say, "God, she doesn't want me!" To overcome this, he then tackles mother's legs, clings and cries, and demands to be picked up and loved. Mother finally gives up and picks the child up with noticeable reluctance, puts him down, and pushes him back outside. This time, the stay outside is even shorter, since there are feelings that maybe mother really didn't want the child around. So he charges back in, demanding more attention. In fact, he can demand so much attention that when mother gets a minute to herself, she mops her brow, says a prayer of thanks, and tries to do something quickly before he comes in again.

The result of this situation is that children find that when they demand attention, they get it; and that if they don't demand attention, they don't get it. So they demand more. This leads to a legitimate need for mother to get away from the child in order to finish her work. Soon it becomes a parody, with an anxious, crying, clinging child pressuring a harassed and more and more unloving mother.

Dr. John Richards believes that, "When crying and clinging behavior interferes seriously with work that must be done, unceremoniously put the child in a safe place such as the bedroom (locked if necessary), or a play pen. Then finish your work. Isolation doesn't increase the child's feeling of rejection as much as scolding and spanking."

There is a way out of this vicious cycle. You should give the attention when they demand it, but you should recognize that that sort of attention is somewhat unsatisfying. The best attention is given free. So, several times a day, pick a time when they are doing something neither particularly good nor particularly bad, and when they are not looking for attention, drop what you are doing for a minute and give the child some "free love." You don't have to make a big thing out of it: a smile, a hug, or tousling the hair will help. Let him know that he doesn't have to come to you—that you love him for what he is, not for what he does. Ultimately, this will relieve him of some of the necessity to chase you, and will result in more free time for you and in better feelings for both you and your child.

Helping Your Child Build Self-Confidence

There are other ways of reducing fears and building a confident adult. Pediatrician Neil Henderson points out that children *want* to be helpful and do grownup things:

> Given the opportunity, many children by the age of two will have learned how to undress themselves properly. By the age of three, they ought to be able to dress themselves, except for the more difficult tasks of buttoning buttons and tying shoes. Mother can help by putting out the clothes she wants them to wear, and by providing places where they may put their dirty clothes. When children are

young, the parents can start teaching them about putting things away by making a game of it. This is where your shoes go; this is where your dirty clothes go. By the time they are four years of age, they should have developed these habits. However, before they are capable of carrying out directions, you must lead them through the routines. As soon as children are capable of accepting responsibility, hand it to them in increasing doses, commensurate with their ability.

Giving them these opportunities is teaching and discipline of the best sort, comments child psychiatrist Robert Herman: "It shows the way. On top of that, it assures children that they are able to function in a grown-up manner and it helps build their self-confidence."

Three-year-olds are in the "bandaid stage." They become acutely aware that they have the capacity for pain. Their appreciation of pain must be regarded with mild skepticism, but don't ignore it completely. A three-year-old, told by his mother that his wounded finger really didn't hurt, responded with, "It does too, feel it!" Dr. Robert Burnett suggests

Figure 37   *"I'll do it myself!"*

that the reaction to such hurts provides an opportunity to teach the child positive thinking. "Certainly some sympathy is in order, but tell the child that the hurt will go away and that he will be all right. A hurt child certainly deserves to be reassured by his parents. However, avoid showing too much sympathy or anxiety over minor cuts and bruises or you may increase his sensitivity and fears."

When dealing with the insecure child, don't judge his fears and behavior too much from an adult standard. Remember that children are children and not adults, says Dr. John Richards:

A parent may complain, "The slightest correction triggers a fit of crying in my son. He often runs home sobbing over insignificant disagreements with other children. He breaks down and cries when things don't go right at school. What can we do to make him act more like a man?"

A little boy is not a man. Let him cry. In our culture, little boys are often unreasonably expected to be brave, to hide their feelings and act "manly" in situations where little girls may cry freely, without criticism. But crying is often a necessary safety valve to relieve normal feelings of frustration, fear, and anger.

However, if a child uses tears too much of the time for attention, in order to control those around him, or as a means of avoiding unpleasant responsibility, correction of his behavior is in order. Don't give him what he wants. Ignore the crying, and a child will soon stop using such undesirable behavior if it no longer works.

Teaching Your Child to Control Fears

One of the first steps in helping a fearful child is to make him aware that fear is normal. Even the tough ones have fears. So do parents. What counts is how logical the fears are, and, when logical, how you use or control the fear. On a day to day basis, children need to be gradually conditioned to learn to stay alone, and to face challenges such as going shopping alone, joining a group, talking to strangers, and many other essential activities. However, parents must avoid giving the impression that their aim in pushing these activities is to escape the child; rather, play on the fact that parental absence at times is an acceptable and unavoidable necessity. These are teaching tasks that parents should plan for in the day to day care of the child—both short-range and long-term. On the other hand, there are adults who have never outgrown their childish fears. This is another area of challenge to parents, and one of the many facets of child rearing which keeps the task interesting and stimulating, for parents can and do help modify their children's personalities for the better. Such positive parenting is largely expressed in a positive attitude of ultimate faith that the child *will* grow up and overcome his fears and lack of self-confidence. However, I have seen children go through stages of severe overreactive fear only to conquer these fears by themselves. Meanwhile, it is of worth to establish a long-term plan to build the child's confidence. Praise the child for what he tries to do. Let him make choices. Let him shop for you and give him responsibilities. Leave him at home alone or in charge of smaller children for longer and longer times. Let him make choices and take the consequences, so that he gets many chances to learn that we don't always succeed and that the world doesn't usually fall apart because we don't.

HATE, AGGRESSION, ANGER, JEALOUSY, QUARRELING, AND FRIENDS

Much of the preadolescent's time and effort is spent on learning how to deal with hate, anger, quarreling, jealousy, and friends. The ways they deal with these issues, and the ways they learn to behave, set the stage for adolescence and for the lifetime personality of the individual. To deal with people successfully requires not only self-control but understanding of these emotions. The first control and understanding is on the part of parents. One of the most difficult things for parents to cope with is an expression of hate from their children.

Hate

What should you do if your child says he hates you? Basically, don't be hurt. Three-and four-year-olds are still "wild wolf puppies" and greatly resent the way they are treated. They become furious at the limits and demands placed on them by the grownups and at playmates who won't do things their way. Those with a lot of temper will express this; many more will feel it but not show it; and, in keeping with our variable natures, some won't care. Dr. Merritt Low suggests that "I hate you" may be the verbal testing, by the insecure child, of a vacillating parent. This, he says, can be taken care of by reassurance, consistency, and love in action and word.

Of course, that doesn't mean that we should ignore the outbursts or simply do what the child wants. Three-and four-year-olds suffer the fact that they *are* three-and four-year-olds, and they do require limits and demands. The parent should point out this fact—and then offer the observation that the way the child feels is "too bad" for the *child*. The fact that a child cannot control his temper proves the point—that he must be treated like a child. Send him to his room until he can control himself and his feelings.

Then you should look at what precipitated the hate. Often, a child's hate is the result of parental hate or anger. Perhaps you have been too harsh because you have had a bad day. If so, don't apologize, but instead decide to be more reasonable with your children and less angry—starting now. Look for a time to give a little extra tender loving care when they don't expect it.

Dr. Lendon Smith points out:

> Four- and five-year-old children test out the magic of words on their parents. The wise parent is supposed to remember that it is a developmental step, like learning to walk. A good response is: "Sometimes I don't like what you do, but I always love you."
>
> Some children must be taught to express, verbally, their hates and frustrations in a nonpunitive atmosphere. A parent should be accepting of a child's hates, but he must surely and quickly limit physical aggression. We are humans, not animals.
>
> A child whose hatred and hostility is a way of life may have a psychiatric or neurologic problem. Medication may be a way to calm him enough so that he may be rewarded for socially acceptable behavior.

Much of this can be avoided if you keep in mind that "I hate you" may merely mean, "I don't like what you are making me do." Dr. Charles Hoffman believes: "It is rarely hate directed at the parent personally. Therefore, accept the hate as an expression of resentment at being made to do what he doesn't want to do. Establish the limits of what he is allowed to do—whether he likes it or not or 'hates you' or not."

One mechanism children frequently use to relieve their guilt feelings is to do something that they know will result in punishment. You spank him and then he feels better. "I hurt you and you hurt me and now we are even," he says by his actions. Often, after a spanking, a child will be relaxed and happy—he can start over. But a problem may be created by such a guilt–punishment mechanism. Some criminals, no matter how smart, leave subconscious clues to their crimes in order to insure that they will be caught and punished. It is possible that this psychological mechanism has its onset in childhood and could be altered by handling the "hateful child" differently. Pediatrician A.S. Hashim believes that reason helps:

> First, look at your demands and see if they are too tough. If not, and if the child says "I hate you," then tell him, "You do not hate me, honey, but you do hate doing so and so, and that's because you are lazy and do not want to move (or whatever he's supposed to do); now my lovely boy will do what I asked of him and we will love each other again."

Such an approach, at a more mature level, depending upon the child's age, works well. Perhaps the child is hungry for reasoning—and reasoning may solve the problem.

Alicia Herman of The Parent Effectiveness Training program confirms this: "If you practice fairness to your child as a human being, there will be less hate. Take enough time to help the child make 'bridges' to necessary action, just as you would to help a not-easily-moved friend or old person."

Remember that the child's hate is usually initiated by your limiting or forcing him to do something which he doesn't understand as being reasonable. Occasionally he is right, at least by his thought process, so you should examine your demands. But most of the time *you* are right. Then, the key to his behavior in response to your demand is not so much what you say as *how you say it*. If you say it in a matter of fact way, without anger and hostility, he will be more likely to obey and less likely to become angry. If that doesn't get results, then discipline him. But make his action his problem, not yours. Let his action dictate the results. If he does have to be punished, let him make the choice. You do this by honestly offering him a choice: Either he does what you say or he will have to be punished—without anger. You should not punish just to relieve *your* feelings. If you are too emotional to do a reasonable job, talk it over with your physician and see if he believes you need more help.

Aggression

There are many views on aggression. Many pediatricians believe that aggressiveness is normal. Dr. Neil Henderson explains: "Young children exhibit aggression by hitting each other; by playing wild Indians, and cops and robbers; and later on, by enjoying violent comic books. A child needs to act out all these aggressive stages until the normal rules and regulations of society are learned. As the child grows up, these aggressive instincts are channeled into sports, competition, and striving for success in business." If aggression is normal, Dr. Charles Hoffman reminds us that everyone is not normal: "Not all children are very aggressive and some must be protected from the aggressive or overaggressive kid."

Why are children aggressive? A common reason is simply for attention—an ego boost. Regardless of its cause, it needs to be controlled. Much of this is accomplished by discipline. Television pediatrician Lendon Smith believes that if discipline doesn't work, medication might:

Children need love *and* limits. Those who are not taught the rules of successful social living grow up to be impossible, petulant, and selfish. Many so-called "hyperactive" children have never been told to behave and are virtually asking for limits. However, some impulsive children have been "disciplined" in the standard way—silence, spankings, and separations—and still seem to be spoiled brats. It is not cheating to medicate these children so they become more tractable and can then be rewarded for compliance. [Medication for behavior should *always* be given only at the recommendation of a doctor who knows the child and his problems, and should never be used as a simple solution.]

Another approach has to do with television programs which feature violence. There is evidence of a relationship between televised violence and aggressive behavior. Violence in television programs aimed at children still occurs. This is another reason to limit total and selective television watching time for your children.

Anger

Anger is a major source of aggression and hate. But what if you can't express anger or open aggression? Most children, when angry at their parents, cannot say, "I hate you." They are afraid that the hate might hurt the parent, or that the parent might hate them in return. One way out for children is to do things that they know the parents dislike, such as whining or soiling their pants. To prevent this subtle but sometimes devastating angry behavior, some specialists urge expression of anger. Dr. Neil Henderson says:

A parent who observes that his child is angry should encourage him to express these feelings. The child must learn that it is safe to express angry or negative feelings as well as positive feelings. If angry feelings are kept inside, because of fear of retaliation by the parents, the child may establish a behavior pattern that will prevent him from expressing negative feelings as he grows older. This may interfere with his ability to use all of his natural resources. In the future, he may not be able to give an honest opinion.

The parent who becomes angry—and there are many justified reasons—should carefully consider the proper way of expressing himself. The use of threats, such as "If you do it once more, you can't go swimming," is ineffective. The child only hears "Do it once more," and thus the parent encourages misbehavior. A threat serves as a challenge to the child, and he must meet this challenge in order to live with himself.

There are ways of expressing anger that correct behavior. For example, a young boy was given a rubber suction cup dart set. Instead of throwing the darts at the board, he threw them at his sister. The parent said, "Shoot at the target board, not at your sister." The child did it again and the dart set was taken away. The parent said: "People are not targets." The child learned from his parent's behavior, as the alternatives were obvious—throw at the target or lose the privilege of having the dart set.

Such an approach bothers other pediatricians, including A.S. Hashim, who doesn't agree about children expressing the feeling of anger. He says:

> The child should have a *reasonable degree* of freedom of freedom of expression, as do the parents. But encouraging the child to express feelings of anger may lead to a troublesome brat who in turn becomes a discipline problem.
>
> If there are reasonable grounds for the parents to become angry, they should express themselves, and MEAN IT. If they have threatened, the threat should be carried out: *Consistency* will pay a good dividend in the long run.

Note that Dr. Hashim's anger is tempered with great kindness. What makes it work is his emphasis on consistency and fairness. His type of anger is in the child's best interest.

Jealousy

Little children are often jealous of any attention given to anyone but themselves. We expect such childish behavior; and by dispensing love and attention fairly, we usually teach them that there is no need for jealousy. But what about jealousy between older children? Dr. Henderson says:

> Children are made secure by feeling they are accepted and loved for themselves and not for what they do. They have to be loved uniquely, not uniformly. In dealing with sibling rivalry, it is best to avoid comparisons. Superior ability in school may cause envy, but it is the parents' excessive praise of that ability that causes jealousy.
>
> Allow children to resolve their own differences without interference. Interfere only to protect life and limb, or because quiet is necessary in the household. Avoid placing the blame for a fight on one child or the other.
>
> Children of different ages should have different privileges. If the younger child is envious of these privileges, deal with his feelings by understanding them. For example: "You want to stay up late to watch television. You wish you were older. I know, but it is time to go to bed." Do not try to explain the facts.
>
> It would be nice if children thought that sisters and brothers are for loving, as parents like to think. The vast majority of children are

striving to be "number one" with their parents. When siblings are in competition with one another, it hardly leads to a feeling of closeness.

Jealousy is a normal emotion. It can be developed into a useful emotion so that as a child grows up he will be able to master rivalry that may occur in a business situation or in the so-called friendly game of golf.

Meanwhile, it helps to praise the child's *efforts* rather than the degree of his success, says Dr. Charles Hoffman: "This helps avoid the situation where the more successful child always gets the praise—and children are always looking for praise and approval from parents. It reduces one cause of jealousy."

The Sensitive Child

Frequently, a child is labeled as "sensitive." Such a word certainly means different things to different people, but to most it means that the feelings are easily hurt—as measured by the reaction to the hurt, such as withdrawing, sulking, becoming angry, or crying.

Of course, if by "sensitive" one means that some children are acutely aware of the feelings of others, then it is a somewhat different "problem." Here, we are talking about children who are often miserable because of slights or hurts inflicted by their fellow men. They are more sensitive in that they are more easily hurt.

Living with people always produces some friction. If one allows oneself to be hurt by the imperfections of parents, siblings, friends, and neighbors, then much suffering will ensue. Even the best of people may

Figure 38

not be perfect for you or for me. When we talk about a "good" person, we actually mean it in the emotional and practical sense, "She is good for *me*." The sensitive or easily hurt individuals obviously have decided that whoever hurt their feelings is "bad for *me*." The exceptionally sensitive individual, then, must believe that the world is full of "bad" people. So we are really talking about the way an individual perceives the rest of the people in the world. The remarkable thing about such perceptions is how often a particular individual is perceived as a "good" person by many, yet perceived as "bad" by sensitive individuals. While there is often some realism in such perceptions, just as often "bad" people do not really mean to be bad. They are either unaware that they are "bad" for a particular sensitive friend; or, if they are aware of this label, they resent it as being unfair, for they meant no harm. The next reaction is the not unusual rationalization: "If they are going to blame me, I might as well do it!" Now a vicious cycle has been created where the sensitive individual's fears create their own problems.

How can you help children out of such sensitivity and fears, and out of the problems they create? First, by love. Convince them that they have nothing to fear from you. Second, by our reaction to people and events. If you live under a cloud of fear and always express worry that "something may happen," you convince children that there is plenty to worry about. You can usually obtain better results if you are positive and express confidence in the child's ability to meet and overcome situations. This should be accompanied by training and advice on a logical manner in which to overcome problems. Third, and equally as important, is to help these children reset their thermostats of expectations about people.

Unreal expectations, taken seriously, can make people miserable. The "sensitive" children often expect too much of other people—they would like to have all relationships with other humans be "good." Their attempts to make such relationships good may not be rewarded to the degree they expect; therefore, they are hurt. This hurt leads to negative reactions which make it less likely in the future that the other person will respond well. The sensitive child needs to learn to appreciate what he gets, not to "curse the gods" because he didn't get all that he wanted.

One method of teaching children not to be too easily hurt is to give them "emotional calluses" by teasing them. Teasing is doing something gently that could be done roughly. Children who have learned to take teasing with reasonably good humor will be far happier than those who explode at the slightest teasing. The rule is to make teasing gentle, light, and controlled. Start with small doses—an amused smile will do. Then a brief jibe, and leave it alone. A good laugh is a good third step. Avoid heckling or continuous teasing.

The sensitive child is often the perfectionist who cannot accept criticism because he must always be right. He cannot accept defeat, lack of praise, second best, criticism, or teasing. He must be taught that it is enough to try, and that lack of success is not the end of the world. Teach him to take criticism with a sense of humor at his inexpertness; teach him to try things because they look like fun rather than simply to try to win.

Most of us have to be fairly mature *and* in a good mood in order to accept sarcasm. Many experts will disagree and say that no one, especially parents, should use sarcasm. My philosophy is that if your child knows that you love him, like him, and are loyal to him, he will be able to accept some negative vibrations and will be better for it.

Some don't agree with the concept of teasing at all. Dr. Hashim says that it may be all right for the "average" sensitive child, but that it is not for all:

A few children can be labeled the super-sensitive, and such children are less likely to take teasing criticism; they will burst into tears with slight provocation. Such children ought to have less teasing, and to be accepted for what they are. Such sensitivity might stimulate a child to outshine his peers and zoom in his accomplishment in life.

A five-to eight-year-old child goes through a stage of being easily hurt; he cries for some slight provocation, and may try your patience. Fortunately, this too shall pass.

A mother commented: "Some children, for a variety of reasons, are not willing to or capable of accepting such teasing, especially from others who are not on the same 'wave length.' "

A final word. Everyone is sensitive. Some just don't show it as much as others, although some do accept human friction better than others. The problem occurs with those who make a "federal case" out of each slight or imagined hostility. These children deserve realistic help in learning to deal with life better and more effectively; they do not simply need more protection.

Quarreling

Brothers and sisters routinely, but not inevitably, fight with each other. It probably bothers parents more than the involved children. But whether quarreling between children is normal or not, the question is, will they outgrow it? And in the meantime should you try to reduce quarreling? Pediatrician Charles Hoffman tells his patients: "Children fight with each other whether in or out of a family. If left alone they will correct their own behavior patterns. However, if there is real hate and hurt in their fighting, the basis should be determined and corrected if possible."

Dr. Lendon Smith looks on fighting as a learning experience:

> Quarreling and bickering during childhood are routine ways in
> which children learn to get what they want in adult life without hurting
> another. By a human feedback mechanism, they find out how far they
> can go and still be a "human" human. If parents interrupt fights and
> quarrels, the children may learn that this is a new, effective way to
> get attention.
>
> It is important that each child in a family be encouraged, or
> directed, into a different activity so that he will not compete directly
> with another sibling. If they are all swimmers, someone will lose and
> feel put down. Maybe one could cook, one sew, and one collect stamps.
> Everyone needs to feel he is important and worthwhile, and that he
> can do something.

As you can see, quarreling between children is part of growing up.
However, if they *never* get along, always seem to hate each other, or are
disturbing the rest of the family with constant bickering, it might be
worthwhile to intervene. If you do intervene, never take sides in your
children's quarrels, says pediatrician John C. Richards: "Avoid making
one the 'good guy' and the other the 'bad guy.' Interfere only when you
must—to preserve your sanity or to prevent mayhem. When this point
has been reached, separate them as calmly as possible and isolate each
for a cooling off period. If more severe punishment is necessary, deal it
out equally, with no comment which might justify either child's behavior."

I find that you can at least have a quiet house if you intervene with
parent power and *act* rather than just talk. First, establish the rule that
they can fight outside the house—but not in the house or around parents
or company. If they disobey, then *calmly* offer to help them hurt each
other. Knock their heads together hard enough to hurt a bit, or switch
them both. Tell them either to quit such behavior or to go outside. But
don't make a big deal out of it; don't lecture them; don't become angry;
and don't give them much time or attention as a reward for such annoying behavior. Actions speak louder than words.

One technique for helping older kids control their fighting is to
show them that it is immature behavior which doesn't pay off. Pick a
time when things are calm and you are alone with the older child. Ask
him how old he was when the younger brother was born—usually he was
two or three years old. Point out how two- and three-year-olds act, especially when mothers have to spend so much time with the new baby. The
older one is usually hurt, angry, and jealous. And when the baby became
a year or so old, and, as one-year-olds will, started getting into his older
brother's things, it became even worse. So older brother started fighting

with baby brother, who fought back—and they still, even now, may be acting like one- and three-year-olds.

Ask the child if he wouldn't be happier if he wasn't "bugged" so much by the younger one, who has become a monster under his brother's tutelage. Show the "older and wiser child" that he can change little brother's attitude toward him by taking the lead himself.

All this may or may not help. But in *any* case, don't spend too much time or effort on their quarrels—which will then seem to be of less importance.

Friends

What can you do about your child's friends? "Not much," says Dr. David Sparling:

> Children's habits in choosing friends are as different as their own personalities. Some enjoy and seem to require a large group of friends. Some tend to dominate the group. Others, equally in need of a group, learn easily to share leadership responsibility. Still others prefer, at least for a time, to be followers. Some children will select one close friend who is very similar in personality, while others prefer friends who seem to be total opposites. When his best friend has even poorer speech than your own child, or less confidence, sports ability, or grades, we cannot help worrying. Yet some children, at least temporarily, need the morale booster of not being the worst. Later, they

Figure 39 *"Friends!*

may develop this preference and build their own character by learning to help others.

If your child chooses a friend with objectionable characteristics, such as bad language or dishonesty, you are faced with a difficult and delicate decision. If your reaction is too strong, it may only strengthen the friendship. Children need opportunities to be helpful to others, and also experience in making their own decisions. In this case, unless your child is immediately acquiring the other child's bad habits, it may be best to see what need this other child fills, or to find out if your child feels he is overprotected. He may need more, not less, freedom, coupled with a discussion of personal standards.

Some children's time is imposed upon by having too many friends. Other children's opportunities for friendship seem limited because of the few who live in their neighborhood or because of their special needs. It may take participation in clubs, church activities, Scouts, and sports for them to find those with whom they can share aptitude and interests. Though some children are more self-sufficient than others, all need the opportunity to learn healthy sharing of interests and responsibilities with others nearer their own age.

Pediatrician Lendon Smith points out that children choose friends with whom they feel comfortable. He advises: "Instead of protesting an undesirable (to you) friend, it is best to invite the 'foreign one' over for dinner, a movie, or an outing. If your own child is embarrassed by his friend's performance, he will probably drop him. If a friendship is deepened, you may have learned something of yourself and your child. You cannot legislate taste in friends or art."

Some people need to be surrounded by friends all the time. "Others," says Dr. Charles Hoffman, "like to spend time by themselves, reading, listening to records and so forth. There is nothing wrong with this if the child is happy and at ease with his peers. Some people need people around all the time to be happy; others like to have time to themselves— and there are all degrees between. It is only the complete loner who is ill at ease with people who needs help."

There are many bases for friendship. Says family medicine specialist Raymond Kahn:

One basis is already present, built in, and needs only to be tapped, encouraged, and rewarded—especially when self-initiated. There is an inherent maternalism or paternalism in some children. Such qualities are likely to come from a home where there are love and consideration between parents and children and brothers and sisters. These qualities are often demonstrated to the newly arrived kid on the block, to the new kid in the school class, or to the child of a known poor family or the child of a family with a chronically ill parent. A chance mechanism, such as an overheard parental conversation about the concerned family, may trigger the expression of love and compassion.

No Friends

Before parents can do anything to help the child with no friends, it is necessary to find the cause for the problem. Some children without friends are shy and fearful. Probably the major contribution parents can make in this sphere is to help the child build self-confidence and overcome fears. A prerequisite is that the parent be at peace with the world. The parent who always seems to worry that "something might happen" is more likely to have a fearful child. If a parent fears to leave a child alone a few minutes by the age of three or four years, is afraid to let him go to the park by himself by seven or eight years, or is constantly worrying, the child must feel it is a world filled with dangerous and untrustworthy people.

It usually is best to limit indoor television and to encourage shy children to go outside to play. If they say there is no one to play with, send them out anyway—to the park—or at least just "out." Dr. Hoffman suggests helping younger children "by being handy for moral support until the child feels more at ease in the group of playing children." If the problem seems severe, arrange for social contacts and group activities. Enroll them in Indian Guides, Cub Scouts, Brownies, or whatever.

Figure 40

Invite other children their age for short trips with the family, overnights, parties, and the movies.

Some children seem to be natural "loners" and prefer to play by themselves most of the time. If such behavior started in the toddler age and hasn't deviated, it is probably a part of the personality. If a loner tried to make friends along the way and then withdrew, then it probably represents a correctable "social problem." Some children make up for the lack of friends in their age group by establishing good relationships with the adults and older children in their lives. This type of child usually finds social acceptance with his peers later. In any case, gentle and persistent efforts should be made to expand their boundaries, and opportunities to mix them with other children should be utilized. Parents probably should not interfere too directly with the child's course regarding friends. But it is doubtful if any of the loners really prefer being without friends —although some few may be "natural born hermits."

A different type of child is the occasional outgoing child who has no friends. The most common reason is that the child is not really "friendly" to other people because he is too self-centered and demanding. Such traits are usually the earmark of and results of permissive child rearing, leaving the child with an unresolved omnipotence complex. Such a child needs discipline at home before he requires it outside the home. Dr. A.S. Hashim has kinder words and reassurance for such children, saying: "If a child rejects making friends in spite of many opportunities, he may think he's above others in his performance as a human being and deserves something special. His failure to be part of a gang, or to gain friends and influence people, may become a *stimulus* for a genius character in him in the future. He may develop such personal achievement in compensation."

A prerequisite for all children is that the parent should not be critical of the child. The child raised with criticism must question his own worth—and is likely to be critical of others. The best thing the parent of a child without friends can do is to value him. This love leads to teaching your child how to get along with the rest of the world.

Although we are all different, if your child persists in such a lonely course it might be well to seek an evaluation of the problem.

PROFESSIONAL HELP

Going to a psychiatrist or taking your child to one doesn't mean that you or the child are "mentally ill" or that you are a poor parent or have a real problem child. Actually, the function of psychiatrists is a combination of detective work and education. If you go, it's an education about *you*. But going to a psychologist or psychiatrist is rarely done with ease—reluctance is normal and understandable. In fact, some pediatricians are quite skeptical about sending children to psychiatrists. Dr. Robert F.L. Polley wrote: "Most childhood behavior problems are best handled by the child's physician and parents. It damages a child's self-confidence to find that his teachers or parents suspect he may have mental illness. Premature and unnecessary referral of children to psychologists and psychiatrists is one of the tragedies of our time." Other pediatricians disagree. Dr. Merritt Low comments: "If properly handled, I have never seen referral to psychologists and psychiatrist do any harm—but I agree, lots of time it does little good. Psychiatrists really help people find and cure themselves."

Most parents should start by having a consultation with their child's physician or their family physician about suspected psychiatric problems. Perhaps it isn't all that bad, and relatively straightforward advice can help you solve the problem. If it isn't that simple, your doctor may refer you for psychological or psychiatric evaluation and possible treatment. The cost is always a factor; but, as in many fields, it can be money well spent. And, again as in many fields, it is the most economical way in which to prevent problems or complications. Seek advice early. And don't fear psychiatry or psychiatrists.

How can you decide whether or not a child psychiatrist can be of help? We asked child psychiatrist and pediatrician Dr. Robert Herman, who replied,

This question perplexes many practicing physicians, parents, and school personnel. If you take a child with minor problems to a psychiatrist, will you upset the family needlessly? On the other hand, what if the problem goes on and on? How can you be certain that he will—to use the favorite phrase of the pediatrician—"outgrow it?"

One reason people give for refusal to take a child to a psychiatrist is the worry about "making a mountain out of a molehill," the old "it's just a phase" syndrome. However, if the child is not seriously crippled emotionally, the problem can generally be discovered and solved in a session or two. Such treatment at the appropriate time may be very important and helpful in preventing serious emotional problems in the future. More than once, as a child psychiatrist, I have seen cases of severe emotional distress that might have been more easily handled at an earlier age. It is vital to remember that psychiatrists are not motivated to treat children who are emotionally healthy. And, just as in physical medical care, a clean bill of health for the child after the psychiatric evaluation can be a great relief to the child and to the parents.

When it *is* necessary to refer a child to a psychiatrist, there are ways in which it can be accomplished without devastating the child. First, make certain that the suggestion comes from his doctor, not from the parents. Second, be certain that you as parents are included in the referral—so it is not implied that it is all the child's "fault." Third, present it as an education about "yourself"—and as a parent, look on it as an education about you, as well as about your child. A good psychiatrist doesn't look for "bad" things: He is a detective who uses his skills to figure out why your child, and you, feel and behave as you do. Then he can help by assisting in changing feelings and attitudes.

Going to a psychiatrist doesn't imply "mental illness." It is amazing how much time we spend in school and throughout life learning about "things" and how little time we spend learning about ourselves, about "me." A good psychiatrist is a good educator.

What Happens When You Take Your Child to a Psychiatrist?

Dr. Herman explains:

A psychiatric evaluation consists of three main parts. First is an interview with the child and his parents. The therapist evaluates how the members of the family interrelate with each other. He will obtain a detailed chronological history of the child's development and the history of the family, its growth and development over the years. Interestingly enough, deficiencies in the family that may be passed on to the child have frequently had their beginnings not from the parents, but from the parents' parents. For example, a boy who has trouble controlling himself may have lacked an adequate father because his father's father died at an early age leaving the father without a male to learn from and copy. Unless the effects of this loss are understood and worked out by the father, they will be passed on to the child.

The psychiatrist interviews the child in the second part of the evaluation. In this visit, the therapist tests the child in many ways. He reviews his daily relationships, with family and friends. Does the child see himself as a loner or as one of the gang? Does he see himself as being stupid or smart? Does he value himself? Is he able to control himself during the interview? What kind of relationship does he make to the therapist: Is he cold and withdrawn? Is he anxious or friendly? Can he talk about things?

The therapist pays special attention to the child's emotional development as compared with other children of his age and sex. Is his behavior appropriate? The interview also includes testing for evidence of physical brain problems.

The concluding part of the psychiatric evaluation is a meeting with the parents. Now the child's specific problems are discussed and their relation to the family made clear. At this time, the therapist will discuss a treatment plan, including some idea as to the length of treatment to follow. A simple diagnosis is given, along with an outline of specific ways of correcting the child's faulty behavior. In many instances, a few sessions are all that is needed. However, a child who is more disturbed may be in need of counseling for a longer period of time— anywhere from a few months to several years.

What Children May Benefit From Seeing a Psychiatrist?

According to Dr. Herman, the following are examples of emotional problems in children and adolescents treated by psychiatrists:

A. Children emotionally upset by problems in people around them may have "adjustment reactions" with no underlying mental disorder and can benefit from a brief analysis of their problems and behavior and positive suggestions from a psychiatrist.
B. Emotional disturbances that may permanently change the child's personality and way of dealing with situations.
1. Hyperkinetic Reaction of overactivity, restlessness, distractability, and short attention span, a condition which usually diminishes in adolescence.
2. Withdrawal Reaction, characterized by seclusiveness, detachment, sensitivity, shyness, timidity, and an inability to form close interpersonal relationships.
3. Overanxious children who have excessive and unrealistic fears, sleeplessness, or nightmares. These children are immature, are self-conscious, lack self-confidence, are conforming, inhibited, and dutiful, and seek approval.
4. Runaway children escaping from threatening situations by running away from home for a day or more without permission. Usually, they are immature and timid and feel rejected at home, inadequate and friendless. Often they steal.
5. Unsocial children who appear disobedient and quarrelsome. They are physically and verbally aggressive, vengeful, and destructive. Temper tantrums, solitary study, lying, and hostile teasing of other children is common.
6. Delinquent children and adolescents who identify with a gang. They may steal, skip school, and stay out late at night. This problem is more common in boys than in girls; it usually involves sexual delinquency and shoplifting.

Even when children have severe problems, some parents still worry about taking them for help. One mother asked, "Won't my child's record of having psychiatric problems be a detriment to him now and in the future?" Dr. Herman replied:

That is a good question. Parents are concerned about the effects of going to a psychiatrist: the effects on the children, on their records, and on the family's status in the community.

Regarding records: A psychiatrist's records are kept "strictly confidential." They are not made available, even to the family physician, except with the permission of the parents. The only persons who need to know, ever, about making visits to the therapist, are those directly involved.

Regarding "face": Fortunately, people are becoming more

enlightened about psychiatry. More is written, discussed openly and known about just what a psychiatrist does, about how most therapy "looks" and "sounds," and about what the expected results may be. We are more aware that psychiatrists may be seen for any malfunction: from the most minor discomfort to a serious mental illness. Hence, the label "crazy" is no longer connected with one who sees a psychiatrist. (In fact, some of the best people do.)

Regarding the child, look at it this way: If your child develops pneumonia, would you ask yourself: "Should I treat it myself or ignore it and hope he will overcome it?" No. You call the proper authority: the physician. If a child needs psychiatric help, he will undoubtedly benefit a great deal from therapy (especially if he is brought in early enough). The change in his behavior and his outlook for the future will more than offset any possible slight discomfort arising from going to a psychiatrist.

Well, when are *you* going to see the psychiatrist? Not too often, if you have to pay for it yourself. On the other hand, it is remarkable that we don't spend more money, each of us, finding out about the self. We are educated about all sorts of arcane and often worthless things, but we receive little education about each of us as a very complex individual. If society ever becomes affluent enough, and psychiatry knowledgeable enough, we should each have a course on "me" in school. It would be interesting, at the least, to have a professional "mirror, mirror on the wall" to give us realistic views and constructive outlets for our personalities.

7

WAYS TO RAISE CHILDREN

There are 1,001 ways of raising children and almost everyone is an expert on the subject—especially how *other* people's children should be raised. Most of this advice is well meant and represents the successful experience of the particular "expert." In the case of pediatricians and psychologists it often, although not always, represents sound statistical advice as well as experience. But whatever the advice, whoever the expert, however sound the statistics, it is only good advice if it works on your particular child. You will find some interesting and remarkably different ways of raising children advocated in this chapter. Some readers will be misled by some of the concepts presented here because everyone has a slightly different view and a somewhat different emotional bias. Sometimes parents are misled because we try to oversimplify complex subjects. For example, we were advised by one reviewer to tell our readers that the ways we offer to raise children may be divided into three varieties: authoritarian (harsh), firm (strict), and permissive (easy). As you will see, these labels do not always mean what they seem to; and, even if they do, they only represent words which at best can only attempt to summarize complex ideas.

The problems of trying to label *a* way of raising children are typified by the conscientious parent-to-be who "decides" on such-and-such a child-rearing philosophy, only to see that philosophy swept away in the unanticipated upheavals of the first weeks and months of actual parenting. In fact, even experienced parents constantly alter and adapt their parenting procedures as their children grow up, as new children come along, and as they themselves change and grow. They appreciate the lessons they have learned (including the comforting realization that a child generally survives what they thought at the time were horrendous parental errors); but they also recognize the need to respond to changes in themselves, their lives, and their children.

Although changes in parental attitudes and methods are inevitable, and a flexible philosophy is often desirable, there is an equally strong need for consistency and solid values. Whether we know it or not, we give our children very strong signals as to how we want them to behave, what we want them to believe, and what kinds of people we want them to be. First, there is the example we set in our lives apart from our specific functions as parents. Second, there is what we tell our children—the "shoulds" we seek to instill in them. Finally, and perhaps most effectively, there is the daily interaction between parent and child that demonstrates to children those behaviors and feelings that are acceptable and those that are not.

PERMISSIVE VERSUS STRICT PARENTING

Daily interactions often raise problems in parenting which force us to deal with our own internal inconsistencies and uncertainties, and to test in action some of our strongest beliefs. Let's take the example of a young mother who is dead set against physical punishment; she believes it teaches a child to solve problems by means of physical force, and in fact has told her own little boy not to hit other children. Still, there are times when he seems hell-bent on defying her, and when nothing else seems to work she often has a very strong urge to smack him. At these times, several thoughts are likely to be running through her mind: "He *can't* climb up on that stool; he might hurt himself and break my good vase besides. He *can't* talk that way to his mother; children need respect for authority. If I spank him, he'll stop, but he'll hate me, or he'll become more rebellious, or he'll take it out on somebody else."

There seems to be no way out of this dilemma that will make the mother happy. Spanking may achieve her short-range goal of getting him off the stool, but at a long-range cost of maternal guilt: "What kind of mother am I to be reduced to using brute force? What will it do to him?" Not spanking will leave her philosophical opposition to physical punishment intact, but can generate other worries: "How can I keep him from hurting himself and from tearing the house apart? Won't he be a spoiled brat if he's never made to mind? I am angry, but what can I do about it? And who's in charge around here anyway?"

Over the years, various authorities on child care have attempted to provide parents with answers to such dilemmas. Their advice has been couched in a series of "best" ways to raise children. Each generation of experts seems to react not only to changes in society but also to the preceding set of rules. To put it in perspective, I asked psychiatrist Irving Philips of the University of California's Langley Porter Clinic how the current philosophy of permissiveness got started:

In the 1920s, character formation was thought to be best achieved by a firm and rigid schedule, developed early, rigorously obeyed, and meticulously followed. The then standard text in pediatrics warned that "the practice of playing with infants and exciting them by sights, sounds, and motions until they shriek with apparent delight is often harmful and should be condemned. . . . It is surprising to see what can be accomplished by intelligent efforts at training in these particulars. Regularity of nursing is of great importance. . . . After nursing . . . [the baby] should be returned to his crib and not disturbed for some time."

In the thirties, a counter-movement slowly gained momentum. The work of Freud and Sullivan began to emphasize the importance of childhood experiences in the developmental process, presaging a more liberal approach. American society began to recognize the rights of children, child labor was abolished, aid to dependent children legislation was enacted. In this climate, interrupted by World War II, Dr. Spock's volume imploring the parent first to *enjoy* the child became the bible for many bewildered parents who reflected on the rigidities of their own upbringing. They wished something better for themselves and their offspring. As prosperity and affluence grew, they were able to give more time and consideration to the needs of their children. Of course, there were parents who, because of their own difficulties, contributed to distortions in the rearing of their children by confusing permissiveness with license. Nevertheless, many raised their children effectively to allow for personality development that emphasized responsibility and concern.

From these roots have grown such liberal theories as those of Richard Farson, a psychologist at California's Esalen Institute, who unquestionably falls in the permissive camp. One of the foremost advocates of children's rights, he believes that children should be able to choose their own homes, design their own education, have the right to vote and to conduct their sexual lives with no more restrictions than if they were adults. Farson objects to the assumption that it is the parents' right and responsibility to control the lives of their children. "Parents," says Farson, "are not always good for their children." [1] A.S. Neill's *Summerhill*, written about a child-centered school in 1964, is still a popular book in some quarters. "I believe that to impose anything by authority is wrong," Neill claims, and continues: "The child should not do anything until he comes to the opinion that it should be done." [2] Psychologist Thomas Gordon, author of P.E.T. (*Parent Effectiveness Training*), does not think of himself as permissive. Still, he writes that "children resent those who have power over them. It feels unfair and often unjust. They resent the fact that parents or teachers are bigger and stronger, if such advantage is used to control them or restrict their freedom." [3]

As you can see, there is a broad difference between the permissiveness of Dr. Phillips and Richard Farson. And although Thomas Gordon does not consider himself permissive, he is very permissive when compared to practicing pediatrician William Misbach, who believes that such permissiveness has led to the spoiling of a lot of children and that "we are reaping the 'rewards' of the permissive era now. This is an oversimplification, but I think it is time for the pendulum to swing back toward the middle. A return to the 'woodshed' with firm and consistent demands seems needed, judging by the behavior I see in my office today as compared with that of twenty years ago."

Other experts refused to go along with "permissiveness." Pediatrician G.R. Russell, who has practiced since the 1920s, offered markedly different advice:

A most important element in providing proper discipline in the child is the establishment of regular habits. When they arrive home with a new baby, parents must remember that the cord is severed and the child has started on the long trip to becoming a separate and distinct individual. Whenever possible, the child should be established in his own room, in his own crib, with a regular schedule for eating, sleeping, and all body functions.

When the child becomes a toddler, a line should be drawn barring all destructive action. He may do what he wishes with his own toys, but when he passes beyond this line, disciplinary action should be taken. This disciplinary action varies a great deal with the type of child involved. The very sensitive child may often be kept in line with a stern look or word, while the other extreme recognizes only the "iron hand."

When playtime is over, the child, as part of an organized life, should be taught to pick up his toys and place things in order. He must learn early that life is not merely "a bowl of cherries" but that it also involves an increasing degree of chores and disciplines. These become almost automatic and lead to satisfaction in work accomplished and greater time for recreation.

By the time the child reaches school age and has established regular habits and has a healthy regard for disciplinary measures, he is well on his way to becoming a useful citizen. In addition to his household chores, he learns to adjust to school chores or study and to take his work, play, and exercise periods in stride. This should always be under supervision. Also, it is well for the parent to know where the child is, and in general, what he is doing at all times, particularly when he is away from home.

As the child becomes a youth and enters the adolescent period, the regular habits and disciplinary measures of infancy and childhood will stand him in good stead in learning to conform to conventional customs and mores. Simultaneously, wise parents and the child's physician will do well to stimulate and motivate the consideration of a life time appropriate career.

As you can see, Russell still believes in strictness. His advice upsets some pediatricians who are more permissive than he. One of our other contributors said of Russell's advice: "It's easier said than done to teach a toddler to pick up his toys. Anyway, should a disorderly mother expect more of her child than of herself?" Of course such a mother herself may be the result of permissive child raising. If you can see an advantage in strict discipline, such as helping your child to become a more competent future adult, then you may decide to be strict. If you see no such advantage, you, like psychologist Gordon, will reject strictness in child rearing. If you decide against strictness, it might be because you believe that if you simply love and communicate with your children enough that things will work out—children raised with love should return that love and will grow into warm, self-respecting, competent adults. Not so, says psychologist James C. Dobson, author of the best selling book, *Dare To Discipline:*

> Perhaps the most common parental error during the past twenty-five years has been related to the widespread belief that "love is enough" in raising children. Every good and worthwhile virtue was expected to bubble forth from this spring of loving kindness. As time has shown, that was wishful thinking. Although love is essential to human life, parental responsibility extends far beyond it. A parent may love a child immeasurably, and then proceed to teach him harmful attitudes. Love in the absence of proper instruction will not produce a child with self-discipline, self-control, and respect for his fellow man. Affection and warmth underlie all mental and physical health, yet they do not eliminate the need for careful training and guidance.
>
> If it is desirable that children be kind, appreciative, and pleasant, those qualities should be taught—not hoped for. If we want to see honesty, truthfulness, and unselfishness in our offspring, then these characteristics should be the conscious objectives of our early instructional process. If it is important to produce respectful, responsible young citizens, then we should set out to mold them accordingly. The point should be obvious. *Heredity does not equip a child with proper attitudes; children will learn what they are taught.* We cannot expect the desirable attitudes and behavior to appear if we have not done our early homework.[4]

Dobson thus concludes that the results of permissive child rearing are often bratty, unhappy children who can grow up to be lazy, irresponsible, self-indulgent adults unable to conform to social order. On the other hand, advocates of permissiveness harshly criticize the authoritarian approach which, some assert, is based on the idea that you believe children are little animals bent only on satisfying their own selfish needs. The "authoritarian" parent would thus use absolute standards for the child's behavior and punish a misbehaving child without discussing the reasons. Authoritarian parents would give harsh commands, attack the personality of the child rather than the issues, verbally and physically abuse children, and discourage their independence.

But if this definition of authoritarian parents is correct or fits your stereotyped concept of strictness in child rearing, neither Dobson nor Russell is authoritarian. They avoid attacking the personality of the child, are not harsh, and certainly do not advocate abusing children. And although some read Dobson's advice in *Dare To Discipline* as authoritarian, I don't believe it is. He certainly believes in authority, parental power, and spanking if needed; but he is acutely aware of the dangers that people may misinterpret his advice and abuse their children by harshness, coldness, demeaning criticism, or even physical punishment. On the opposite side of the coin, if Farson's and Neill's theories are taken as being permissive, then Dr. Benjamin Spock, the best known authority representing permissiveness in the public eye, is not permissive. Yet critics have accused him of ruining an entire generation of American children. Because he has become the symbol of permissive child rearing, I asked him to clarify for you what he meant by permissiveness in the past and to tell what he thinks of it now.

WHAT'S PERMISSIVE? *

There is no agreement on the meaning of the word "permissive" as applied to child care. Now-a-days a majority of those who use the word—editorial writers, politicians, and other citizens—are expressing disapproval. They mean parents who let their child interrupt adults' conversation, refuse parents' requests, demand service, and make rude remarks. They are angry at the children for their arrogance and they are angry at the parents for letting them get this way.

But we've also heard the word permissive used approvingly. I myself formerly used the word permissive in a mildly approving way to indicate a relaxed kind of parental management as opposed to a more severe one. I sometimes use the word overpermissive as a label for those parental approaches which I think lead to spoiling. But during the anguished controversy over American involvement in Vietnam, several prominent supporters of the war accused me of having created what they called the undisciplined, irresponsible youths who balked at military service. They blamed it on "instant gratification." That was nonsense, because anyone who has used my

* Benjamin Spock, M.D.

book *Baby and Child Care* knows that there's no instant gratification in it. The book urges parents to give their children firm guidance and to ask for respect and cooperation: This makes children not only better behaved but happier, too. The mistaken accusation of "permissive" is still being made, though always by people who admit that they haven't used my books.

I now dissociate myself from the word permissive in order to make it clear that I've always been trying to help parents to avoid spoiling, and to help them to develop responsibility, self-discipline, and politeness in their children.

What is it that traps some parents into letting their children become pests? It's that the parents are afraid, for any one of a variety of reasons—some obvious, some obscure—to stand up for their rights and to guide the child sensibly.

I've known an occasional baby who became a disagreeable tyrant by the age of six or eight months. He would demand to be walked in the mother's arms all evening and a good part of the day. When the mother, exhausted, tried to lay him down in his crib, he would glare at her and bellow angrily until she gave in and resumed the walking. Most often it happens with a first baby. The parents are excessively conscientious people, unsure of themselves, overwhelmed by their new responsibilities, and familiar with the general psychological concept that babies are vulnerable to lack of love and attention. So they feel that, when in doubt, it's wiser to give in. The baby feeds on their submissiveness.

Other parents are made submissive by other factors. A father who in childhood experienced an unusual amount of mutual hostility between himself and his own father may easily run into the same uncomfortable relationship with his son, which makes him dread taking definite stands. A mother who resented a certain pregnancy and wished or tried to end it may feel guilt toward that child or she may exhibit anger toward a daughter who reminds her of a sister whom she resented.

There is a general tendency among many conscientious parents now-a-days to worry about every step of child development which, they've heard, may cause parent–child tension. They may anticipate trouble and feel guilty ahead of time. In a child-rearing study in which I participated, we found, for instance, that a majority of the parents who were college graduates considerably delayed achieving toilet training with their first child because, they later confessed, they dreaded that mutual hostility might develop if they went at training too firmly. It was revealing that training was finally achieved in several cases, as the child approached three years of age, when the mother finally lost her temper one day after an accident and loudly demanded that the child grow up and use the toilet. The child looked surprised, as if to say, "Why didn't you say so in the first place" and became trained from that hour.

A common factor in parents' hesitancy today is the sense of

inferiority that they've acquired as a result of all the books and articles written by professionals in the child care field. The literature and the lectures give parents—especially those who've been to college and acquired a great respect for "experts"—a conviction that only professionals know the answers, and that parents, because they haven't studied child development in a university, are apt to make serious mistakes. Parents with much less education, here and around the world, don't have this problem. They assume that they, and the grandparents, are the experts. That makes for a more comfortable state of mind.

Some parents fear that their children will resent them if they impose firm discipline. (You may have seen a parent who always wilts and gives in when a child shouts, "I hate you!") The trouble is that every parent has expectations about how a child should behave—and these expectations are different, of course, in every parent. If this behavior isn't forthcoming, the parent will inevitably be irritated or even alarmed. So there is no getting away from the absolute necessity —if family life is to run smoothly—for the parent to be clear and firm in giving directions and corrections.

There's another factor that sometimes makes for *over*permissiveness. During investigation of delinquent children, it was discovered that the parents, though law-abiding on the surface, often showed unconscious toleration of their child's misbehavior, which the child could sense. For example, the father of a very young runaway, himself a long distance truck driver, complained officially of his child's repeated disappearances. But it was apparent at the same time that he took great pride that such a young child could cover such great distances and take care of himself successfully.

I recall a four-year-old child, the daughter of unusually polite, considerate parents, who infuriated all the adult neighbors by treading on their toes, knocking over drinks at their cocktails and meals, glaring at them, and speaking rudely to them. Yet the parents, instead of correcting her, would beam on her proudly. It was the contrast between the parents' own considerateness of neighbors and their allowing their child to repeatedly irritate them that suggested that the parents were, without realizing it, getting vicarious satisfaction from permitting their child to misbehave as they had never been able to do in childhood—or adulthood.

Many parents who are overly permissive don't recognize this because so much of the time they are using a cross tone of voice which, they assume, means sternness. Actually, an irritable tone is more often an expression of frustration. The parent feels chronically frustrated by not being able to get the desired behavior from the child. And yet the parent is inhibited by guilt.

I've been discussing families in which the parents are overly permissive, and know it—but don't know how to get out of the trap. There are other parents who have no awareness that their children are spoiled, that they themselves are submissive, and that they have largely created the situation. Their placating is so automatic and instantaneous that they lack the detachment with which to view their child's behavior objectively.

The solution for overpermissiveness is easy enough to write down in words. But in actuality, it's difficult to break out of an overly permissive habit. The parents first have to recognize that *the central problem is their own hesitancy.* But the ideal alternative for them is not to become overbearing, though there's always a temptation to swing in that direction when they realize they've been door mats. All the parent has to do is to be clear-cut, positive and prompt in giving directions and corrections—before the situation has had a chance to deteriorate. It is also important for the parent not to use a nagging tone which rubs anyone, young or old, the wrong way. But if the parent is controlling the situation instead of being imposed on, there is really no reason to have that frustrated, nagging tone.

If you and your child have fallen into a pattern of chronic mutual resistance and irritation, you may feel sure that the child will never conform unless you are disagreeable. It may help you to think for a minute of some military leader like Lincoln. Is it plausible that they got their orders obeyed by being cranky with their subordinates? It isn't likely. Leadership of a vast army or a small child requires a combination of self-confidence or self-respect, and a respect for subordinates. The job of the parent is harder than that of a general. The general was being trained in leadership from his first day in West Point; and his subordinates have all been thoroughly trained to accept authority. Most parents have had no leadership training; and the only training their children have had in being subordinates is what their parents were able to give them.

I've used such words as spoiled and pesky to describe the children of overly permissive parents. But the interesting development that I've observed is that most of them have their irritating traits rubbed off them as they move through school and the university. A great majority end up as responsible citizens and agreeable companions. It's in childhood that they are nuisances—and mainly to their parents.

The next type of parental attitude I want to mention, very briefly, to round out the discussion, I'll call authoritarian. Authoritarian parents don't think of children as striving by themselves to grow up and become more mature. They think of them as naturally preferring to stay childish, be lazy, avoid constant watchfulness, bossing, threats, scolding, and punishment—by parents and teachers—which civilize children, all of whom have to be dragged by the ear into maturity.

Authoritarian parents feel this mistrust of children because they themselves were brought up by parents who had the same mistrust. Throughout their growing-up, they took their parents word for it that they were more naughty than good; that when they behaved themselves, it was because they were being made to. They learned, you might say to mistrust themselves. An authoritarian parent says to a child, "I'll be listening to hear whether you're doing your practicing." I remember a new mother who, when her just-born daughter was brought to her for the very first time with her thumb in her mouth, said crossly, "You bad girl!"

There are really two sub-types of the authoritarian parent. The first is only mildly mistrustful, but is not really hostile. Under this influence, children can grow up quite friendly, and only slightly handicapped in regard to initiative and creativity. At the other extreme is the parent who is hostile and therefore apt to produce hostile children, and whose marked mistrustfulness will be apt to limit significantly the self-assurance and initiative of the children.

I've been writing as if there were four distinct parental attitudes— overly permissive, trustful, mildly authoritarian, and hostile–authoritarian. Of course there are only a few parents who belong to such distinct types. I sketched the extremes to make my points.

A great majority of us parents have mixed attitudes. We may be overly permissive about one or another aspect of our children's rearing, perhaps about soft drinks and other junk foods, or about procrastinating at bedtime. (The children do all their arguing with parents in the areas in which the parents are hesitant, never in those in which the parents are sure of themselves.) Yet at the same time, we were made very anxious in our own childhood. For instance, I was ashamed of being a sissy as a child, and as a result was much too severe with one of my sons when he was going through a weepy period at three years of age. On the other hand, I was overly permissive in not daring to be firm about certain chores: so about these I nagged instead of leading.

Between the intensely authoritarian and the frustratingly permissive approaches is a *trusting* approach. It might also be called relaxed or democratic. Parents with a trusting attitude aren't the least bit submissive to their child. They don't kow-tow or accept any rudeness. They respect themselves fully and don't have to maintain their own sense of worth by putting down their child. They see children as usually eager, hard-working, honest, and creative, as wanting most of the time to please, and as striving by themselves to become more mature and responsible. They respect children's feelings and individuality.

Of course, even parents with a trusting approach know that children, because of their inexperience and impulsiveness, require a lot of leading, guiding, reminding, and correcting. But as long as their child is getting along well, their trustfulness makes it easy for them not to interfere. This non-interference fosters independence, initiative, and creativity.

Most trusting parents find that they don't need to punish— physically or otherwise. The child's desire to please the parents (most of the time), and the parent's prompt suggestion or correction are generally enough to keep the child on the right track. Because the parents have matters under control, they don't need to get frustrated or angry. The lack of hostility in the family atmosphere keeps the child pleasant-natured, and cooperative. Children brought up in an atmosphere of mutual love and respect acquire a trust in themselves as dependable people and a general trust in most other people as well. So they bring out the best in those they deal with.

The pendulum swings first one way, then the other. The direction depends on such factors as the sense of economic security and civil tranquility which favor the trustful attitude, or domestic and international crises during which leaders and people demand stern measures. Unusual prosperity brings a lot of overpermissiveness to the surface, because parents are reluctant to deprive their children of anything.

The most striking development in young people in the past ten years, to my mind, has been the assurance with which they've been able to make up their own minds, independently of what their elders think. They've drastically changed their hair styles, their clothes styles and, more importantly, their life styles. They've created a revolution in the way they look at sex and the relations between men and women. (I'm thinking of their openness about sex and the marked decrease in the exploitation of each sex by the other.) They've persuaded many colleges to become coeducational and others to become less rigid. They've helped to open up colleges, fraternities, and sororities to minority groups. They've had no hesitation in coming to their own conclusions about political matters.

They can't be intimidated. I know because I tried to intimidate the first year class in the medical school at which I taught, about coming to lectures on time and not bringing coffee. In spite of becoming quite severe, I failed completely to decrease the tardiness and the coffee toting. I only succeeded in making the class critical about the course of which I was so proud.

Many adults find this seemingly defiant attitude offensive and alarming. I did at the time, because I couldn't control it. But later, when I was no longer teaching that course and could be more detached, I changed my mind. In the first place, I decided that these students were not deliberately rude. When I taught them in small groups, they were attentive and cooperative. It's mainly that youth today is not impressed by—or really aware of—adult attitudes, especially disapproving ones.

Spock doesn't believe in overpermissiveness, yet he doesn't speak too harshly about some of its apparent results. If young people are defiant of their elders, have created a sexual revolution, and ignore disapproving attitudes—then many hard learned lessons of mankind will have to be learned over again, from scratch. Of course, it is true that youthful rebellion is not new, and Socrates in 400 B.C. had the same complaint: "Children are now tyrants, not the servants of their households. They no longer rise when their elders enter the room. They contradict their parents, chatter before company, gobble up dainties at the table, cross their legs, and tyrannize over their teachers."

How much of society's problems are due to permissiveness—or to the tyranny of either the young or the old—is a pertinent question, but one that isn't easily settled. On the other hand, the fruits of permissiveness have been documented on an individual basis. At the height of the permissive era of the 1960s, Marguerite and Willard Beecher wrote a book, *Parents On The Run,* in which they said: "The morale of parents throughout this country has sunk to a notable low. They seem to be falling from exhaustion and uncertainty. Their hearts are weary. Their children are out of hand." [5] This may seem melodramatic, but it was a fact of life for many. Pediatrician Robert F.L. Polley points out what permissiveness did to the children. He contends:

> It deprived youngsters of the opportunity to discover one of nature's most precious commodities—self-control. Maturity and self-confidence are closely tied to the experience and practice a child has in mastering the art of self-control. Many a competent child becomes a continuing problem to himself and to others because a permissive childhood leaves him labeled with the reputation of being an independent but unreliable class clown, sorely lacking in maturity, stability, reliability, and self-confidence. Permissive child care borders on child neglect when the experience leads to the development of inadequate self-confidence, an unsavory reputation, and a dubious self-image.

There are wide differences between the permissive and the strict methods of child rearing. In practice, however, these differences are often not as marked as they appear in print. It is easy to take sides and politically "Watergate" the opposition, especially when you don't really know the individuals. For example, "authoritarian" Dick Russell is a mild mannered quiet man, and "permissive" Ben Spock is firm and forceful. This may not help you to make up your mind, but it does present a caution: Don't read too much into the various views expressed. Both Russell and Spock agree in substance with Dr. John Richards's advice on parental attitudes that can encourage children to develop into mature, responsible, and successful adults:

> First—*Respect your child as a person.* Regardless of behavior, everyone deserves to be treated with respect. Your child may do things which you consider wrong or express ideas completely contrary to

your own opinions. In these circumstances, it is important to show the same consideration for your child's feelings and point of view that you expect to be shown toward your own.

Second—*Be reasonable* in your expectations for good behavior. A two-year-old cannot be expected to understand the rules and limits of a five-year-old. Nor can a self-centered, impulsive, thirteen-year-old, who is overwhelmed and frightened by the pressures of adolescence, act with the self-control expected of an adult. Learn what behavior is reasonable during each stage of your child's development.

Third—*Be patient.* Don't expect a small child to jump to your command like a marine recruit reacting to his drill sergeant. Every child knows that some rules of behavior are more important than others. He just isn't always sure which ones can be stretched the most, so he'll often test them all.

Even when trying to cooperate and to do what he was told, a child can become distracted by something which, at the moment, seems much more interesting than the task at hand. He might have every intention of obeying, but just isn't able to see the importance of doing it "right now."

Fourth—*Reward good behavior.* A smile and a pleasant reaction or statement show your appreciation for his efforts. Every child wants to please his parents. If desirable behavior is taken for granted and ignored, he may have to resort to disruptive behavior in order to gain recognition. Unpleasant attention is often better than no attention at all.

Fifth—*Don't invite disobedience.* When giving directions to your child, try to phrase your words in a way which won't invite him to defy and test you. If you say, "Pick up your toys and put them back into your room," he can say "no" and there's little you can do to force him to obey. You may threaten or spank, and yet he still won't pick up his toys. He has successfully defied, frustrated, and angered you.

It is better to say, "Before you go out to play, pick up your toys and put them into your room." He might say, "no", but then he must accept the consequence of his disobedience and give up the privileges of going outside to play with his friends. In other words, he has punished himself without having achieved the satisfaction of seeing his parent react to his defiance with anger and frustration.

Sixth—*Be sure your child understands what is expected of him.* When instructions are too complicated, a small child may be confused. If a command is given harshly or in anger, a child may be so immobilized by fear that he neither hears nor comprehends what was said. When completely involved in play, some children just don't hear a parent's voice. So be sure your child is paying attention when you give directions, and if he often seems to misunderstand, have his hearing checked by your physician.

Seventh—*Don't punish the rest of the family.* For example, when you say, "We won't go on our picnic until you have made your bed," he might refuse, knowing that in order to be fair to others in the family you'll give in and go on the picnic in spite of his disobedience. Or, if you don't go, he achieves the satisfaction of having punished the entire family by his act of defiance.

Eighth—*Correct misbehavior immediately.* Don't wait until the fifth "stop doing that" before you discipline. Usually, when a parent has said, "stop" for the fifth time, the discipline and punishment which follows are given in anger. Consequently, the child has learned that he can successfully disobey as long as his parent doesn't become angry and that the punishment will be caused by his parent's anger rather than by his own disobedience.

Ninth—*Admit your mistakes.* Don't be afraid to change your mind and admit to your child that you are wrong if you have made a hasty decision which you later realize was unfair and unreasonable. Of course, don't give in and change your decision just to preserve peace when he cries and nags to have his way.

Tenth—*Work together, as parents.* Don't let your child play the "parent game," playing one parent against the other to get what he wants. Nor should he be able to avoid one parent's discipline by playing on the sympathy of the other. Every child quickly learns how to manipulate the adults in his home. Parents must agree on discipline and their expectations for a child's behavior. When there are differences, each must compromise some of his own beliefs. Obviously, total agreement is impossible, but uncertainty and doubt lead to childhood behavior problems.

Eleventh—*Set good examples for your children.* A small child imitates what he sees and hears in his home. His parents' example is of primary importance in learning desirable behavior.

Honesty, patience, respect for others, and any other virtue which you hold important is best learned by your child through observation of you.

There will be times when it seems that in spite of your efforts to be a "good" parent, nothing has worked. You set good examples, teach important values, and try to understand your child's problems; yet he rejects all of your values and seems destined for a life of delinquency. Don't let such setbacks discourage you. They are probably temporary. Go ahead confidently doing what you feel is right, following the principles you know are important. Eventually you'll be pleasantly surprised to discover that you have raised a child who is a good person. Not perfect, but good.

HOW DO YOU CHOOSE?

Although we all generally subscribe to such attitudes and methods of child rearing, the results will be colored by our basic concepts of the proper way to parent. As we have seen in the chapter on parents, much of our attitude comes from our individual background. And, in the chapter on the growth and development of children, we saw that whatever our background, each child is unique and reacts somewhat differently. This adds up to the fact that parenting is not simple. It is an engrossing, challenging, and occasionally trying occupation. And we can generally use all the help we can get from the family, from society, or from the experts. It would be comforting to believe that we can trust the experts' theories on child rearing to be absolutely correct and applicable one hundred percent to our children. One would assume that careful scientific experiments, with the results validated by practical experience, would produce such guidelines for parents.

Guidelines are available. For example, psychiatrist Richard Robertiello offers "The specifics of child raising" in his book, *Hold Them Very Close, Then Let Them Go*. His advice comes from the "tremendous explosion of knowledge in psychoanalysis" over the past ten years; and on this basis he tells us how to be "authentic" parents. He does, however, admit that, "I am certain that ten years from now another such book will have to be written to amend this one." [6] If this is so, I guess it means that when today's infants are ten years old we will have to scrap the theories and methods under which they were raised and then start over. Or we can hope for a twenty year cycle of theories that will allow our children to grow up and leave before we found out that what we did was wrong.

There are, of course, other sources of advice. But it often turns out that an expert's advice on parenting is really based upon his personal traditions, instincts, and experience with his children or with children and parents who have trouble. At best, this offers a limited view of parenting. Pediatricians and family practice physicians (who aren't just "sick baby doctors" and whose expertise is the growth and development of children) get to know children and their families over a period of years. They probably have more experience in the effects of various types of parenting and discipline in a normal population than other types of experts. Yet pediatricians disagree on some aspects of discipline, because, being people, they measure the results in different ways. Psychologists, psychiatrists, and social workers who see only problem families often get distorted views of what is going on, and are likely to ascribe bad results to practices that are widely used with good results by the rest of the population.

It is because of this type of confusion about child raising that University of California psychologist Diana Baumrind's research is so welcome. A member of the Institute of Human Development, Dr. Baumrind did some badly needed objective investigations on the effects of different kinds of parenting on children. She established a model of the "ideal" child as one who is generally competent, with the ability to set goals, to adapt, and to work toward these goals, and as one who has a good self-image and is able to live comfortably in a world of just laws. Then Baumrind went to a group of normal representative children and measured various aspects of their competency. Following that, she went to their families and found by interview and observation how the families actually raised their children and what sort of discipline they used.

By far the most competent children came from what may be called rational firm parents who offer the child reasons for the standards used and who encourage questions and discussion. They value the child's initiative and drive as well as disciplined behavior. As Baumrind describes them:

> Rational (authoritative) parents control the child firmly when the child's actions are not acceptable but do not hem the child in with restrictions. They believe that the parents have their own special rights as adults, but they also recognize and respect the child's individuality and personality. They value the child's qualities, but set higher standards for future conduct. They use reason as well as power to achieve their objectives. They value both obedience to adult requirements and independence in the child. They listen to the child, but do not base their decisions solely on the child's desires or on a group vote; also, they do not regard themselves as infallible or as divinely inspired.[7]

Baumrind uses the word "authoritative." From one standpoint the choice of words is unfortunate because it can easily be confused with the rigid authoritarian parent who believes that the child must accept the parents' words and beliefs without question. We have editorially substituted the term *rational* for authoritative.

Balancing Firmness and Permissiveness

The control of children by a firm parent can be exerted in many ways, including physical punishment if necessary. This control and authority is justified by the parents' expertness and responsibility—acting in a manner which is seen in the long-term best interests of the child. For such control not to be stifling, the parent should not only be able to explain the reasons for his or her values and goals to the child but must also value the child's self-assertion and prepare the child to become independent of parental control. In order to achieve this independence and freedom, the child must accept responsibility for his own behavior, which in turn requires that he believe that the world is orderly. The child must also believe that he lives in a world susceptible to reason, and that he can develop the skills needed to manage his own affairs.

Traditional Parenting

Baumrind's results indicated that liberal permissive parenting doesn't generally produce competent children. But that was only one study. Baumrind's model parent is close to what many of us would call a traditional parent. However, our traditions vary, so it becomes difficult to understand the significance of the term. Richard H. Blum, a Stanford psychologist who has done extensive investigation of drug-abusing children, found that there is a distinct correlation between drug use and permissive child rearing. He defines traditional parents as being more religious; having more stable marriages; emphasizing work, duty, discipline, love of parents; supervising their children more closely, and acting more conventional. The traditionally raised child is far less likely to go on drugs.[8]

When To Be Permissive

In thinking of a labels like traditional parent or rational firm parents, it is well to remember that Baumrind's work describes only some parents, as they appeared in her study. Whether this type of parenting appeals to you or not, there is considerable danger of oversimplifying the description and the results. I, like Baumrind, believe that parents have the right and duty to set models and goals and to insist on high standards of behavior for their children. In spite of this, I advocate permissiveness in some areas of life and in many areas of child rearing. First, as an expert in parenting, I am permissive with most parents— they can and will raise their children the way they like and they may not heed my advice. I encourage this, for I don't believe in the omnipotent expert. Second, there are some key areas where we know from *experience* that permissiveness works well in raising healthy children and that authoritative edicts do not. These are areas which have to do with *basic human rights*. It was an exercise of these rights which started the decline of the British Empire. Mahatma Gandhi rallied the Indian people to passive resistance, which ground India to a halt in spite of all the force of His Majesty's Army. Basically these are inalienable rights— as an example, they couldn't force the Mahatma to eat. No one can or should try to force *you* to eat or to go to the toilet. By the same token, you should not try to force your child. Pediatricians have seen eating and toilet training as the two most common problems of toddlers. They are the result of strict parents who insist that a child should eat or go to the toilet at the parents' bidding. Certain functions are innately personal and beyond the control of anyone outside of self. If these functions are directed by forces outside of one's self, it may smother the sense of self-worth. It is in this area that toddlers find their first ability to control themselves—their first victories. Living in a world directed by giants, being at the bottom of the totem pole, unable to assert themselves, toddlers find that they do possess *some* power. They cannot be forced to eat or to go to the toilet. If they are forced, they can be damaged severely.

Another area where parents should be as permissive as possible, in the opinion of conservative pediatrician Bryon Oberst, is in the areas of exploration, communication, expression of feelings, creativity, and development of talents:

> The child needs to explore, create, learn, understand, and question without interference. Encourage the child to do things for himself. On occasion, he will be stymied and not be able to proceed. Parents should allow the child to cope with this challenge for a while to see if he can surmount it by himself. If the child seems to be in a cul-de-sac and does not have the insight to ask for help, parents should then step in and lend a helping hand. As the child surmounts this obstacle, they should step out of the way so the child can proceed again in an independent fashion. By allowing the child to cope with challenges, ask for help, and receive help when bogged down or overwhelmed, the parents help the child to give and receive within his environment, his home, and his community. The assumption of independence, dependence, and interdependence are essential growth needs to the child, youth, and adolescent. The individual person should be able to develop to his ultimate potentials spontaneously and with inner motivation.

Problems from Lack of Permissiveness

Baumrind has stated that scheduled feedings and firm toilet training did not appear harmful to the child in her study, although she recognizes that harm may occur. Certainly many children respond well to firmness in these areas and do well. Yet I know of others who have starved themselves rather than give in and eat, because it became a demand of parents rather than an exercise in individual rights. Stubborn? Certainly. I have seen adults, raised to go to the toilet at the demand of their parents, who developed anal fixations, and who, in spite of good intelligence and being otherwise sane, would push all manners of things up their rectums, from carrots to bottles. You can't really force people to stop sucking the thumb, twisting their own hair, biting their fingernails, picking at the skin, nor can you force them to sleep when you insist they should.

When To Be Firm

Permissiveness is fine if it means freedom to develop one's talents, to try to satisfy one's desires and needs, to explore life. However, even if permissiveness, as defined, rules out license, it is at best only half a loaf. To raise children requires that they become disciplined. They need the disciplines of reading and writing and arithmetic and later of chemistry, history, and geometry. At home, they need the discipline of manners, of minding parents and teachers, and of dress and deportment. To fully develop into an adult, in the total sense of the word, requires a lot of guidance in this complex world. Our children require freedom, but they also should be disciplined to the needed skills and behavior patterns in order to enable them to become responsible adults. This discipline requires that parents use power.

I have raised four children and am quite comfortable in believing that parents naturally have not only the power, but the right and responsibility, to discipline their children. Discipline is essential to keep children out of trouble and to teach them to live with the rest of the world. To do this, parents need to have their children under control, a control that is exerted in the children's best interest. This control recognizes and treats the child as a unique individual with certain personal rights, and with the ability to earn full social rights by demonstrating competence and responsibility. The aim of discipline is, gradually and carefully, to free the child from parental control and to grant the gift

CHANGING BALANCE OF POWER AND FREEDOM WITH AGE

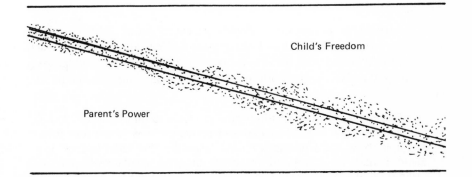

Age in Years

Figure 41 *1 year, 10 years, 20 years*

of respect and self-determination. To achieve this, the parent must continually assess the effect of various forms of discipline (rewards, punishment, and freedom) upon each child. It requires that parental methods and attitudes be modified when needed in order to get the best results. The prerequisites are discipline with confidence and love.

Even as I write this, however, I realize two things: First, that this approach to parenting may not suit other parents whose personalities, backgrounds, and lives are different from my own. Second, I know that some readers will seize on such words as "power," "children under control," and even "discipline" as advocating authoritarian child rearing. What I advocate is firmness with fairness, and the use of power with the child's best interest at heart.

HOW TO DISCIPLINE

Whether we philosophically agree or disagree with Spock, Farson, Gordon, Baumrind, Russell, or others about various types of parenting and their results, we can all agree that a major task of parenting is preparing children to assume the responsibilities and freedoms of adult life. Children start life completely dependent upon the power and love of the parent. How that power is used and how much is used is one of the major differences between authoritarian, firm, and permissive parents. But regardless of these philosophies, words, and methods, the development of responsibility and freedom in a child entails the progressive reduction of parental power.

Parents All Use Power

Regardless of philosophy, all parents exert power, whether physical, or by attitude. By attitude I mean your feelings and how they teach your child. Whether you believe yourself to be permissive and passive, or firm and active, your children will learn from you. Baumrind declares:

> Parents teach their children how to relate to others, whom to like and emulate, whom to avoid and condemn, how to express love and animosity, and when to withhold response. The child learns to aspire toward the noble and the ideal—or to be satisfied with the ordinary and the tangible. The child, by seeing himself through his parents' eyes, learns to know his own characteristics and what value to place upon his attributes.

If we think of discipline as teaching, then it goes without saying that parents are constantly disciplining their children, whether they make a conscious effort or not. When things are running smoothly, discipline is an indistinguishable part of normal, everyday family life: Parents set examples, make suggestions, and in general respond positively or negatively to aspects of their child's appearance, behavior, or accomplishments. When problems arise—when the "student" fails to conform to the expressed desires of the "teacher"—discipline assumes a more prominent role: Rules are asserted more strongly, lectures are given, and punishment is meted out. Sometimes the teacher prevails, sometimes the student; sometimes compromises are worked out, and sometimes the problem is swept under the rug in the hopes that it will disappear of its own accord.

When people talk about forms of discipline, they are usually referring to the more active functions such as lectures and spanking, but in fact these constitute just one part of the total disciplinary process, and, in the opinion of some child care experts, the least effective part at that. It's true that children learn what they are taught; it's also true that some parents are unaware of the many subtle and powerful ways they unwittingly teach their children how to think, to feel, and to behave. For example, a parent may teach just what he advises against, as in the case of the chain-smoking father who worries because his teenage daughter won't heed his nonsmoking directives. Discipline becomes more complicated when the goals are less tangible—giving the child a sense of himself as competent and worthy of love; encouraging a sense of trust in himself and in others; developing such values as responsibility, honesty, thoughtfulness, and patience. These may be harder goals to teach or reach.

As an example, all parents want their children to have "good" values. Children usually respond well to family values which are clear, consistent, and well integrated into family life. Even when they respond by rebelling (as they may well do at various stages of their growth), they have the two-fold advantage of being exposed to the *value* of values (values that could come, for example, from being exposed to religious training), and they have something concrete to rebel *against*.

How, then, does one explain children whose parents have taught them all the "right" values and who still refuse to adopt them? Part of the answer lies in the fact that parents are not the only influence on their children: They must compete with their children's friends and teachers, other adults, television, books, and movies. But there may also be other factors at work, other subtle lessons a parent unknowingly gives a child which counteract his or her best overt teaching efforts. Developing honesty provides a good illustration of how this process can operate. Two honest parents can instruct their child in the virtues of honesty—and still be left with a son who cheats regularly on school examinations. Why? One explanation is that the parental emphasis on achievement creates fear of failure in the child. If his parents have given him the message that they love him for what he does (rather than for what he is), he cannot then risk failing—for to fail is equivalent in his mind to losing his parents' love. At one level he wants to be honest, but at a deeper level he fears the consequences too much to take the risk. By stepping up the punishment for cheating, his parents may be able to stop him in the future—but it will be from a fear of being punished and not from a truly internalized decision he makes on his own. This example is perhaps oversimplified—children can generally benefit from the nudge of occasional punishment to help them solidify good habits—but it does illustrate the many influences at work in the task of teaching a child values.

Discipline As a Team

If you are uncertain about some of your values, your children will soon know, and you will have taught them a lesson of sorts. A more difficult problem can occur if you and your spouse differ markedly in your values or in your approach to discipline. Family life runs more smoothly when both parents agree on disciplinary matters, but such accord is not always possible. Parents are separate people, after all, and do not always react in the same way to a child's behavior. Nevertheless, it's a good idea to be in basic agreement on house rules, whatever they are. One parent who sides with a child (to be the good guy, to get back at the other spouse, to avoid confrontations) in clear violation of these rules is playing into the child's game of divide and conquer. Individual parents do have their own styles, limits, and preferences, however, and a child is quick to detect these differences, no matter how parents seek to hide them.

It is helpful for the parents to discuss their attitudes, philosophies, and methods of discipline and come to a compromise that both can agree upon. If there are disagreements, try not to argue about them in front of the child or use these disagreements about child rearing as part of a marital battle. Some suggest that parents can openly discipline in different ways as long as they don't let the child play one parent against the other. However, my personal observation is that it is often better for one parent to do the "wrong" thing as a team with his or her spouse rather than for each parent to discipline in separate "right" ways that most often end up in a parental battle.

Associate editor Julie Oliver elaborates:

> It is vital that parents talk to each other, at least once in
> a while, about sharing the responsibilities of discipline. Who does
> what, when, and how? Specific duties need to be discussed and

decided upon. The following sample agreements may give you some ideas as you go about making these decisions in your own ways.

1. Mom agrees not to "save up" discipline all day and present Dad with a list of offenses when he walks in the door after work.
2. Dad agrees to take an active role in discipline so the child knows these are home rules, not just Mom nagging—also because Dad may want a more active role in nurturing and guiding his child.
3. If one parent is better at certain situations, that parent should handle the problem, with the other backing up the effort.
4. If one parent will not share in discipline, the other parent must not give up but should do the best job possible, and avoid making an issue of it, especially in the presence of the child.
5. Avoid making excuses like, "Your Dad's tired," or "Mother doesn't feel well." This is the adult's problem, not the child's.
6. Parents agree to make decisions privately instead of hashing them out in the presence of the child. This especially includes criticism of the spouse's handling of problems.
7. Problems will be handled on the spot by the parent who is *present* instead of "Wait till your Mom hears what you've done. She'll give you a spanking.
8. Use the term "we" whenever it is appropriate.
9. Agree not to use your child's misbehavior to get back at or criticize your spouse. "You're just as messy as your father."

Try to make sure that your rules include all the principles you each believe most important. Be as honest as you can when discussing these ideas, and try not to spring any big surprise on your spouse while he or she is in the middle of handling a problem with your child. "Well, I think you're being too harsh. I don't really think good grades are all that important!"

Try to help each other improve the way you carry out discipline. Your spouse *may* be able to view your behavior more objectively than you at times. You might even be able to give each other some gentle constructive criticism, and some much needed praise, comfort, and encouragement. Share your feelings of guilt, fear, frustration, and anger (as well as joy, achievement, and hope!) with your spouse, not your child. The best kind of parent power is plural.

Discipline by Reward

We all respond to rewards, and among the most valuable awards for children is parental approval. There are two basic types of approval. The first is unconditional approval of the child as a person. The second is approval of what the child produces in the way of behavior, grades, materials, and services. Most important is the unconditional approval by the parents of each child. Unconditional approval is a good part of what parenting and marriage are about. It is a common source of un-happiness if the reward of approval is only given for accomplishments. It is as if the child must "buy" parental love and approval. Uncondi-tional approval comes from unconditional love and loyalty. Such ap-proval is the bedrock of self-esteem. And children must have self-esteem: It helps them trust their own feelings and abilities, and, even-tually, to develop their own sense of right and wrong. Then even if they stray from the path, they know within themselves where that path lies.

A child should feel confident in his parent's continuing love for him, no matter what he may do; with the assurance of unconditional parental love, a child can usually deal with parental disapproval of a specific act without feeling devalued as a person. This approval is to a large degree shown by praise.

Praise
The praise that comes from unconditional approval praises the child himself for what he is. To be effective, it helps to praise specific char-acteristics: "Mary has a great sense of humor!" or "Johnny is one of the friendliest people I know," or "Susie has such pretty hair!" It may be better to praise a child indirectly and casually while talking to others at a time when the child can hear it. That way, there is no implied de-mand on the child to behave in a certain way—it is just a statement of fact and respect.

It may sound mixed up to talk of a punishing reward, but that is what happens in some cases. An example is in the attitude and words of three different parents who are pleased that their child's grades im-proved from C's to B's. To show approval, one parent may say "I am proud of you," another parent, "That's good, but you could do better!", while a third parent might angrily offer, "At least you got a B!" The latter two parents punish the child at the same time they reward. What matters here is the underlying parental attitude. A positive accepting at-titude is vital for the child's healthy optimum emotional growth and practical competence later in life. So an important parental task is for each of us to discipline ourselves to think positively and to feel posi-tively about our children.

Praise should also be given for specific accomplishments that we ap-preciate, such as helping with the housework, earning money, or help-ing a brother out of a tight spot. In giving praise for accomplishments such as good grades or winning competitive events, it is wise to make it as clear as possible that you recognize that the child is serving his own best interest. "Johnny, that is a good report card. People respect people who know how to study effectively." Indirectly, various parental values

—for example, teamwork—can also be inculcated by praise. "Joe, it is great that you won. It really helps the team. We are all proud of you."

Material Rewards and Allowances

Many parents struggle with whether or not to give material rewards for good behavior. However, psychologist Dobson calls the use of such rewards "miracle tools." This should not be surprising when we face the fact that most of our daily rewards are material. Children are not that much different. It is possible to buy good behavior from children: for instance, paying Susie to get good grades or to stop teasing her little sister. However, a problem can arise from paying children for good behavior. They may perceive that this behavior is good for you, so much so that you are willing to pay. In the minds of some children, this means that their good behavior is in the parent's best interest, not necessarily in the child's best interest. Such behavior patterns may not then be internalized as part of the child's conscience but may instead be added to the child's armamentarium as potential bargaining weapons.

Buying good behavior may also teach some lessons parents are not comfortable with, such as the power of material goods to influence others, and "being good" as synonymous with "pleasing others." Still, most would agree that there is probably no harm done if paying for good behavior is not overdone; in any case, it's hard for children living in our society to avoid learning the power of material possessions. But there is no question that Dobson is right when he says: "Behavior that achieves desirable consequences will occur." (On the question of rewarding good behavior with food; it should probably be avoided. Such a pattern of discipline may mark the beginning of overeating and obesity in later life. Food from parents, like love, should be unconditional.)

How to Give Rewards

As important as the reward itself is how and when it is granted. Because even the best behaved children have a hard time being good every minute, it's a good idea to reward steps in the right direction instead of waiting for the final accomplishment. It is the little things in life that count, and it is too long to wait for perfection. If a reward becomes ineffective, change it so it becomes a step toward a desirable award for the child. So if gold stars on a chart cease to have meaning, award five gold stars with a gift or a new privilege. Over the period of the child's growth, he will hopefully learn to act in his long-term best interest, which realistically also includes the best interests of family and society. Thus his actions become aimed at more than making parents happy or acting just for material rewards. We teach "good" behavior by praise, by encouragement, by understanding, and by emphasizing the positive rather than the negative and granting increased privileges—often in the heady form of allowing a child to assume responsibilities. The advantages of the carrot over the stick need no elaboration here.

Discipline by Teaching

Ready or not, a parent begins teaching as soon as a child is born. The parent is the infant's world and model. However, the most rewarding form of teaching is stimulating, guiding and instructing the child about the world. But for many parents who may not even know how to live comfortably with a small child, this may sound like fancy theory. Some fall back on their own schooling experience and attempt formalized teaching, not recognizing that play is probably the most important method of learning for the preschool child.

A group of experienced mothers in Illinois used the self-motivating rewards of play in order to expand children's horizons and make rainy day living more tolerable for parent and child. Calling themselves Parents As Resources (P.A.R.), they adopted a light-hearted, enthusiastic, low-key approach that encourages children to participate in learning experiences. For equipment they use common household items and discarded junk, a little imagination, and the accumulated experience of many mothers. These ladies produced handbooks of techniques and ideas that run the gamut from making the backyard into a vacation center, keeping children constructively occupied on a rainy day, to making a walk around the block a memorable educational experience. Their *Recipes for Fun* and other books can be obtained from the P.A.R. Project, 464 Central, Northfield, Illinois 60093.

Discipline by Non-Reward/Non-Punishment

There are times you can't reward yet you don't want to, or can't, punish. One method is the non-reward of just ignoring bad behavior. Associate Editor John C. Richards believes that, "whenever possible, you should ignore behavior that is only annoying or messy but not dangerous or destructive. Try to anticipate behavior that may lead the child into trouble so that you can take corrective action before things get too far out of hand. Above all else, give attention for good behavior so that bad behavior won't be needed as often." But some types of bad behavior, such as sneaking cookies, have their own reward. Moreover, Baumrind has pointed out that the very presence of mother may be taken by the child as tacit approval of his behavior if mother ignores the behavior.

Teachers have developed non-reward/non-punishment techniques to help them control children. One way is to cue a child to remember to act at a specific time by reminding him when the action is expected rather than criticizing him later for non-performance. Here, timing is critical and heckling should be avoided. The reminder should be pleasant. Another method is to teach that behavior which is unacceptable at one place, such as in the home, can be acceptable at another place. The child who runs in the home can be sent out to do his running outside. Some undesirable actions can be avoided by allowing or insisting that the child repeat the action until he tires. For example, a child who plays with matches can be pushed into spending several hours of lighting matches until he is very tired of the game. Another worthwhile technique is to keep a child busy doing something acceptable when he might otherwise be getting into mischief.

Discipline by Punishment

As the preceding principles demonstrate, discipline by reward can take many forms. Sooner or later, however, parents have to punish in order to protect their child's safety, to insure their own well-being, and to help the child learn to handle the overwhelming urges and feelings which can erupt within him and scuttle his best efforts to behave well. There comes a time when reason doesn't work; and parents must teach their child in terms that he will understand and remember. Children need to know where they stand; they deserve clear, consistent rules so that they know where the limits are. Punishment which is clearly associated with transgressing these limits (and *not* accompanied by shaming, belittling, ridiculing, or embarrassing) not only stops unacceptable behavior, it teaches children to be responsible for their own actions. The message a child receives from punishment under these conditions is: "You should not do that. Because you did, you now have to be punished to help you remember not to do it again."

When Should You Punish?

Dr. David Friedman points out that, "even under ideal conditions, punishment is sometimes necessary. Children have different temperaments and respond differently to expectations—no matter how clear—and to limits—no matter how appropriate. A parent may be able to communicate with and cope with one child and not with another, and may have to resort to punishment more often with one child than with the other. But punishment is what adults resort to when other forms of discipline fail."

Some of us feel that punishment is inevitable, and psychologist Baumrind makes a telling point: "It is more reasonable to teach parents who wish to learn to use punishment effectively and humanely how to do so than to preserve the myth that punishment is ineffective or intrinsically harmful."

Punishing by Scolding

Scolding is finding fault and blaming with angry words or looks—it is a withdrawal of approval. It is perhaps the most ineffective form of discipline. No one likes to be scolded. In older times, scolds themselves were often punished by being ducked in ponds. Anger, blame, and fault heaped upon a child can hardly make a child feel loved, or wanted, or taught that he is anything but bad. Luckily, most children quickly learn that although many parents scold a lot, they act on their scolding rather infrequently. So the child learns to ignore the words and live with the tone which makes him believe the parent doesn't like him. Thus most scolding represents more of an emotional outlet for the parent than an effective tool to improve a child's behavior. Oh, it works sometimes, but usually children block it out and develop the disease called "parent deafness."

There are ways of "scolding" and expressing disapproval of a child's behavior that are less likely to make the child feel unworthy. Whether these ways are really scolding is not the issue; they work better as teaching tools. Let's call them criticism of behavior. The first characteristic that differentiates criticism from scolding is that you avoid telling the child that he is bad, that you are angry at him, or, by your tone of voice, that you don't like him. The way you criticize behavior will vary with your personality. Some criticize with just a frown or a grimace. Some criticize gently and cooly, and the gentleness mutes the assumption of personal disapproval.

Some people are good at using humor in criticism—which says, in effect, "What you did wasn't all that bad," and expresses some understanding and acceptance of the child while letting him know the behavior is unacceptable. A few parents control their anger and criticize icily and deliberately, which may or may not get across that the child is acceptable, although the behavior isn't. Others scream their heads off and then feel sorry and hug the child. Actually, discipline can even be fun if you learn to laugh at yourself. In any case, it needn't always be done with great solemnity. Have enough faith in yourself and your child that you can be sure things will turn out well in spite of current problems. It helps to avoid making a "big deal" out of your child's misbehavior. Remember that children are children and will do childish things. And we all made mistakes and still grew up. One thing I am grateful for is the patience and forebearance of my parents. I remember when they used to laugh and tease me a little for some of my misbehavior rather than take it too seriously. Humor is a good way to put things in perspective, to teach that unwise childish actions are not usually all that terrible. Sometimes nothing clears the air like a good laugh together. Of course, laughter and teasing can be done in an unloving attitude to put a child down. That can be worse than a spanking. It is when we talk of spanking that most people think of discipline, even though when we talk of attitudes such as love and anger we are talking of powerful disciplinary tools.

Spanking

I personally believe that if and when you spank, you should spank with love not anger. This may not work for you; it hasn't always worked for me. But since parents are bound to spank, you might as well develop a technique for meting it out in educational quantities rather than in heated, angry outbursts. Spanking in anger is not education, it is simply a way of venting parental frustrations. It tells the child that the parent has the power to hurt. It does not give the child a model for self-control or self-discipline but instead offers the spectacle of what can be almost an adult temper tantrum. From the child's standpoint, it offers an excellent way to get even. As the child sees it, whatever the "bad" behavior was, it really must have hurt the parent to have evoked such a hostile reaction. So if the child then wishes to punish the parent, all that has to be done is to act "bad" again. Thus, the child experiences the power to manipulate and hurt the parent through bad behavior.

The middle-of-the-road view on physical punishment is that a younger child can be lightly swatted or spanked once in a while with no long-range harm done. Spanking frequently clears the air, lets off parental steam which might otherwise explode later in a more frightening outburst, and tells the child quickly and effectively to stop what he is doing. There are, however, several necessary conditions to this limited approval of physical punishment: (1) The child's behavior is in clear defiance of what he knows is expected of him; (2) the parent is in charge of his feelings, whether he is angry or not, and is confident they will not escalate beyond his control; (3) physical punishment is not a habitual response to a child's misbehavior; and (4) it is carried out in such a way as not to inflict physical injury.

Warning

If you or your spouse were beaten or abused as children, avoid spanking if you can. Parents who were beaten as children frequently have an unreasonable compulsion to beat their own children. For such parents, their emotions may take over and the child can be damaged. This does not mean that *most* parents should not spank, but that none of us should spank in anger—and that we should follow the "rules" about spanking. There are other ways to discipline.

Problems with Spanking

Some people who "refuse" to spank because of their permissive orientation are often driven to spank out of desperation and in anger. Sometimes they then damage the child more than their conscience allows and feel considerable guilt. Other people have a lot of chronic anger, and fear they will lose control if they start to spank. Certainly such individuals should not spank. However, only two out of 150 average families studied by Psychologist Diana Baumrind said they didn't spank. Psychologist Thomas Gordon of P.E.T. fame also admits that power "strangely enough remains the method of choice for most parents, no matter what their education, social class, or economic level." Yet he argues against the use of power and punishment (spanking) because he believes it leads to "resistance, defiance, rebellion, negativism, resentment, anger, . . ." and on and on.[9] Alice Ginot, in her column, "Being a Parent," wrote: "Punishment does not discipline, it only enrages and humiliates. It breeds revenge fantasies. Children who are punished are preoccupied with the need to get even. And there are many ways that children can get even with their parents. They can fail in school; go on drugs; get pregnant; leave school; run away or commit a crime. They can make their parents' lives miserable." [10]

All these things are true, *if* physical punishment is capricious, continual, vindictive, and directed at the child himself rather than at something he has done. Of course, a similar list of awful negative childish reactions may occur if you *don't* physically punish. The classic example of "What's mother to do?" when the child gets out of hand and deliberately flouts parental authority results from the well-meant advice of permissive experts who see themselves reducing child abuse. Dobson's advice for such a situation is that there is no substitute for a spanking when the circumstances demand it.

Pediatrician Thomas Conway has another perspective:

> Spanking has been with us a long time and will continue to be a popular part of child raising. It is a persuasion usually imposed by the stronger and perhaps wiser on the weaker. Many children never need spanking; some adults never need to spank. The event, when it occurs, serves as a release for the "spanker" and is educational to the child, who learns you can push people in authority only *so* far. Kept within bounds, spanking probably hurts neither party very much.

Guidelines for Spanking

If you spank, what sort of guidelines should you use? When we get to specific ways to discipline children at different age levels you will find that I don't believe you should ever spank or shake a baby under nine months, and that spanking should rapidly diminish between the ages of five to ten years and should probably never be attempted on adolescents. I become upset when I hear of people spanking babies too young to really understand. Of course, others become upset with me when I advocate premeditated spanking for most toddlers starting between nine months to a year of age. Associate Editor John C. Richards believes spanking shouldn't start till between twelve to fifteen months. Both of us agree that the important points are an unangry attitude, and, while the spanking has to hurt, that it not inflict any real damage. My defense is that premeditated spanking works well, that children will obey, that they are not made into fearful puppets, and that they suffer no physical or psychological damage. Under nine months they *are* damaged. One of the major reasons I advocate rational spanking is that it is one of the most effective ways to avoid spanking, and even child abuse. Most children, if they know you mean it when you say you will spank, will be far less likely to challenge your power than if they aren't certain that you mean what you say. So don't threaten to spank unless you are willing to follow through.

Dobson suggests that a useful tool in child rearing is knowing when to punish and how excited one should get about a given behavior:

> First, the parent should decide whether an undersirable behavior represents a direct challenge of his authority—to his position as the father or mother. Punishment should depend on that evaluation. For example, suppose little Walter is acting silly in the living room, and he falls into a table, breaking many expensive china cups and other trinkets. Or suppose he loses his bicycle or leaves Dad's best saw out in the rain. These are acts of childish irresponsibility and should be handled as such. Perhaps the parent should have the child work to pay for the losses—depending on the age and maturity of the child, of course. However, these examples do not constitute direct challenges to authority. They do not emanate from willful, haughty disobedience.[11]

Pediatrician Sid Rosin advises: "Spanking should be avoided except when the child does things that are dangerous. Then a good spanking is in order. Hitting the hands or fingers when a child reaches for restricted objects may work temporarily, but, unfortunately, most children will soon slap back at your hands. If you have lost your temper and you are frustrated, put the baby in a restricted area and walk away until you cool down."

I recommend that you settle the issue well in advance so the toddler knows that if you say you will spank unless he obeys, that you *will* spank. In that case you will rarely have to spank; and when you do spank, if you know in advance why you are spanking and how to spank, there will be less likelihood that you will fall into the trap of spanking in anger.

Punishment by Withdrawal of Love

If you don't spank, what can you do? Psychologist Alice Ginot, in her column "Being a Parent," presented the case of a six year old who threw food at the table and did not respond to words or yelling. His father sent Jeremy to his room without dinner. Ginot objected because, she says, "Punishment does not discipline." Her alternative? "Father could have said, 'Jeremy, I see words don't help. I am getting more upset. I am not enjoying my dinner with you. I have decided to take my plate into another room where I will be able to digest my food peacefully. When you are ready to be more pleasant, I hope you will come and fetch me.' " [12] Ginot's rationale is that "when their parents leave them, children become sufficiently upset to change their behavior. They are faced with the consequences of their unpleasantness. They improve *in order to win back their parent's love*." Possibly Ginot's "ideal" parent doesn't leave the child angry, but how withdrawal of love is perceived by the child may be another story. Open anger and action might be healthier.

Punishment by Guilt

While psychologist Diana Baumrind researched and reported that most parents who use their natural authority firmly and fairly produce highly competent and satisfied young people, psychologist Thomas Gordon found that many problem cases he saw in his practice frequently improved as he helped open communications between parent and child. Gordon decided that the communications techniques he used should be taught to parents and would increase parent effectiveness. He wrote a book, *Parent Effectiveness Training,* and has established P.E.T. courses throughout the country. His permissive theories are the opposite of Baumrind's and those of psychologist James Dobson in that he specifically advises parents to avoid the use of power and punishment. Rather, he urges, you understand by communication and you trust the child to handle a situation constructively—to respect your needs. Then you give the child a chance to start behaving positively. Gordon "avoids" confrontation by telling the child how his behavior affects the parents. One example he gives in his book is of two possible types of parental response after a child kicks the parent in the shin:

> "Ouch, that really hurt me—I don't like to be kicked." "That's being a very bad boy. Don't you ever kick anybody like that!" [13]

Gordon advises the first response. His point is that the child can't argue with the first message but can argue with the second message. He contends that this approach helps the child learn responsibility for his own behavior. Unsaid is the fact that the basic motivation for the child to change behavior is guilt. Punishment by guilt is probably better than punishment by withdrawal of love. However, guilt is a poorly tolerated discomfort. Often it leads to superficial rationalizations, to anger, and, if severe enough, to depression. Unsaid also is that this approach will require sainthood or psychotherapy for a parent who will put up with a physical assault without responding in kind or by spanking the child.

Still, I have found that Gordon's and Hyam Ginot's communication techniques help a lot of families. However, in my experience, for communication to be really helpful it must culminate in some sort of action. In the eyes of many children, the P.E.T. technique of avoiding confrontations over obvious misbehavior is looked on as a sign of parental weakness. Children who perceive their parents as weak lose respect for them. Also, the P.E.T. communication techniques offer some children a handy tool for manipulating their parents and an almost guaranteed method of being center stage. An example of this sort of reaction to the "fairness, communication, and guilt" technique is related by Dr. James Dobson in his book *Dare To Discipline*.[14] Dobson also sees problem cases, including problems caused by the advice of other psychologists.

Dobson's example is the case of Sandy, a defiant three-year-old whose mother asked for help:

> She had realized that her tiny little girl had hopelessly beaten her in a conflict of wills, and the child had become a tyrant and a dictator. On the afternoon prior to our conversation, an incident occurred which was typical of Sandy's way of doing business: The mother (I'll call her Mrs. Nichols) put the youngster down for a nap, although it was unlikely that she would stay in bed. Sandy is not accustomed to doing anything she doesn't want to do, and naptime is not on her acceptable list at the moment. On this occasion, however, the child was more interested in antagonizing her Mom than in merely having her own way. Sandy began to scream. She yelled loudly enough to upset the whole neighborhood, fraying Mrs. Nichols' jangled nerves. Then she tearfully demanded various things, including a glass of water. At first Mrs. Nichols refused to comply with the orders, but she surrendered when Sandy's screaming again reached a peak of intensity. As the glass of water was delivered, the little tigress pushed it aside, refusing to drink because her mother had not brought it soon enough. Mrs. Nichols stood offering the water for a few minutes, then said she would take it back to the kitchen if Sandy did not drink by the time she counted to five. Sandy set her jaw and waited through the count. " . . . three, four, five!" As Mrs. Nichols grasped the glass and walked toward the kitchen, the child again screamed for water. Sandy dangled her harassed Mom back and forth like a yo-yo until she tired of the sport.
>
> Mrs. Nichols and her little daughter are among the many casualties of an unworkable, illogical philosophy of child management which has dominated the literature on this subject during the past twenty years. This mother had read that a child will eventually respond to patience and tolerance, ruling out the need for discipline. She had been told to encourage the child's rebellion because it offered a valuable release of hostility. She attempted to implement the recommendation of the experts who suggested that she verbalize the child's feelings in a moment of conflict: "You want the water but you're angry because I brought it too late"; "You don't want me to take the water back to

the kitchen"; "You don't like me because I make you take naps"; "You wish you could flush Mommie down the toilet." She has been taught that conflicts between parent and child were to be perceived as inevitable misunderstandings or differences in viewpoint. Unfortunately, Mrs. Nichols and her advisors were wrong! She and her child were involved in no simple difference of opinion; she was being challenged, mocked, and defied by her daughter. No heart-to-heart talk would resolve this nose-to-nose confrontation, because the real issue was totally unrelated to the water or the nap or other aspects of the particular circumstances. The actual meaning behind this conflict and a hundred others was simply this: Sandy was brazenly rejecting the authority of her mother. The way Mrs. Nichols handled this confrontation would determine the nature of their future relationship; she could not ignore it. To quote the dilemma posed by a television commercial, "What's a mother to do?" [15]

A lot of us could tell the mother of Sandy what to do—with the caution not to take all of her accumulated frustrations out in one long overdue spanking. All that has to be done is to convince Sandy that mother has and will use the power to punish defiant behavior. This takes a logical demonstration—a moderate but firm spanking to prove the point. Similarly, most of us could offer some other types of parental response to the boy who kicked the parent in the shins. If nothing else, the child ought to know, by example if needed, how it feels to be hurt. Certainly, very few people in the world, aside from a sprinkling of psychologists and some propagandized mothers, will tolerate such behavior. In spite of my disenchantment with many of Gordon's theories, I have seen some parents helped by his techniques. For a few parents it offers, for the first time, a way to really communicate with their children and understand their feelings. It can reduce fruitless parent–child conflict, and often allows the child his first chance to start behaving constructively. The P.E.T. techniques for active listening and the "no-lose" methods of preventing conflicts are practical skills which can be helpful to people in any walk of life, including parents. For many families, P.E.T. can help achieve more harmonious living because anger and hostility are reduced.

To better understand P.E.T. in action, we asked P.E.T. instructor Alicia Herman to tell us in her words how P.E.T. works. She explains:

We have a tendency, when faced with our children's problems, to think of them as *our* problems and to put what we hear through *our* senses, *our* experience, *our* fears, and *our* expectations. In some cases, this can either magnify a problem out of proportion or unjustifiably make light of it. It is best to let the child struggle with the problem so he can talk about what is bothering him, get his feelings out without blame, criticism, judgment, probing, advice, or preaching, so he may be able to get a better grasp of what is going on. Then the child is better able to find his own solutions and handle the problem himself.

What better way is there to build self-esteem and responsibility? All of this may come as welcome relief to many parents who can now recognize that they don't always have to have just the right answer and can admit that they are not all knowing.

It is important to recognize that Gordon started with families with problems. If they had no problems, or thought they didn't, they were unlikely to go to a psychologist. Other families with problems went to psychologist James Dobson, who tells parents to listen, judge, and then "dare to discipline." Many parents with problems have been helped by Dobson's techniques. In fact, both Gordon's and Dobson's books have each sold over a half a million copies. Their theories and techniques are complete opposites, yet both have messages of value. One is that there are in fact, 1,001 ways of raising children. Another is that no single way is likely to work for everyone. Still, psychologist Baumrind's study was of an unselected group of ordinary children and families who varied from permissive to authoritarian in methods of discipline. She found that firm rational parenting produced the best results. This type of parenting philosophy is much closer to Dobson's than to Gordon's.

Anger in Discipline

As we saw, permissive parents usually spank, and when they do it is usually in anger. Harsh, authoritarian parents also spank in anger, as do rejecting parents and child beaters. Even normal parents spank in anger on occasions. The question is, does the anger help or hurt good discipline? Although spanking with care and for good reason can be an effective tool for discipline, I feel that spanking in anger is more often ineffective. But then anger itself is often ineffective as a tool for discipline. Many will argue this point—certainly spanking in anger can clear the air, and afterwards both parent and child are often calm and ready to make up and try again. Pediatrician Neil Henderson writes:

> I see nothing wrong with *occasionally* spanking a child. The parent's anger is quickly released and the child will no longer feel guilty. Having broken reasonable rules and regulations, he pays the penalty. Don't worry about the anger. It is perfectly normal for children occasionally to have angry feelings about their parents and vice versa. These are legitimate feelings. There should be no feeling of guilt about this, as angry feelings are universal. Birds fly, fish swim, and people have feelings.

A pediatrician thoroughly involved in the fight against child abuse, Dr. David Friedman, writes: "Experts tell us that punishing in anger is probably not a good idea, but parents are human and children must understand that their parents have feelings, too. Thus, an occasional punishment meted out in anger is not a catastrophe and may be a growth experience for the child." [16]

In my experience, the issue is less the spanking, which is a release, than the anger. Anger expressed by shouting, threats, or even icy calm can be frightening to children, possibly more so than a spanking. But even more important than the fright is the counter-reaction of anger in the child. I believe that the bad behavior problems Gordon and Ginot describe are due more to the anger than to the isolation or spanking. When parents have a lot of anger and cannot control it, I suggest that they take a P.E.T. course. But more than that, I suggest that they learn *not to be angry*. Now I hasten to repeat that I have gotten angry at my children at times. However, I have found for myself, and for a lot of parents over the years, that children are best disciplined without anger; and that discipline in anger is usually ineffective. "But," you may say, "anger is normal."

It is not easy to control anger. As one mother told me, "I tried, but here I am!" Some psychologists believe that you should "let it all hang out," because many problems come from holding in anger and bad feelings because of a fear that if you don't, you will not be loved. The theory is that letting out such feelings make you feel better about yourself and therefore able to feel better about others. Of course, there is a catch. If you have a lot of angry feelings and let them out, other people, includ-

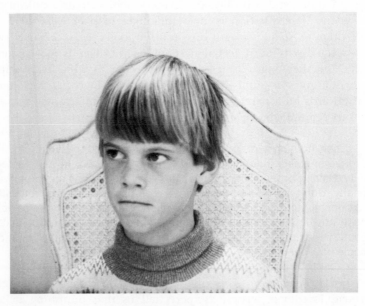

Figure 42

ing your kids, may *not* love you. And even if they do "love" you, they react in anger, and the family arena becomes a boxing arena rather than a place of security and a tranquil refuge which recharges the soul and rests the spirit and body.

In order to understand the reverse effect of anger in discipline, put yourself in the shoes of a four-year-old who is trying very hard to be big and important. Four-year-olds frequently become quite angry at their parents, who are always telling them what to do and what not to do. But if a child is angry at a parent, what can he do? The parent is too big to hit; and if he did hit his mother or father, he would feel even worse because he does love them. So the child is caught with a bundle of confused feelings, including anger, resentment, and frustration, that he doesn't know how to handle. What usually happens, at first by accident, is that the child behaves in a way that sends the parent "up the wall." The child then senses that here is a way that he can punish the parent and "pay him back" for being so bossy. So he continues this misbehavior—usually some sort of immature, annoying habit. A child often feels it is a sort of victory, even when the parent becomes angry enough to spank him. When this happens, the child psychologically "wins" by doing the wrong thing.

So discipline in anger may produce less than desirable results. Regardless of who starts it, most of us respond to anger or annoyance with anger or annoyance in return. Children punished in anger may come to regard discipline as a fight. Then the only way a child can win in this fight, or get some licks in, is to do the wrong thing. If the child submits to the parental demand, he loses a fight even if the child realizes that what the parent wants is in the child's best interest. If the parent is forceful, or if the child loves the parent a lot, the child may do what he is told, but in so doing he loses vital self-esteem. As open rebellion is dangerous, the child finds that he can rebel against hostile discipline in a variety of indirect ways. Usually, this takes the form of some annoying immature behavior that upsets the disciplining parent. It is *because* such behavior upsets adults that many children continue to misbehave. To avoid these traps I suggest that parents use the technique of neutral discipline—that is, that the parent sets the rules, offers the options, and then allows the child to make the choice without the parent becoming emotionally involved.

Most parental decisions on behavior are in the child's long-term best interest. Discipline should be established in such a way that the child (not the parent) wins if he does the right thing and the child (not the parent) loses if he does the wrong thing. This can be achieved by a parental attitude of neutrality and firmness, of calmly offering the child his choice. Tell the child, in effect, "If you stop hollering in the house (obey), it shows you are growing up and becoming big and responsible.

If you don't stop hollering in the house (disobey), it is because you are still a little child. It is all right if you want to be little, but little children have fewer privileges: They have to go to bed earlier, or perhaps take a nap, or not be allowed to ride their bikes." If this is explained to the child in an accepting manner, without annoyance or anger, then it truly becomes the child's unhampered choice. Usually, the child will choose the course that is in his own best interest.

Of course, some children may throw "a fit" if you tell them to take a longer nap. If the child defies you, then you may have to spank him. In a relaxed way (not through clenched teeth), explain: "If you don't go to bed like I told you, then you are acting so little that I may even have to spank you"; and then ask, "Do you really want a spanking?" Again, *really* let it be the child's choice—without your choice showing, one way or another. If the child is too upset to mind, give him a spank and then forget it. He paid for his misbehavior, and the slate is clean. Neutral discipline teaches the child to make decisions and choices which will benefit himself rather than the parent. As an example, if a child doesn't pick up the toys in the living room, the parent calmly offers options: "If you pick up your toys like a big boy every day, we can allow you to have a shorter nap. If you are too tired or too young to pick up your toys you will have to go to bed earlier." If the child does not pick up the toys, then the parent calmly picks them up and the child is put to bed earlier that night. Done neutrally, this really leaves the problem of making the choice up to the child and leaving the enforcement or reward up to the adult. If the child makes the wrong choice and the parent becomes angry, then the problem has become the parent's. So, even though Gordon and I disagree about the use of power and spanking, we end up with a similar principle—that the problem must become the child's problem rather than the parent's. Unfortunately, such a principle can be easily misapplied if one gives open-ended choices to small children, many of whom are unable to comprehend the possible results. The limits should be clearly set, with simple choices for preschool and grammar school children.

Still, it may be that we can discipline effectively in anger *if* the child knows that the anger is justified. You probably can spank in both anger and love. Certainly most of us remember responding to parental anger by "shaping up." Experienced pediatricians and parents like John Richards are comfortable and successful with some anger in their discipline. He says:

> I don't believe neutral discipline is possible. Although behavior can usually be controlled by the dispassionate application of a painful spanking, it is unrealistic to expect a parent, who is after all a victim of his own emotions, to maintain an unemotional attitude when

spanking. Probably I can, now that I have over twenty-five years of parenthood behind me. But, in looking back, I doubt seriously whether I could have been that detached and "grownup" as a parent when dealing with my first child's misbehavior. Not even if I had realized, then, that when disciplined in anger the only real lesson learned by my child was "when Dad gets mad, I get punished." One should not assume that neutral discipline is necessarily the best means of creating a "civilized" adult from an undisciplined child.

However, if the child's attitude toward the parent is basically negative, then the anger can be used as a weapon against the parent. Conversely, guilt and withdrawal of love are weapons parents can use on children. Guilt as a basic mechanism to punish children is the foundation of Parent Effectiveness Training and withdrawal of love is the foundation of Ginot's methods of dealing with unacceptable behavior. A different approach is used by Baumrind's rational firm parent who allows the child to pay for misbehavior by punishing with withdrawal of privileges or spanking, therefore leaving the child with no residual guilt feelings. I have been impressed that children of harsh authoritative parents seem to have better feelings toward their parents, in spite of open or subtle rebellion, than children of permissive parents. It is interesting to compare and observe the wide variation of approaches to the problem of misbehaving children advocated by authorities, from the Bible to the *Ladies' Home Companion*. Personally, I favor neutral discipline.

A major key to neutral discipline is to avoid, when possible, the *reasons* for anger. We must recognize that conflict is inevitable; that almost all children try to establish their independence, if not domination, in this world; and that the degree of independence allowable for children must be limited until they mature enough to use their freedom safely and constructively. The way to reduce anger and impatience on the part of the child is for consistency (strength) on the part of the parents in their handling of the child's bids for freedom. If children know where they stand and expect certain legitimate reactions from parents, even though they may challenge the parental limits, they will respect them and will have less reason to react in anger.

Conversely, if you as a parent know that you can expect childish behavior, challenge, misbehavior, and childish actions such as lying, stealing, fighting, sulking, anger, bossiness, breaking things, demands, center stage, sassing, bad words, and so forth, then you can plan on it and prepare yourself. You will then have less reason for anger from unexpected hurts and misbehavior. It also allows you to establish a family community of law and justice in which to raise your children—just as we live in a larger community regulated by laws and in which we constantly strive for justice. It is, after all, our task to prepare our children to live in a law-abiding society.

Child Abuse

Many experts, aware of the child-abuse problem in this country, hesitate to endorse even mild spanking for fear that parents will assume they have the go-ahead to beat their child. Even Dobson warns against abuse of physical punishment: "Much sound advice has been written about the dangers of inappropriate discipline, and it should be heeded. A parent can absolutely destroy a child through the application of harsh, oppressive, whimsical, unloving and/or capricious punishment." [16] There is evidence to suggest that many parents lose control when they punish their children. The child could remind them of a part of themselves that they don't like, or perhaps their anger is really directed at their spouse. When the child does or says something that triggers this kind of anger, a parent should never express his feeling in physical punishment. There are alternatives:

- Get away from your child for a short time.
- Call someone: your spouse, the doctor, a "hot line" for child abuse problems.
- Take your child and visit a neighbor or go somewhere where you won't be alone together.

If these steps don't work, seek further help through professional counseling. Child abuse has received a great deal of attention from family and child care experts. They feel the causes lie in the parent's own experience as a child; almost without exception abusive parents were neglected or abused to some degree during their own childhoods. Often, they were belittled and scolded by their own parents, who expected too much too soon. As a result, they feel unloved, and were not able to develop either a basic trust in others or a sense of their own worth. When they become parents, they may find themselves repeating the pattern. They often feel unhappy, and that everyone (including their baby) has let them down. Even their children seem to criticize them, just as their parents did; some even come to think that their child is actually evil or is possessed by the devil. Or they may simply feel they have to show the child who is boss, and to bear down hard to make the child obey. They may not want to "give in" to their baby when he cries, or to let him get away with things. Almost all parents have moments when they feel some of these things; but if you find yourself obsessed with such feelings (and increasingly tempted to act them out in physical punishment against your child), you should talk over your problem with your child's pediatrician, with your doctor, or with a psychological counselor. They can help you come to understand and control your feelings.

But what do you do meanwhile if your child is out of control and requires discipline and restraint? One good technique is to set the child in your lap facing you and to hold him against you physically and tightly with his arms down for five or ten minutes until he ceases struggling. Often this leads to love as well as to mutual security, and it may save you from abusing your child.

DISCIPLINE AT DIFFERENT AGES

From Birth to Crawling

The first goal of discipline is to teach your newborn to trust. Neurologically, an infant is a bundle of instincts. If he doesn't get what he wants, he cries, gives up, or goes to sleep. Do what you can to meet his needs; you can't spoil him in the first several months of life. The more you talk to and hold your baby, the more nurturance you can give him, the more you will be repaid with your baby's love and happiness. Such unconditional giving can wear down parents during this period: A baby who seems to cry for no reason can drive a parent to worry, frustration,

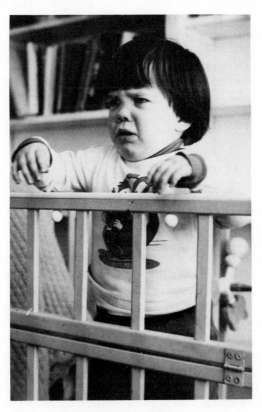

Figure 43 *Jailed!*

and anger. Punishment won't help, however; in fact, violent shaking can cause serious brain damage. Fortunately, somewhere around the age of three to six months, an infant will begin to tolerate some delays in gratification. One mother solved the "hold them or leave them" dilemma by patting her baby when he cried, talking to him, turning him over, and then leaving him for a few minutes. Later, she would pick him up and change him, and even if his demand was for food, lay him back down for a minute while she got the bottle ready. Gradually, she found that her baby learned not to expect instant results from his crying.

By two or three months, most infants have at least one long wakeful period every day, usually lasting from one feeding to the next. Use this wakeful period for play, bathing, and talking to and enjoying the baby. After five or six months, you may find that your baby spends much of the day wide awake and ready for play. This is the time to start using the playpen for short periods. You may not be able to get into long, time-consuming jobs, but you can leave the baby alone for ten to fifteen minute periods while you do shorter chores. Afterwards, pick up the baby, whether he is crying or not. If the baby is playing happily, it is tempting for a mother to use this quiet time to do something else, but if the baby is only picked up when he cries, he may soon learn to cry and scream immediately upon being deposited in the playpen. Ideally, both parent and baby are learning to discipline themselves during this stage not to think of crying as the only means of getting attention. Begun in infancy, this lesson should be gradually expanded and reinforced as the child grows older.

From Crawling Through the Toddler Stage

The faster a baby gets around, the greater the chance he will get into trouble and hurt himself. Incidences of accidents and poisoning reach a peak during this period, if parents do not take steps to create a relatively trouble-free environment for their child, and to lay down (and enforce) rules of safe behavior. This entails baby-proofing the house to remove dangerous (and valuable) objects from baby's reach so that he will be able to explore more freely and you won't have to spend your time worrying and saying no. "No" can become the parents' constant refrain at this age of their child. If it bothers you always to be so "negative," take a look at some of the things you are saying "no" to. You may decide you can tolerate those activities which are merely messy and noisy (as versus dangerous and intrusive to you). One of the reasons one- and two-year-olds get into so much trouble is that they need to explore, to learn, and to try things out. Within limits, why not let them? They can be put in playpens for short periods of happy play when the parent is busy with something else. However, Harvard researcher Burton White found that crawlers and toddlers who were allowed to follow their mother around the house and explore and try out new things while she did chores, developed more competence, curiosity, and learning ability than those shut in too much. Mother should be ready to stop what she is doing for a moment when the baby wants or needs attention. Sometimes, it is just helping the baby with a problem, or showing him a new way of handling objects, or just talking with the baby.

There are many children who can be disciplined without the use of punishment. This comes naturally, as they are cooperative and sensitive to adult actions and reactions. They trust their parents, and if told gently not to play with the light cords, or if these objects are removed from them a few times, they will leave them alone from then on. Some children have such an urge to please, even as toddlers, that they will only get into "mischief" if they don't know that what they are doing is bad. Such children require only quiet explanations, and from then on they avoid bad behavior. They can be a joy to raise, and they make parenting an easy and happy experience. All you have to offer such children is love and explanation. Of course, all children do not respond like this, and, for many, you will have to use other methods. But try love and explanations before you use isolation, scolding, or spanking.

When "no" or modern methods don't work (as they often don't), when alternative activities are not possible, when your baby is irritating you, or when he is endangering himself or his environment, what can you do? Here is some personal advice from a number of pediatricians,

Figure 44   *Curiosity can kill.*

starting with a method I have found works well for a lot of children: I believe that spanking will help a child know that when you say no, you mean it. Once he understands this lesson, you may never have to spank again. Start with situations that could endanger his safety. When a toddler heads towards a plug in an electric outlet, for example, say "no" firmly but without scolding. Usually he will smile at you and keep going toward the electric cord outlet. If he continues, say "No, or I will spank." Repeat this while you get the small spanking switch (best hung on the wall in plain sight). Pull up his trouser legs and spank the calf of the leg, hard enough to produce hurt feelings and crying. Then put up your switch, and pick up your child to show that you are not angry at him, and that you are sorry he had to be spanked.

Dog trainers tell you not to spank your dog with your hand, for the dog doesn't know whether he will be petted or hit when you raise your hand, and he'll cower. I have seen children cower when a mother raises her hand to do something else. However, Associate Editor Dr. John Richards doesn't like the use of the switch. He says: "The hand that feeds,

Figure 45   *A wooden spoon has many uses!*

caresses, and loves is also the hand that wields the switch. Perhaps your pet dog is fooled, but I am certain that children aren't. A child's rump can be pretty hard—especially when protected by several layers of clothing. I suspect that the only real advantage offered by the use of the switch when punishing is that it saves one from considerable discomfort and from the indignity of a bruised hand." However, even if I accepted Dr. Richards's argument as valid, I can point out another advantage of the switch. If you take time to go for the switch, it gives you time to cool off a little if you are angry. Some agree and others disagree with me about the use of the switch. A few have visions of lacerated legs, or they may remember being beaten with a belt as a child and resenting the brutality. Yet I have had many parents use the switch, in spite of their initial reluctance, because the toddler wouldn't mind otherwise. Their results were good. The child finally learned that the parents *meant* what they said and *acted* on it instead of simply hollering or talking. Spanking should *not* be brutal; and certainly the switch shouldn't be used in anger. But I have seen children bruised from being swatted with the hand by an angry parent. It may be that it doesn't matter so much whether you swat the child, switch him, isolate him, or take away privileges in order to enforce your rules. What probably does matter is the way you do it. It is best to discipline with love.

Dr. Sidney Rosin suggests that spanking be saved for dangerous acts, and that "no" be reserved for important occurrences:

> If a child continues the behavior after you have said no, pick him up with authority and dispatch, and put him in a restricted area, such as his bed or crib. (I know there are those who believe this will turn the child against the bed, but in practice this does not seem to happen. I have yet to find a child who does not know the difference between when they are in bed to sleep and in bed to be punished.) After he has stopped crying, enter his room and tell him not to repeat the behavior. After a little loving, take him back to the "scene of the crime" and see if he has learned his lesson. If not, repeat the process.

Dr. Charles Hoffman emphasizes the importance of sticking to your guns:

> Saying "no" when a baby touches a vase may slow him down but only temporarily. If you are satisfied to keep on saying no until you get tired and *then* spank, a child will look at you with wonder as if to say, "What's up? The last time I touched it was no big deal." In my office, I will frequently have to put a child down as many as fifty times before he or she lies still for an examination. Each time I do it without anger or inflicting pain, and at the end I give him or her a hug and explain, "What a good baby you were." I rarely have the same problem on subsequent visits.

Dr. William Foster recommends that, "whenever possible, parents should avoid stepping into a problem situation and instead allow the child to figure things out for himself. Toddlers want to gain mastery and control over their lives; as they see rewards in more positive behavior, negative behavior will decrease."

The Preschooler

For this age group, discipline requires patience, persistence, and an occasional spanking, but mostly love and understanding. Three-year-olds often seem neither very civilized nor considerate of other people; yet they are quite rational, they are developing their verbal skills, and they will respond to reason. Since they are beginning to imitate their parents, we must temper our discipline with kindness. If we are not kind, they will not learn kindness. This is the time to introduce your child to the world of rules, and the freedom to operate within these rules. He needs the freedom to test his abilities and to assume larger doses of responsibility. Try to set things up so that by doing the right thing he wins, and by doing the wrong thing he loses. If, for example, you have a front yard, let him play in it but make sure he understands that he is not to wander off. If he seems unable to stay put, tell him that he will have to play in the back yard until he is old enough to play in the front. Don't be deterred by his howls; make it clear that his choices are to play in the back yard, stay quietly inside, or sit in the corner.

We may get a lot of vicarious satisfaction from watching these egocentric little creatures explore their world with no thought of the consequences. However, for their immediate safety and also for their development into civilized beings, we will have to step in from time to time and point out the consequences. For this reason, it is important to make the punishment fit the action, and not the results of the action. If, for example, a child tries to get into a forbidden cookie jar, or if he gets into it and happens to break it, the punishment should be the same. It is unreasonable to expect a small child to anticipate all the consequences of his actions.

The School Age Child

As children grow older, discipline should shift from parental force towards a greater concentration on teaching children self-control. At this age, your child is more sensitive and receptive to you than ever before; he or she will respond to explanations of "why not." This is the time when the parent can begin to step aside and let his children suffer the natural consequences of their actions, if they don't involve permanent damage. Not getting good grades may keep them from playing on the school team; the quality of their school work therefore becomes *their* problem, not yours.

Rather than adopting an "I'm in charge so I always win" stance, give them the chance to "win" when adopting correct behavior. Start by assessing "bad" behavior: Who is it really bad for? Generally, bad behavior is immature behavior. Without adopting the "when are you going to grow up?" approach (which creates a sense of shame and regression), explain to your eight-year-old that he must act like an eight-year-old in order to earn privileges appropriate to his age. If he acts like a five-year-old, then make it clear he won't be allowed to ride a two-wheeler or stay up after dinner. If he throws a tantrum, point out that he is now acting like a two-year-old. Make him go to his room or sit in a chair. If he persists, quietly yet firmly offer a spanking. Dr. Richards objects to spanking being the culmination of discipline. Certainly there are children on whom a spanking will not work. For some it may take isolation, and you as the parent have many choices, including those advocated by P.E.T.

Consistency is important at this stage: consistent punishment for unacceptable behavior followed by a positive response from you so the child won't mope over why you said "no" to him. Rewards become more effective than punishment for the pre-teen child. To avoid having to punish, try reminding your child, just before a particular action is expected, of the kind of behavior you want. Don't go overboard in your discipline. As Dr. Charles Hoffman points out: "If I were to see two children in my waiting room, one whose parents were too strict and another whose parents were too lenient, it would be impossible for me to tell which was which in most cases. They would both behave equally badly. The child of the overstrict parent has learned that he must defy authority in order to express himself. The child from the oversubmissive family does not know right from wrong, and so does as he pleases."

It is with the school age child that I believe Parent Effectiveness Training is of real value. P.E.T. helps the child come to his own conclusions about his behavior. It requires that the parent learn to listen to the child, and gradually to drop directing the child's behavior so that the child can take over this function. Basic is the parents' respect for their child and a demonstration of their own parental values in action. I would go a step further and make certain that the child suffers the consequences of his wrong choice—because it is part of the parenting task to teach the child the bad as well as the good consequences of behavior. I also believe that the parent is equally responsible to see to it that there is some sort of reward for basically proper choices by the child, even if circumstances in life don't always reward "good" choices.

Instilling Good Habits

Discipline is teaching, and there are many habit patterns that children should be taught. These include good manners, neatness, doing chores, and even enjoying work. Actually you can teach a child almost anything if you desire and if you have the patience and persistence. Learning a few techniques about how you deal with these common problems may also help you deal with other traits you desire for your children. Most of these techniques start with a demonstration by you.

Teaching Children to Work

Part of discipline involves teaching children to work. This is a worthwhile value to hold for the children and a practical help for the family. It is often easier for the adults to do the chores themselves, but this establishes a situation in which the children's efforts do not seem needed or wanted. Daryl V. Hoole, in her small book of sound advice, wrote:

> A mother should not be a slave to her family; she must not do all the work alone. Besides her having neither the time nor the strength to do so, the children need to learn how to work and accept responsibility. They need to feel a part of the family by sharing in the responsibilities of a home. They must realize the benefits of team work.[17]

Allowances

Dr. Neil Henderson believes in allowances:

> When children are six years old, I believe it is wise to start a small allowance. Twenty-five cents a week, or a lesser amount, compatible with the family's budget, is enough. The allowance is given because children are members of the family group. It should not represent payment for specific chores or a reward for good behavior. However, all children should have specific chores, such as emptying the garbage every day or bringing in the evening newspaper, because they are members of the family group.
>
> All allowances do is provide children with important experience in the use of money. They should feel free to do with it as they wish. However, it may be given with the understanding that it is to cover certain expenditures such as school supplies, bubble gum, and, as children grow older, toiletries and inexpensive articles of clothing. Naturally, allowances should grow with children, as well as the expenditures it is supposed to cover. No parent is perfect in the handling of money, and perfection should not be looked for in the child. If gross errors are made, they should be discussed in a friendly, noncritical manner.

The principle of saving may also be taught through the use of an allowance. If children do not have the money to purchase something they want immediately, they will learn that it is wise to save for future needs.

I don't believe you should give allowances. It appears to me that unearned things means less to us than things we work for to achieve. So if the child wants money, have several tasks available above his routine chores. Pay him only for completion of the tasks, not for just working a while. Make a verbal contract and stick to it. Point out that everyone in the family has responsibilities. If the child doesn't want to, don't force him to work. However, withdraw some of the privileges of the age. A five- or six-year-old who isn't able to take out the garbage isn't old enough to ride a bicycle. A ten- to twelve-year-old who won't weed the garden isn't old enough for Saturday afternoon movies. Be very matter of fact about refusing new privileges and stick to your decision. Do not deny privileges while angry, frustrated, or disgusted. Do not punish children for refusing to act grown-up. That is their problem, not yours.

Discipline is for purpose. Home is a training ground to prepare children for life. Work is a requirement, and the satisfaction of fulfilling one's obligations and duties is a reward that children should have as well as adults. Other methods of getting children to work are suggested in Daryl Hoole's book, *The Art of Homemaking:*

1. A family should learn that they must all work together, then they can all play together.
2. Help your children to understand that if they cooperate with you in carrying out your work and schedule, you will cooperate with them and be considerate of their plans. If some of your requests are not particularly appealing to them, remind them that it isn't exactly pleasant for you to bait a hook with a wriggling worm or to put up with grasshoppers in bottles in the house for them!
3. It is wise to not overload your children with jobs. Start out gradually; one job completed is worth six on the list.
4. Let your children have a variety in their work. Let them have a change of jobs every day if necessary. It's also a good idea sometimes to give them a choice as to what their duty should be or to let them draw their assignments from a hat.
5. A novel way to ask a child to do a certain job is to pin a note to his or her pillow or tuck one in a lunch box. Note writing is also an impressive way to thank children for a job well done. Children thrive on sincere appreciation expressed for their efforts.
6. Our little daughter learned to keep crayons off the floor when I began throwing away each crayon I found lying on the floor.
7. A child will remember to make his bed before leaving for school if he returns home and finds his bed completely stripped.
8. Children need to learn that they must follow through and complete their tasks. One mother was exasperated because her young son did things only

halfway. Finally the situation was corrected when she served him a half cooked dinner.

9. A way to encourage your children to care for their toys is to have them leave one of their previous year's toys under the Christmas Tree for Santa to see.

10. Pre-teens and teenagers, with their homework and activities, often lose sight of helping around the house. A wise parent is considerate of their outside interests and helps them to plan their household obligations accordingly. For instance, it might be better for them to do their helping early in the morning rather than after school. If teenagers have been taught since early childhood the value of work and the importance of carrying their share of responsibility in the home, and if their work is organized so they can do it easily and in a minimum of time, they can and will help. They may gripe and complain at the time, but the day will come when they will appreciate what they have learned and praise you for teaching them.

11. Children should learn to help because it is their duty to do so. If they fail to perform a specific duty, they should be penalized in some way that is related to their misdeed. Depriving them of something they want to have or do is frequently an effective way of impressing upon them the importance of carrying out responsibility.[18]

DISCIPLINE OUTSIDE THE FAMILY

Another type of discipline involves the child's activities in organized groups outside of the family in areas such as sports, music, dance, drama, and so on. Pediatrician William Foster outlines how participation in organized groups helps build self esteem, decision making skills, and social awareness:

For children to become independent, confident, and self-reliant, they must be given chances to make small decisions first, take the consequences for errors, analyze risks, and use the information gained to make gradually increasingly more complicated decisions. Ideally, this is done under the protective wing of the parents and possibly of older siblings who provide sage advice and satisfy the child's normal dependency needs. The parents protect the child against making catastrophic decisions, but on the other hand do not attempt to protect them totally against failure or adversity. Parents may at times interfere with a child's decision making process if a situation appears *to them* to be an unusually unfair one, but this must be done very cautiously. I believe parents should basically err on the side of allowing the child to handle even unfair situations, as these must be faced at some time.

An area which permits children to make such decisions where mistakes cost little and yet allow the child to develop a feeling of gradually increasing control over what happens to him/her is in skill-building fields.

Numerous advantages accrue to the child involved in such programs:

1. *The child has to relate directly to adults outside the family (coaches, teachers, directors, etc.)* and acquires an ability to deal with diverse personalities.
2. Acquisition of basic skills improves one's own self-image relative to peers. The understanding that you win some and lose some, and that you're better at some things than others, helps to produce a realistic self-appraisal.
3. The child acquires an understanding of commitment to a short-term goal, as well as the value of practice and perseverance in achieving this goal.
4. The natural competitive and aggressive instincts which are present in varying degrees in all children are permitted healthy expression. Competition can be with a standard, with oneself or with others, depending on the child and the activity preference.
5. Social relationships are enhanced via the learning of values and necessity of teamwork: sharing of responsibilities and the feeling of belonging, sharing in the frustrations and successes of the particular organization or individuals.
6. Lastly, skills and abilities learned as children provide those persons with the basis for a more interesting and meaningful life as adults.

Teaching Neatness

Dr. Bruce Valentine offers very practical advice on how to teach a child neatness, beginning at a young age:

> Children generally play in the family room and usually leave toys scattered around. They use the family rooms to play in, which is natural; and they must be taught to remove their toys each night, so that the rest of the family can use the room. There must be adequate provision for storage of the toys and objects, and it must be suitable. Obviously, they must be able to use it: It must not be too high, or the lid or door too heavy for them to use by themselves. The dictum must be repeated often enough to become "law"—which equals "Clean up the floor and room so the rest of us can safely walk and use the room before you go to bed." If there are repeated lapses, then the warning may be given that the toys will disappear. After an appropriate time, they do disappear and may only reappear as "new" toys, suitably wrapped at a birthday or at Christmas, as the time suits. If there are further repeated lapses, then the toys may have to disappear permanently, despite the wailing response after their loss. In this way, they learn to respect the rights of others, that is, the use of the family space by others.
>
> When they grow up and have their own rooms, the problem becomes one of caring for themselves. If the room is impossible to care for due to "dropped clothes," the answer may be two-fold. Let them do their own picking up and placing in the wash on their own, or let them run shy of clothes since they neglected to put them in the

laundry in time, on their own. Or, use the alternative of refusing to clean the room, since it cannot be done properly due to "handling things on the floor," but then the room must be cleaned by them under these circumstances.

Teaching Good Manners

"Good manners do not just happen," says Dr. Marvin McClellan:

Children learn good manners if their parents lay down good ground rules. They also learn by watching the people of their community. If children see their parents misbehaving toward each other, either at home or in public, then they, too, will misbehave. If they see adults doing unmannerly things, they assume that such behavior is all right for them, too. If you wish your child to have good manners, practice good manners in front of him at all times. Be polite, be courteous to each member of the family, and treat each other with respect.

WHEN DISCIPLINE DOESN'T WORK

If your child's behavior doesn't respond to your discipline, or to discipline in the school, you need help. Regardless of the cause, it is a sign that you need a fresh approach toward that particular child. The child may or may not want help; some get considerable emotional satisfaction out of harassing a parent. But whether he wants help or not, the child needs it. The fact that you may need help doesn't mean you are a poor parent. Even professionals need help with problems involving their own children—probably as much as the average parent. I find it is easier to tell someone else how to handle their child than it is for me to follow my own advice. This doesn't mean that professionals can't help you with *your* parenting problems. They can look at your problems objectively, and "hear you out." Usually, it only takes a minor change in attitude or method of handling. I suggest you read our section on what psychiatric help means. On a less professional but very understanding basis, our Editor-Mother Julie Oliver offers the following advice:

Don't berate yourself because you screamed at your child in total frustration, or spanked in anger, or failed to discipline your toddler, or are faced with behavior problems in a second grader. Begin new, today. Look back only long enough to see what you did wrong and decide to change. Then change the way you handle yourself and your child today. It is never too late to begin again. If you think of yourself as a flop as a parent, you'll act like one. If you believe you can change and do a better job, you've taken the first step toward real development.

Program yourself and your child to succeed. You can't lose fifty pounds in one week and you can't become a great, successful disciplinarian overnight. Pick one problem and concentrate on that. Success in small, possible stages will give you and your child increasing self-confidence. Huge, unrealistic goals produce unrealistic frustration and guilt. You know your child needs praise for accomplishment—don't forget yourself.

Give yourself a pat on the back for the discipline you handle well today instead of concentrating only on the situations you mishandled yesterday. Also—don't forget a pat on the back when your spouse handles something well. Disciplining children is hard, important work. We all need all the encouragement we can get.

Too Much Discipline?

You may want to consider the possibility that your child may be spoiled by too much discipline, if not too little. Dr. John Richards describes the spoiled child as:

> One who uses undesirable behavior to get what he wants, *too much of the time.* Children can also be "spoiled" by too much discipline, too little discipline, and by unreasonably harsh forms of discipline. Every child tries to get his way by using undesirable behavior some of the time, and most parents are at times too lenient, too firm, inconsistent, or unreasonable. It is when such patterns of behavior, on the part of children and parents alike, become a "way of life" that real problems may develop.
>
> Another type of spoiled child learns to "con" his parents by being too cute, too funny, or overly nice. Even though attention gained for these reasons is usually pleasant, too much attention may cause unhappiness or interfere with the needs of other family members. Parents who spend too much "fun" time with a child eventually become frustrated and resentful because they find that it is almost impossible to leave the child alone when other needs demand attention.

You may wonder how a child can "get what he wants" when there is too much discipline. This occurs when the child finds that he can get the parents to react to him any time he behaves in a "bad" (for the parent) manner. This allows the child to manipulate the parent at will, and assures the child the center of the stage in the family.

Is It Allergy?

Yet another possibility is that your child's behavior problem is partly due to allergy. If this sounds far fetched, read Saskatchewan professor John W. Gerrard's presentation in *The Parents' Medical Manual* and note the similarity to the following case reported by Dr. William Crook:

> There were multiple complaints about ten-year-old J.H.: fussy, irritable, unhappy, awake at night, dribbling urine, tense—and he had a stuffy nose. He had unpredictable fluctuations in daily behavior, varying from wild to normal. No physical disease was found. The mother found that citrus fruit, chocolate, and cola made him irritable. Further testing showed that he reacted to rice with bedwetting, crying, and hyperactivity. Careful diet control reduced all of these symptoms, but mother reports, "If there ever was a Dr. Jekyll and Mr. Hyde, it's Jim. He's a wonderful little guy, loved by everyone, as long as he doesn't get hold of something that disagrees with him. But when he does, look out!" [19]

Too Much Nagging?

Dr. William Foster reminds us that too much nagging can result in the opposite behavior from what is desired: "A common reason for the failure of discipline is an excessive number of minor requirements, resulting in constant nagging of the child by the parents. This tends to produce a child with a negative self-image who feels he or she can never do anything right and who will never look good in the parent's eyes. This leads to an image of a child who is 'expected' to be bad, and many such children eventually live up to this negative expectation."

Is It Your Inconsistency?

The principles and practice of disciplining toddlers and two-year-olds remain valid and can be used throughout adult life. However, as the child gets into the three- to four-year-age group there should be an expansion of discipline to more sophisticated methods which teach self-control and self-reliance.

One problem that occurs is that children, as they grow, find more sophisticated methods of testing their limits. If the three- to four-year-old won't mind, it may be because his testing and his analysis of the parents' response gives him no good clues as to what to expect. Georgia pediatrician Martin H. Smith says:

> On analysis of the child's day-by-day behavior and the parents' response to situations, we find that the ingredient most often missing is a consistency in the response of the parent. The parent is often deterred from reacting as he should have reacted because of the pressure of time or circumstances. A similar circumstance on another day produced an entirely different reaction, and perhaps on a third day, because the parent was tired or already angry, it produced still another reaction. The child would be less than human if he did not continue testing his parents.

In any situation that requires discipline, the parents should pause long enough to ask themselves if the reaction is appropriate, and "if this is the way I reacted yesterday and is it reasonable for me to react this way tomorrow?" If the answer to these self-queries are all "yes," then you should proceed with the discipline and know that you are being consistent.

Is It Persistence?

"Some children are timid and respond almost too quickly to a harsh voice," says Dr. Robert Herman. "Others are very persistent in wanting things their way. With persistent children, try to control the most urgent behavior; other behavior may be irritating but not physically harmful to the child or the family. To handle the persistent child requires that you be more persistent than the child. If you keep children under control, they will gradually develop self-control."

If Your Child Doesn't Listen to You

If your child doesn't mind you, maybe it is because he doesn't hear you. Maybe you talk too much. Children develop parent deafness as a protection against constant demand, reproach, criticism, and scolding. Try using fewer words. Use a cowbell for a "come home call." Have the children write down their own reminders.

On the other hand, maybe your child *really* doesn't hear. Julie Oliver offers suggestions on parent deafness:

If your child really doesn't hear what you say quite often, you might ask yourself:

1. Could my child have a hearing problem? If you have any real doubt at all—have your doctor check.
2. What is the noise level in my home? If you can't "hear yourself think," others can't hear you talking.
3. Do I talk "at" my children so often that they've turned me off in self-defense?
4. Have I substituted a cranky, whiny tone of voice for stating my wishes calmly and clearly?
5. Do I nag incessantly instead of following up with punishment when I get no response?
6. Does my spouse have the same problem? If not, why not?
7. Have I failed to follow up with appropriate punishment so often that my children know they can safely ignore anything I say?
8. Am I so critical and full of "no's" that my child gives up trying to obey because there's no way to stay out of trouble anyway?

9. Am I unreasonable in my behavior expectations and overdemand that all orders be followed instantly? The drill sergeant approach?"

Too Much Love?

Baumrind says that self-sacrificing mother love leaves the child unprepared to deal with the world if he is accustomed to immediate gratification: Parents who give the child only kindness, self-sacrifice, and understanding, while demanding nothing of the child in return, allow the child to be selfish. If the child identifies with the parents, who are unselfish, it leads to a sense of shame and an unhealthy conflict within the child as to what he should become.[20]

It is not that anyone is against kindness and understanding, it is just that to be effective *for the child,* parental love is probably best given with demands for improved behavior, self-discipline, and development of skills. These demands may require some use of parental power in such a way that the parent will be admired by the child in the long run, rather than resented. It may be easier not to demand and to grant the child unearned freedom in the hope that he will straighten himself out. Many do just that. But your results will probably be better, and be far more appreciated, if you actively parent and exert the effort to control and aid the child's development. Adults look back on the demanding teacher with far more respect than they do on the permissive teacher. The same occurs with parents. The key is that the child knows, during the time he is controlled, when power and punishment are exerted, that the parent does this in the child's best interest.

Do You Lack Confidence?

Probably the most common reason that discipline doesn't work is uncertainty on the part of the parent. Lack of confidence stops a parent from acting firmly and decisively when it is needed in order to make discipline effective. You *can* become an authoritative or rational parent. As a start, don't forget that in relation to the child the parent *is* an authority. It is helpful to increase your knowledge about child raising; but regardless, you already know far more than your child does. What you may need to do is have a conference with your spouse and establish ground rules for handling your children. What techniques you use may be less important than your consistency and attitude. Look on yourself as a teacher who has information that the children must learn.

Make Your Choice

We have considered Dobson's strict method of parenting, Baumrind's rational firmness, Gordon's P.E.T., and my "neutral" discipline.

One of these will probably work for you on your particular child. If you cannot settle successfully on a method, or if you do and the methods don't work, then you and your spouse should arrange for a consultation with a pediatrician or a psychologist. But keep in mind that you *are* the parent and that it is *your* responsibility, not theirs.

Do You Need to Discipline Yourself?

Unless you have some self-discipline, it is rather hard to discipline your children. You will learn self-discipline as a parent if you haven't learned it before. It isn't that we *want* to grow up, it's just that, as parents, we *must* grow up. Parenting is one of the more maturing experiences of life.

How you go about it is personal, but that really doesn't help. There is a limited amount of help that we can give you, but we did decide that Associate Editor Julie Oliver should take this task, by a two to one vote of the three editors. She came up with some tips for parents:

1. Keep reminding yourself which of you is the child and which the parent.
2. Don't ask questions that your child can't answer. Your two-year-old may not understand his sudden urge to fling oatmeal at the wall. If you must ask "why," be prepared to accept the obvious instead of a Freudian analysis. "Why did you cut the heads off all the flowers?" "Because I wanted to."
3. Don't take all misbehavior personally. David did not pour your new bottle of perfume down the drain because he hates you, he just liked to hear the gurgling sound.
4. Don't make misbehavior personal for your child. Criticize the behavior, not the child. "This is a very poor grade in spelling," NOT "You're so stupid!"
5. Avoid the eternal and the total. "You *never* mind." "You'll never amount to anything." "You always lie."
6. Don't criticize a child for not being something impossible. "If only you were more like your sister." "Why can't you grow up?" "My family all made good grades."
7. Don't push the "Do as I say, not as I do" idea too far. It is possible to encourage some things in your child that you are unable to do yourself. But— it's a whole lot harder to get through to your child about the importance of picking up toys while you are busily laying a trail of clutter yourself. After you've heard your toddler sprinkling playtime conversations with swear words, you never again have to ask yourself whether the model you set is important.
8. Program yourself and your child for success. Try to use your hindsight and your foresight to make sure conditions are as conducive as possible for good behavior. Hanging up clothes is rough when you can't reach the hooks. Perching a little one on a satin chair with nothing to do while you indulge in a lengthy visit at a friend's house is unfair and is asking for it. Try child-proofing your schedules and expectations as well as your home.
9. Don't play poor pitiful put upon parent. "How can you leave your room so messy when you know I've slaved over the years taking grease stains out of your permanent press slacks?" "After all we've done for you, how can you act like this? Why, your braces alone cost $3,000 and now you stay out until 2 A.M. without calling."

10. Don't drop the A-bomb for minor disobedience—and vice versa. Being grounded for two months is too high a penalty for leaving a bicycle out in the rain. Yet a gentle no-no doesn't cut it for throwing rocks at baby sister.

11. Try to be consistent. Egging them on for showing off the first time, ignoring it the second, and coming down like a ton of bricks the third doesn't teach much except the unpredictability of adults, which many children accept as a fact of life.

12. Your public and private behavior expectations should be as similar as possible. Don't throw a fit if your child doesn't use perfect manners at Grandmother's when you haven't worked on and demanded their use at home. Don't be surprised if your child plays kick ball with a friend's needlepoint cushion if you haven't taught "hands off" at home.

13. Expect children (especially small ones, but also those from one to ninety years old) to be quite literal. If you scold because a child fails to tell you about a visitor at the front door, don't be surprised one day to have a repairman brought directly to the bathroom while you're having a bath. When you work hard at teaching your child never to lie, you may one day cringe to hear a tiny voice saying: "My Daddy can't come to the phone. He's busy fighting with Mommy." This is a great chance for you to dig out your sense of humor. Unfortunately, this literal interpretation never seems to apply to instructions such as "Clean up your room!" "Go to bed," or "Turn off the lights!" Still, it is sometimes wise to qualify your commands. "You must sit in the corner and not leave your chair for ten minutes. Of course, you may leave if you are wetting your pants, if you see smoke pouring out of the kitchen, or if I call you."

14. Give marching orders one at a time. Even adults can't always remember a rapid fire list of different errands. In fact, you may forget what you asked and fail to follow up. Keep it clear, keep it single, keep it simple—and make sure your child understands what you want. Try to avoid procrastinating with discipline. If you wait till Susan has failed to feed the dog for the eleventh straight day, you're more likely to blow up and Susan may have developed the habit of *not* feeding the dog.

15. Don't compare your own childhood behavior with that of your child. "My father would have slammed me against the wall if I'd talked back to him like you do to me." You'll just leave the child wondering why you don't insist on the same respect. "I was always helpful and obedient," may cause your child to decide: "I could never be as good as you were; I must be a big disappointment to you."

16. When your child misbehaves, count to ten before you do anything. If your child has done something that really gets your goat, give yourself enough time to calm down. There are obvious exceptions to this rule, such as when the child is endangering his or her own safety, or that of someone else, or flushing your pearl necklace down the toilet. Speedy response is mandatory in these cases. Start discipline early. A very wise elementary school principal, Walter Bollinger, used to tell beginning teachers to "start out tough and you can loosen up later. If you start out loose and then have to toughen up, the children will never respect you." Paddle now and relax and enjoy later.

17. You are a tour guide, introducing children to a new world. They'd be lost without you. They would miss much, and enjoy a great deal less. When everything goes wrong, and you're sure you can never be the kind of parent you want to be, sit down and reassure yourself. "I'm not perfect, but I know

more than my children do, so I must have something to teach them." After all, you have been living longer, and experience is a valuable asset for any job.

WAYS TO RAISE CHILDREN

We had a lot of problems writing about ways to raise children. Everyone has his own ideas; it almost seemed as if there *are* 1,001 ways of doing it. But we all agree that the key is that you do it! Whether you can discipline neutrally or not is up to you. It did help in the following true case. A six-year-old kept peeing on his bedroom walls: The family brought the child to his doctor, considerably bruised, having decided that they would murder him if they didn't get help. The child was the oldest of a large brood and was, in fact, rather ignored. The parents agreed with the doctor's assessment that the child wanted to be babied, too; and they followed the advice to put him in diapers and baby him thoroughly but restrict him from the privileges of a six-year-old. Three days later they were in a panic because he was being happily spoonfed in a high chair. Soon after, however, he announced he wanted to go out to play. Given the fact that if he peed on the wall he was acting like a baby and had to wear diapers, and therefore was too young to go out and play, he decided to grow up and use the toilet in place of the handier wall. Soon he was out playing with the other kids and getting his bruises there rather than from his parents. This child survived and learned. Yes, there are many ways.

The principle remains that regardless of the various ways to raise children, you must exert your power to discipline and you must have the proper attitude—an attitude of love. Discipline should involve very little spanking or other punishments if you teach them early that you *will* spank and that you *mean* what you say. This sets the stage for a more pleasant existence with your children. If they understand that they have choices of action which dictate whether they get punished or rewarded, they will usually go for the reward. However, beware of the trap of the negative reward. Children can win by getting parents upset. They often regard the spanking or scolding as a confirmation of victory. "I got her goat!" they say with considerable satisfaction; and they will go to almost any lengths, as you can see, to get the parent's proverbial goat and attention. So, when possible, reward negative behavior as childish and unworthy of much attention. If you let children know that they can make you mad, it offers some of them too good a means of manipulating you for them to ignore.

The preferable way to discipline is in a controlled yet relaxed fashion that allows you to treat undesirable behavior for what it is—immaturity. Withdrawal of privileges should come before isolation, and isolation before spanking. Set it up so that when they mind, act grown up, and do the right thing, they win your respect. We all want respect, and this is probably the most potent factor in the drive toward maturity and self-discipline.

Everyone has deep and cherished feelings about the what, how, and why of discipline. I don't think there is a truly scientific approach to the subject. Perhaps someone will come forth with a controlled study one day. I doubt it, but even if one can show that a certain method of discipline can be statistically proven to work, I will object. "Statistical proof might show that a particular method of discipline can work for the majority, but that is numerical proof: It works for the greatest number. It is not human proof: It may not necessarily work for you and your child.

The parenting experts who have written for *The Parent's Guide*, and all those we quote in it, respect and prize children. Just how that respect is shown, however, is a matter of considerable difference. What really counts to your child is the respect you have for him as a person, regardless of his age or talents. If you have that, he will be more content and you will enjoy actively disciplining him in his best interest. But don't take all the credit or all the blame yourself. Solzhenitsyn said:

> Some children take after their parents, others grow to be quite different from them. Some assume our views and habits as though they could wish for none better. Others, though apparently given all the right guidance at every step and though outwardly obedient, evolve, with the unswerving persistence of a tree trunk, in a direction which is wholly theirs and not ours.[21]

8

SCHOOL AND LEARNING PROBLEMS

When the child starts school, mother's function and life change. First there are the pangs of separation and the accompanying exhilaration of independence felt by both parent and child. Then there is the concern over how well or how poorly the child will learn and adapt to his teachers and classmates. Many things are at stake, including the effect of the educational process on the child's future, his personality, and his character. Then there is the more immediate question of "Is life in school good or bad?" Some children enjoy school to the hilt and face the challenges of learning with confidence and poise. Others detest school, its teachers, some of their classmates, and face learning with uncertainty, inability, or rebellion. The problems that can occur are complex—now even more complex than the already complex individual child—for the effects of the particular school system, a teacher, and sometimes certain classmates are added to your parental reaction. Most of the time it works out, and usually parents are reassured and somewhat settled down when the child graduates summa cum laude from kindergarten. Some children, however, don't graduate from kindergarten with honors, ready to overwhelm the first grade. And others get to the first grade only to find that they have real problems sitting still or learning. Parents then begin to feel that "Something is wrong with my child! Or the school! Or the teacher. Or something!"

WHY DOESN'T JOHNNY LEARN?

Why don't some children learn easily? Even with good teachers and a good educational system, they have difficulty. Part of the problem may

Figure 46 *Learning!*

be that a "good" system for most children isn't good for all children. Children aren't turned out like General Electric modular products—they are as individual and unique as people. So one of the major problems with the school age child is getting him with the right teacher and in the right system. Both normal and abnormal children can have problems in school, and because school is such an important portion of a child's life, the difficulties can be significant. They were with me. I did so well learning to read in the first grade that my teacher graduated me to cleaning erasers. That may not seem significant to you, but it was to me—I went downhill from there until I was rescued by some fine and dedicated teachers in the fifth grade and restarted on the road to learning. We will talk more about teachers, but one thing should be kept in mind: A good teacher is worth her weight in gold, even if we don't pay them that handsomely. How we value our children is to a degree reflected in how we pay and respect their good teachers.

Can you tell if your child will have learning problems when he goes to school? There are a number of characteristics that seem to be associated with later school failure problems. If your child has any of the following problems, it is wise to consider early intervention in order to prevent later school difficulties:

- Hyperactivity: Aside from an inability to sit still long enough to learn anything, there may be special problems in arithmetic, spelling, and handwriting.
- Family history of reading problems: This usually occurs in males who read late or poorly; at times the history goes back generations but isn't talked about.
- Speech problems: Children whose speech sounds "funny" may develop reading problems later.
- Prematurity: Language problems are not uncommon in the premature child.
- Slow development: This may carry over into school.

Figure 47

- Immaturity: Children who are too young chronologically or developmentally tend to later failure in school.
- Permissive parents: Children who are indulged may be self-confident but are aggressive, impulsive, and inconsiderate of others, leading to school problems.
- Over-strict parents: Children who are overdirected and not trusted may lack initiative and confidence in school.
- Alcoholic or constantly quarrelling parents: psychic conflict in the home life may reduce learning potential.

WHAT IS THE ROLE OF PARENTS IN SCHOOL AFFAIRS?

All parents have the responsibility of knowing what their children do in school. It is for each parent to decide how involved to become in this critical aspect of upbringing. From nursery school to college, parents must evaluate the leadership, personnel, curriculum, and the degree of responsibility assumed by the school for their offspring's education.

It is up to the parents to see that their children receive a good education. This may require parental intervention, either through formal or informal channels or even through withdrawal and new placement for the child. Parents should also give positive support to these educational elements which are successful.

If your children aren't learning knowledge, discipline, or how to learn, and if they are losing self-esteem and educational opportunity, then the parent should intercede. Parents know their children, and the results of the schooling on their children, whether or not the parent knows about the system. We can say the same about medical care—I believe it is the parents' responsibility to evaluate the results and seek another source of care if they are unsatisfied.

Teacher Jan Canby says: "The earlier parents and teachers become acquainted, the better. Parent–teacher conferences are helpful to find out the goals and expectations of your child's teacher. The teacher can help direct the parents' efforts with the child at home. If problems occur, most teachers want to be approached directly by the parents. Then, if a solution is not reached, they can go to the principal."

Are You Angry at Your Child's Teacher?

Children are subjected to many pressures in school. They must obey the rules. They have successes and failures. Teachers make them study, test them, and judge them. Rarely is it all roses. Sooner or later, a major or minor crisis occurs in the teacher–student relationship. Your instinctive parental bias may cause you to defend the child, too often in anger.

The teacher may or may not deserve an angry reaction; but, deserved or not, the angry reaction rarely produces the desired results. Teachers are professionals, but, like parents, they are also subject to human emotions. Ideally, they should be able to deal with the irate parent in an objective manner. Most can. But teachers are also individuals. Education does not always change their personality or their ability to control instinctive responses.

As a parent, you have a right and duty to intercede if it is in the best interest of your child. When you intercede, do it for maximum positive effect. Make it worthwhile. Control your anger, fears, and frustrations. The teacher, too, wants the best for your child. So don't start by putting the teacher on the defensive. Assume that your child's teacher is willing to work out a rational solution to your child's problem. Occasionally, it is best to go straight to the principal. Give the facts and tell how you feel. Try to be fair. Remember that there is a superintendent of schools and a school board for appeal, as well as your local Parent Teachers Association, if you are not satisfied. Your doctor may be able to help. These are *our* schools. Let's work with them as much as we can. Meanwhile, at home, don't let the child and his peers become involved or even aware of a parent–teacher hassle. That creates even bigger problems.

GENERAL PROBLEMS WITH EDUCATION

The first teacher your child has is you. Your child's view of self, the world, and of life and learning starts with you. This takes time, and it cannot simply be left to a child care center. You should include your child in your life, including your work and your activities in the home or in your job whenever you can. They need a lot of time for play, but they also need an adult to help, to admire, and to copy. They need to work and feel needed. Their horizons should be expanded beyond television and four-square. It isn't necessary for you to teach your preschooler to read, but you can offer him the chance. It isn't necessary to give your child lectures about the world but it is necessary to take him to meet the neighbors, to read to him, and to talk with him about his world and yours. Ideally, your child will have spent a year or two in nursery school prior to kindergarten. But nursery school or not, the time comes to go out into the world. We asked pediatrician Henry Richanbach how he responds to the question, "Is my child ready for kindergarten?" He writes:

Many a bewildered parent presents the pediatrician with this dilemma: The school says our son, a "typical boy," is immature. We are considering keeping him out for a year, having him repeat the same grade (if he is already in school), or moving to another community to hide our shame. What should we do?

Note that the student is a boy. Kindergartens, by and large, have been designed by females, are run by females, and are best suited for little girls. Boys and girls vary tremendously at this age. Boys, for whatever reasons, seem less well equipped for school as it is now set up than do girls.

Children need certain skills in school. A major one is the ability to sit still and pay attention. The "skill" of standing in line is one prized beyond all others. Also, one mustn't talk, one must avoid running, and one must learn not to touch. If a child wants to go to the bathroom, the act must be preceded by a hand raising ceremony. Who said childhood is a time of freedom?

The mind must work in all the wondrous ways that permit man, of all nature's creations, to read, cipher, and communicate via the spoken word. Are all children's variations in intelligence developed sufficiently to allow them to function well in the classroom? Did God provide children in uniform units of thirty, all ready to do page seventeen, paragraph three on November 19th at 11:15 a.m.? It seems unlikely. It is up to you and your school to find out where each child "is at," so that they can be helped to learn in their own ways, even as they "mature," and learn and develop the other needed skills.

Good school systems are increasingly aware that it is their responsibility to find out what children need and to provide it for them. Such planning does not imply excessive permissiveness or lack of solid educational goals. It simply recognizes that children vary a great deal. Some read when they enter kindergarten. Others may need years more time. All children deserve the particular kind of help they need for solid achievement—not just more time to mature.

Many countries don't start formal education until the children are seven or eight years old, yet these countries still produce their share of scholars. Don't think that your child is doomed to scholastic oblivion if he can't read French fluently at eight. Don't leave town, we need you here.

I don't think we should knock standing in line. Without that basic training, we would have anarchy in society as well as in schools. A mother who experienced the problems that can occur if your child goes to school before he is ready commented: "If your child is not ready for kindergarten and you keep him out, you do him a tremendous favor—you give him a gift of time. If he gets into school and is not ready, a sense of failure may develop right there in that cheerful colorful classroom."

Characteristics of Kindergarteners Who May Have Learning Disabilities

* Usually boys
* Immature emotionally
* Short attention span
* Poor muscle control and coordination
* Poor social adjustment
* Highly impulsive
* Delayed speech

Girls, too, can have some problems of maturity, although generally they are far more ready for school than boys at this age. There are no hard and fast rules to help you make your decision. Your pediatrician is often in the best position to help you make an overall evaluation of your child's readiness for school. Many pediatric offices do school readiness screening tests, and some schools offer screening evaluations prior to kindergarten.

WHY DOESN'T YOUR CHILD WANT TO GO TO SCHOOL?

A not uncommon problem is that little Johnny decided that school is very nice, thank you, but "I think I'll stay home." After all, it *is* a jungle with thirty other little relatively untamed "wild animals" in that classroom who can do all sorts of things like pushing in line and being mean; and there are also teachers who make you do lousy things like "sit down in the chair!" This happens in all areas of the world we know of, including South Australia. "There, also," says Australian pediatrician Eric Sims:

> Some children try hard to avoid going to school. They rarely voice and may not understand their true reasons. It usually isn't really due to a dislike of school. School phobia, or fear, is usually a family problem, and may require family counseling before it is ironed out. Disturbances in the home may make the child insecure; he may fear that something disastrous will happen while he is not at home to keep an eye on things.
>
> But, regardless of the cause, the child must return to school as quickly as possible. The longer he stays at home, the harder it will be for him to resume normal life. Yet getting such a child to school, in spite of all his protests, can be quite an upsetting business for everybody involved. Parents will find allies among teachers, the child's school friends, and the family doctor—and the parents may well need all the help they can get.

If the problem becomes severe enough, says Indiana pediatrician Thomas Conway:

> School phobia can produce such symptoms as headache, sore throat, loss of appetite, abdominal pain, nausea, and vomiting. These symptoms vanish rapidly when the threat of leaving home for school has passed. It is possible that causes other than family tension explain this disturbance. There may be big dogs, bullies, or other obstacles between home and school. School itself may pose a real or imagined threat to the child.
>
> I believe that parents must force school attendance upon children affected by school phobia. Armed with anxiety allaying medication or whatever else might be necessary, the child should return to school at once. Their parents and the teacher must realize that this child sees withdrawal from a threatening situation as the logical answer to the problem. It is far better, in my opinion, that the child suffer now, rather than postpone a confrontation with reality.
>
> The physical and emotional problems induced by fear of going to school make it necessary to involve the child's physician. He is usually in a good position to assess the problem, to help get the child back to school, and, perhaps, to involve the parents and teachers in a search for the cause and the cure of the condition.

IF THE SCHOOL SAYS "NO!"

Now that you have gotten your child into kindergarten and have convinced him that school is a fact of life, that you will not disappear when he is in school, and that you will be there when he gets home, you relax. Then, what if the school says, "No!" and wants to expel your child. There can be many reasons; and, when going through the potential problems, try to keep your cool—because the school may be right. It is rarely as serious as it sounds. In kindergarten, it could be that your child just needs another year to mature. Even if it is more than immaturity, you can get help and rectify the situation.

It is shocking to parents when this happens, just as the child shocks the school. Most school personnel bend over backward to avoid such drastic action. If the school wants him out, usually the child's behavior is terrible indeed. Most often, a consensus is reached by classmates, teachers, and principal, indicating that the child is uncontrollable and undesirable, and is making it impossible for the rest of the class to function. A kindergarten dropout! Why?

The usual litany of complaints may include sassing or paying no attention to the teacher, refusing to stay in his seat, interrupting other children's work, talking out of turn, hitting other children, blaming others for his problems, fighting, refusing to play games by the rules, lying, cheating, stealing, destroying things, and insisting on being center stage or first in line all the time. A real monster. When a child behaves in this way, others react with dislike and disapproval, causing the child to act even worse. As he continues to respond with violence or withdrawal, a vicious cycle evolves which culminates in exasperation and expulsion. Yet this child can be very bright and may be lovable. The specific causes for such behavior are unique to each child, but there are some general explanations worth exploring.

Some children from strict homes harbor hostility because of severe limits imposed by unsmiling parents. If they get into a class where no real discipline is required, they "run wild." At first, they may act up to find the limits of behavior; but, if the school vacillates in its approach or finally invokes hostile punishment, the children often remain out of control.

Another type of "bad" child comes from an extremely permissive home. The child can get away with almost anything, is center stage most of the time, manipulates the adults in his life, and may overwhelm brothers or sisters. Often, the parents in such a home do not consider themselves permissive. They may confuse their anger and hollering and swatting at the child with being strict, but in fact, the child is not under their control. They are victims of a child who uses their fruitless negative reactions as a toy. A variation of this situation occurs when parents serve as slaves to their children. They literally jump to meet the child's demands, believing that, in order to be a good parent, they must do whatever it takes to gratify the child.

It isn't always the child. Another cause of severe misbehavior is the "permissive" school or teacher who accepts misbehavior and seems to believe that the child will somehow ultimately become civilized without discipline and firmness. Children don't—they require limits and control. Parental intervention and rule-setting for "in school" behavior may remedy this situation. The fact that problems developed at all is an indication that the parents and the school should reassess their methods of handling the child.

In some cases, the personality of the teacher and the child may clash, or there may be clever "little monsters" in class who incite poor behavior in others or who force fights. Each case is different. Confer with the teacher and principal in a controlled manner. If necessary, go to your child's physician for advice. Things can usually be worked out!

Hyperactivity is not an uncommon cause of problems in school. Some children simply cannot work in a large group environment: They mean to behave, but simply cannot turn off their motors. Teacher Jan Canby suggests: "The school may precipitate and complicate such a problem. A child this uncontrollable is in need of more help and individualized attention than can possibly be offered in a usual classroom situation. Special programs to meet the needs of such children should be available."

Yet another cause, writes Dr. Richanbach is that "some children are not trained in the kinds of behavior needed by their school. Some schools, particularly in the economically disadvantaged areas, provide this kind of teaching. Headstart attempts some of this, and the "early Childhood Education" programs recognize the problem."

One significant cause of school problems may be that the child has a learning disability which makes him a failure in school. The authors of *Something's Wrong With My Child* state:

> Much of what the learning-disabled child does is not willful or intentional on his part. He is not in control of his behavior or his inadequate learning performance. His physiological impairment seems to "short-circuit" what would be normal behavior and learning. Now he begins to develop emotional problems on top of his learning difficulties. He learns about social rejection. Children can be cruel to the youngster who still uses baby talk, who can't climb the monkey bars, catch a ball, or swing a bat. Adults dismiss him as unruly, spoiled, or worse, neurotic. Because he is intelligent, the learning-disabled youngster is acutely aware of his failures. He becomes frustrated, assumes he is worthless, and gives up on himself and school.[1]

Many children do suffer from the inability to control behavior or learning performance. For many, their weaknesses do not seem to be helped by the usual teaching and parenting techniques, and the learning-disabled child has become the center of great efforts by teachers, legislators, and volunteer groups.

The "Turned Off" Child

However, there is a considerable segment of educators, pediatricians, and parents who believe that many of these children simply suffer from poor teaching and poor discipline at home and at school. When this happens, these children frequently disrupt the classroom by becoming class clowns. Or, depending on their personality, they simply become quiet intellectual dropouts. In my experience, the class clowns are generally rather bright and aggressive, and are likely to get an education in spite of the system. Others who are turned off simply turn up at school, patiently or impatiently, and put in their time. These intellectual dropouts seem to suffer the most. About half of all school and learning problems are from the class clown syndrome, claims pediatrician Robert F.L. Polley. I agree, if we include the quiet ones, and the ones who aren't really "clowns" but whose passive rebellion gets them in trouble.

Dr. Polley's observations and his personal success in treating many of the cases of learning and school behavior problems runs counter to the current emphasis by educational specialists on learning disabilities and hyperactive children. Still, many teachers and parents believe Polley is right. I have seen some children who were class clowns and who responded to common sense pressure. Other children who seem similar on the surface have other problems. Regardless of the origin of their problems, I suspect that many children who have trouble in school can benefit from Polley's approach:

THE CLASS CLOWN

Up to the age of nine or ten years, children behave pretty much as they *think* they are expected to behave by the audience. Their actual performance is not the direct result of inherited traits, but is more often due to the type of audience present, its attitude and expectations.

The child's audience, which influences and determines the development of behavior habits, includes the adults and children in the home, school, and neighborhood. Brothers and sisters, playmates and classmates are often among the most influential members of the child's audience.

Otherwise normal children who develop the unfortunate habit of playing the role of a *Class Clown* probably account for over 50% of school performance problem cases. One could estimate that 10 to 15% of all boys have symptoms of "Class Clown Syndrome," while fewer than 5% of school girls do.

Any child might fall into the Class Clown category who can be described as intent, sensitive, intelligent, versatile, imaginative, cunning, shrewd, dramatic, creative, witty and impulsive. These qualities are also indicative of a very competent child of course. Any child who has developed a bona fide Class Clown reputation is likely to be one of the most capable children in the class, despite being an academic failure. It requires a lot of mental agility and spiritual independence to sidestep the regulations of home and school. However, despite good mental ability, this child lacks intellectual honesty and drive. If unchecked beyond ages nine or ten, the class clown's habitual failure to recognize the time for work and the time for play can develop a performance pattern which may signal the beginning of a tragic career. It is frightening to listen to the childhood study of a hardened drug addict or felon and to hear emerging the word picture of a typical Class Clown boyhood which failed to develop in the child the qualities of reliability and integrity.

Some Ways and Means of Controlling Class Clown Behavior

1. *Action, not words, counts most.* A lengthy "dialogue" in response to Class Clown antics has the general effect of audience applause. Corrective measures should be specific, brief, and without fanfare. Sending the Class Clown to his room to pout, amid a barrage of words by the adult, is interpreted by the child as success on his part and hesitancy on the part of the adult. A firm ear lobe pinch or arm grasp gets a message through to the play-actor with more speed and clarity than any lecture.

2. *Avoid asking the child whether he "likes" school.* If the Class Clown is constantly reminded that we are anxious to keep him happy, he quickly learns to turn on simulated sadness as a whitewash for his misbehavior.

3. *Don't buy a ticket to his show.* Most class clowns will identify their potential audience, adults or other children, by catching their eye before opening the bag of tricks. And nothing will discourage him more than complete non-recognition by his audience when he is putting on a show. A Little League coach, faced with molding a group of unruly boys into a baseball team, is a past master at making his young athletes think he is unaware of their presence when they are "horsing around." Direct eye contact and recognition by the coach is reserved for those who act with some maturity. Before long, most team members are behaving themselves because they realize they are expected to act like reliable ball players.

4. *Encourage mature behavior.* Then, when it happens, take it for granted. Applause for good behavior is evidence that the child was really expected to act otherwise.

5. *Remember that, deep in his heart, the Class Clown does prefer order.* The three- or four-year-old boy who can pull his stunts on everyone in the family except perhaps an impatient, firm teen-age sister, will often choose *her* to take him to the park or the zoo! Even at that age, he senses, the wisdom of business-like conduct and the resulting pleasure of an outing free of the crises which seem to accompany supervision by a permissive adult.

6. *Turn off misbehavior and disobedience at once.* When the Class Clown deliberately defies the rules, the adult supervisor should win the round promptly with a minimum of talk and a maximum of action. Children are greatly influenced by parents' attitudes and example. They are much less impressed by what parents say.

7. *Paternal deprivation (boys) and maternal deprivation (girls).* A factor of major importance concerning the development of boy Class Clowns is that the women in charge of his life at home and at school are often unable to see through his antics and recognize them as such—and hence they inadvertently became his receptive audience. Girl child Class Clowns also seem to have greater success using their dramatic skills on male supervisors. The presence of mature male supervision for the boys, and mature female supervision for the girls, usually produces the best results.

For fatherless boys, the Boy Scouts, Boys' Clubs, community and church organization, and in particular the Big Brothers of America, provide a most valuable service.

8. *The Pedestal Program.* We respect a policeman's authority because he has City Hall behind him. We don't expect him to give a detailed description of the law and of our wrongdoing before he writes out a speeding ticket. Likewise, the mother who has been placed on a pedestal of respect and authority by the father can control most of her children's activities with ease.

It should be a firm family ground rule that it is absolutely inexcusable for the children's actions to upset and embarrass their mother. And mother, firmly in place on her pedestal of respect, should conduct herself accordingly. Stepping down off her pedestal too often to engage in physical or verbal combat with the children can quickly destroy her reign of respect.

9. *"Make him cry."* The three-word rule "make him cry" is worth considering in the correction of Class Clown traits. All children are individuals, of course, and quite unique. Therefore one approach can hardly apply across the board. But the ground rule above is often useful. Its use in handling Class Clown children with reading failure, for instance, would be an example.

A second grade Class Clown has fiddled his way through kindergarten and first grade, gaining no significant reading ability. He becomes aware of his predicament in the second grade, but by now he also feels some confusion and panic because his occasional attempts to "catch up" with his classmates meet with embarrassing failure. Frustration and despair set in. Vaguely realizing that the intellectual agility which saved him earlier from the tedious work of learning letters and sounds is now unable to rescue him, he retreats to a "won't read" status and there sets up his camp.

As the tutor approaches the situation, the Class Clown non-reader's defense proceeds like this: (1) He uses his personable, "con-artist" wiles to charm the tutor out of the task at hand. This failing, he then (2) adopts a helpless "I can't" posture and clings firmly to this. If the tutor presses on, he then (3) play-acts with a dramatic, firm, and vehement "I won't" attitude and supposes that his victory has been won. However, if the tutor seems unimpressed by either 1, 2, or 3, the Class Clown then unveils his biggest weapon: He breaks down and cries. Many tutors retreat at the 1, 2, or 3 level, and certainly most give up when (4) appears. The problem reader's eyes, of course, twinkle behind the tears as the tutor beats a final retreat.

The knowledgeable tutor, however, rolls over 1, 2 and 3 without breaking stride. He is ready to meet and neutralize weapon (4) by producing a handkerchief when tears appear. With a smile, he indicates that now that the preliminaries are out of the way, it is time to get down to work. This completes the sequence, demonstrating that the greatest act of confidence on the part of the tutor can be the ground rule "make him cry." Once the Class Clown realizes that the tutor is confident that the child can do the job, he decides to use his wits to show the tutor he was really only fooling—in fact, he intended all along to learn to read when he got around to it. He had just not yet decided that it was time to try! A final act of confidence on the part of the tutor is to take this mature behavior for granted, quickly forget at 1, 2, 3 and 4 ever took place, and help the child learn the tools of a reader.

10. *Brief comments about discipline.* Effective discipline represents giving the child an opportunity to practice self-control. It should be brief, firm and without fanfare. Again, it is a matter of action, not words. Confining the culprit to his room or withholding privileges while the family "news media" busily spreads the word is ineffective because of the publicity associated with it. This plays into the hands of the Class Clown.

The child should be given the opportunity to learn "mature behavior," which is nothing more than self-control. All children are capable of *some* self-control. The Class Clown simply has to be given extra time and repeated opportunities to learn to control himself, to learn that there is a difference between play and work time. He has to be given the chance to acquire enough self-control so that he can complete routine tasks and duties at home and at school.

The development of mature behavior consists mainly of learning to stretch short periods of self-control over longer and longer time spans until the child can meet their responsibilities.

An example of helping the child acquire self-control could be the establishment of a firm family ground rule that says "Walk, don't run in the house." In addition to cutting down on chances for accidental injuries, this gives the clown an ongoing opportunity to exercise self-control. If a child does behave well, the parents should indicate that they have noticed it. This feed-back should be subtle, and should stress that they understand that being good is not always the easiest thing to do. Emphasize that the *chore* and *effort* of being good is more important than the *act* of being good.

11. *School evaluation vs. family evaluation.* Satisfactory conduct at school should be expected of a child. However, the family should not panic when a teacher's evaluation is less than ideal. The family should never make the child feel that his entire worth in their eyes is tied directly to the teacher's evaluation.

Teachers can be way off target in their estimate of a child's conduct and ability, particularly in the lower grades. Many children are grossly misunderstood by inexperienced teachers. School problems often die on the vine when the child enters another grade where the teacher understands children and has them routinely eating out of his hand. Children who are considered difficult to manage in the lower grades are often prime examples of the rule that a child's performance is the result of the way he thinks the teacher expects him to behave.

Furthermore, a child is at home, and responsible to his family, eight hours for every one hour he is at school. Don't forget to let him know how important he is as a member of the family.

It is important, therefore, to refrain from evaluating a child's worth because of what the teacher has to say. The parent must consider as well the way the child responds to circumstances and duties as a member of the family.

Too often the academic failure of a child at school coincides with the failure of the *parent* to assist at home in mastering the 3 R's and related subjects. You can be sure that the young lad who is first string on the Little League ball team practiced many hours at home with his father, *before* the season opened. Most assuredly with children, success promotes success.

Finally, don't overrate the importance of school matters to the child by talking at length about report cards and parent–teacher conferences. The young student should not be expected to be continually thrilled by his school experience. The family attitude should expect reliable school behavior and honest academic effort as two of the routine duties of life. The child should learn that school, like any assignment, is far less unpleasant if he gets down to business and does a good job. School becomes a complicated and bothersome burden when the teacher, parent, and student delay the development of this attitude. A permissive kindergarten or first grade, coupled with the parent's anxiety to have a child "enjoy" school, can give the child the idea that school is just fun and games.

12. *Immaturity promoted by medical handicaps.* An understandable prolongation of childhood immaturity can occur when illness or medical handicaps have resulted in some overprotection and permissiveness by the parents. Prematurity, chronic eczema, asthma, allergies, and eye surgery are a few of the many medical situations associated with subsequent Class Clown behavior. Side-stepping discipline during the preschool period at home helps develop a habit pattern which can result in varying degrees of academic failure later. Children who have had eye surgery, in particular, often use their awareness of adult concern as an excuse for indifferent efforts at reading. Quick correction of errors in visual interpretation helps train the normal child to be more accurate in describing what he sees. Adult doubt concerning a child's ability to see correctly can make him feel he is not expected to try. Once he knows his ability is in question, his progress grinds to a halt. Many people with real visual handicaps have gone ahead to become competent in the classroom because they were not constantly reminded that they were expected to have difficulty in reading.

13. *Misconceptions regarding love and security.* We adults speak of *love,* but our interpretation of its actual meaning is often vague. Children can be understandably confused when parents refer to "love" and attempt to use it as the pivot point for child–parent relations.

Children have no trouble recognizing such qualities as *loyalty,* dignity, privacy, and honesty, however. Again, actions speak louder than words. Once children have determined that an adult is genuinely loyal to them, their response to this person becomes predictable and reliable. Children's concepts of loyalty include providing them with the training in conduct which will permit them to taste success and develop self-respect. Many a child, showered with permissiveness, wanders uncertainly until some genuine loyalty appears on the scene. Therefore, *loyalty,* to a child, can mean *love.*[2]

Whether the child reacts by being the class clown, the class bully, or the school truant, or just walls himself off and daydreams through school, something has to be done. The first step is to decide which children are simply misbehaving because it is easier than really trying to learn, and which children really have serious trouble learning.

Clowning Is Frustration

We asked San Francisco pediatrician and learning specialist Louise C. Taichert to comment on Dr. Polley's concepts.

The *Class Clown* is described above as a normal child who is shrewd enough to manipulate his environment to avoid academic demands. No attempt was made to explain why the child needs to be a clown. Clowning is a symptom of frustration. It generally stems from real problems. Probably the most common problem is the inability to develop learning skills on a neurodevelopmental basis. Another source of frustration is a feeling of physical inadequacy. The child may be shorter, taller, fatter, or otherwise different than his classmates.

Other children live in a family where their clowning acts as comic relief for an otherwise depressed family.

The child with underlying learning problems is usually the *Class Clown* because he is unable to perform a "straight act." He is unable to do what is being asked of him in the classroom. Generally, clowning is a form of avoidance behavior. This behavior becomes the only way the child can win acceptance from other children and from his parents. To blame the parents for this behavior is too simple, and is unfair. The parents are probably unaware of the ways they encourage this behavior and why they do so. Many parents enjoy the "liveliness of a clown" or encourage the child to act "silly" to help him and themselves avoid or deny significant learning problems or family dysfunction. Unfortunately, the clown is allowed to amuse others at his expense, and is usually encouraged by non-verbal communication: parents' laughter, subtle amusement shown by a smile, or failure to intervene or comment altogether. The mother may smile and laugh while the father remains uninvolved, or the father may secretly enjoy the silliness in the younger child and the acting out in the older child because he had similar problems as a child and is angry with the establishment.

Clowning is a symptom that should be taken seriously and indicates a need to investigate some underlying problem. The jolly fat child who clowns has the façade of happiness. This child, to be sure, is sad, empty, and lonely—and is at a distance from his or her feelings.

Dr. Polley replies: "Dr. Taichert's appraisal of the Class Clown Syndrome provides a number of worthwhile observations. However, one must caution against the proposal that a child is 'unable to behave in a responsible manner,' or that he 'needs' to be a clown because of some underlying excuse or cause. The time and effort devoted to investigating and publicizing the 'cause' of his clowning seriously weakens a consistent corrective program by reminding both the child and family of too many 'good excuses' for the misbehavior."

Author Sylvia Richardson says this about the Class Clown in her book, *Something is Wrong With My Child*:

There is an inner confusion and sense of unfitness resulting from the failure and frustrations of the learning-disabled child which leads to doubts and self-criticism. A ten-year-old with an I.Q. of 140 told his teachers "I'm stupid, stupid, stupid." There are other reactions, for the learning-disabled child is very vulnerable to stress. He finds the world less well organized for him, more confusing, more unsettling. His ego must find ways to mediate effectively between his impulses and desires and the pressures exerted by his environment. To survive, he must find some way—some defense mechanism. He makes the best deal he can. One deal might be withdrawal. Seeing that people do not accept him, do not find him lovable, he comes to feel that the best thing to do is to get away. If he's alone, he doesn't have to prove anything. So he pulls into himself.

Other children become clowns—silly, loud, obstreperous. It is as though this child were saying, "If I'm going to lack control and inhibition, I might just as well make a big deal out of it. People might not like me, but they won't shove me out of the way or forget about me. Maybe then I'll be considered a person, after all. I'm even a hero to some of these kids. I make them laugh. I put the teacher down and make her uncomfortable." He gets perverse gratification from irritating, upsetting, enraging. Believing himself to be weak and powerless, he can at least show he is effective in manipulation, getting others to do what he wants, or getting them so unnerved that they simply "don't know what to do with him." This negativism and power struggle emanate from a child's belief that he is basically incompetent.

No matter how loud and aggressive this youngster is, under it all he is still beset by his fears of inadequacy and of punishment and retaliation—for both what he does and what he wishes.[3]

Demand Their Best

Whatever the cause, those who are turned off in school require help. They cannot be allowed to give up. If necessary, a tutor must "make him cry." No ineffective and defeating sympathy should be given. It requires that parents and teachers teach, and that they will not be put off by protests or tears. It is essential that the best he can produce be demanded of each child, regardless of apparent disability. Teachers working with slow or damaged children have learned to continue to stimulate, to try again and again to draw out the best in a child. It is often surprising what an apparently hopeless case can learn. It is usually inspiring to see what an intellectual drop-out or class clown can accomplish in learning, given enough teacher determination, effort, and talent.

It is important to remember that, in Dr. Polley's experience, half of the children with learning problems *do* have various perceptual disorders, dyslexias, and a multitude of specific or general learning problems that require more than parental or teacher firmness. Most of these children can be helped by proper diagnosis and by a combination of teaching techniques. However, if a child isn't doing well in school, whether he is a class clown or not, it is important not to label him as learning-disabled without a thorough investigation. A lot of normal children do poorly in school. I believe that most of them are simply not mature enough to realize and understand the ultimate value of schooling. They are childish and don't like to "work"—they become bored. Here is an area where a good teacher can really shine. It is amazing how few learning problems there are in some teachers' classes and how many there are in other teachers' classes. It isn't simply making learning fun for the children, although that helps. They can learn with proper handling: pressure, leadership, and psychology. The good teacher convinces the child that learning is important *for the child*, and that it is a satisfying experience to master or even partially master a subject that is

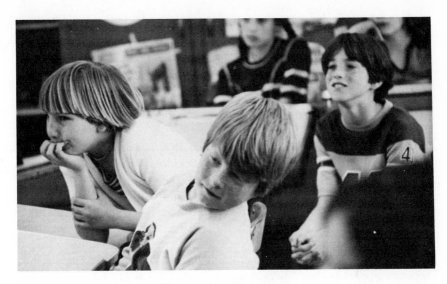

Figure 48   *Learning!*

difficult for the child. After all, learning and developing mastery of self and of knowledge and skills are very rewarding experiences. Once children discover that they *can* learn, they can rarely be kept from learning on their own from there on in. Pride in self-improvement (not *just* in excelling above all others) is the key to life-long learning, regardless of whether you start out with mental retardation, a specific learning disability, a bored child, a class clown, or a genius intelligence. However, in spite of talented teachers, dedicated parents, and great efforts, a sizable portion of children have real innate difficulty in learning.

DEEP LEARNING PROBLEMS

Separating those children with more superficial learning problems from those with deeper problems is not easy. It cannot be simply done by psychological and aptitude tests, although these can help. It requires an in depth assessment of each individual child, involving the parents, the teachers, and the psychologists—and, quite often, the child's physician. Such children represent a difficult challenge. The various deeper learning problems can be roughly divided into several categories. However, there is so much overlap between these categories in any individual child that the divisions serve more as an approach to general understanding than as a finely tuned diagnostic method. In fact, problems in one area commonly cause problems in another area. For example, the student who fails because of an underlying specific perceptual learning problem develops emotional problems and then turns off. So as you read through here, don't jump to conclusions—even if you see your child's problems rather accurately described. Humans, and children, are too complex and too varied for simple answers.

If you line up a hundred children, you have a hundred different heights, a hundred different brains, and a hundred variations of academic talent. Some children are short and some tall, some children are mentally quick, and some are slow. Such slowness does not necessarily mean they are unintelligent; but, in a classroom where they must keep up with the others or fall behind and fail—some fail. Under other teaching circumstances they may do better, and if there is determination, they may ultimately catch up. It can be somewhat comforting to know that there is not a good correlation between academic excellence in school and later success in life.

Whatever the cause, when a child has a problem learning, it soon becomes apparent that "Something Is Wrong With My Child." Dr. Sylvia Richardson, a leading pediatric learning disability specialist from Cincinnati, teamed up with two educators to explain that learning disability is a mystifying handicap:

> [Learning disability] encompasses an incredible variety of problems gathered under the same umbrella. . . . It is the most common of the more than fifty names that experts have attached to this collection of impairments. Some of the other names most commonly heard are: minimal brain dysfunction, perceptual impairment, hyperkinetic, hypokinetic, dyslexia, aphasia. . . . Learning disabilities are the most common and pervasive neurological problem among children. Estimates range from one to 40 percent of all children in the United States. . . .[4]

I suspect that learning disability covers 98% of the population. We all have our talents and our weaknesses. The children we talk about under this heading are the ones who come to our attention. Yet each of us could probably benefit from a good assessment of our strengths and weaknesses. To achieve maximal growth and development, every child should be individually assessed as to whether "something's wrong" or not. Disability is a matter of degree. We will discuss this confusing potpourri of labels and intellectual disabilities under the following headings.

- Mental Retardation and Mental Slowness
- Minimal Brain Dysfunction
- Learning Disability
- Perceptual Handicap
- Emotional Handicap
- Hyperactivity

OVERLAPPING CAUSES OF LEARNING PROBLEMS

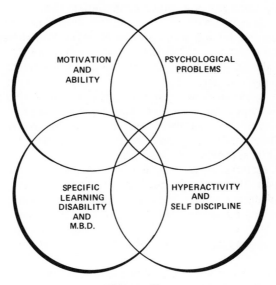

Figure 49

Dr. Sylvia Richardson, when reviewing this chapter, made the point that the reader might easily come to believe that each of these types of disability is distinct. In fact, they overlap so much that we cannot consider one without considering the others. Part of the reason for the overlap is that we don't yet know enough about the field. Another reason is that people are complicated, and that if something is wrong in one part of the intellect, or brain, the effects can cause symptoms of another sort. Thus, varieties of hyperactivity can result from all of the conditions in this section plus another dozen or so known or suspected causes we discuss under hyperactivity. Then there is the fact we must face that none of us is perfect, that we are all mentally retarded to some degree in some way, and that we are all mentally slower than many other people in other ways. Does this indicate brain damage? One way out of that uncomfortable thought is to change the labels, and, if we have problems, to call them Minimal Brain Dysfunction. Or should we all just admit to partial retardation?

Is It Mental Retardation, Mental Slowness, or M.B.D.?

Many children are, in fact, mentally retarded. Pediatrician D. Kerr Grant, whose expertise includes retarded children, is careful to sort out of the mentally retarded children those whose problem is only minimal brain dysfunction (M.B.D.). Some people think of both conditions as resulting from brain damage. Others disagree. Dr. Grant comments:

"Brain damage" is a rather controversial term, but one which, especially when coupled with the tag "minimal," has nonetheless enjoyed a considerable vogue in recent years. Sometimes, to cool it a bit, people will talk of "minimal brain dysfunction," or M.B.D. Controversial or not—and there are some who believe these labels should be discarded entirely—I believe they serve a useful purpose.

There exists a sizable group of children who are "different," sometimes even different at birth. They have a mixed bag of behavioral characteristics which set them apart from the majority of their peers. Thus, in infancy, they may be nervous, irritable, poor sleepers or feeders, or have prolonged colic. Later on, they may be unduly impulsive, restless, overactive, distractible, unpredictable, and difficult to discipline. They may, or may not, be clumsy. In their school years, their short attention span, coupled with reading, writing, and speech problems, may make the educational process puzzling and painful for the child, teacher, and parent alike. These traits may perhaps be regarded as exaggerations and distortions of usual childhood behavior.

These children act this way because it is the way they are, not because of the way they were brought up. Environmental circumstances may modify their behavior in one direction or another, but do not basically affect the underlying patterns. M.B.D. is as real as a broken leg.

Pediatrician Henry Richanbach puts the label and the fact of mental retardation into some perspective:

M–R is the abbreviation for "mentally retarded." The term is descriptive; it does not refer to an irreversible situation. Many of us function at different—even retarded—levels in different areas. Have you ever considered challenging Bobby Fischer to a game of chess? The apparent performance of your child may be deceiving. Psychological tests, although necessary as a starting point, do not provide final or complete answers. It is best to find out what your child needs in the way of love, respect, self-confidence, and achievement. Then do your best to meet these needs.

How to Help a Mentally Retarded or Brain Damaged Child

For the truly mentally retarded, Dr. Grant counsels:

It is of overwhelming importance to assess and manage such a child individually. Rather than trying to change such a child into someone fundamentally different from himself, try to help him to become the best person that *he* can be. Emphasize his strengths and his good points; gloss over his weaknesses with sympathy. Build up his confidence in himself as an individual being. It will not be easy, but in this way lies the best chance to success and happiness.

Again, remember that it's not his fault, let alone yours. This is not to sanction over-permissiveness, but rather to counsel against undue confrontation. Feel your way with patience and understanding. There are no magic answers; don't look for them.

As in the case of other children with on-going functional problems, joining a parents' group may offer helpful support, as long as you do not go there seeking a miraculous cure.

For any child with learning problems, or for one who is retarded, slow, or suspected of having M.B.D., Dr. Richanbach suggests:

You can turn to special education services. In many school districts, there are programs for children with hearing loss of varying degrees, with vision problems, with cerebral palsy, with degrees of retardation, with speech and language problems, and behavioral and emotional disorders. Your district may offer special classes, special schools, tutorial or remedial services, and consultants. Find out what your child needs. If your school district does not offer it, find out where it is offered. If your child is somehow not equipped to perform in the "normal school situation," do not demand that he stays there—this will be self-defeating.

It should be carefully noted that many severely brain damaged cerebral palsied children can and do function beautifully in school, have good intellects, and learn beautifully. Some children who are retarded can and do learn rather well in certain areas. So, regardless of the diagnosis, don't give up without a good try.

Learning Disabilities and Minimal Brain Dysfunction

As we have seen, the terms Minimal Brain Dysfunction and Mental Retardation can vaguely overlap. This is unfortunate, for some people assume that a child with minimal brain dysfunction is retarded, when, in fact, most of them are very bright. But bright or not, they have problems learning, explains Dr. Richanbach:

Minimal brain dysfunction means a failure to function normally. It may best be thought of as delay or uneven maturation and development of the brain. Hyperactive, impulsive four-year-olds can get along, but if they are still that way in the third grade, they have problems. A little upside-down or backward writing is acceptable in kindergarten, but if this condition persists it will make the printed page a hazardous place.

Problems that fall into the M.B.D. category include hyper- or hypoactivity, learning disabilities, attention span problems, perceptual disorders, impulse control problems, and in many, clumsiness. Children with severe brain damage, such as cerebral palsy, may not exhibit M.B.D. symptoms, while some gifted athletes may do so.

An evaluation of M.B.D. must start with a complete physical examination of your child by his own doctor, who will then suggest more detailed assessments, which might include a neurological evaluation, psychological testing, speech and language consultation, or perhaps psychiatric evaluation. Emotions, after all, play a large role in how well we do in school. Electro-encephalograms may be helpful to a physician. Then he may be able to prescribe specific treatment, recommend consultation with other specialists, or, at appropriate times, prescribe medication.

Some seemingly bright children grow up unevenly. Problems impair their school success. Waiting for them to "grow out of it" can sometimes lead to falling behind and to failure.

Types of Learning Disability

Dr. Richanbach continues:

There are many intermediate and long-range causes of learning disabilities. Labels such as "slow learner" are neither helpful or scientific. We must turn instead to specifics such as general intelligence, good health, motivation, family, social, and ethnic behavior, and particularly to hyperactivity, short attention span, and distractability. Or it may be possible to identify specific performance skills which affect the learning experience:

Poor visual perception means that children "see" incorrectly—not with their eyes, but in their brains: To perceive well, they must be able to reproduce accurately the various geometric designs that make up the printed page.

If they perceive letters and shapes backwards, then p's and b's and d's may look alike.

Visual memory may be deficient if they have to scan the blackboard twenty times to remember what the teacher wrote.

Auditory memory may be at fault if they remember what they see but not what they hear.

Immediate recall memory is required for a learning process such as phonics, which requires a particular kind of sequencing. A simple test: A five- or six-year-old should be able to repeat five numbers forward, for example, 4,2,9,1,6 is 4,2,9,1,6; and three in reverse, 3,2,5—which is 5,2,3.

Auditory discrimination is the confusion of sounds, such as those occurring in the words "bat," "cat," "that," "rat"—even though hearing is good.

If a specific learning disability is found in your child, you can be comforted by two facts. First, *you* now know where to put the special effort. Second, he will learn better if you and his teachers can teach him a *way* he can learn.

Good school psychologists fill many functions in addition to testing for learning disabilities. They serve as consultants to teachers; they monitor special education programs; and they often provide educational counseling. It is necessary for you to consent to any significant involvement of your child with the school psychologist, so you can know what your child's symptoms are, what the results of the psychologist's intervention are, and how these results can be used to help your child. Make sure that the psychologist explains clearly to you what tests he has administered and how he has scored them.

What Is a Perceptual Handicap?

To confuse the picture further, one type of learning disability is called a perceptual handicap. This describes a group of learning-disabled children who have been found to have problems because their brains are unable to process, use, or reproduce information accurately. Its cause may be genetic, arising from intrauterine damage, or from brain damage after birth. Here is how a government committee describes children with learning problems:

> Children with specific learning disabilities exhibit a disorder in one or more of the basic psychological processes involved in understanding or in using spoken or written languages. These may be manifested in disorders of listening, thinking, talking, reading, writing, spelling, or arithmetic. They include conditions which have been referred to as perceptual handicaps, brain injury, minimal brain dysfunction, dyslexia, developmental aphasia, and so forth. They do not include learning problems which are due primarily to visual, hearing, or motor handicaps, to mental retardation, emotional disturbance, or to environmental disadvantage. Children so affected are often restless, distractable, and unusually active. They frequently have difficulty controlling their impulses. They interrupt conversations and wander around. They are often emotionally unstable, easily hurt, and overexcitable. Consequently, they are anxious and angry, because they are unable to cope with the world, especially with school.

Health Related Learning Problems

Many of the cases of M.B.D. are medical problems. Some, it is suspected, suffered brain damage. A few may have a form of hidden epi-

Figure 50 *Learning can be difficult.*

lepsy. Whatever the cause, a thorough pediatric work-up is in order for children with learning problems. Although it is rare that dramatic diagnosis and instant cures can be made by doctors, such events occasionally occur. We will discuss many specific conditions and a few treatments that work. Probably the most common and currently most popular medical and school diagnosis is hyperactivity. It owes its popularity to the fact that a good number of cases can be quite effectively treated by the doctor with medications.

HYPERACTIVITY

A visit to any playground will convince most adults that *all* children are hyperactive. A visit to any classroom will convince us that some children are indeed hyperactive when they shouldn't be. They wiggle and squirm, talk when they shouldn't, get up and wander around the room, tease others, maybe pick fights—and they can drive a teacher crazy. One must admit, however, that hyperactivity is in the eye of the beholder, and some of us have little tolerance for the normal energy of children while others aren't fazed by these children's incessant activities.

The particular adult perception of hyperactivity is significant because it is possible to give drugs (Dexadrine, Ritalin, Cylert) which will cure some hyperactive children when they are on the drug. In some, it works like magic. In others, it does no good or it suppresses the child so much that it does more harm than good. Those children on whom the drug works especially well usually were born hyperactive or were even noted to be hyperactive in the uterus before birth. They are easily distractable, have a short attention span, and often get into trouble because of a lack of self-control. Dr. Sidney Adler believes that many delinquent teenagers file off to prison "because they did not receive proper guidance and medical treatment in their formative years." [5] He has found that many children whose "emotional" problems were blamed on the parents actually were born hyperactive. I have seen children change from "Peck's bad boy," about to be expelled from school as incorrigible, to proudly achieving scholars and citizens overnight when given one of these drugs. And I admit that I, too, had thought that the problems were emotional. This doesn't mean that most "Peck's bad boys" are simply hyperactive children in trouble. Nor does it indicate that all hyperactive children get into trouble nor that all hyperactive children are congenitally hyperactive. But for those children who are helped by the "smart-pill" (as the children often call them), it is a Godsend. Before you consider using the pill for your hyperactive child, though, it will be wise to be aware of the many possible causes of hyperactivity.

Causes and Treatments for Hyperactivity

Although all preschool children are very active, some are probably hyperactive. This can be a real problem for some mothers. Later, when these children start school, the practical dividing line between normal activity and hyperactivity is when the excess activity creates problems for the school or for the child. For the school, a hyperactive child disrupts the classroom and makes learning difficult for others. For the child, it results in academic underachievement and, frequently, in rejection. In the classic hyperactive child, there is a short attention span and easy frustration, yet under other circumstances these children learn beautifully. They have good intelligence and no specific learning disabilities. Some such children become class clowns; others react in different ways and to different degrees. One of the most critical points in helping hyperactive children is to determine the cause of their hyperactivity. But that is not easy nor is it always possible. There is considerable disagreement among the experts, and multiple causes and treatment are proposed. It may turn out that one or another of these possible causes will be proven to be the most statistically common. Regardless, what counts is the cause for *your* particular child's hyperactivity, be it common or uncommon. So be open minded as well as skeptical in looking at opinions on cause—do as much of your own detective work as you can.

You may find the clue that will help your doctor or your child's teacher make the right diagnosis.

Possible Causes of Hyperactivity

The first three common causes of hyperactivity have to do with teachers:

1. A permissive teacher who allows children to misbehave and get away with it. It has been said that there is little hyperactivity in strict parochial schools.
2. A boring teacher who cannot keep the children interested in learning. In either case, the entire class may appear hyperactive to an outside observer.
3. Then there is the possibility of a teacher–student personality clash. We can't expect everybody to get along with everybody else, and sometimes personalities simply clash—even teachers are human!

School consultant and pediatrician Henry Richanbach has seen children with hyperactivity ensuing from a variety of other causes:

4. Tight underwear or a plugged up nose which may keep children on the move. Or they may have trouble sitting still and producing if they were up watching the horror movie at midnight, if their mother had to leave for work without fixing their breakfast, or if they got squeezed into another quarrel between their parents.
5. Children's life style, whether ghetto, farm, or suburb. It may not have included the skill of learning to "Sit Still and Pay Attention." Maybe no one ever asked them to sit still before.
6. Boredom or bewilderment. Maybe they already know all that stuff, or maybe they are bewildered by its complexity and strangeness.
7. A developmental problem. They may have a nervous system which is hard to train. The internal controls that we expect with maturity may be late or inadequate in developing. It is especially hard for these children to limit their activity, focus their attention, or keep their hands off of interesting objects (and people). They are easily distracted by activity and noise.
8. An organic brain difference. Some hyperactive children outgrow their hyperactivity as they develop. Others don't, and there are hyperactive adults, frequently with an obvious family history of hyperactive people. The cause is probably that there is something physically or chemically different about the brains of these children which causes their behavior. They are impulse-ridden, constantly on the go, unable to sit still, easily distracted, and have little power of concentration.
9. Another cause is emotional, and manifests itself only if the child is under stress and is disturbed. It is intermittent and not constant.
10. Then, of course, there is the child who is *called* hyperactive. His parents were over 35 when he was born, or they are parents who believe that children should *always* be seen but not heard. Perhaps the most unfortunate is the child whose parents didn't want him and resent the upset he causes in their lives. Whatever the cause, the parents are unable to cope with a normally active child, so *in their eyes* the child is hyperactive.

Dr. William Crook says that allergy may cause hyperactivity:

> Hyperactivity may be caused by allergy, with symptoms of irritableness and nervousness leading to a short attention span. This results in bad grades, teaching scolding, and *loss of confidence and self-esteem*. Children are criticized and pushed, and they fail—often resulting in a secondary misbehavior problem at school or at home. Before you label your child and treat him with drugs, make sure that allergy is not the problem.[6]

For examples, read the cases presented by Dr. Gerrard in the chapter on allergy in our companion volume, *The Parents' Medical Manual.*

Pediatric allergist Ben Feingold believes that he has found the answer to the increase in hyperactive children over the past decades. He points out that the diagnosis wasn't prevalent prior to World War II. Since that time, there has been a massive growth of the food coloring, preserving, and flavoring industry.[7] There can be no question but that we eat a remarkable number and quantity of chemicals in our food; this is verified by pioneer allergist Lockey in the chapter on allergy in *The Parents' Medical Manual.* Food additives are known to cause allergy in many unfortunate individuals and mental changes in some. The question is, do they cause hyperactivity or learning disorders in children? Dr. Feingold believes that they are a major cause. Genetically, certain people don't tolerate these synthetic chemicals, which are manufactured from petroleum. I have asked the parents of over sixty hyperactive children to put the children on Feingold's salycilate-tartrazine free diet. Of them, six were significantly helped. Now, Feingold has expanded his diet to exclude *all* artificial colors and flavors. The scope of the problem of trying to avoid such chemicals can be appreciated by examining Dr. Lockey's diet lists in *The Parents' Medical Manual.* However, it is possible to avoid most of these chemicals if you use natural foods and avoid mother nature's foods which contain "organic" salycilates.

If Lockey's estimate that 12% of the population are potentially allergic to synthetic coloring and flavoring agents, and Feingold's contention that the hyperactivity caused by these synthetic agents is not due to allergy but is due to an indirect chemical action, then a lot of people are being damaged by these chemicals. It may be that growing children are the most susceptible. The concept is certainly worth serious thought, and the diet worth a try. For a few children, and for their parents, I am sure that the diet is worthwhile.

In order to balance the picture we should recognize that this is a typical statistical bell curve problem. A percentage of the population is abnormal and reacts significantly to chemicals that don't seem to have much effect on the rest of us. It speaks strongly to the need for stronger federal laws requiring full disclosure of the contents of any foodstuffs on the labels. Aside from the tragedy of the results on some hyperactive children and the occurrence of hives in possibly up to 12% of the population from petroleum products put in the food, a careful look should be taken at the reality of the need to color our food. I have been a little turned off of hot dogs since I learned that the nice red color may come from beetle wings from India. If we insist on an unanemic red glitter to hide the dull grey of the natural contents, then we will continue to eat beetle wings or some such coloring. These issues are, to a degree, settled in the market place. On the other hand, children in my practice have developed eczema from common food preservatives. Without such preservatives, we would probably have less food. Aside from that, keep in mind that it isn't just man who contaminates food. Mother nature has her own "additives" and poisons in large numbers of plants, including many commonly used ones.

Feingold's partially substantiated theories do not now explain all or most hyperactivity. We often find a family with a history of such traits as hyperactivity, dyslexia, and the inability to concentrate that have been passed down from generation to generation. Some of these problems predated the time when such additives began to be used. There are probably multiple causes of hyperactivity or learning disability, just as there are of pneumonia. Avoid rushing into oversimplistic solutions. Read Dr. Oettinger's article at the end of this chapter on the long-term use of drugs for learning, and reflect on the complexity and potential of the problem. Take whatever clues or information you can to your child's doctor in order to help unravel what the facts or factors are that apply to your particular child.

Too Much Civilizing and Too Little Love Create Hyperactivity

Another possible cause of hyperactivity in children is raised by Dr. Arvin Henderson, who has worked with a team of psychologists on parent–child relationships. He believes that a large amount of hyperactivity in infants and children may be caused by reactions partly brought on by our civilized customs of child rearing.

Most of the symptoms of overactivity, distractability, and behavior problems are manifestations of tension. This, of course, varies with the individual. Some infants are tense and hyperirritable at birth, and are not calmed down by the usual amount of holding and soothing. Others of average temperament may have tense, apprehensive parents whose manner of handling them is alarming and overstimulating. When infants are fussy and hard to soothe, they exhaust and worry their parents, perpetuating the tension.

Perhaps this is avoided in those primitive peoples where there is almost continual contact between the infant and the mother. It is more typical of the industrialized societies, however, that the infant spends many hours apart from the mother, usually in an immobile crib. Thus, the "civilized" infant may experience considerably less tactile stimulation, feelings of movement, and body contact with the mother. The variety of early visual and auditory experiences is much less than that afforded the infant strapped to and carried by the mother. We feel that the human nervous system develops optimally under conditions which include close physical contact.

Normally, children seek their mothers in order to be comforted when they are distressed, just as infant monkeys run and cling to their mothers. The feel of the mother soothes and comforts them. With hyperkinetic children, on the other hand, the comfort-contact from the mother is not calming; rather, it has been found that holding and cuddling may even cause tension and distress. The child may find this uncomfortable, and attempts to avoid it; thus, he fails to look to mother as a source of comfort and security.

In the most commonly observed pattern, a child's increased tension causes restlessness and resistance to being held and cuddled. The mother perceives this resistance as a rejection, and this may cause her to cease offering such comfort and to become conditioned not to hold and cuddle the child. Parent–child, and, later, other relationships, easily become characterized by tension and difficulties: As the tension persists, the child's behavior may become purposeless, disorganized, and out of control. This may spiral into school learning difficulties and anti-social activities.

LEARNING FAILURES FROM EMOTIONAL HANDICAPS

One way of looking at learning failures is with a "retrospectoscope." Academic underachievement in spite of good intellect is common in higher education. This most likely started when the young person was a child, whether from personality, circumstance, or emotional reaction. These problems may come into sharp visibility in the college age group, writes college physician Henry Bruyn:

> We generally expect our young people to go at least two years to college, hoping that a college degree will guarantee them a fine position and career. Learning problems represent the primary and most significant cause of academic underachievement.
>
> Competition is important in scholastic achievement, yet many young people are afraid to compete. The cause may be due to relationships with parents. In a healthy normal relationship, the young adults learn to conquer their fears of competition within the family and then enjoy or tolerate competition in school.
>
> Some young adults, however, require, as an incentive to learn, expres-

sion of recognition and appreciation from their families. If the parents are deeply engrossed with their own personal affairs, such young people feel that they are working in a vacuum, and interest in their studies will diminish. Some students feel so insecure with this problem that they become involved in a variety of extra-curricular activities that distract even more severely from their time for academic effort.

Other patterns of child raising contribute to problems in learning. In high school and college, overprotected individuals lack the maturity to mobilize for academic battle. They have never had to struggle for anything, and they certainly do not wish to struggle for academic achievement.

The strong mother/weak father team gives boys a problem in establishing an adequate masculine identification and a normal aggressiveness. Or a boy may have trouble identifying with a strict, critical, punitive, and emotionally distant father—so he may identify with mother and become more passive.

Some young people have a great deal of trouble becoming involved. This leads to an unconscious defense against emotional closeness and a fear of winning in a competitive situation. Such a student is literally "accident prone" and makes mistakes on examinations in a resistance to getting deeply involved.

Another type of academic under-achievement results when a young person is trying to be what someone else wants him to be. Parents may have pressured their children to excel as a means of gratifying parental need for status. Young people feel this as a threat to their automony; but, being unable to express rebellion openly, they resort to academic failure as a retaliatory gesture and as an outlet for hostility.

Tension and restlessness from non-academic personal problems will certainly make studying difficult for young adults. In the structured situation of study, any anxiety the young people may have concerning a disappointing love affair, the illness of a close member of the family, or some other personal problem will seriously handicap their ability to concentrate on their academic work.

Aside from these basic causes for academic underachievement, there are times when the motivation for a college education is consciously and totally lacking. These students are in college simply in order to avoid adult responsibilities. They are far better off out of the educational field and in some sort of gainful employment.

Certain personality characteristics may be associated with successful academic achievement:

1. Willingness to commit oneself emotionally to things and to people, not afraid to become emotionally involved, not afraid of closeness.
2. Can remain positively oriented towards things and people.
3. Feels adequate in regard to scholastic achievement, can tolerate his work being judged.
4. Faces problems and scholastic endeavor by being active and competitive.
5. Strives to meet his personality needs.
6. Minimum inner rebellion to demands put upon him.
7. Time well organized.
8. Not overly anxious, but enough so to do academic work.
9. Performs well enough so that he does not feel guilty.
10. Good self-discipline.

There are, in contrast, certain personality characteristics which lead to scholastic anxiety and underachievement:

1. Hesitant about becoming involved, must remain distant, fear of closeness to things and people, often lonely.
2. Constant tug of war between positive and negative attitudes towards study and other people (ambivalence).
3. Does not feel adequate in scholastic endeavor; feels he or she will be harshly judged.
4. Wishes to be passive, does not wish to get in a fight.
5. Personality needs unmet, requires praise or special recognition for certain accomplishments.
6. Much inner rebellion at demands of the teacher—a foot dragger.
7. Time unorganized, a time waster, a procrastinator.
8. Anxiety makes him restless, with an inability to concentrate.
9. Guilt and tension over failure to get at his academic work.
10. Self-indulgent.

All these factors contributing to academic underachievement require very special and individualized types of treatment, ranging from an improvement in relationships to parents to more formal treatment by a therapist. Supportive therapy can include a wide variety of factors in young people's lives. It should be emphasized that underachieving young adults do not feel right about themselves. Indeed, they are busy making themselves miserable. It is an unrealistic and unhealthy solution to solve problems by means of failure. For successful therapy, the students need some understanding of their life situations and a desire to get rid of bad habits. When they want a better solution to their problems than academic underachievement, they can be helped.[8]

Associate editor Julie Oliver adds: "Many girls and women fear academic competition and success because of social pressures—including fear or resentment of boys and becoming handicapped in the marriage market."

Dealing with most of these problems is not easy. This is especially so in our current society, when far more graduate from college than society can use. Ph.D. taxi drivers and people holding Bachelor's degree and clerk's jobs are not that uncommon. Perhaps some of the college dropouts are smarter than they look. But college drop-out or not, all of us want our children to develop to their maximum. And if they have emotional problems that block learning or function, their life will be quite different than what it might have been. If there is a possibility that your child, now, suffers a significant emotional problem which interferes with learning or happiness, then get some professional help. To prevent such problems and get the best development out of your children requires your best in parenting. As a start, I believe you should set high goals, use firm, fair, and dispassionate discipline, and enjoy stimulating your child's best efforts.

TREATMENT OF LEARNING DISABILITIES

The first step in obtaining help is to admit that there is a problem. It isn't easy to separate the learning disabilities of children who are simply "turned off" from those with deeper problems. Elementary school teacher Jan Canby explains why troubles aren't found and taken care of before children get in a hole:

> It is very difficult for parents to accept that a child cannot perform as well as his or her classmates. The guilt some parents burden themselves with can block even the best intentions. It may force them to view the school psychologist as a threat. They blame previous teachers for not recognizing the problem or for not doing anything. Sometimes they simply don't hear what the teacher tells them. They may insist that the child can produce if only the teacher makes him do it. At times, it takes years of repeated failures for the parents to accept that there is probably a specific problem with the child's learning ability. By then, several years of specialized help has been lost, and the child has slipped even further behind.

What Can Be Done for the Learning Disabled Child?

Dr. Sylvia Richardson sums up what can be done to help:

> By a combination of techniques, a group of qualified professionals—chiefly in psychology, medicine, and education—can find most of these children. If the diagnosis is positive, education—in the form of tutorial assistance, or, for children with more than mild impairment, special classes—becomes the key to improvement. *This remedial training consists of finding the area in which the learning-disabled child is weak and then giving him exercises designed to improve his skills in that area. No one knows why such exercises work or what happens inside the child's brain.* Educators have a number of ideas concerning the learning-disabled child, how his areas of weakness can be found, and how special methods and teaching materials can be used to help overcome them. Their approach is pragmatic; in much the same way, a headache sufferer takes aspirin, although science has no sure knowledge of how aspirin functions to reduce the pain.[9]

What Can Parents Do for Children with Learning Disabilities?

First, realize that special class placement is usually a help, not a threat. Then make certain that you coordinate your activities with the teacher. Home life should be structured, not permissive. Help your child develop basic skills to organize homework. Start with a preparation period to get books and papers in order. Then, establish a routine time of short duration to do homework. Don't overburden a child; exercise firm control with gentleness. Create small achievable tasks.

Start with short periods and gradually increase the time, depending on the child's interest and progress. Do not allow the child to manipulate you by arguing, fooling around, getting "sick," or even ignoring you. Firmly force the issue and make him actually pay attention for the total allotted time, even if you have to stay at the task longer. Give the child time to understand the task, then tell him to do it "now." Make the child look at your eyes and at the work. Simplify the task as much as possible. Break complex tasks into their basic elements if necessary. Relax and teach the child to relax, at least for short periods of time. Set readily apparent guidelines for behavior.

These children have usually experienced failure. It is vital that their social life offer a good chance of success. This can frequently be accomplished through group activity *if* the group leader is understanding and mature. Find this out before you place children in a group situation. Then let them do the best they can without your becoming overinvolved. It is their life.

Dr. Henry Richanbach points out that as parents, you can "fix things" at home to help your hyperactive child:

1. Training and discipline are required. The secret here is to understand enough about the child so you do not ask for more than can be produced, yet you demand all you can get. If, for example, you know that they will not retain two instructions, for example, turn off the hose and bring in the paper (they leave the hose on and bring in the paper), then ask for one thing and see that it is done. Success ensues: They did what you wanted at least once that day!

2. Let activities fit the child. Bowling or swimming with Dad may be more rewarding than an afternoon waiting for fish to bite at a secluded spot by a previously quiet brook.

3. Don't let the child "con" you. Most children will eventually learn to use behavior problems as cop-outs. If they "can't remember" what they do, they will soon learn not to hear you. When you can differentiate between the put-on and the real thing, you will have arrived.

There are ways to help a hyperactive child function better in school. Good teachers and schools have always recognized that children are different, just like people. It must have been great for hyperactive children in a one-room country school house—if they couldn't sit still, they could go out and chop wood or run a while. (a.) Sit hyperactive children at the front of the room rather than at the back, so their focus is on the teacher and the school work. (b.) Reward success and good behavior instantly. (c.) Keep the classroom simple and free of distractions, with only the materials needed at the moment

348 *School and Learning Problems*

in sight. (d.) Small classes and specially trained and motivated teachers are ideal.

As you think of all the things you can do to help the learning disabled child, keep in mind that there are other children in the family to be considered. A hyperactive child can make things awfully rough on them. Enlist their help and understanding and don't let them get lost in the shuffle while trying to help the special child.

Choosing a Pediatrician to Treat Your Hyperactive Child

Pediatricians who are interested in behavior problems and learning disabilities in their daily practice can best help these children. All children with hyperactivity need help. First, help is needed in sorting out the cause. Then, it must be understood that when the hyperactivity is organic—from having a different type of brain or from reacting to food additives and so forth—that punishment, psychotherapy, or conversation won't help. Sometimes the "smart pill" helps, other times special diets are necessary. Check with your local medical society, school district, or local parent organizations—such as the Association for Children with Learning Disabilities (A.C.L.D.)—for recommendations.

How Do You Treat Hyperactivity?

From the preceding discussion of causes or possible causes, it can be seen that treatment must depend upon cause. Hyperactivity *without* school or learning difficulties is first of all a medical problem. Report to your child's doctor. Hyperactivity *with* school, social, family, or learning problems is a combined problem. Your doctor will need to talk to the teachers, may request psychological testing or consultations, and will require a thorough work-up and considerable thought before suggesting treatment. Some of the work-up may involve trials such as elimination diets or different approaches to handling the child.

Treating Hyperactivity Physically

As you have seen, there are many treatments for hyperactivity. One experimental approach we alluded to earlier in the chapter involves simply holding the child. Pediatrician Arvin Henderson explains:

Much hyperactivity is a manifestation of tension, and regardless of how it starts, it is difficult for parents to cope with. Exhausted, worried parents make both parents and children more tense. Children who don't receive soothing when alarmed become chronically hyperactive because they help make their environment more alarming.

To escape this trap, we teach parents to change children's behavior by insisting on close physical contact until the child finally finds comfort in the physical closeness. The technique of holding depends on the age, strength, and resistance of the child. In most cases, the child is willing to sit on the parent's knees face-to-face, and talk about his specific problem. If the parent is not tense, the child will relax in time and enjoy the contact.

The results of teaching this approach to parents are good so far. In most instances, there is a decrease in hyperactivity and associated symptoms. We have been able to take some children off of drugs successfully. Further research will be required, however, to prove scientifically the worth of this very old "new" method of handling children.

Treatment of Hyperactivity With Drugs

To treat children with drugs is bothersome. It might be helpful to know that successful drug treatment for hyperactivity was found accidently in the 1930s when a doctor in a retarded children's home started using Dexedrine for a weight reduction program for some of the more obese M.R.'s. To his astonishment, many of these children ceased acting retarded and became less hyperactive (as some retarded are), and better able to concentrate—and they began to learn. Considering that Dexedrine makes most people more active and jittery, the results were astounding. Decades of work on this phenomenon has simply shown that many hyperactive children calm down, are able to concentrate, and act like normal children when the drug is in them. Indeed, the drug doesn't act at all like a drug. It isn't habit-forming, doesn't require increasing doses for continued effectiveness, and it acts more like a vitamin or hormone that is needed by the body for normal function. It even helps some children who are not hyperactive but who have trouble concentrating and learning or who are discipline problems often in trouble because of a lack of self-control. The children who benefit from the drug and who have few or no side effects from it often call it "the smart pill." However, the idea of using chemicals to treat hyperactive children does not set well with some.

We asked pediatrician Robert Burnett to tell us why we shouldn't treat hyperactive children with drugs:

Before an answer can be given, let's consider some adjacent questions: Is "hyperactivity" just a popular cliche applied indiscriminately as "fact?" Is there an increase in the number of children who are born with hyperactivity? Are parents and educators becoming less tolerant of this behavior pattern? Has medicine really found a cure or a safe effective method of controlling the symptoms of hyperactivity?

Hyperactivity as a word (or definition) has become popular, and I believe is often misused as a diagnosis to indicate any child who is more active than a particular teacher or parent can easily tolerate or control. If used to mean that the activity both interferes with learning and is poorly tolerated by teachers and peers, then the onus is on the child. Sophisticated educators use it often, yet I doubt that there is an increased reproduction of hyperactive children; rather, the most significant cause for concern about hyperactivity is that society has changed.

Today, we live in an urban, crowded, physically restrictive society. Children are physically closer to adults most of the time. Little physical effort is required or demanded of children to aid the family. At the same time, we place great emphasis on academic achievement, requiring children to "live up to their intellectual capacity" at all times. Often, such demands start at the preschool level. These conditions impose an expectation of "ideal" behavior that is inconsistent with the nature of many children.

Why is there a decrease in the tolerance of parents and educators to hyperactivity? Perhaps the increased tensions of a more complex society cause increased strain on family relationships which make parents less tolerant of childhood behavior in general. The educator's short-term concern for evoking maximum performance from the child, coupled with oversized classes and increased stresses on teachers, may lower tolerance for hyperactive behavior at school. The result is increased sensitivity to hyperactivity.

The key to what, if anything, should be done about hyperactivity lies in the brain, a complex organization of trillions of cells, responsible for behavior. Brain cells are stimulated by the world around the child and respond by producing an electro-chemical discharge which is integrated with billions upon billions of discharges from brain cells to form an individual's behavior. Individual differences in behavior, which are apparent in infancy, change with age. The *brain* of a two-month-old cannot program the muscles of a two-month-old to walk. That of a five-year-old cannot program its body to shoot baskets with the proficiency of a professional, or to be as still and attentive as a twenty-year-old. This change in function of the brain is called maturation.

Maturation means that the cerebral cortex (the conscious portion of the brain) develops greater control over the individual's functions. But the rate and uniformity of maturation is highly variable. Children who are hyperactive at five may not be at ten, if their hyperactivity is solely due to slower maturation of the particular cells most concerned with activity. Hyperactivity is not measurable on an E.E.G. (electroencephalograph).

Drugs affect the function of the brain cells, but a given drug does not affect all brains in the same manner. The amphetamines, for example, make most adults more active or wakeful yet have the opposite effect, especially on children who are hyperactive. We do not understand how brain cells are altered by amphetamine or why it has a greater effect on the brain of many hyperactive children than on non-hyperactive children. That it does is evidence that perhaps different metabolic processes are occurring in hyperactive children.

If one out of thirty children is hyperactive in the eyes of their parents or teachers, then there are nearly two million children in the country to be given amphetamines to calm their behavior. We must consider the philosophical implications of such an action on our society, as well as the effects on the individual child. If we give amphetamines to hyperactive children, then perhaps we should give tranquilizers to negative children and mood elevators to lethargic children. In essence, the brave new world of Aldous Huxley will have reached our society ahead of schedule, for we would be chemically creating a great deal of "sameness" and eliminating some problems of individuality.

On the other hand, if children's hyperactive behavior has the deleterious effect of constantly getting them into trouble at school or at home and if it interferes with their ability to learn, they need help— and amphetamines are justified. Treatment should be continued until some future date when the maturation of the brain develops enough for cerebral cortical control. However, this teaches the parent and child that pills are a way to control behavior—an unhealthy side effect of the medication.

Before resorting to drugs, it is vital for the parent, educator, and physician first to evaluate all the factors that produce the child's behavior pattern. The evaluation should include assessment of those who say the child is hyperactive: What is the attitude of the parents and teacher toward normal children as well as toward hyperactive children? Can the child be handled in a different way which may achieve the desired results? Is psychological evaluation or psychiatric counseling in order? Perhaps a different approach to discipline will induce self-control in the child. Altering children's behavior in this manner allows them the opportunity to learn to make adjustments in their own behavior patterns.

There are some children who will remain so incorrigible, in spite of diets, environmental and attitude changes, counseling and discipline, that drugs will have to be used. Still, long-term effects of the drugs are not thoroughly understood, and their actions are not uniform, so they should be used only in situations of dire distress. The complex question of hyperactivity is of logical concern to parent and teacher. If a workable solution is to be reached, a thorough and extensive evaluation by the child's physician must be accomplished—a task more complex than suturing a corneal graft on an eye. But equally important, a major commitment of time and effort—of involvement—must be made by the parent and by the educator.

Use Drugs When They Are Needed

Pediatrician Henry Richanbach takes a more positive view of drug use:

> The goal of medicating hyperactive children is to help them to use their own abilities better. *There is no drug which will make them any smarter or better.* If a desirable change can be accomplished with the aid of medication, then the parents and teachers can be more effective. Any improvement from drugs must be capitalized on and rewarded in order to make it worthwhile. The treatment should be viewed as part of the teaching process.
>
> Yet we hesitate to use drugs because we live in a society that uses, misuses, and overuses a variety of chemicals to an alarming degree. We are urged to use analgesics for headaches from tension and distress; one set of medicines for a runny nose, and more, if there is a cough. There are preparations to alter odors (normal, abnormal, and all, presumably objectionable) at all body openings and surfaces. Different brands of cigarettes are pushed for ladies, he-men, nonconforming horsemen, or for outdoor types who need menthol by the waterfalls. It is no wonder that the kids turn to organic apples to protect themselves and marijuana to expand their minds, even as their parents load up on prescription tranquilizers to keep the lid on their own minds.
>
> Some of the medications that are used to help children with hyperactivity and attention problems "work" far better than any of those above. They may help children to change their entire life style. They should be used only with careful observation and management to capitalize on any change, with the understanding that children are using medicine to help themselves and not being made better because of a pill. The "better" child was there all the time. Such medication should be regarded as a useful training device. The drugs can only be prescribed by doctors. It is a most heavy responsibility.

I regard amphetamine as a crutch to allow children to keep up while their brains and their control mature. Like crutches, they can be misused, or they can be of great help. Like crutches, they should not be prescribed lightly. Nor should children be given the drug because it functions as a crutch for parents and teachers. Dr. Richanbach adds three major points to our knowledge about the use of amphetamines in hyperactive children by posing the question, "What harm can occur from using amphetamines in hyperactive children?"

1. Are they habit forming? For practical purposes, no. They may be used for years and stopped with little effect, although one can get used to and dependent on the *effect.* As children mature and become productive and

successful, they easily outgrow the need for medication, if their total management has been appropriate.

2. Can these drugs be used to control children's minds? No. First of all, only
doctors can prescribe them. They don't control the mind but they do control
hyperactivity and actually free the mind from overreacting to impulses, thus
allowing it to function fully and normally.

3. Will it lead to drug abuse when they are older? The evidence so far is that
the children who have been helped into success by medication seem to have
far less of a problem misusing drugs as adolescents than the average population. Drug abuse is a "people problem" as much as a drug problem. The
drugs are not addicting or habit-forming when used as described. Unsuccessful
people are more likely to look for chemical solutions, with alcohol, uppers,
downers, psychedelics, and marihuana, as a way of avoiding dealing with
their problems.

The Long-Term Outlook on Pills
for Minimal Brain Dysfunction

A pioneer with thirty years of experience in the use of drugs to treat
hypeactivity and learning disabilities is Dr. Leon Oettinger. He offers a
look at both the past and the future in drug therapy.

There is a popular myth, believed by many and perpetuated by the
hopeful attitude of physicians and teachers, that all children who suffer
from minimal brain dysfunction (MBD), and associated learning and
behavior disorders, will recover when they enter adolescence.
Particularly with reading difficulties, the advice has been given "he'll
grow out of it," or "boys are slower than girls," or "we must not
compare children." As with all myths, there is a kernel of truth in these
assertations. Nevertheless, complete recovery occurs in only a few
individuals.

Investigators have found that if children had problems in
kindergarten, three out of four of those studied during adolescence
still gave their parents difficulties. They would not obey rules, were
moody, lacked self-esteem, were aggressive, and were still having
social and scholastic problems. Even adults, at age twenty-five or
older, who had been studied in childhood still had serious problems.
Problem behavior as a child predicts problem behavior as an adult. All
of the studies suggest strongly that children with MBD do not outgrow
learning and behavior disorders. This leads to the conclusion that
treatment should be started early in life and continued, in many cases,
into adult life.

When making a decision as to what treatment should be
undertaken, and for how long, it is necessary to understand the basic
causes of MBD and learning disorders. Many theories have been put
forward: Poor teaching, emotional problems, inter-family conflicts,
developmental lag, "bad parents," and brain damage have been blamed.
Unquestionably, there is some basis for each of these theories, and, in

some cases, treatment must be directed toward one or more of these factors. However, the best evidence suggests that MBD has a high genetic incidence. Many workers in the field feel that the problem is often a biochemical one in which there is a disturbance of chemical substances which react in the metabolic processes of the brain. It is felt that drugs, particularly the so-called "stimulants," act primarily to regulate these substances, much in the manner that insulin regulates diabetes.

Many children whose problems are not severe or who have learning problems secondary to poor teaching, or a poor start, respond and do well when remedial teaching is begun early enough. "Perceptual" training occasionally seems to work and must be considered by educators, physicians, and psychologists; but proof is lacking that these methods are effective in a significant number of children. Psychiatric intervention has proven to be a dismal failure, except in handling the emotional overlay which accompanies learning disorders. Behavior modification techniques have been shown, convincingly, to bring about improvement in MBD; however, although behavior modification is effective, medications have proven to be more satisfactory. Using a combination of behavior modification with medication appears to be the most effective treatment of all.

The use of medication for the treatment of learning and behavior disorders is the best documented of all the methods, with the possible exception of psychiatric intervention. Dozens of well conducted studies indicate strongly that behavior is improved in children with MBD when they are treated with appropriate medication. The preponderance of evidence also suggests improved academic achievement.

It must be emphasized that a drug is not given to quiet the child or to decrease aggressive behavior. It is not given to "stimulate" or "depress." It follows, then, that, if the purpose of the drug is to improve brain function, the drug should be given seven days a week. The concept of a "drug vacation" makes little sense. Drugs should be continued for as long as they are needed. Although medication is required long after adolescence begins in many children, a large proportion of patients on drug therapy for MBD have been able to discontinue the drug and function successfully later, but some may require medications throughout their lives.

All of the drugs used for MBD have some toxicity. Their use requires close supervision by a physician during the entire period of therapy. Although the toxicity of medications has been emphasized by some, the "stimulants" are among the safest of those used in all drug therapy. Under conditions of abuse, when fifty to one hundred times the therapeutic dose is taken, these drugs are clearly dangerous; but the same is true of most other drugs prescribed for medical therapy, even common aspirin.

One of the most important findings in studies of patients on medication for five years or longer is that there has been no increase in the amount of drug required when they became adults, and, in some, the dosage has been reduced. Since an important factor in drug addiction and habituation is that increased amounts are required in order to achieve the same results, one can state flatly that this has not been a problem. No author who has used drugs over a long period has reported any increase in drug abuse, and most feel that there is less.

Recent reports of growth failure in children who have been on long-term therapy presents a real potential problem area, but when the amount of loss in growth is projected to adult males it represents only a loss of three fourths of an inch to an inch. There is evidence that much of the loss is temporary and is regained during a catch-up period after the drug is discontinued. I have found no growth loss in a group of adults who were still on medication.

There have been a few reports of hallucinations with stimulant drugs, but these are rare and disappear upon stopping therapy. Convulsions have occurred when the drugs were suddenly discontinued, but this is extremely rare and seems to occur in individuals who are seizure prone.

Extensive evaluation of patients who have been on long-term therapy has demonstrated no abnormalities in blood pressure, thyroid and liver function, or blood chemistries. Overall, it would seem that the use of drugs in MBD is considerably safer than a long trip in an automobile.

To summarize, there is evidence that medication can help control the symptoms associated with MBD in both adults and children, and that this is achieved by stabilizing some of the metabolic processes of the brain.

There are some toxic effects, but in general these are minor and can be controlled. There is little danger of addiction or habituation if the drug is carefully monitored by a physician and doses stay within the medical ranges. Drugs should be started when the need becomes obvious and continued until they are no longer needed. The use of other therapeutic approaches, particularly behavior modification techniques (and tutoring) in conjunction with drugs, increases the incidence of success in the management of this challenging problem.

As you can see, learning problems are about as complex and as different as humans. Even as this is written new theories are being promulgated and old ideas resurrected. My friends Drs. William Crook [10] and Lendon Smith [11] believe that hypoglycemia is a not uncommon cause of learning and behavior problems—even though most physicians, including me, remain skeptical. Low blood sugar may be the problem with a few— more to the point, is it a problem with your particular child? Some children are being subjected to special tactile and coordination exercises by some physical therapists and to eye muscle exercises by some optometrists. Much of this, I believe, proves that if you give a child extra attention he will learn better. Meanwhile, there is a swing back toward basic grammar schools where the 3 R's are taught, children are made to mind, and many learning problems seem to vanish. Perhaps traditional schooling has always been a form of behavior modification. In any case a good portion of learning problems stem from permissive education theories that require the first grader, like a college student, to take the responsibility for his own education. Give complete freedom of choice I wonder what percentage of children would go to school, and if they went, would finish their education. Meanwhile, magic pill or no magic pill, individual parents and individual teachers will continue to try to educate their particular charges. They do this by using the greatest magic of all, determination to do the best for each child.

9

SEPARATION: DIVORCE AND DEATH

Being abandoned is a major fear of most children. It starts at the time they realize that they can be separated from their parents by their own efforts—when they develop that deeply satisfying talent of walking. Throughout *The Parents' Guide* we have discussed various phases of separation fears, from stranger fears (which usually peak around nine months) to "leaving home worries," the necessary emotional recognition that the time will finally come to leave home. Concern over such future separation usually occurs during the five to twelve age span and culminates in the practical separation process that starts during adolescence. How parents help their children to handle these feelings about the problems and opportunities of separating has a lot to do with their success as parents. How children adapt to these worries and excitements has a lot to do with their ultimate adjustment. Thus, our childhood reactions also serve as the basis of our adult parental reaction to problems of separation—such as divorce or the death of a child. In this brief chapter, we will consider children's death fears and the child's problem of losing a parent through divorce, as well as the adult's problem of losing a child.

When a child discovers that he really can be separated from his parent, he worries. But there usually is an underlying faith, and always an underlying hope, that the child will find the parents or that the parents will find the child. Then comes the shocking realization that separation can be final, at least in this world: that there is a process called death. With this realization, worry changes to a fear of death, which usually peaks in the four-year-old.

DEATH

When three- or four-year-olds discover the concept of death, they have trouble believing that it can happen. So they question and question. "Where did grandmother go?" or "Where is our dog now?" They worry the idea like a loose tooth, and the more they see it or hear it, the greater its reality and threat. Adults often think that they can help a young child handle death fears by instilling faith in the child. And they frequently succeed. The child may feel that he is going to heaven in a golden Cadillac with angels playing harps all the way. But even the child who accepts this isn't about to go on *that* trip! But then, who of us is really ready to go? Very few. The instinct for and love of this life and the love of their parents block the acceptance of death or the welcoming of even a glorious afterlife for most children.

How do children handle death fears? There are two major mechanisms. Most bury it, quit talking about it, and either forget it, or, if the stimulus is enough, have nightmares or odd fears that are really death fears surfacing. Other children find ways to protect themselves from death. In my practice, when doing health supervision checks, I often hold up the growth chart and say to the child: "See how big you are growing." Not too uncommonly, a six- to nine-year-old will reply, almost angrily, "I'm not going to grow up!" When I ask why, they impatiently explain, "If you grow up, you get old and you die!" I guess it is the Peter Pan in all of us—childhood forever. It is a comforting precept that attracts almost all of us. The Peter Pan myth serves a good purpose. It is a safety valve that protects children from undue exposure to one of the harsh realities of life: that we are mortal and must die. Fairy tales are a lubricant that eases the child into accepting fact and a safety valve that protects the vulnerable developing psyche from too much and too early stress. And facing death can be far more stressful for a child than it is for an adult.

The child who is taken to funerals before he has mastered his separation fears of childhood may be permanently scarred. The initial fear and grief may become chronic grieving with a sense of abandonment, hopelessness, and anger at a God (or parent?) who allows such things to happen. Acute reactions can go on for years, blighting years of the child's life. Or the entire frightening prospect of separation by death may be buried. During routine discussions of the death fears of four-year-olds, I have had a good number of parents volunteer that they had chronic anxiety or depression springing from overexposure to death and funerals when they were children between five and twelve. Several parents had buried these fears so deeply that it took years of psychotherapy to un-cover them.

Because of such vivid examples of problems due to an overexposure to death, I suggest that you shouldn't take young children under twelve years old to funerals—not even to funerals of close relatives. Some psychiatrists disagree with my stand. They see adults with problems stemming from bottled-up grief and an unrealistic refusal to face death. But I doubt that adult rationalizations or ventilations about death fears will help most children. A child who believes in fairy tales and in Santa Claus is not ready for exposure to death. Let children be children—they will face such realities soon enough. All things in good time! Protect your child from exposure to death as much as you can. When you cannot, then give him the minimal and factual details about the loss, and about your own faith or feelings about life after death. Although you cannot protect your child completely from the concept of death, you can at least minimize the trauma. Don't allow the child to question you interminably about the meaning of death. Divert his attention to the appreciation of good memories and things left by those who have gone, and to the joy of living that the deceased, and the rest of us, desire for each child. Once mourning is over, let the dead rest in peace—and also let the living continue to live in peace.

If a child loses a parent, even by death, there may be a real feeling of abandonment. The separation fears of the child—the feelings that the parent may not have loved him—may all erupt. Thus there can be anger, as well as a feeling of grief and loss. It may be of worth to tell the child that the parent couldn't help dying and that he didn't really want to leave the child. On the other hand, some children may even feel that they were somehow responsible for the parent's death. Small children often have uncontrolled anger and may "death wish" a parent in the height of a tantrum or when being punished. If the parent then dies, the child may be guilt stricken and feel responsible. It may help to tell the child that our feelings about each other are often mixed, and that we all go through, and get over, many feelings of all sorts. Most all of us are occasionally angry at people we love.

It can also be of help to let the child know that the deceased parent wouldn't want the child to grieve too much or to feel too bad about the loss; that the parent "in heaven" will be happier if the child enjoys life than if the child grieves. A little bit of grief is necessary, but life is to be lived today and anticipated for tomorrow, not just spent in concern about the past. You don't have to philosophize, indoctrinate, or explain to the child as much as you show by attitude—by what you don't do and by what you do.

DIVORCE

Another separation problem facing children is divorce. Divorce is hard on everyone, and it is especially hard on the children. It represents, of course, the end result of many factors. I think that the most common factor is self-centeredness—an often mutual syndrome of not recognizing or effectively meeting the needs of a spouse. This same factor frequently affects the children, who may feel that they, too, are being divorced. This causes psychological problems that can run the gamut from rebellion to unexpected school failure. It also may cause medical problems, from stomach ulcers to headaches. Many of the problems created by divorce spring from the child's underlying feeling that he is personally responsible for the divorce. This may seem an unlikely event to the adults involved, but it is not unreasonable to the child. Few children have a realistic understanding of their effect upon their parents. They do understand that they can cause many types of parental reactions. Some of these reactions initially come as a surprise to the children. Others are expected, and may even be orchestrated by a child. In general, the child sees that his feelings, which are usually on the surface, cause the parents to react in certain ways. He may then reason that almost *all* of his feelings, as well as his childish actions and desires, have an effect on the parents. It is for this reason that a child often feels that it is his fault if the parents are angry at each other. Sometimes this is because the parental anger at a spouse is triggered by the child's misbehavior and obviously then becomes directed at the spouse once the child is dealt with. At other times, a child may be angry at a parent and expect counter anger, only to see one parent become, instead, angry at the other parent. A more significant cause for a child to assume the blame and guilt for parental quarrels is if he believes that one parent loves him more than the other parent. Here, the child may think that the less-favored parent is angry and attacks the spouse out of jealousy and hurt. At times, this is true. Even when no divorce is contemplated, if parents quarrel with each other and if the child senses the anger and hurt, the child may be more damaged than the adults involved. When parents fight, they should take great care to do so when the children are not around. This is especially so if the fight is about how to handle the child.

If a divorce is a possibility, it is best not to mention it until the parents have finally firmly made up their minds. A child whose parents are discussing divorce often feels that he must somehow help the parents solve their problems, or that he is supposed to choose sides with one of them. In either case, then, the child actually becomes part of the divorce fight. So, when parents have decided upon divorce, it is best to present it to the child as a final act. This unburdens the child from the self-im-posed task of uniting or separating the parents. In fact, if there has been fighting and uncertainty, the child may occasionally welcome the divorce as a resolution of his problems—especially if both parents are truly com-mitted to the child and reassure him of their continuing love. It may also be welcome if one parent abuses or hates the child.

It is, of course, natural for a parent to want the child on his or her side. The parents are usually lonely and hurt and want the child for comfort and security. And whether parents try or not, the child usually ends up picking one or another according to the circumstances. Still, this picking of sides should be avoided as much as possible. One way is for both parents to inform the child that the divorce is "none of his busi-ness!"

How do you explain a divorce to your child? First, do you really understand it yourself? Hopefully you both will have had some profes-sional counseling when you first recognized your problems. Often the underlying reasons for hurt and anger come out and are resolved. Other times, they are not resolved. The genesis of most divorces is personal dis-satisfaction. Often, it results in regression: a try to recapture childhood or adolescence without obligations or commitment, a search for freedom. The result of refusing to accept responsibility may be freedom, but it usually creates a burden of guilt. Of course, there are people trapped in destructive marriages with an unchangeable and unreasonable partner whose needs they will never meet, and for some divorce is healthy. But, still, how do you tell the children?

Perhaps one of the best ways to explain to the children why you are divorcing is to tell them briefly, and then listen to them and try to answer their questions. Reassure them of their own innocence, and firmly reject their intervention into the situation. Most important is that you reassure the child that the child isn't losing a parent, that it is the parent who is losing a spouse. The child should feel that he will still have his parents, even if he doesn't have them together.

During the stress of divorce, it is especially important for each par-ent to remain aware of the needs of the child. This is better demon-strated than talked about. Continue or increase whatever positive rela-tionship you have with the child—whether it is taking him shopping with you (if he likes it), or fishing, or to a scout meeting, or even helping with the homework. Help the child's stability by changing as few things as possible. Try to let him stay in the same school, on the same team, and with the same friends.

Once the parents have separated, it is wise not to try to make up for feelings of guilt and loneliness, or to one-up the ex-spouse by being the "good guy." Many parents with visiting privileges come armed with presents in order to cover their guilt. Be positive, but be as normal as possible.

When a divorced or separated parent starts to date, many problems can occur. Remember that the children were not around when their parents were dating; and keep in mind that the child is shielded from parental sexual activity during marriage. Parents should have a private life apart from the children. And when a divorced parent sleeps with a friend, it is best to keep this away from the child. This is especially true early in the divorce when the parent may be meeting and dating many people. In any case, the parent's love life and sex life should be private. At least don't rub the details in the child's face.

Until a parent has firmly decided to marry a new spouse, it might be best not to let the child attach to the friend as a surrogate mother or father. If the marriage does not materialize, then it amounts to another divorce for the child who has become attached. Of course, it is equally important to mix with people and enjoy life. But don't force the child to conclude that a love commitment—or marriage—is a temporary thing.

If a child doesn't want to visit a parent, it may be because he is afraid of what he may see in the parent's home, or afraid of what might happen to the parent he leaves while he is gone. Often the child becomes quite possessive of one or the other parent and jealous because he fears the parent may divorce him. A sensitive child can *feel* rejected even if the parent is not, and has no intention of, rejecting him. Thus the mainstay of the child in divorce is the parents' acute awareness of the child's needs and the love and commitment that sees to it that these needs are met as well as is possible.

TERMINAL ILLNESS AND DEATH

Children aren't the only ones who must occasionally suffer the loss of a loved one. Parents occasionally have to suffer the loss of their child. One of the most shocking losses is the unexpected loss of a baby, for example, by miscarriage or by death at birth. Such losses have been common throughout human history until recently. The marked increase in the average human life span has come about largely because we are able to save most infants from the risk of birth trauma and most infants and children from the risk of accidents and infections during the first five years of life.

Although the loss of newborns was common a century ago, the parents grieved. They continued to have babies, and lavished their care upon the living, thus mostly healing the hurt and assuaging the inevitable parental feeling of guilt that occurs when a baby or child dies.

Sudden Infant Death Syndrome—
S.I.D.S. (Crib Death or Cot Death)

Looking at the most common, yet still unlikely, cause of death in the first six months of life today, we find that it is the sudden infant death syndrome. Over 10,000 infants in the United States die of this mysterious malady each year, and over 20,000 parents are left in a state of shock and disbelief, with feelings of suspicion, anger, and guilt.

Infants between the ages of two weeks and six months can suddenly die in their sleep during the night. These deaths are not expected—the infants seem well. In spite of massive research which is trying to find the cause, we still don't know why they die. Because we don't know what causes these deaths, we cannot yet prevent them. Sudden Infant Death occurs among infants receiving excellent parental and medical care. Emeritus pediatric professor Ed Shaw discusses some of the various speculations about the cause of these tragedies and some of the ideas proposed for dealing with the situation:

Most of these babies have been progressing normally without previous evidence of respiratory difficulties. Characteristically, a well child is put to bed and in the morning is found dead. Fairly often, the infant has had a very minor respiratory infection beforehand or perhaps some mild upper respiratory infection may have just started and gone unnoticed. However, autopsy findings fail to reveal the cause of death.

There have been many explanations proposed—none has been generally accepted. In Biblical times it was believed that the mother "overlaid" her baby and smothered him, and this idea persisted until fairly recent times. Causes which have been thoroughly disproven include:

1. Smothering from bedding, clothing, or pillows
2. Enlargement of the thymus gland
3. Vomiting of food with aspirations
4. Injury to the spinal cord from mild trauma
5. Abnormalities of the thyroid and the thymus, plus dozens of vague surmises

It is even difficult to determine the proper areas for research. One theory is that death is due simply to the infant's momentary failure to breathe, something which does happen without fatal results in the newborn nursery where the babies are under close observation. Many infants less than six months old can only breathe through their noses, and if their nostrils are gently held during sleep they will simply stop breathing, at least for one-half a minute. Obviously, however, this experiment cannot be prolonged in order to see if the infant will die, or if he will gasp and breathe! Experiments with monkeys have not been conclusive, and this type of research has not been extensively supported.

One surmise, which was extensively reported in the lay press, was that the infant who has been fed until he falls asleep over his bottle and is then put to bed later gives an enormous belch after he falls asleep and that the large amount of air expelled is too much for his upper airway to handle. It can do no harm to be certain that the infant is well "burped" before he is put to bed, but this idea has not been accepted by most scientists.

It has been proposed that monitors for the baby be provided which could sound an alarm when there was an interruption of breathing. These might be of value if there was some way to determine in advance which babies are at risk; but the devices are expensive, are subject to many false alarms, and would be a source of tremendous anxiety to parents who would do well not to live in dread of this disaster. There are a few instances in which the sleeping baby has been found to be blue, where resuscitation has apparently averted sudden death, but these instances are few, and, again, are unpredictable. There is good reason for parents not to hover continuously over the child's bed.

Dr. Shaw's observations reflect the common experience of pediatricians. Many believe that the death occurs because the nose is plugged and infants cannot breathe well through the mouth. Babies have a small lower jaw, and usually a large tongue set back in the mouth, making it anatomically difficult, if not impossible, to get enough air through the nose if it is plugged. Further, because the nasal passages are so small, it takes only a minor amount of mucus or swelling to plug them up. There is some hope that many sudden infant deaths can be prevented by changing the sleeping position, elevating the head of the bed so that there is less likelihood of the tongue or food or milk blocking the baby's airway. Elevation of the head of the bed also reduces congestion in the nose from puddled mucus or the swelling of edema that moves to the head when we lie flat. Autopsy studies of S.I.D.S. reveal a high incidence of unsuspected viral "colds." The use of prescribed decongestants by mouth or of baby nose drops for colds, along with elevating the head of the bed, may also be of some help. However, it should be emphasized that these new theories have neither been extensively tested nor completely proven. As of now, S.I.D.S. is still unexplained, unexpected, and unpreventable. Cases of sudden infant death, however, share enough features in common that it is a medically accepted condition or disease.

I believe that the most preventable part of the tragedy of the sudden infant death syndrome is the feeling that the parents, or whoever was around, were responsible. Dr. Shaw observes: "Understandably, parents who are confronted with this situation are devastated by it and usually seek some fault of their own, either commission or omission, which might have prevented it. Sometimes neighbors and, until recently, police, have been equally suspicious of the parents. It is most essential that all concerned know that this event cannot be predicted or prevented by any known means."

The suspicion, guilt, and anger aroused by the death of a previously healthy baby can do terrible harm. It should be recognized that S.I.D.S. is caused neither from neglect nor murder. The family should be left with a clear conscience. It is helpful to talk to other parents who have gone through this sorrow. Material on S.I.D.S. and help is available from the National Sudden Infant Death Syndrome Foundation, 310 South Michigan, Chicago, Illinois 60604 (phone 312-663-0650); and from The International Council for Infant Survival Inc., 1515 Reistertown Road, Suite 300, Baltimore, Maryland 21208 (phone 301-484-0111).

It is also helpful to work for funds and to push for research on this condition. Meanwhile, life goes on; so don't forget the rest of your family, and try not to dwell on the unfortunate past.

Facing the Death of a Child

The death of a baby from S.I.D.S. is shocking, difficult and is over and done with, leaving you to recover. But what if you have a child who is ill and will probably die? Every minute can seem an hour, for you not only have your own suffering to contend with but you also have to decide what to tell the child, and how to carry on. For advice on this very difficult situation, I asked Australian pediatrician Dr. Eric Sims, "Should you tell your child?"

Death is a fact of life, but unless a child has had unusual experiences, he is unlikely to comprehend such a permanent sleep. You, on the other hand, do understand what this parting will mean. Naturally, you are distressed that he is going to miss so much that you have enjoyed in life. You are bewildered that such a thing can happen, and numbed at the thought of a future without him. The big task for you is to make the rest of his life as normal and happy as possible. The challenge is to carry on with an outwardly cheerful countenance towards him, in spite of the numb feeling inside you. Continue to show your usual affection for him but resist the big temptation to overindulge him in an attempt to make his remaining time doubly happy. This is not only impossible, but also your apparently inexplicable behavior might puzzle him. His happiness is best served by following his usual routines, including school if possible. He will not be helped by being told things he cannot grasp; and he is unlikely to force you into false statements by directly questioning you. Nevertheless, you and your doctor should discuss this possibility and have some agreed explanation, short of the truth, to offer your child about his illness and its outcome.

If you have a faith, this should be a source of strength to you. You will also find the love of your spouse, your family, and your friends an essential support. Although your main distress is your regret that your child is to be deprived of so many opportunities in life, you would be less than human if you did not feel sorry for yourself as well. No one can pretend that your loss will ever be forgotten, and no words can really comfort you; but his short life has been sweet, and you will always have your memories of him, in perhaps what were to be his sunniest years. Young lives ended without complete fulfillment are always tragedies, but at least "age shall not weary them, nor the years condemn." So many of us are spared, to suffer many long years of misery greater than youth ever dreamed of.

But what do you tell the other children? I believe children usually adapt better to the loss of a playmate or brother or sister with less difficulty than the parents. Dr. Sims suggests:

Your attitude to your other children at this time will depend upon their ages. If they are old enough to cope with the knowledge, they could be told the truth about the illness, and their knowing will be some help to you. If they are too young, they should merely be given some simple explanation in keeping with their beliefs about this life and the hereafter. Young children do not feel bereaved for long; but they may be deeply disturbed if they perceive their parents' prolonged grief.

You may find that during the next few months you will gradually adjust to the sense of impending loss. The situation is very different for those parents confronted with the sudden death of a child by accident. This is a shattering thing, often compounded by the guilty feeling that, with some forethought, the accident could have been avoided. Vain recriminations against themselves or each other will not help the unhappy parents. Only with mutual sympathy and support can such a heartbreak be faced together.

SUMMARY

Separation, death, divorce, and illness are difficult subjects to handle —especially in a book. Each individual's reaction to the problems or the suggested solutions is likely to be somewhat different. Advice can rarely be universally applicable. When you have such problems, we suggest that you talk them over with your family, true friends, and your "family" physician—whether he is a pediatrician, family practice specialist, internist, or obstetrician. Further help is available from other specialists, including psychologists, psychiatrists, and counselors as well as ministers, rabbis, and priests—and often from various lay organizations. But do look for help: It is rarely healthy to suffer in silence.

As to universally applicable advice, there is precious little. It does help to try to understand the other's viewpoint and to recognize that the basic premises on which we base our lives differ from individual to individual. But the effort must be made to try to understand each other's needs as well as the reasons for their actions. And once some understanding is achieved, then positive action is usually possible. Sometimes, however, it is difficult to be positive when you are hurt or angry. For these situations, it is helpful to turn to the teaching and philosophies that have been handed down over the centuries by religious and intellectual leaders whose devotion was to smoothing human relations and helping us to live with the fact that we are, physically at least, mortal. It is the human spirit that counts, and that is strengthened by the way we live our lives today, and the ways in which we can strengthen others in turn. Be of good spirit.

NOTES

Chapter 1

1. Rose Zeligs, "The Physician/Psychologist Partnership," *Feelings and Their Medical Significance, 18*, No. 1 (1976), p. 1.
2. Some thoughts about childrearing. In U. Bronfenbrenner (Ed.), *Readings in the development of human behavior.* New York: Dryden Press, 1972.
3. DONALD CAMPBELL, "On the Conflicts Between Biological and Social Evolution and Between Psychology and Moral Tradition," *American Psychologist* (December 1975), p. 1103.
4. BURTON WHITE, *The First Three Years of Life* (Englewood Cliffs, N.J.: Prentice-Hall, Inc., 1975).
5. DR. THOMAS GORDON, *P.E.T. Parent Effectiveness Training* (New York: Peter H. Wyden, Inc./Publisher, 1970), p. 21.
6. DONALD NAFTULIN, "Identifying Styles of Family Interaction," *Physicians Associate* (April 1972), pp. 39-41. Reprinted by permission of The Williams and Wilkins Co., Baltimore.
7. BURTON WHITE, "Reassessing Our Educational Priorities," *Oral presentation, Educational Commission of the States Early Childhood Education Symposium,* Boston (Aug 3-4, 1974).
8. JAMES DOBSON, Ph.D., *What Wives Wish Their Husbands Knew About Women* (Wheaton, Illinois: Tyndale House, Publishers, Inc., 1975), p. 52.
9. ESTELLE RAMEY, "Boredom: The Most Prevalent American Disease," *Harpers,* 249 (1974), p. 14.
10. ALAN JAY LERNER and FREDERICK LOEWE, "If Ever I Would Leave You," from *Camelot* (New York; N.Y.: Chappell and Co., Inc., 1906).
11. MARY C. HOWELL, M.D., "Effects of Maternal Employment on the Child," *Pediatrics,* 52, No. 2 (1973) pp. 252-263, 52, No. 3 (1973) pp. 327-343.
12. *Palo Alto Times,* February 16, 1976, p. 5.
13. The Committee on Infant and Preschool Children, *Recommendations for Day Centers* (Evanston, Illinois: Academy of Pediatrics, 1973).

14. ERIK H. ERIKSON, *Childhood and Society* (New York: W.W. Norton and Co., 1950).
15. MARGARET MEAD, *Blackberry Winter* (New York: Pocket Books, January 1975), p. 310.

Chapter 2

1. LEO BELL, M.D., THOMAS CONWAY, M.D., and DAVID SPARLING, M.D., "The Parents' Almanac" (unpublished, 1975).
2. Peninsula Oral School for the Deaf, Redwood City, California 94061, California Association of Parents of Deaf and Hard of Hearing Children, "Instructions to Parents," Pamphlet (1975).
3. ROBERT F.L. POLLEY, M.D., *Call the Doctor* (821 McGilvra Boulevard East, Seattle, Washington: Family Handbooks, 1971), p. 42.
4. KAREN PRYOR, *Nursing Your Baby* (New York: Harper & Row, Publishers, 1963).
5. La Leche League International, 9816 Minneapolis Avenue, Franklin Park, Illinois 60131.
6. POLLEY, *Call the Doctor*, p. 25.
7. DR. LEE SALK, *What Every Child Would Like His Parents to Know* (New York: Warner Paperback Library, 1973), p. 22.
8. GLENN R. STOUTT, JR., M.D., *The First Month of Life* (Oradell, New Jersey: Medical Economics Company Book Division, 1977), p 1.
9. Committee on Infant and Preschool Children, Advertising of "Toys That Teach," *American Academy of Pediatrics Newsletter Supplement*, Vol. 24 No. 2 (March 1973).

Chapter 4

1. E. NEIGE TODHUNTER, Ph.D., "Food Is More Than Nutrients," *Food & Nutrition News*, Vol. 43 (1972), pp. 6-7.
2. NATHAN H. AZRIN, Ph.D., and RICHARD M. FOXX, Ph.D., *Toilet Training in Less Than a Day* (New York: Simon and Schuster, 1974).

Chapter 5

1. *Palo Alto Times*, May 24, 1975, Peninsula Living Section, p. 7.
2. DR. HAIM G. GINOTT, *Between Parent & Child* (New York: The Macmillan Company, 1965).
3. DR. THOMAS GORDON, *P.E.T. Parent Effectiveness Training* (New York: Peter H. Wyden, Inc./Publisher, 1970), p. 29 and p. 103.
4. DIANA BAUMRIND, Early socialization and the discipline controversy. *University programs modular studies*. Morristown, N.J.: General Learning Press, March, 1975.
5. JAMES DOBSON, Ph.D., *Dare to Discipline* (Wheaton, Illinois: Tyndale House Publishers, 1973).
6. RICHARD H. BLUM and Associates, *Horatio Alger's Children* (San Francisco: Jossey-Bass, Inc., Publishers, 1972).
7. Committee on Public Education, "The Joys and Sorrows of Parenthood," *Group for the Advancement of Psychiatry*, Volume VIII, Rep. No 84, (May 1973), pp. 247-48.
8. Reciprocal rights and responsibilities in parent-child relations. In N. Fesh-

bach & S. Feshbach (Eds.), "The changing status of childhood: Roles, rights, and responsibilities," *Journal of Social Issues*, in press.

9. JAMES DOBSON, Ph.D., *Hide or Seek* (Old Tappan, New Jersey: Fleming H. Revell, Company, 1974), p. 12.
10. JOHN MONEY and PATRICIA TUCKER, *Sexual Signatures* (Waltham, Massachusetts: Little Brown and Co., 1975).
11. ELEANOR MACCOBY and CAROL JACKLIN, *The Psychology of Sex Differences* (Stanford, California: Stanford University Press, 1974), pp. 277-302.
12. *Newsweek*, "Do Children Need Sex Roles?", (June 10, 1974).
13. GLEN GRIFFIN, *You Were Smaller Than a Dot* (575 Medical Drive East, Bountiful, Utah, 84010: Better Books, 1972).
14. DOBSON, *Discipline*, p. 173.
15. MARVIN GERSH, *How to Raise Children in Your Spare Time* (New York: Stein and Day, 1966).
16. BETTY ROLLIN, *Mothers are Funnier Than Children* (Garden City, New York: Doubleday, 1964).
17. ASHBY JOHNSON, *Communion With Young Saints* (Richmond, Virginia: John Knox Press, 1959).
18. BLUM, *Horatio Alger's Children.*
19. BURTON WHITE, *The First Three Years of Life* (Englewood Cliffs, N.J.: Prentice-Hall, Inc., 1975).

Chapter 7

1. RICHARD FARSON, *Birthrights* (New York: Macmillan Publishing Company, Inc., 1974).
2. A.S. NEILL, *Summerhill* (New York: Hart Publishing Co., 1960), p. 114.
3. DR. THOMAS GORDON, *P.E.T. Parent Effectiveness Training* (New York: Peter H. Wyden, Inc./Publisher, 1970), p. 177.
4. JAMES DOBSON, Ph.D., *Dare to Discipline* (Wheaton, Illinois: Tyndale House Publishers, 1973), p. 20.
5. MARGUERITE AND WILLARD BEECHER, *Parents on the Run, The Need for Discipline in Parent-Child and Teacher-Child Relationships* (New York: Matrix House, Ltd., 1955), p. 1.
6. RICHARD ROBERTIELLO, M.D., *Hold Them Very Close, Then Let Them Go* (New York: Dial Press, 1975), pp. 1–13.
7. Effects of authoritative parental control on child behavior. *Child Development*, 1966, *37* (4), 887–907. Current patterns of parental authority. *Developmental Psychology Monographs*, 1971, *4* (1), Part 2.
8. RICHARD H. BLUM AND ASSOCIATES, *Horatio Algier's Children* (San Francisco: Jossey-Bass, Inc., Publishers, 1972).
9. GORDON, *P.E.T.*, p. 174.
10. *San Francisco Examiner and Chronicle*, April 6, 1975, p. 6.
11. DOBSON, *Discipline*, p. 28.
12. *San Francisco Examiner and Chronicle*, April 6, 1975, p. 6.
13. GORDON, *P.E.T.*, p. 118.
14. DOBSON, *Discipline*, p. 28.
15. DOBSON, *Discipline*, p. 11.
16. DOBSON, *Discipline*, p. 29.
17. DARYL HOOLE, *The Art of Homemaking* (Salt Lake City: Deseret Book Company, 1963), pp. 132–38.
18. HOOLE, *The Art of Homemaking.*

19. WILLIAM G. CROOK, M.D., *Your Allergic Child* (Jackson, Tennessee: Professional Books, 1973).
20. Parental control and parental love. *Children*, 1965, *12*, 230–34.
21. ALEXANDER SOLZHENITSYN, *August 1914* (New York: Farrar, Straus and Giroux, 1972).

Chapter 8

1. MILTON BRUTTEN, Ph.D., SYLVIA O. RICHARDSON, M.D., CHARLES MANGEL, *Something's Wrong with My Child* (New York: Harcourt Brace Jovanovich, Inc., 1973), pp. 3 and 4.
2. ROBERT F.L. POLLEY, M.D., *Call the Doctor* (821 McGilvra Boulevard East, Seattle, Washington: Family Handbooks, 1971), pp. 94-100.
3. BRUTTEN, *Something's Wrong*, p. 48.
4. Ibid.
5. SIDNEY ADLER, M.D., with KEITH C. TERRY, *Your Overactive Child: Normal or Not* (New York: Medcom Press, 1972).
6. WILLIAM G. CROOK, M.D., *Can Your Child Read? Is He Hyperactive?* (Jackson, Tennessee: Professional Books, 1975).
7. BEN FEINGOLD, M.D., *Why Your Child Is Hyperactive* (New York: Random House, 1975).
8. HENRY BRUYN, "An Interpretation of Academic Underachievement," *Journal of the American College Health Association*, 18 No. 2 (December 1969).
9. BRUTTEN, *Something's Wrong*, p. 98.
10. WILLIAM G. CROOK, M.D., *Are You Bothered By Hypoglycemia?* (Jackson, Tennessee: Professional Books, 1977).
11. LENDON SMITH, *Improving Your Child's Behavior* (Englewood Cliffs, N.J.: Prentice-Hall, Inc., 1976).

BOOKS FOR PARENTS

General Information
1. *Call The Doctor, Questions Parents Ask About Children.* (Family Handbooks) by pediatrician Robert F. L. Polley. A practical, direct and colorful exposition of Dr. Polley's views about a variety of issues concerning children, their illnesses and their problems. (Sold by direct mail, $3.00 post paid, 821 McGilvra Blvd. East, Seattle, WA 98112)
2. *The Encyclopedia of Baby and Child Care* (Prentice-Hall, Inc.), by television pediatrician Lendon Smith. A comprehensive book that covers the basic scientific information available about the diseases, growth, and development of children.
3. *Baby and Child Care* by the famous Benjamin Spock. This traditional best seller covers a wide variety of information on childhood illness and child rearing in Dr. Spock's own pragmatic style.

Child Rearing—Basics
6. *The First Three Years of Life* (Prentice-Hall, Inc.) by Harvard psychologist Burton White represents a lifetime of practical research and offers valuable insights into the effects of parenting practices on young children.

Liberal Child Rearing
5. *Parent Effectiveness Training* (Peter H. Wyden, Inc.) by psychologist Thomas Gordon offers the basics of Gordon's philosophies on why parents shouldn't use power or punishment and how they should communicate with their children.
6. *Freedom-Not License* (Hart Publishing Co.) by A. S. Neill, a frank advocate of permissive child rearing explains the difference, as he sees it, between freedom and "excessive permissiveness."
7. *Hold Them Very Close, Then Let Them Go,* (Dial Press) by Richard C. Robertiello, M.D. A psychiatrist points out the errors and results of raising children by past permissive theory and now offers a new theoretical psychoanalytical basis for child rearing.

Conservative Child Rearing

8. *Dare to Discipline* (Tyndale House) by pediatric psychologist James Dobson. A no-holds-barred landmark book advocating firmness and commitment in parenting.
9. *Hide or Seek* (Fleming H. Revell) by pediatric psychologist James Dobson. An excellent book offering a positive view on how to raise confident and psychologically healthy children.
10. *Call The Doctor.* Offers conservative views on discipline.

Learning Problems

11. *Call The Doctor* by Polley contains constructive and conservative advice on children's learning and school problems.
12. *Can Your Child Read? Is He Hyperactive?* (Professional Books) by pediatric allergist William G. Crook. Suggestions for helping children who have diet and allergy-caused learning and behavior problems. (Sold by direct mail $5.50 post paid Box 3494 Jackson, Tennessee 38301).
13. *The First Three Years of Life* by White is an eye-opening study of how parenting in the first three years can affect later learning.

Sex Education

14. *The Encyclopedia of Baby and Child Care* by Lendon Smith has scientific sections on sex and sex education for children.
15. *You Were Smaller Than A Dot* (Better Books) by pediatrician Glen Griffin. A delightful, small book of cartoons and text that offers parents a way to introduce sex education to young children. (Sold by direct mail, $3.00 post paid, 575 Medical Drive East, Bountiful, Utah 84010).

INDEX

375

Parents (*Cont.*)
  tasks beyond biology, 12–13
  teamwork, 13
Parents As Resources (group), 280
Parents' Medical Manual, The, 341
Parents On The Run (Beechers), 266
Pediatrics (journal), 24
Poarch, Ruth, 183
Poison-and-accident proofing of home, 41
Polley, Dr. Robert F. L., 75
Price, Sandra, 11
Professional help, 250–54
  damage to child's self-confidence, 251
  "fault-free," 252
  psychiatry, 252–53
  records of, and "face," 253–54
  and tests, 252
  urgency of, 251
  who benefits, 253
Pryor, Karen, 94

Quarreling, between siblings, 245–47
  and competition, 246
  if constant, 246
  as immaturity, 246–47
  intervention in, 246
  as learning experience, 246

Ramsey, Estelle, 21
Recipes, 171–72
  applesauce, 172
  carrots, 172
  egg yolks, 171
  lamb, 171
  peas, 172
Recipes For Fun (Parents As Resources), 280
Responsibility between parents and children, 205
Richanbach, Dr. Henry, 226
Richards, Dr. John, 72, 183
Robertiello, Robert, 269
Role of parents in school affairs, 317–18
  anger with teachers, 318
  cooperation with school, 318
  responsibility of, 317
Rousseau, Jean-Jacques, 5
Russell, G. R., 258

Safety, in first four months, 139
Scherz, Robert, 73
School and learning problems, 315–56 (*see also* Learning disabilities, Learning problems)
  change of mother's function, 315
  difficulties in school, 316–17
  "Why doesn't Johnny learn?," 315–17
Scofield, Bambi, 91

Sehring, Maxine, 212
Self-esteem and confidence, 205–9
  and acceptance, 207
  and beauty, physical, 205
  building of, 206–7
  excess involvement, 207
  fame, 205
  identity crisis, 208
  and intellect, 205
  jobs, 208
  mathematics instruction, 205
  money, 205
  and school, 206
  self-doubt, and parental guilt, 206
  skills, 208
  social realities, 207
  spontaneous attention by parents, 207
  sports, 205
  and values, 205
Sensitive child, 243–45
  dealing with, 244
  emotional calluses, 244
  fears, in vicious circle, 244
  and friction with others, 243–44
  "good" vs. "bad" definitions of, 244
  perfectionism, 245
  sarcasm, 245
  unreal expectations, 244
  usual definition of, 243
Separation, 357–67
  abandonment fears, 357
  death, 358–59
    causing abandonment fears, 359
    faith in afterlife, 358
    fears of, 358
    funerals, bad effects of, 358
    and guilt, 359
    muting of, 359
    Peter Pan myth, 358
    questions about, 358
  realization of death, 357
Sex (*see also* Sexual identity)
  education in school, 213
  information about, 212–13, 215–17
  for three-year-old, 210
Sexual identity, 209–218
  "adequate" values, 214
  anti-incest instinct, 218
  awareness of physical differences, 211
  biology of, 213
  and genital play, 210
  "hang-ups," avoidance of, 217–18
  heredity, 209
  honesty about, 213
  and intercourse, 212
  latency of in children, 215
  parent favoritism, 217–18
  parents' footsteps, 210
  problems of, 213–18